A Geographical And Historical Description Of Asia Minor, Volume 2

John Anthony Cramer

A

GEOGRAPHICAL AND HISTORICAL

DESCRIPTION

OF

ASIA MINOR;

WITH A MAP.

BY

John Antony

J. A. CRAMER, D.D.

PRINCIPAL OF NEW INN HALL, AND PUBLIC ORATOR OF THE
UNIVERSITY OF OXFORD.

IN TWO VOLUMES.

Νῦν δ' αὖ παρραλίης 'Ασίης πόρον ἐξενέποιμι
'Ος ῥά τε πρὸς νότον εἰσιν, ἐφ' 'Ελλήσποντον ὁδεύων
Καὶ ποτὶ μηκίστου νότιον ῥόον Αἰγαίοιο.
DIONYS. PERIEG. v. 799.

VOL. II.

OXFORD,
AT THE UNIVERSITY PRESS,
MDCCCXXXII.

CONTENTS

OF

THE SECOND VOLUME.

SECTION VII.

PHRYGIA AND LYCAONIA.

MIGRATIONS and history of the Phrygians—Different parts of Asia Minor to which the name of Phrygia has been applied—Greater Phrygia, its boundaries and divisions—Topography—Lycaonia—Sketch of its history—Description.   Page 1.

SECTION VIII.

GALATIA.

Account of the migration of the Gauls into Asia, and their occupation of a large portion of ancient Phrygia—Their division into Tectosages, Tolistoboii, and Trocmi—Conquest of Galatia by the Romans—Conversion to Christianity—Description of the province.   79.

SECTION IX.

CAPPADOCIA AND ARMENIA MINOR.

Origin of the Leucosyri or Cappadocians—Sketch of their history under the Assyrian, Median, and Persian empires—Cappadocian dynasty—Roman province of Cappadocia—Its boundaries and geographical features—Description—Armenia Minor—Its several districts and topography.   105.

SECTION X.

CARIA.

Origin and early history of the Carians—Princes of Caria—
Brief sketch of the principal events in the annals of the
country, from its first conquest by Crœsus to its becoming a part of the Roman empire—Boundaries and geography of the province—Dorian colonies, and other towns
on the coast—Interior—Islands of Cos and Rhodes. 163.

SECTION XI.

LYCIA.

Origin and history of the Lycians—Boundaries and maritime topography—Interior—Milyas and Cabalia, districts
of the ancient Solymi—Cibyra.   240.

SECTION XII.

PAMPHYLIA AND PISIDIA.

Origin of the Pamphylians—Description of their coast and
towns—Pisidia—Account of its inhabitants—Boundaries
and geographical features of the country—Topography.
                                                     273.

SECTION XIII.

CILICIA.

Origin and history of the Cilicians—Boundaries and division of the province into Trachea or Aspera, and Campestris—Chain of Taurus and mountain passes—Topography.   315.

SECTION XIV.

CYPRUS.

Origin of its inhabitants—Sketch of its history from the
earliest period to the fall of the eastern empire—Natural
history, productions and principal geographical features
of the island—Periplus of the coast—Interior.   366.

SECTION VII.

PHRYGIA AND LYCAONIA.

Migrations and history of the Phrygians—Different parts of Asia Minor to which the name of Phrygia has been applied—Greater Phrygia, its boundaries and divisions—Topography—Lycaonia—Sketch of its history—Description.

HERODOTUS relates that Psammitichus, king of Egypt, having made an experiment to discover which was the most ancient nation of the world, ascertained that the Phrygians surpassed all other people in priority of existence. (II. 2.) The story itself is childishly absurd; but the fact that the Egyptians allowed the highest degree of antiquity to this nation is important, and deserves attention. What the Greeks knew of the origin of the Phrygians does not accord, however, with the Egyptian hypothesis. Herodotus has elsewhere reported that they originally came from Macedonia, where they lived under the name of Briges, and that when they crossed over into Asia this was changed to Phryges. (VII. 73.) This account has been generally followed by subsequent writers, especially Strabo, (VII. p. 295.) who appears to quote Xanthus and Menecrates of Elæa, Artemidorus, and other writers, who made the origin of nations and cities the object of their inquiries. (XII. p. 572. XIV. p. 680. Cf. Plin.

V. 32. Steph. Byz. v. Βρίγες.) It is certain indeed
that there was a people named Briges, or Bryges,
of Thracian origin, living in Macedonia at the
time that Herodotus was writing; (VI. 45. VII.
185.) and tradition had long fixed the abode of the
Phrygian Midas, who was no doubt a chief of this
people, near mount Bermius in Macedonia. (Herod.
VIII. 138. Cf. Nicand. ap. Athen. XV. p. 683. Bion.
ap. eund. II. p. 45.) Again, the strong affinity which
was allowed to exist between the Phrygians, Lydians, Carians, and Mysians, who were all supposed
to have crossed from Thrace into Asia Minor, serves
to corroborate the hypothesis which regards the
Phrygian migration in particular[a]: but whilst there
seems no reasonable doubt of the Thracian origin of
this people, it is not so easy to establish the period
at which they settled themselves in Asia. Xanthus
is represented by Strabo as fixing their arrival in
that country somewhat after the Trojan war; (XIV.
p. 680.) but the geographer justly observes, that,
according to Homer, the Phrygians were already
settled on the banks of the Sangarius before that
era, and were engaged in a war with the Amazons;
(Il. Γ. 187.) and if mythological accounts are to have

---

[a] Brig, or Briga, a word
allowed on all hands to be Cel-
tic, is reported by Juba (ap.
Hesych. v. Βρίγες) to have been
used by the Lydians in the sense
of a "free man." The name of
Midas seems also to have been
common to the Lydians, since
Midas, according to some accounts, was the husband of
Omphale. (Clearch. ap. Athen.
XII. p. 516.) So also Tantalus and Pelops, Atys and Cotys,
which again are Thracian. It
is not improbable also that the
Bebryces, (Βέβρυκες,) who are
spoken of in the poets as the
aboriginal inhabitants of Bithynia, were the same as the
Bryges. The name of the Berecyntii, an ancient Phrygian
tribe, may be only another form
for Brigantii.

any weight, the existence of a Midas in Asia Minor, long before the period alluded to, would prove that there had been a Phrygian migration in times to which authentic history does not extend. (Cf. Conon. Narrat. ap. Phot. Cod. 186.)

Great as was the ascendency of the Thracian stock, produced by so many tribes of that vast family pouring in at various times, there must have entered into the composition of the Phrygian nation some other elements besides the one which formed its leading feature. I have already stated in the introductory section, as well as in the one immediately preceding this, my belief that the Thracian Bryges found the country, which from them took the name of Phrygia, occupied by some earlier possessors, but who were too weak to resist their invaders. What name this people bore cannot now be ascertained, but there can be little doubt that it was of Asiatic origin: probably they were Leuco-Syrians, or Cappadocians. At the time that Herodotus wrote, the Halys was the boundary of those nations which appeared to claim a European descent, and those which owned Asia for their mother-country. The Phrygians, who were on the left bank of the river, were the last of the Europeans in point of situation, but in order of time I conceive they were first, as the direction of the stream of migration, setting in from the Thracian Bosphorus, was from west to east. Herodotus, however, has stated a circumstance which, if true, must be allowed to overthrow what I am seeking to establish respecting the current of migration. In the muster he makes of Xerxes' myriads, he states that the Phrygians and Armenians were armed alike; the latter being, as he observes, colonists of the former. (VII. 73[b].)

Herodotus is, I conceive, quite singular in this statement, which is moreover at variance with all received notions on the subject. The Armenians are a people of the highest antiquity, and we must not seek for their primitive stock beyond the upper valleys of the Tigris and Euphrates: in other words, they are a purely Asiatic people; and if there existed any resemblance between them and the Phrygians, I should account for it rather by supposing that the latter were not altogether Europeans, but mingled with an indigenous breed of Asia, whose stock was also common to the Armenians. The greater part of the Phrygian superstitions, those especially which related to the worship of Cybele, or Rhea, and the Corybantes, were supposed by Strabo, who has entered largely into the account of those mysteries, to have been imported from Thrace, with whose religious rites they exhibited a striking similarity. (X. p. 466—474.[c]) On the other hand, there are traces of a mythology which is certainly Asiatic. The worship of Sabazius, or Bacchus, which became mixed up with the mystic ceremonies of Rhea and Dindymene, is confessedly of that character. Again, that of Men, or Menes, which answers to Lunus in Latin, and which was so widely

[b] Ἀρμένιοι δὲ κατά περ Φρύγας ἐσεσάχατο, ἐόντες Φρυγῶν ἄποικοι.

[c] Cf. Heyn. Relig. et Sacr. cum furor. peract. Orig. Comment. Soc. R. Gotting. tom. VIII. p. 1. Ste Croix Mém. pour servir à l'histoire de la Religion secrete. Dupuis, Origine de tous les Cultes, tom. II. b. 2. p. 60. Freret, Rech. sur les Cabires, Acad. des Inscr. et B. Lett. tom. XXVII. p. 10.

spread throughout Cappadocia, Phrygia, and the contiguous provinces, is certainly derived from Syria, or Armenia.

The Greeks concerned themselves but little about the real origin of nations, or received without discrimination such traditions as reached them on this head. In many cases their national vanity led them to assign to people, however distant or barbarous, a Greek consanguinity, founded solely on a mere approximation of names, and divested of all historical evidence, and even probability. We are not to expect therefore from them any philosophical investigation of the question which is here considered. They regarded the Phrygians as one only among the barbarous tribes which occupied Asia Minor under the dominion of the great king, and their language was too rude and uncouth for them to bestow much pains on analyzing its origin and structure; and yet this, I conceive, is the only method by which we could ascertain at all satisfactorily the elements of their population. At a later period, when Asia Minor had been overspread, as it were, with Greek colonies, and some barbarous words had, by a natural consequence of these relations, been rendered familiar to Grecian ears, we find among others some Phrygian terms preserved by the lexicographers; but they are too scanty to furnish a basis of inquiry [d], without some further aid; which, considering the remote period to which it must ascend, is hardly to be expected [e].

[d] These have been collected by Professor Jablonsky, in his Disquisitio de Lingua Lacaonica, among his Opusc. Acad., tom. III. Leyd. 1809.

[e] The remarkable inscriptions, copied by Col. Leake, on the tombs of the kings of Phry-

We must also keep in mind the constant changes which were taking place almost daily in the population of the peninsula, both before and after the siege of Troy; a circumstance which renders it impossible that any one language should have flourished above the rest, where all were exposed to the same vicissitudes and migrations[f]. As the Phrygians appear to have occupied Asia Minor at an earlier period, and to have been more widely diffused than the other tribes, whose origin is referred to Thrace, their dialect would probably be more worthy of investigation than the rest; but as it does not appear ever to have been a cultivated language, the speculation, however it may amuse the antiquary, could scarcely be expected to confer much advantage either on literature or science. The political history of the Phrygians is neither so brilliant nor interesting as that of their neighbours the Lydians. What we gather respecting them from ancient writers is, generally, that they crossed over from Europe into Asia under the conduct of their leader Midas, nearly a hundred years before the Trojan war. (Conon. ap. Phot. Cod. 186.) That they settled first on the shores of the Hellespont and around mount Ida,

gia, (Asia Minor, p. 23,) are certainly in Archaic Greek; and it is extremely probable that the language of the Bryges, imported from Thrace or Macedonia, was what might perhaps be called a dialect of the old Pelasgic tongue; but this must have been mixed up in process of time with the more ancient remnants of Asiatic languages, so as to make a barbarous tongue, which would not be intelligible to Greeks of the age of Xenophon and Plato.

[f] We know from Strabo that several Phrygian tribes had disappeared long before his time: the same might be said of the Lydians and Mysians. The Chalybes, too, had shifted their abode in a surprising way, so that Ephorus, and other respectable authors, hardly knew where to place them. (Strab. XIV. p. 678.)

whence they gradually extended themselves to the shores of the Ascanian lake and the valley of the Sangarius. It is probable that the Doliones, Mygdones, and Bebryces, who held originally the coasts of Mysia and Bithynia, were Phrygians. The Mygdones were contiguous to the Bryges in Macedonian Thrace, and they are often classed with the Phrygians by the poets. (Cf. Strab. XII. p. 575.) Driven afterwards from the Hellespont and the coast of the Propontis by the Teucri, Mysi, and Bithyni, the Phrygians took up a more central position in what may be called the great bason of Asia Minor. Still preserving the line of the Sangarius, they occupied to the south-west of that great river the upper valleys of the Macestus and Rhyndacus, towards the Mysian Olympus, and those of the Hermus and Hyllus on the side of Lydia. On the west they ranged along Catacecaumene and ancient Mæonia, till they reached the Meander. The head of that river, with its tributary streams, was included within their territory. To the south they held the northern slope of mount Cadmus, which with its continuation, a branch of Taurus, formed their frontier on the side of Caria, Milyas, and Pisidia, as far as the borders of Cilicia. In this direction are to be found the Lycaonians, who, though a distinct and peculiar people, will, for the sake of convenience, be included within the present section. To the east of the Sangarius the ancient Phrygians spread along the borders of Paphlagonia till they met the great river Halys, which divided them from Pontus, and further south, from Cappadocia and Isauria. This extensive country was very unequal in its climate and fertility. That which lay in the plains and valleys, watered by rivers, exceeded in richness and beauty almost every other part of the peninsula; (Herod. V. 49.) but many a tract was rendered bleak and desolate by vast ranges of mountains, or uninhabitable from extensive lakes and fens impregnated with salt, or scorching deserts destitute of trees and vegetation. The Phrygians appear at first to have been under the dominion of kings, but whether these were absolute over the whole country, or each was the chief of a petty canton, is not certain. I should rather imagine the latter to have been the case, since we hear of Midæum and Gordium, near the Sangarius, as royal towns, corresponding with the well known names of Midas and Gordius; (Strab. XII. p. 568.) and again, Celænæ, seated in a very opposite direction, near the source of the Meander, appears to have been the chief city of a Phrygian principality. (Athen. X. p. 415.) The first Phrygian prince whose actions come within the sphere of authenticated history, is Midas, the son of Gordius, who, as Herodotus relates, was the first barbarian who made offerings to the god of Delphi. He dedicated his throne of justice, the workmanship of which, as the historian affirms, was worthy of admiration. (I. 14.) At this period the Phrygians were independent, but under the reign of Crœsus the Lydian we hear of their being subject to that sovereign. (I. 28.) History has not acquainted us with the particulars of this conquest; but it seems to have cost the Lydians but little trouble, and the conqueror was probably content with exacting from the Phrygian chief an avowal of his inferiority, in the shape of a tribute or tax; for the tragic tale of the Phrygian Adrastus affords evidence that the ancient dynasty of that

country still held dominion, as the vassals of Crœsus. (I. 35.) Adrastus is said to have been the son
of Gordius, who was himself the son of Midas. The
latter was probably the grandson of the Midas who
dedicated his throne to the shrine of Delphi, and is
called son of Gordius; so that we have a regular
alternation of monarchs bearing those two names
from father to son, for seven generations [g]. The
first Gordius is probably the one who is indebted
for a place in history to the puzzle which he in-
vented; but which, if it had not fallen into the way
of Alexander, would probably never have given rise
to the proverbial expression of " the Gordian knot."
(Arrian. Exp. Alex. II. 3.) According to Arrian's
account, Gordius himself was a man of humble birth
and means, but Midas, his son, was created king in
compliance with an oracle. After the overthrow of
the Lydian monarchy by Cyrus, Phrygia was annexed to the Persian empire, and under the division
made by Darius formed part of the Hellespontine
or Bithynian satrapy. (Herod. III. 91.) In the par-
tition of Alexander's dominion, it fell at first into
the hands of Antigonus, then of the Seleucidæ, and
after the defeat of Antiochus was ceded to Eumenes,
king of Pergamum, but finally reverted to the Romans. (Polyb. XXII. 27. 10. Liv. XXXVII. 56.)
At that time Phrygia had sustained a considerable
diminution of territorial extent, owing to the migration of a large body of Gauls into Asia, where they
settled in the very centre of the province; and having succeeded in appropriating to themselves a considerable tract of country, formed a new province

---

[g] These two names are so
common that they would seem
to have been appellatives, rather
than proper names.

and people, named Galatia and Galatæ, or Gallo-græci.

The Phrygians are generally stigmatized by the ancients as a slavish nation, destitute of courage or energy, and possessing but little skill in any thing save music and dancing. (Athen. I. p. 27. Virg. Æn. XII. 99. Eur. Alc. 678. Or. 1447. Athen. XIV. p. 624—629.)

Phrygia, considered with respect to the territory once occupied by the people from whom it obtained its appellation, was divided into the Great and Less. The latter, which was also called the Hellespontine Phrygia, still retained that name, even when the Phrygians had long retired from that part of Asia Minor to make way for the Mysians, Teucrians, and Dardanians; and it would be hazardous to pronounce how much of what has been included under Mysia and Troas belonged to what was evidently only a political division. (Strab. XII. p. 563, 571. Arrian. Exp. Alex. I. 13. Diod. Sic. XVIII. 3. Polyb. Exc. Legat. XXII. 27. 10.)

The present section will be devoted to the consideration of the Greater Phrygia, such as we find it defined by the authors above cited, and according to the limits we have laid down in tracing the progress of the Phrygian settlements throughout the peninsula. Following Strabo as our guide, we shall make a threefold division of this part of our subject, namely, into Phrygia Epictetus, Major, properly so called, and Parorius. It will be right to mention, that besides this ancient classification, we find in the Lower Empire the province divided into Phrygia Pacatiana, and Phrygia Salutaris.

PHRYGIA EPICTETUS.

The name of Epictetus, or " the Acquired," was given to that portion of the province which was annexed by the Romans to the kingdom of Pergamum. It would appear from Strabo that the Attalic princes were themselves the authors of that appellation; (XII. p. 563.) and it is also evident from his account that it included not only some districts of the Hellespontine, but others also which must have belonged to the Greater Phrygia. (XII. p. 571.) It would be vain to attempt any accuracy of demarcation, when this geographer has himself apologized for the imperfection of his divisions. We must content ourselves with tracing out those places he has assigned to Phrygia Epictetus, and comparing his account with such information as may be collected from modern travellers of the actual state of this part of Asia Minor. This district was obtained principally from the territories of Prusias, king of Bithynia, (Strab. XII. p. 563.) consequently we should expect to find it lying between the latter province and Mysia. And here, in fact, Strabo's description leads us. South of the Mysian Olympus, and on the borders of Lydia, we find a chain of mountains, which divides the waters flowing towards the Propontis from those which run in a south-westerly direction to the Ægean. The rivers which have their termination in the Propontis have been already spoken of under the names of Macestus and Rhyndacus in the section which treated of Mysia. But Strabo has taught us to look upon their sources as belonging to Phrygia. The Macestus he reports to flow from Abbaï-

Abbaites Mysi.

tis, (XII. p. 576.[h]) a district apparently belonging to the Mysians. For the coins with the inscription

Ancyra.

ABBAÏΤΩΝ ΜΥΣΩΝ, can, I think, only be referred to that canton. The principal town of this people was Ancyra, situated at the head of the Macestus, and which Strabo elsewhere assigns to Phrygia, and places in the vicinity of Blaundus, a town of Lydia. (XII. p. 567. Cf. Ptol. p. 120. Plin. V. 32.) As no traveller has visited the upper valley of the *Sousougherli*, which represents the Macestus, it is impossible to identify the position of Ancyra with any modern site. The Notitiæ class this town among the sees of Phrygia Pacatiana. (Hierocl. p. 668.[i]) From some ecclesiastical documents adduced by Wesseling, it appears that Ancyra was united to the see

Synnaus.

of Synnaus, which consequently cannot have been far removed from thence: and, accordingly, we find that town named by Hierocles immediately after Ancyra. It is also noticed by Ptolemy and the ecclesiastical historians. (Socrat. VII. 3. Nicephor. XIV. 11.) This place was probably seated between the sources of the Macestus and Rhyndacus, and not far from *Simaul* on Major Keppel's route [k]. Strabo places near the head of the Rhyndacus, which

---

[h] In the text of Strabo the name is written 'Αβασίτις, and elsewhere the geographer speaks of the Ablites Mysi to the east of Pergamus, who are doubtless the same people. In both cases we ought to read 'Αββαΐτις and 'Αββαΐτες, as may be seen from the coins, and an inscription found in the country by Major Keppel. Travels, tom. II. p. 244. Ὁ Δῆμος ὁ Μυσῶν 'Αββαεί-των. Sestini is therefore mis-

taken in assigning these coins to Aba of Caria.

[i] There are coins of Ancyra, but it is not easy to distinguish them from those of Ancyra in Galatia: the epigraph is ΑΓ-ΚΤΡΑΝΩΝ. Sestini, p. 117.

[k] Tom. ii. p. 260. It is to be regretted that this traveller did not explore the course of the Macestus, as well as those of the Rhyndacus and Hyllus.

flowed to the east of the Macestus, the Phrygian city of Azani, or Aizani, which is also noticed by several writers. (Strab. XII. p. 576.) Herodian the grammarian, cited by Steph. Byz. (v. Ἀζανοὶ) affirmed that it had been founded by Æzen, the son of Tantalus, and wrote the name consequently Æzani, Αἰζανοὶ, which, from the inscriptions discovered recently as well as the coins of the town, appears to be the more usual orthography [1]. Hermogenes, who is also cited by Stephanus, accounted for the origin of the word very differently, but his etymology is not worthy of being repeated. It might seem, from a passage in Pausanias, that the Azani of Phrygia were supposed by some to be connected with the Arcadian people of the same name. (Arcad. c. 4. Phoc. c. 32.) Azani is also noticed by Ptolemy and Hierocles : (p. 668.) but the ruins which have recently been visited and described by Major Keppel, give a greater idea of its size and importance than we should otherwise have been led to fancy from the casual mention of it occurring in ancient authorities. Major Keppel, travelling south-west of *Kutaieh*, arrived at " *Tjaudere Hissar*, a village built " entirely of the splendid ruins of the ancient Azani. " These ruins," says he, " occupy the banks of a " river, which, on my return to Constantinople, I " ascertained to be the Rhyndacus. Over this stream " are two ancient bridges, raised on elliptical arches ; " a superb quay connects these bridges together. " On the right bank of the river is the temple. " Tracing its north front at about a quarter of a

Æzani, sive Azani.

---

[1] Tom. II. p. 204. The epigraph on the coins is AIZANEITΩN, and sometimes EZEANITΩN, as in a medal of Julius Cæsar, or Augustus. Gest. p. 116.

" mile distant is the theatre, and a little to its north-
" west angle are the remains of a building con-
" structed of huge blocks, standing on a low hill."
These ruins are further detailed by the Major, with
accompanying plans and sketches furnished by Dr.
Hall [m]. The numerous inscriptions found at *Tjaudere* prove beyond a doubt that it represents Azani;
they appear, together with the temple, the principal
building, to be of the reigns of Hadrian and Antoninus [n]. From Dr. Hall's account it would appear
that the Rhyndacus has its source in the mountains
above Azani [o].

Cade.

Proceeding from this town towards the south-
west, we find a small place named *Kedous*, or *Ghediz*, which has long been conjectured to occupy the
site of Cadi, a city commonly attributed to Phrygia,
but reckoned by others within the confines of Mysia.
(Strab. XII. p. 576. Ptol. p. 119. Steph. Byz. v.
Κάδοι.) This conjecture has now been fully verified
by the researches of that enterprising traveller Major
Keppel, who found its site to agree with the information afforded by Strabo, and observed several remains of antiquity. According to his account, *Ghediz* " occupies the base and slope of two mountains.
" It contains 800 houses. The town is celebrated
" for its scammony, which is abundant. It is watered
" by a river called the *Ghediz-tchai*, which name it
" retains until it disembogues into the Archipelago,
" a little above Smyrna: this stream I have ascer-

[m] This gentleman, then travelling under the foundation
and bequest of Dr. Radcliffe,
was the first to discover the site
of Azani. Appendix to Keppel's
Travels, p. 444.

[n] Travels, p. 221—233.

[o] Keppel's Travels, note to
p. 234.

" tained to be the Hermus of ancient history, having
" travelled along its banks from the source to the
" whole extent of its course." The antiquities of
Ghediz consist of capitals of pillars, and marble
fragments with inscriptions. The principal mosque
is built of large blocks of stone, which are supposed
to have belonged formerly to an ancient temple.
Among the stones of which the bridge is built are
the fragments of two very fine white marble statues [p].
Cadi is generally supposed to be referred to in
these verses of Propertius. (IV. 6, 7.)

Spargite me lymphis, carmenque recentibus aris
   Tibia Mygdoniis libet eburna Cadis.

Stephanus Byz. gives Καδηνὸς as the Gentile deriva-
tive of this town, but the legend on its coins inva-
riably exhibits ΚΑΔΟΗΝΩΝ [q]. Hierocles and the
Acts of the Councils prove it to have been an episcopal see. (p. 668.)

Major Keppel, proceeding northwards from *Ghediz*, came, in three hours' march, to what he con-
ceived to be the source of the Hermus. He says it
issued from a circular aperture, about twelve feet in
diameter, in the mountain, a little below the road
on which he was travelling. The mountain itself, Dindyme-
now called *Morad-Dagh*, is the Dindymene of He- ne mons.
rodotus, who says, distinctly, that it gives rise to
the Hermus; (I. 80.) and he is followed by Strabo.
(XII. p. 626.) I am inclined to think, however,
that the source which Major Keppel saw was not
that of the Hermus itself, but of a tributary stream;
for he says, " In three hours' march we crossed a
" bridge over the Hermus, and at some distance

[p] Travels, t. II. p. 239—247. of these reference is made to
[q] Sestini, p. 119. On some the river Hermus.

"from the road saw a village called *Deulis-Sandik*.
"We then lost sight of the river for a short time,
"but soon after fell in with a fine limpid stream
"running in a southerly direction [r]." It is evident,
from this account, that the fine limpid stream is different from the Hermus; and I cannot help suspect-
Peucella fl. ing that it is the stream called Peucella by Pausanias, who states that the Phrygians, who lived near
it, shewed to strangers a remarkable cave named
Steunos. (Phoc. c. 32.)   He describes it as circular,
and of a respectable height; and he adds, that it
was sacred to Cybele, and contained an image of the
goddess.   These Phrygians were supposed to be descended from the Azani of Arcadia, clearly because
they belonged to Azanitis of Phrygia. (Arcad. c. 4.)
Steunos   From whence I conclude that the cave Steunos could
antrum.   not be far from *Tjaudere-hissar*, and most probably
was the aperture observed by Major Keppel.   The
sacred character of the spot would lead naturally to
the idea that the stream which issued from it was
the Hermus; but Pliny thought that this river rose
more to the north-east, in the vicinity of Doryleum;
that, however, is much too far. (V. 29.)   Mount
Dindymene, or Dindyma, was celebrated in antiquity, in connexion with the superstitious rites of
Rhea, or Cybele. (Cf. Strab. X. p. 469. Steph. Byz.
v. Δίνδυμα.)

> O vere Phrygiæ, neque enim Phryges, ite per alta
> Dindyma; ubi assuetis biforem dat tibia cantum.
>
> Æn. IX. 617.

Major Keppel describes the country around as very
beautiful: "A rich plain is bounded by abrupt
"mountains, which are thickly clothed with every

r P. 256.

" species of evergreen [s]." The same traveller journeying from *Kutaieh* to Azani, observed several places
which bore evident marks of former Grecian habitations, but only one contained written monuments, by
which the locality could be identified. It was found
at *Tatar-Bazarjik*; and the termination of the inscription, τοῖς Βεννῖταις, points evidently to a town Benna.
named Benna; the only indication of which, besides
the record traced by Major Keppel, is to be found in
the Notitiæ Antiquæ, which class Bana, or Beana,
(Benna,) among the episcopal sees of Lydia [t].

Kutaya, or *Kutaieh*, a Turkish town of about Cotyæum.
8000 souls, has succeeded to the ancient Cotyæum,
or Cotiæum [u], assigned by Strabo to Phrygia Epictetus, (XII. p. 576.) as well as Pliny (V. 32.) and
Stephanus Byz. (v. Κοτυάειον.) Suidas says that, according to some accounts, it was the birthplace of
Æsop. (Κοτυάειον.) Alexander, a grammarian of great
learning, and a voluminous writer, was also a native
of Cotyæum. (Steph. Byz. in v.) It appears, from
Socrates, (Eccl. Hist. IV. 5.) to have been a bishopric, though not noticed by Hierocles. The Notices
place it in Phrygia Salutaris [x]. Late Byzantine
writers term it the metropolis of Phrygia. (M. Duc.
p. 7. A.) In the Table Itinerary the name is corrupted into Cocleo. It does not appear that there are
any remains of antiquity of consequence at *Kutaya* [y].

Ptolemy places on the northern frontier of Phry-

[s] P. 256.
[t] Keppel's Travels, tom. II.
p. 220.
[u] The latter, judging from
coins, would be the more correct mode of writing the name
of the town; the legend being
always KOTIAEΩN. Sestini, p.
121.
[x] Geogr. S. Paul. p. 244.
[y] Keppel's Travels, tom. II.
p. 184.

Cidyssus. gia towards Bithynia, consequently in the direction of Cotyæum, a people named Κυδησσεῖς; and Hierocles acknowledges Cidyssus among the episcopal towns of Phrygia: (p. 668. Cf. Notit. Ant.) there are also some coins which prove its existence in the time of Domitian and Caracalla[z].

Acmonia. The Table Itinerary furnishes a communication between Cotyæum and Philadelphia, to which we have already referred in the preceding section. The first station south of Cotyæum is Acmonia[a], at a distance of thirty-five miles from thence. Frequent mention is made of this town by Cicero in his oration for Flaccus; (§. 15, 16.) whence it would appear to have been a place of some consequence. In Pliny's time it came under the Conventus Apamenus. (V. 29. Cf. Hierocl. p. 667.) Alexander Polyhistor, in his account of Phrygia, ascribed its foundation to Acmon, the son of Manes. (ap. Steph. Byz. v. Ἀκμονία.) The site of Acmonia has not hitherto been identified; but it must have been near the source of the river Thymbres, now *Pursek*, which flows near *Kutaya.*

Alydda. Alydda, which the Table lays down twenty-five miles further towards Philadelphia, is also mentioned by Ptolemy; (p. 119.) but he appears to place it towards Mysia and Bithynia. It is probably the same town which Steph. Byz. calls Attalydá, though he assigns it to Lydia. (v. Ἀττάλυδα.) There is less certainty of its being identified with Attuda, a town

---

[z] The legend on these monuments is ΚΙΔΥΗΣΣΕΩΝ. Sestini, p. 120.

[a] We have coins of Acmonia, both autonomous and imperial: the inscription is both ΑΚΜΟΝΕΩΝ and ΑΚΜΟΝΩΝ. Sestini, p. 116.

of Phrygia, known only from its coins [b], and the Ecclesiastical Notitiæ and Acts of Councils [c]. Ptolemy names with Alydda the town of Præpenissus, Præpenissus. which the Ecclesiastical Notices assign to Phrygia Salutaris [d].

Returning to Cotyæum, and proceeding along the banks of the Thymbres, we shall arrive, not far from Doryleum. its junction with the Sangarius, at the Turkish town of *Eski-sher*, generally allowed to occupy the site of the ancient Doryleum [e], which Strabo fixes in Phrygia Epictetus, (XII. p. 576.) and the Table Itinerary on the road leading from Nicæa through the heart of Phrygia into the south-eastern provinces. Doryleum is alluded to by Cicero in the Oration pro Flacco, (c. 17.) and noticed by Pliny, (V. 29.) Ptolemy, (p. 120.) and Stephanus Byz. (Δορυλάειον.) Athenæus speaks of some warm sources which were to be found near it: (II. p. 43.) and this, as Col. Leake has observed, affords another indication of its identity with *Eski-sher*, which is celebrated for its hot baths [f]. Doryleum is often mentioned by the Byzantine writers. It was a beautiful city under the Greek emperors: being adorned with baths and other buildings; the climate was delightful, and it was surrounded by rich plains, through which flowed the rivers Bathys and Thyaris, abounding with fish. It was afterwards nearly destroyed by the Turks, but restored by Manuel Comnenus in forty days. (Cinnam. p. 172–3. Nicet.

[b] Sestini, Attuda. Epigraphe, ΑΤΤΟΥΔΕΩΝ. Cultus Mensis Cari. MHN. ΚΑΡΟΥ. Imperatorii, Augusti indeque Vespasiani, Hadriani, &c. p. 118.

[c] Geogr. Sacr. p. 242.

[d] Geogr. Sacr. p. 243.

[e] This is satisfactorily established by Col. Leake, Asia Minor, p. 18, 19.

[f] Asia Minor, p. 18.

Ann. p. 114. B.)   A great battle was fought here
by the crusaders against the Turks. (Ann. Comn.
p. 317. C.)   The river, called Thyaris by Cinnamus,
is doubtless the *Pursek,* which flows near *Eski-sher,*
and joins the Sangarius to the north-east of that

Thymbres fluvius. town.   It is the Thymbres, or Thymbrius, of the
Ancients.   Livy says it united with the Sangarius
on the borders of Phrygia and Bithynia. (XXXVIII.
18.)   Pliny calls it Tembrogius. (VI. 1. [g])   The

Bathys fl. Bathys is the little river probably which traverses
the town of *Eski-sher,* and afterwards joins the
Pursek [h].   There are but few vestiges of antiquity
at *Eski-sher* [i].

The Table Itinerary places to the east of Dory-
Midæum. leum, and twenty-eight miles from it, Midæum,
which Strabo also assigns to Phrygia Epictetus.
(XII. p. 576.)   It evidently derives its name from
Midas, a name so common with the ancient kings
of Phrygia, of whom it was probably once the residence. (Cf. Strab. XII. p. 568.)   We learn from Dio
Cassius that Sextus Pompeius fell here into the
hands of Marc Antony's generals, and was afterwards put to death. (Dio Cass. XLIX. p. 403.)
Hierocles and the Notitiæ reckon it among the
episcopal churches of Phrygia Salutaris, (p. 678.
Cf. Plin. V. 32. Ptol. p. 120.)   Mannert conceives
it to be the Mygdone of Ammian. Marcell. (XXVI.
8 [j].)   The site of Midæum should be sought for on

---

[g] This was probably according to the Galatian way of pro-
nouncing the name.

[h] Col. Leake's Asia Minor,
p. 18.

[i] The coins of Doryleum are
of the reigns of Augustus and

Titus.   The legend, ΔΟΡΥΛΑ-
ΕΩΝ. Sestini, p. 122.

[j] Sestini gives the following
description of the coins of Midæum: Imperatorii tantum a
Trajano, usque ad Philippum,
Inn.   Epigraphe, ΜΙΔΑΕΩΝ.

the left bank of the Sangarius, near a village called *Caragamous*. Beyond was Tricomia, known from Ptolemy, (p. 120.) and the Table Itinerary, which places it twenty-eight miles from Midæum and twenty-one from Pessinus. The latter, though originally a Phrygian town, is considered to belong to Galatia, and will therefore come under our notice in the following section.

To the south of Doryleum we have to point out Nacolea, which Strabo includes within Phrygia Epictetus. (XII. p. 576.) It is frequently mentioned by later writers; and we may infer, from their accounts, that it became a place of some importance under the eastern emperors. Ammianus reports, that the usurper Procopius was here defeated by Valens. (XXVII. 27. Cf. Zosim. IV. 8. Socrat. Eccl. Hist. IV. 5. Sozom. IV. 8.) Under Arcadius Nacolea was occupied by Tribigild, chief of some Goths garrisoned in the town, and who revolted against the emperor. (Philostorg. XI. c. 8. p. 542.) This town is also noticed by Hierocles, (p. 678.) Ptolemy, (p. 120.) and Steph. Byz. (v. Νακολία [k].) The Table fixes its situation twenty miles south of Doryleum; and Col. Leake is disposed to identify it with a ruined fortress called *Pishmesh-kalessi*, near *Doganlu*, where he observed some most remarkable monuments, apparently sepulchral, and, from the inscriptions, leading to the idea that they were the tombs of the Phrygian sovereigns[l]. As Nacolea, however, does not seem to have been a place of sufficient antiquity or note to accord with the de-

Conditor Midas, ΤΟΝ ΚΤΙCΤΗΝ-ΜΙΔΑΕΩΝ. Mentio situs a fl. Elate vel a fonte sacro ΕΛΑΤΗΣ in Trajani nummo, p. 125.

[k] The epigraph of its coins is ΝΑΚΟΛΕΩΝ. [l] P. 21—24.

scription of these monuments, I think we must refer them to some other site; especially as they appear to be removed from any regular line of road, which was not so with Nacolea.

PHRYGIA MAGNA.

Having now exhausted the towns which Strabo assigns to Phrygia Epictetus, we will pass on to consider what belonged to central Phrygia. This, as far as we may conclude from Strabo's rather hurried description, was formed of several valleys connected together; beginning from the Hyrcanian plain, near the junction of the Hyllus and Hermus, Cyri Campus. and the Cilbianus Campus, towards the head of the Cayster, he names successively the plain of Cyrus, which was so called by the Persians, but whether from the elder or younger Cyrus, he does not mention. (XIII. p. 629.) It is perhaps the same as the Campus Peltenus. Castoli Campus of Xenophon. Beyond was the plain Peltene, which belonged to Phrygia: that of Cyrus must therefore have been in Lydia. It derived its Peltæ. appellation from Pelte, the principal town in this part of the province, and situate, according to Xenophon, one day's march from Celænæ, at the head of the Meander. (Anab. I. 2. 10.) The historian describes it as a well inhabited city, and states that the army of Cyrus remained there three days, during which, games and sacrifices were performed; this implies a rich and fertile district. The Table confirms the topography of Xenophon, by placing Peltæ[1] twenty-six miles from Apamea Cibotus, which subsequently replaced Celænæ. The march of Cyrus, as described by Xenophon, presents consider-

[1] Falsely written Pella.

able difficulties, so that many critics have been led
to imagine that there has been some confusion in
this part of the narrative, from the carelessness of
transcribers, or some other cause[m]. The true way,
however, of considering this part of the Anabasis,
is to look upon these operations of Cyrus, not as a
straight-forward march towards the ultimate object
of his expedition, but rather as a circuitous pere-
grination through his dominions, for the purpose of
collecting supplies of men and money from the different districts, at the same time that he kept moving, and both supplied his troops and deceived the
enemy as to his real project. Thus we find him
moving from Sardes to the Meander, and along that
river up to its source; then northwards, by Peltæ,
up to the confines of Mysia, and subsequently along
the northern part of Phrygia and Galatia, into Lycaonia. This, I say, must be taken into the account
fully, and when we find the historian mentioning
places, the names of which are strange to us, we
are not therefore to conclude that there is any error
or confusion in the narrative, unless it is so palpable
that we cannot be mistaken. As I shall have occasion to revert again to the march of Cyrus, I need
not pursue the subject further at present.

Strabo ranks Peltæ among the smaller towns of
the province. (XII. p. 576.) It is also enumerated by
Ptolemy. (p. 120. Steph. Byz. v. Πελταί.) Pliny
states, that in his time Peltæ was under the jurisdiction of Apamea. (V. 29.) The Notitiæ name it
among the episcopal towns of Phrygia Pacatiana[n].
We must look for this ancient site to the north of

---

[m] Palmer. Exercit. in Auct. Gr. p. 59.   [n] Geogr. Sacr. p. 240.

the Meander, and probably in the valley and plain formed by the western branch of that river, now called *Askli-tchai*, but formerly Glaucus[o]. The Table places north of Peltæ, but without any indica-

Eumen'a.tion of distance, Eumenia, which probably derived its name from Eumenes, king of Pergamum. (Steph. Byz. v. Εὐμένεια.) Pliny, if his text be not corrupt,

Cludrus fl.says that this town was situated on the river Clu-
Glaucus fl.drus, but names immediately after the Glaucus, which is also referred to on the coins of the place. (IV. 29[p].) We collect from Hierocles and the Notitiæ, that it was the see of a Christian bishop, (p. 667.) Pococke observed at *Ishekle*, or *Ashkli*, where there were some ruins, an inscription with the name of Eume-

Lysias.nia. Lysias, which Pliny names together with the Glaucus, must have been in this vicinity and on the borders of Caria: I should be inclined to place it therefore south of Peltæ and Eumenia. It is perhaps the station marked in the Table under the name of ad Vicum. (Cf. Strab. XII. p. 576. Ptol. p. 120. Notit. Episc.) The coins of Lysias imply its foundation or restoration by Alexander[q]. It is in this direction, about the Glaucus and Meander, on the borders of Caria, that Pliny (V. 29.) places the Berecynthian district, which took its name from the

Berecyn-
thii.Berecynthii, a Phrygian tribe celebrated by the poets in connexion with Cybele, so often styled " Berecynthia mater." Xanthus, the Lydian histo-

---

[o] The coins of Peltæ lead us to suppose it had received at one time a Macedonian colony; the legend being ΠΕΛΤΗΝΩΝ ΜΑΚΕΔΟΝΩΝ. Sestini, p. 120.

[p] Sestini, p. 122. ΕΤΜΕΝΕ-ΩΝ ΑΧΑΙΩΝ. Mentio situs a

Glauco Fl. ΓΛΑΤΚΟΣ. Summus Pontifex Asiæ in nummis Neronis.

[q] Epigraphe, ΛΤΣΙΑΔΕΩΝ. ΒΟΤΛΗ. ΑΛΕΞΑΝΔΡΟC. ΚΤΙCΤ. Sestini, p. 124.

rian quoted by Strabo, (XIV. p. 680.) said the Berecynthii crossed over from Europe into Asia, after the Trojan war; but Strabo proves, from Homer, that there were Phrygians in the latter continent before that period. He elsewhere speaks of the Berecynthii as no longer existing in his time; but he censures Æschylus for placing them around Ida and Sipylus, as if those mountains were close to each other. (XII. p. 580. Cf. X. p. 469.) The same geographer speaks of another extinct Phrygian tribe, named Cerbesii, alluded to by the poet Alcman, but Cerbesii. of whom no other memorial remained, but a charonium, or hole, which emitted noxious exhalations. It was called the Cerbesian foss, but Strabo does not tell us where it was situated. (XII. p. 580.)

Eucarpia, according to the Table, was thirty miles Eucarpia. from Eumenia; (Cf. Strab. XII. p. 576.) it owed its name doubtless to the fertility of the country which surrounded it, and an ancient writer, quoted by Stephanus Byz. (v. Εὐκαρπία,) gave a marvellous account of the size of the grapes it produced. Pliny says Eucarpia was under the jurisdiction of Synnada. (V. 29. Cf. Ptol. p. 120. Hierocl. p. 676.) The site is unknown[r].

Conni, another Phrygian town, is placed by the Conni. Table between Eucarpia and Nacolea, thirty-two miles from the former, and forty from the latter. Pliny calls it Conium, (V. 32.) Ptolemy, Conna, (p. 120.) and Hierocles, Coniopolis, (p. 666. Cf. Notit. Episc.) This place was probably situated not far from *Altuntash,* near the source of the *Pursek.*

[r] There are coins of Eucarpia, both autonomous and imperial; the latter from the reign of Augustus to that of Treb. Gallus. The inscription is ΕΤ-ΚΑΡΠΕΩΝ. Sestini, p. 122.

Ceramo-
rum Fo-
rum.

The town called Κεραμῶν ἀγορὰ, Ceramorum Forum, by Xenophon, in the Anabasis, (I. 2. 11.) was more to the west, on the borders of Mysia, or rather that doubtful part of Lydia which was called Catacecaumene, and which some writers assign to Phrygia. It may be observed, that when Xenophon wrote, the Mysians were in the habit of making inroads on their neighbours, and were otherwise troublesome to the Persian king. It is possible that the town we are here considering may be the same as Ceranæ,

Ceranæ.

Synnada.

noticed by Pliny. (V. 32.)   We now come to Synnada, the most considerable town of this part of Phrygia, at least in Pliny's time, since it was then the capital of a Conventus Juridicus, which included all the surrounding boroughs; (V. 29.) Forum Synnadense, as Cicero terms it. (Ad Att. V. 21.) Strabo, however, speaks of it as a small town, situate at the extremity of a plain, about sixty stadia long, and planted with olives.   It was, however, greatly famed among the Romans for the beautiful marble furnished by the neighbouring quarries, and which was commonly called Synnadic, from the town, but the people of the country gave it the name of Docimites from Docimia, the precise place where it was excavated from the quarry. This beautiful substance, so much prized by the Romans, and celebrated by their poets, was of a light colour, interspersed with purple spots and veins[s].

> Sola nitet flavis Nomadum decisa metallis
> Purpura, sola cavo Phrygiæ quam Synnados antro
> Ipse cruentavit maculis lucentibus Atys.
>
> STAT. SILV. I. 5. 36.

[s] For a full description of this costly marble, see the learned work of Blasius Caryophilus on ancient marbles, and the authors quoted by him.

It is elegantly described by Paulus Silentiarius, in his Poem on the Church of S. Sophia.

Καὶ Φρύγα δαιδαλέοιο διέθρισεν αὐχένα πέτρου,
Τὸν μὲν ἰδεῖν ῥοδόεντα μεμιγμένον ἠέρι λευκῷ
Τὸν δ' ἅμα πορφυρέοισι καὶ ἀργυρέοισιν ἀώτοις,
Ἀβρὸν ἀπαστράπτοντα.

(Cf. Plin. XXXV. 1.) The central position of Synnada made it a place of passage and commerce[t]: it communicated with Celænæ, or Apamea Cibotus, as we learn from the Itineraries and the march of the consul Manlius, in his expedition against the Gallo-græci. (Liv. XXXVIII. 15. Cf. XLV. 34.) Cicero writes to Atticus, that he passed through Synnada on his way from Ephesus, by Laodicea and Apamea, into Cilicia; he stayed there three days. (Epist. V. 20. Cf. ad Fam. XV. 4. III. 8. Ptol. p. 120. Steph. Byz. v. Σύνναδα. Hierocl. p. 677[u].)

Docimia, whence, as we have seen, the Synnadic Docimia. marble was extracted, appears from Strabo to have been at the extremity of the plain in which Synnada was situate, and the Table places it to the north of that town, on the road to Doryleum. The accompanying number XXXII. denotes, I conceive, the distance which separates the latter city from Docimia, though it is placed between that town and Synnada. Strabo's description leads to the idea that Docimia, in his time, was but a small place; but it must have subsequently increased considerably, from the celebrity of its marble, and the price affixed to it; especially in the time of Hadrian. We learn

[t] See Col. Leake, Asia Minor, p. 54.
[u] There are numerous coins of Synnada; the epigraph, ΔΗΜΟC or ΒΟΥΛΗ CΥΝΝΑΔΕΩΝ. On one appear the words ΑΔΡΙΑΝΙΑ. ΠΑΝΑΘΗΝΑΙΑ. The series of emperors extends from Augustus to Gallienus. Sestini, p. 127.

from its coins that it had a senate, and a prætor or archon, as magistrates; besides which, we collect from the same source, that it had received at one time a Macedonian colony[x]. (Cf. Steph. Byz. vv. Σύνναδα, Δοκίμειον.) It was a bishopric of Phrygia Salutaris. (Hierocl. p. 677.) According to Col. Leake, there are appearances of extensive quarries between *Kosru-khan* and *Bulwudun,* which he is inclined to identify with those of Docimia; consequently, Synnada could only have been a few miles to the south, or south-west. It is not, however, improbable that

Santabaris. *Doghanlu* answers to Docimia. Santabaris, which Anna Comnena notices in the expedition of the emperor Alexius, (p. 470,) beyond Doryleum, was perhaps near *Seid Ghazi,* where there are some ruins[y]. To the south of Synnada, the Table places

Euphor-bium. Euphorbium, at a distance of thirty-seven miles from that city, and thirty-six from Apamea. Pliny, too, assigns the Euphorbini to the Conventus Apamenus; (V. 29.) but besides these two authorities, there are no other vouchers for its existence, that I am aware of. It is commonly supposed, that this place corresponds with the site of *Sandakli*[z], on a river which most probably is the Orgas of Pliny, if

Prymnesia sive Prym-nessus. that of *Ishakli* is the Glaucus. Prymnesia, or Prymnessus, was another small town in central Phrygia, according to Ptolemy's notation. (p. 120.) We learn from Hierocles, and the Ecclesiastical Notices, that it was the see of a bishop. The former writes the name Prymnesus; (p. 677[a].) Pococke found an in-

---

[x] ΑΠΜΟC vel ΙΕΡΑ CΤΝΚΛΗ-ΤΟC – ΔΟΚΙΜΕΩΝ – ΜΑΚΕΔΟ-ΝΩΝ. Sestini, p. 121.

[y] Pococke's Travels, p. iii.

c. 15. Otter's Travels, I. *c.* 7.

[z] Col. Leake's Asia Minor, p. 165.

[a] On the coins it is Prym-

scription near *Afiom Carahissar*, in which mention was made of Prymnesia [b].   Metropolis is another Metropolis. Phrygian town in the vicinity of Synnada, as we collect from Athenæus, who mentions having himself travelled from one town to the other. (XIII. p. 574. Cf. Liv. XXXVIII. 15.)   It is also noticed by Ptolemy, (p. 120.) Stephanus Byz. (v. Μητρόπολις,) and Hierocles. (p. 677.) Pliny assigns it to the Conventus of Apamea; (V. 29.) and it appears from Artemidorus, quoted by Strabo, to have been situate beyond that city, on the great road leading from Ephesus to Cappadocia and the Euphrates. (XIV. p. 663.) Elsewhere he enumerates Metropolis among the smaller towns of the province. (XII. p. 576[c].) The position of Metropolis evidently depending on that of Apamea, nothing can be ascertained respecting it, till that of the latter has been determined.   But if Apamea stood at *Dinare*, or *Dinglar*, as Col. Leake is inclined to think, and many other antiquaries with him, there would then be little doubt that Metropolis was situate to the east of that place [d]. General Lapie, in his map, fixes it at *Tchoulabad*, and Prymnesia at *Afiom Carahissar*.   Between Synnada and Metropolis was a small place, named Melisse, rendered interesting by Melisse sive Melitæa. the circumstance of Alcibiades having been interred there, by the affectionate care of his mistress Theodote, after he had fallen by the hands of the Persians.

nessus; these are not uncommon, and the mention of Midas implies a place of some antiquity. Epigraphe, ΒΟΥΔΗ, or ΣΥΝΚΛΗΤΟΣ ΠΡΥΜΝΗΣΣΕΩΝ ΜΙΔΑΣ ΒΑΣΙΛΕΥΣ. Sestini, p. 125.

[b] Travels, p. iii. c. 15.

[c] The coins of Metropolis lead to the idea that it was a more considerable place under the later emperors. Sestini, p. 124.

[d] Col. Leake, Asia Minor, p. 55, 56.

By order of Hadrian, a statue of that great man, in Parian marble, was afterwards erected on the tomb, and a yearly sacrifice of an ox offered to his shade. (Athen. XIII. p. 574.) I am inclined to think that the Melitara of Ptolemy (p. 120.) is the same as the Melisse of Athenæus; and on this hypothesis I should be disposed to alter in the former the name to Melitæa, Μελιταία instead of Μελιτάρα. Livy, in his narrative of the expedition of Cn. Manlius against the Gallo-græci, places between Metropolis and

Diniæ. Synnada a spot named Diniæ, (XXXVIII. 15.) of which no notice is taken by other writers; unless some trace of it should be thought to lurk in the word Χελιδονίων, applied by Strabo to a place which stood beyond Metropolis, on the great central road which traversed Asia Minor, from Ephesus to Tomisa in Comagene. (XIV. p. 663.) The generality of critics are of opinion that Χελιδονίων is a corrupt reading, and Palmerius would read Φιλομηλίου; but that town is mentioned below. Mannert proposes Κελαινῶν; but this conjecture, though nearer the text, is geographically inadmissible. The position of Diniæ answers sufficiently to that of the supposed Chelidonia, but it leaves the former part of the corrupt reading unaccounted for; perhaps another name is disguised under this likewise, and I should not think it improbable to be Cilla, or Cylla, which gave its name to a Phrygian plain in this direction. Strabo names it, together with the plains of Cyrus, Peltæ, and Tabæ. (XIII. p. 629.) Of this district, I find no mention made by other geographers, except Pliny, who briefly alludes to it in his description of Galatia, as a canton bordering on Pisidia. His words are, (V. 42.) "Attingit Galatia et Pamphyliæ Caba-

" liam et Milyas, qui circa Barin sunt, et Cyllanti-
" cum, et Oroandicum Pisidiæ tractum." The MSS.
read " Cyllanicum," which comes nearer to the Κιλ-
λάνιον of Strabo: and since, according to Pliny's
geography, the Cillanian district bordered on Pisidia, Galatia, and Lycaonia, it must have been somewhere between Metropolis of Phrygia and Antioch
of Pisidia, and it might therefore have some reference to the faulty reading, Χελιδονίων, discussed above.
Finally, I may observe, that the Cillanian plain may
possibly answer to the valley of *Sitshanli*, situated
north-east of *Dombai* and *Sandukli*, and which is
described by modern travellers as fertile and well
inhabited[e]. Holmi is another place mentioned by Holmi.
Strabo, on the road to Lycaonia, beyond Chelidonia;
it was at the foot of a chain of mountains, and dis-
stant 920 stadia from Carura, and 500 from Philomelium. D'Anville identifies it with *Houma*. (Strab.
XIV. p. 663.)

Polybotus, a place mentioned only by Hierocles Polybotus.
and the Byzantine historians, Procopius, and Anna
Comnena, is thought, with great appearance of probability, by Col. Leake, to answer to the site of *Bulwudun*[f]. (Hierocl. p. 677. Procop. Hist. Arc. c. 18.
Ann. Comn. p. 470.)

Philomelium was beyond Metropolis, on the same Philome-
great road to Iconium and Cappadocia, being men- lium.
tioned as such by Cicero, (ad Fam. III. 8. XV. 4.)
and Artemidorus, cited by Strabo. (XIV. p. 663.)
It was on the borders of what Strabo calls Phrygia
Parorius, that is, which stretches along the mountains, being situate in a plain of considerable extent

[e] Gen. Koehler's Journal in Col. Leake's Asia Minor, p. 139.
[f] Asia Minor, p. 53.

from west to east.   The chain of mountains above
mentioned was a branch of Taurus, on the south
side of which was Antioch of Pisidia. (Strab. XII.
p. 577.) Philomelium, according to Pliny, was under
the jurisdiction of Synnada. (V. 29.) Cf. Hierocl. p.
673. Ptol. p. 120.) It is often alluded to by the
Byzantine historians in the wars of the Greek emperors with the sultans of Iconium. (Ann. Comn.
p. 473. Procop. Hist. Arc. c. 18. Nicet. Ann. p.
264. B.)   From a coin struck under the emperor
Decius, it would appear to have been seated near a
river named Gallus [g].   It is probable that Philomelium was situate near the modern *Ilgun*.   Close
to this place is a lake which answers, as Col. Leake
observes, to the lake of the Forty Martyrs referred to
by Anna Comnena. (loc. cit.[h]) The same Byzantine
writer mentions Mesonacte and Zyganium as being
places in the same district. (p. 473, 480.) The latter
is probably the Cingularium of Nicetas. (p. 264. B.)

Julia.   The Table places beyond Philomelium, on the
road to Iconium, a spot named Jullæ, which Col.
Leake is inclined to identify with Juliopolis, named
by Ptolemy in Phrygia, (p. 120.) with Synnada and
Melitœa.   At the same time he observes, " that
" there can be little doubt that so fine a position as
" that of *Ak-shehr* was occupied before the time of
" the Cæsars by some important place, which, on
" its being repaired or reestablished, may have as-
" sumed the new name of Julia, or Juliopolis."
Pliny assigns the Julienses to the Conventus Synna-
dicus. (V. 29.[i])

[g] Sestini, p. 125. Epigraphe,
ΦΙΛΟΜΗΛΕΩΝ. Imperatorii ab
Augusto ad Gallum. Mentio si-
tus a fl. Gallo ΓΑΛΛΟC (sic) in

nummo Decii.
[h] Asia Minor, p. 59.
[i] The name of the town appears from its coins to have been

Laodicea, surnamed Catacecaumene by the Greeks, Laodicea. Catacecaumene. Combusta by the Latins, was twenty-eight miles from Philometium, according to the Table Itinerary. It is assigned by Ptolemy to Galatia, but Hierocles and the ecclesiastical writers name it among the episcopal sees of Pisidia. (Hierocl. p. 672. Socrat. Eccl. Hist. VI. 18.) According to Strabo, who quotes Artemidorus, it stood on the great road which led from Ephesus to the Euphrates, and at that period it belonged to Lycaonia; but previously it must have appertained to Phrygia. Ancient authorities are silent with respect to its foundation, but it was evidently built by some prince of the Seleucid dynasty. (Strab. XIV. p. 663. Steph. Byz. v. Λαοδικεία.) It obtained its surname of Catacecaumene from the volcanic nature of the district in which it was situated. Laodicea retains the name of *Ladik*, and exhibits, as we are informed by Col. Leake, numerous remains of antiquity dispersed throughout the modern town, which is considerable, and famous for its manufacture of carpets [k].

In this part of Phrygia, but probably nearer Synnada, we should seek for Ipsus, celebrated for the Ipsus. great battle fought in its plains by Antigonus and his son Demetrius, against the combined forces of Cassander, Lysimachus, Ptolemy, and Seleucus. We have no detailed account of this decisive conflict, in which Antigonus lost all his conquests and his life. The reader may consult Plutarch in his life of

Julia, and not Juliopolis: the epigraph being ΙΟΥΛΑΕΩΝ. They are not anterior to the reign of Nero. Sestini, p. 123.

There are a few imperial coins belonging to Laodicea, of the reigns of Titus and Domitian. Sestini, p. 95.

[k] Asia Minor, p. 43, 44.

Pyrrhus, Appian in his history of Syria, and the mutilated narrative of Diodorus, as the best authorities to be procured ; but little is to be gained from them respecting the position of Ipsus. Hierocles (p. 677.) and the Acts of Councils afford evidence of its having been the see of a Christian bishop in the seventh and eighth centuries[1].

Beudos Vetus.

To the north-east of Synnada, and distant from it about five miles, was Beudos, surnamed Vetus, to distinguish it probably from a town of more recent foundation. Livy says, that the army of Manlius, marching from Synnada, came to Beudos, having scarcely performed five miles in one day; it was so encumbered with booty taken from the surrounding towns, whose inhabitants had deserted them on their approach. (XXXVIII. 15.) Beudos, I suspect, is the same town which Nonnus calls Budea.

Καὶ Φρύγες ἐστρατόωντο παρ' ἐγρεμόθων στίχα Λυδῶν
Οἵτ' ἔλαχον Βούδειαν ἀειδομένην τε πολίχνην
Δενδροκόμον Τεμένειαν, εὔσκιον ἄλσος ἀρούρης.

DIONYS. XIII. 511.

Temeneia.

Temeneia, which the poet connects with it, is unknown, unless we should suppose Eumenia, or perhaps Metropolis, is signified by that name. The epithet ἀειδομένη implies that it was a noted place.

Dresia.

Dresia was also another place which the poet Dionysius in his Bassarica, as well as Nonnus, introduces with Beudia.

Βουδείαν, Δρεσίην τε καὶ οἱ μηλώδεα γαῖαν.

(ap. Steph. Byz. vv. Δρεσία, Βουδεία.) The latter

[1] Numismatical writers assign a coin, with the epigraph ΙΨΤ, supposed to be unique, to Ipsus. Sestini, p. 123.

connects it with the Obrimus, or Obrimas, one of the tributary streams of the Meander.

Οἱ Δρεσίην ἐνέμοντο καὶ Ὄβριμον ὅστε ῥεέθροις
Μαιάνδρου σκολιοῖσιν ἐὸν παραβάλλεται ὕδωρ
Καὶ δάπεδον Δοίαντος ἐπώνυμον.

The Dœantius Campus, mentioned in the last line, is perhaps only another name for the great plain of Peltæ, and the fertile country about Eucarpia and Euphorbium: (Cf. Steph. Byz. v. Δοίαντος πεδίον.) and perhaps Dœas, which gave its name to it, is the Diniæ of Livy. From Beudos, which is, with great probability, thought to agree with *Beiad,* Manlius marched on to Anabura. In another day he came to the sources of the Alander, and on the third to Abassus, on the frontiers of Galatia. The Alander appears to be an inconsiderable river, which rises somewhat to the north of *Beiad,* and falls into the Sangarius to the north-east of *Eski-sher,* or Doryleum. Abassus is certainly the Ambasus of Steph. Byz., (v. Ἄμβασον,) and perhaps the same with the Alarnassus of Hierocles, (p. 678.) or Amadasse of the Councils [m]. Following the Alandrus, the Roman army halted successively at Tyscon, Plitendus, and Alyatti. This part of Phrygia was named Axylos, (Ἄξυλος,) from its being so destitute of wood that the inhabitants used cow-dung for fuel. (Liv. XXXVIII. 15.[n]) Having advanced some way, the consul came to Cuballus, a fortress of Gallo-Græcia,

(marginal notes): Dœantius Campus. Anabura. Alander fl. Abassus. Tyscon vicus. Plitendus. Alyatti. Axylos regio. Cuballus.

[m] See Wesseling's note to Hierocles.

[n] We must suppose the march to have been extremely slow and cautious, in order to adapt the narrative to the map: otherwise we must admit that the Roman army, baffled in its attempt to penetrate into Galatia by the left bank of the Sangarius, retraced its steps and crossed to the other side. It is to be regretted that we have not Polybius's narrative of this Gallo-græcian war.

where he had a skirmish with the Gauls; from thence he reached the river Sangarius, after a continuous march of some days. This river, according to Livy, who copies Polybius, rises in mount Adoreus of Phrygia, and after receiving the Thymbris on the borders of Bithynia, falls into the Propontis. Eustathius, in his commentary on the poet Dionysius, (p. 143.) says, there was a village named Sangia near the source of this river. Ptolemy marks three considerable bendings in the course of the Sangarius: the first takes place near its junction with the Gallus; the second below *Sevrihissar*, near the ancient Gordium; the third below *Yerma*. The Byzantine historians make frequent mention of a bridge at a place called Zompi, or Zompus, which seems to have been on the Sangarius. (Ann. Comn. p. 472. Curopal. p. 836. Niceph. Bryenn. II. p. 52.) We are informed by G. Pachymeres that the Sangarius was subject to overflow its banks, and to change its course. (Andr. Pal. p. 228.) We must now quit the Sangarius, and proceed in a very opposite direction to the valley of the Meander, to explore the course of that river and the towns seated on its banks, which were neither the least celebrated, nor the least considerable in the whole province. If we place ourselves at Tripolis in Lydia, the highest point to which our descriptive tour has led us up the river, we shall gain, on crossing over to the left bank, the great road leading from Ephesus by Magnesia and Tralles into Phrygia, Lycaonia, Cilicia, or Cappadocia. The first town we shall arrive at after quitting Tripolis is Hierapolis, which Strabo is inclined to assign to Lydia; (XIII. p. 629.) but other geographers include within the

Adoreus mons.

Sangia vicus.

Zompi pons.

Hierapolis.

viduals. Among these Strabo mentions Hiero, who, besides greatly embellishing it, left by his will the large sum of 2000 talents; the orator Zeno, and his son Polemo, who was made king of part of Pontus by Augustus. These patriotic citizens amply repaired the damage which their native city had sustained when besieged by Mithridates. (Strab. XII. p. 578. Appian, Mithr. c. 20.) Stephanus, who places this city in Lydia, (v. Λαοδίκεια,) says it was founded by Antiochus, son of Stratonice, and named after his wife Laodice. Pliny reports that it was previously called Diospolis and Rhous: he adds, that, besides the Lycus, its walls were washed by the Asopus Lycus fl. and Caprus. (V. 29.) Strabo also states that the Ly- Asopus fl. cus and Caprus united their waters, and afterwards joined the Meander [r]. The Lycus, the most considerable of the two, had its source in Mount Cadmus, Cadmus which rose above the town; but the river issued from mons. a more distant part of the chain, which prolonged its range to the east into Milyas and Lycia, where it joined mount Taurus. The Turks call it *Babadagh*. Strabo speaks of a small stream, also named Cadmus, which descended from it. The Lycus, ac- Cadmus fl. cording to the same geographer, disappeared not far from its source, and flowed for a considerable space under ground: this was to be accounted for from the volcanic nature of the district, which rendered it full of caverns, and subject to earthquakes. Laodicea was frequently exposed to this calamity, as well as the surrounding towns and villages. (Strab. loc. cit. Cf. Tacit. Ann. II. 79. XIV. 27.) Herodotus states that the Lycus disappeared at Colossæ; and,

---

[r] Sestini, p. 123. Epigraphe, ΛΑΟΔΙΚΕΩΝ. Mentio situs a fluviis Lyco et Capso, ΛΥΚΟC. ΚΑΠΡΟC. in nummis Commodi, Gallieni, etiam in autonomo.

after remaining concealed at most for five stadia, reappeared again and joined the Meander. It is certain that the Lycus does not pass very near the ancient Colossæ; we must not therefore take the historian's expression, (VII. 30.) ἐν τῇ Λύκος ποταμὸς ἐς
χάσμα γῆς ἐσβάλλων ἀφανίζεται, literally, but " in the
" vicinity of Colossæ; in its territory." The modern name of the Lycus is *Djok-bounai*, or *Sultan
Emir-tchai*; that of the Caprus, *Giumiskoi*[s]. Laodicea was celebrated for the breed of sheep which
fed in the plains around it; their wool was even
thought to be superior in softness and colour to that
of Miletus; so that this article was a source of great
profit to the city. (Strab. XII. p. 578.) The history of Laodicea derives further illustration from
Polybius. (V. 57. 5.) Cicero, (Verr. I. 30. Ep. ad
Fam. III. 5. 7. XII. 13. 14. ad Att. V. 15.) Tacitus,
(Ann. IV. 55.) Philostratus. (p. 543.)

The zeal of St. Paul for the church of Laodicea
is attested by the mention he makes of it in his
Epistle to the Colossians. (ii. 1.) " For I would that
" ye knew what great conflict I have for you, and
" for them at Laodicea, and for as many as have not
" seen my face in the flesh." (iv. 16.) " And when
" this epistle is read among you, cause that it be
" read also in the church of the Laodiceans; and
" that ye likewise read the epistle from Laodicea."
From the mention here made of the epistle from
Laodicea, it has been supposed that the apostle had
written a special letter to the converts of that city,
now lost; but most critics are of opinion that this
refers to another of his epistles, either that to the
Ephesians or Timothy I. Others imagine again that

[s] Chandler, p. 284. note.

it was a letter written by the Laodiceans to the apostle; but this is less probable.

The book of Revelations contains a severe rebuke on the lukewarmness of the Laodicenes, and their worldly-mindedness, and threatens them with that ruin which has been so completely accomplished. iii. 14. "And unto the angel of the church of the "Laodiceans write; These things saith the Amen, "the faithful and true witness, the beginning of the "creation of God; I know thy works, that thou art "neither cold nor hot: I would thou wert cold or "hot. So then because thou art lukewarm, and "neither cold nor hot, I will spue thee out of my "mouth. Because thou sayest, I am rich, and in-"creased with goods, and have need of nothing; "and knowest not that thou art wretched, and mi-"serable, and poor, and blind, and naked: I counsel "thee to buy of me gold tried in the fire, that thou "mayest be rich; and white raiment, that thou "mayest be clothed, and that the shame of thy "nakedness do not appear; and anoint thine eyes "with eyesalve, that thou mayest see. As many as "I love, I rebuke and chasten: be zealous there-"fore, and repent."

The Byzantine writers make frequent allusions to it in the time of the Comneni. It was fortified by the emperor Manuel. (Nicet. Chon. Ann. p. 9. 81.) Its ruins are now to be seen a little below *Denisli*, a Turkish town near the junction of the Lycus and Caprus. The site is called *Eski-hissar*, and some-times *Ladik*. "We had crossed the hill," says Chandler, "on which Laodicea stood, coming from "*Denisli:* on our approach to it we had on either "hand traces of buildings; and on our right, of a

" low duct, which has conveyed water. The first
" ruin was of an amphitheatre, in a hollow; the
" form oblong, the area about 1000 feet in extent,
" with many seats remaining. At the west end is
" a wide vaulted passage, designed for the horses
" and chariots, about one hundred and forty feet
" long. On the north side of the amphitheatre, to-
" ward the east end, is the ruin of a most ample
" edifice: it consists of many piers and arches of
" stone, with pedestals and marble fragments. From
" this ruin you see the odeum, which fronted south-
" ward. The seats remain in the side of the hill:
" the materials of the front lie in a confused heap.
" The whole was of marble. Sculpture had been
" lavished on it, and the style savoured less of Gre-
" cian taste than Roman magnificence. Beyond the
" odeum are some marble arches standing, with pieces
" of massive wall; the ruin, as we conjectured, of a
" gymnasium. This fabric, with one at a small dis-
" tance, appeared to have been reedified, probably
" after an earthquake, to which calamity Laodicea
" was remarkably subject. Many traces of the city
" wall may be seen, with broken columns and pieces
" of marble used in its later repairs: within, the
" whole surface is strewed with pedestals and frag-
" ments. The luxury of the citizens may be infer-
" red from their other sumptuous buildings, and
" from two capacious theatres in the side of the hill,
" fronting northward and westward; each with its
" seats still rising in numerous rows one above an-
" other."

About twenty miles to the west of Laodicea, and
Carura. on the frontier of Caria, was a place named Carura,
situate on the great road which followed the Me-

ander from Ephesus, and apparently a town of considerable traffick, as there were many inns for the
accommodation of travellers. There were also numerous warm springs, which gushed forth, some in
the Meander itself, others on its banks: a sure indication of a volcanic country. It was reported, that
on one occasion a whole troop of courtesans, who
were lodged at Carura, were engulphed during the
night by the yawning earth. (Strab. XII. p. 578.)
Near this town, and towards Laodicea, was the
temple of Men-Carus, an object of great veneration
among the surrounding people. Strabo states, that
in his day a celebrated school of physicians, surnamed Herophilii, from Herophilus, who flourished
under the Ptolemies, had been established there.
(XII. p. 580.) Athenæus speaks of a village named
Men-Carus, and distinguishes it also from Carura, Men-Ca-
which he seems to place in Caria; both places had rus.
warm sources. (II. p. 43.)

Returning to Laodicea and the Lycus, and advancing to the north-east, we shall come upon the
Meander again, where, after bending round the hills
of Hierapolis, it returns towards the south. Here
we shall find, at a little distance from its left bank,
the ancient town of Colossæ, mentioned by Herodo- Colossæ.
tus as a large and flourishing town of Phrygia, at
the time of Xerxes' expedition, who passed through
it on his way to Sardes from Cappadocia. (VII.
30.) Xenophon also reports that Cyrus the Younger
halted there, on his march towards Babylon, and he
terms it a populous and wealthy city. (Anab. I. 2.)
Strabo, in one passage, seems to reckon Colossæ
among the minor towns of Phrygia: (XII. p. 576.)
but elsewhere he speaks of the great profit the in-

habitants derived from their wool trade, as did their neighbours the Laodiceni. (XII. p. 578.) In the reign of Nero this city was nearly destroyed, and scarcely retained any trace of its former greatness. Its church however, which had been so great an object of solicitude to the apostle of the Gentiles, though he had not visited it in person, (Coloss. ii. 1.[s]) still flourished even as late as the time of Hierocles, who names it among the episcopal towns of Phrygia Pacatiana. (p. 666.) He writes the name Κολασσαὶ, in which mode of writing it several other authors concur, and numerous MSS. of St. Paul's Epistles, as Wesseling observes[t]. But Herodotus, Xenophon, and Strabo must outweigh the contrary testimony, especially as they have on their side the evidence of coins, whose authority is not to be disputed[u]. Under the Byzantine emperors, Colossæ, being in a ruinous state, made way for a more modern town, named Chonæ, which was built at a short distance from it. This place is chiefly known to us from the account of Nicetas, the Byzantine annalist, who was born there; whence his surname of Choniates. He reports that it was a large town,

Chonæ.

[s] It is certainly said, on the other hand, that he "went all "over the country of Galatia "and Phrygia;" but this may mean only that central and northern part of Phrygia which bordered on Galatia. And in the whole of the epistle there is no expression which leads us to the direct inference that he had visited Colossæ in person. On the contrary he says, (i. 3, 4.) "We give thanks to God "and the Father of our Lord "Jesus Christ, praying always "for you, since *we heard* of "your faith in Christ Jesus." Epaphras is particularly mentioned as having preached the Gospel to them; he being a native of Colossæ, as well as Onesimus. (iv. 9, 12.)

[t] In his commentary on Hierocles. This must have been a late corruption.

[u] The epigraph is ΔΗΜΟΣ ΚΟΛΟΣΣΗΝΩΝ. Sestini, p. 120.

and possessed a magnificent church, dedicated to the archangel Michael, but which was afterwards burnt by the Turks. (p. 115, D. p. 256, B.) The historian Curopalates mentions also its destruction; he speaks besides of the river, (Lycus,) and its subterraneous channel, and an extraordinary rise of the water, which drowned several persons. (p. 834.) Some remains of Colossæ and its more modern successor are to be seen near each other on the site called *Khonas*, or *Kanassi*, by the Turks, to the north-east of Laodicea, and not far from the left bank of the Meander. They have been visited by Pococke [x], Picenini [y], and, more recently, by Mr. Arundell. *Chonos* is a village of about 200 Greek families, situated near the Meander, and under a very high and almost inaccessible hill: the ruins may be traced for the space of nearly a mile. Mr. Arundell, on his way from *Denizli* to *Khonas*, says he came to a beautifully clear stream, flowing close by the side of the road, on the left downwards towards the Meander: soon after, the same stream disappeared at once, or rather appeared to issue, by a subterraneous course, from under a low hill [z]. Mr. A. says, "*Khonas* is situated most picturesquely " under the immense range of mount Cadmus, which " rises to a very lofty and perpendicular height above " the village, with immense chasms and caverns. On

[x] Travels in the East, tom. III. part ii. c. 14.

[y] In Chandler's Travels, p. 298.

[z] A Visit to the Seven Churches of Asia, by the Rev. V. J. Arundell, British Chaplain at Smyrna. London, 8vo. 1828. p. 92. The same traveller was told that the river near *Akkhan*, which is clearly the Lycus of Strabo, disappeared about three hours above that place in a chasm of the ground, and after 300 fathoms reemerged again, two hours from *Denizli*, and two hours and a half from *Khonas*. p. 100.

" the summit of the castle are several fragments of
" old walls, but none of very ancient date. The
" village on the eastern side is of considerable ex-
" tent. The multitude of fragments of marble pil-
" lars almost upon every terraced roof, used there
" as rollers, proved the existence of some consider-
" able ancient town in the neighbourhood." These
are evidently the remains of Chonæ. Those of Colossæ are to be referred to other ruins, which he
was shewn more to the west. He observed a place
where " a number of large squared stones lay about,
" and what seemed to have been a small church.
" Passing through several fields, in which were
" many more stones, he noticed an imperfect in-
" scription. He was told also, that not far off were
" the remains of two churches. Beyond this he
" came to a level space, elevated by a perpendicular
" brow of considerable height above the fields be-
" low. Here were several vestiges of an ancient city,
" arches, &c.; and the whole of this and the adjoin-
" ing grounds was strewed with broken pottery[a]."

To the east of Colossæ, and towards the source of
Anava urbs et lacus. the Meander, was a town and lake named Anava.
The lake was salt, as we learn from Herodotus, who
mentions the fact with reference to the march of
Xerxes' army from Celænæ to Colossæ. (VII. 30.)
No other writer has mentioned this place, at least un-
der the same name; but I imagine it to be the same
town which Strabo calls Sanaus, (XII. p. 576.) and
Ptolemy Sanis; (p. 120.) but Sanaos appears in
Hierocles, (p. 666.) and the Council of Chalcedon.
p. 674.) Mr. Arundell passed by this lake, on his

---

[a] Visit to the Seven Churches of Asia, p. 94—98.

way from *Khonas,* and was told it was called *Hagee Ghieul,* or the bitter lake; that the water was not fit to be drunk, and no fish would live in it. (p. 104, 105.) He reports it to be sixteen miles long by four wide. (p. 106.) The site of Anava probably corresponds with that of *Alan-kevi,* somewhat to the north of the lake. That of *Bourdour,* further to the east, is of greater extent, and is doubtless the Ascania Palus of Arrian, which Alexander passed on his way from Sagalassus in Pisidia to Apamea. He says this lake was so impregnated with salt, that it formed of itself on the top, whence the natives collected it. (Anab. Alex. I. in fin.)

Themisonium was a town of Phrygia, but situ- Themisonium. ate on the borders of Pisidia, and latterly came to be included within the limits of that province. (Hierocl. p. 674.) But Strabo distinctly assigns it to Phrygia, (XII. p. 576.) as well as Pausanias (Phoc. c. 32.) and Ptolemy. (p. 120.) Pausanias states that the Themisonians shewed a cave, about thirty stadia from their town, where, by the advice of Hercules, Apollo, and Mercury, they had concealed their wives and children during an irruption of the Gauls into this part of Asia: in consequence of this they afterwards erected statues to these deities within the cave. Themisonium, according to the Table, was thirty-four miles from Laodicea. Returning to the lake of Anava, and tracing the Meander up to its source, we shall arrive at Celænæ, a city of great Celænæ. antiquity, and celebrated in Grecian mythology as the scene of the fabulous story of Marsyas and Apollo. It was also connected with the legendary tale of Midas, to which Nonnus alludes when he says,

Οἳ Δρεσίην ἐνέμοντο καὶ Ὄβριμον, ὅς τε ῥεέθροις
Μαιάνδρου σκολιοῦσιν ἑὸν παραβάλλεται ὕδωρ
Καὶ δάπεδον Δοίαντος ἐπώνυμον, οἵ τε Κελαινὰς
Χρυσοφόρους ἐνέμοντο.   Dionys. XIII. 514.

Athenæus also speaks of it as the residence of Li-
tyerses, son of Midas. (X. p. 415.) Herodotus is the
earliest historian who gives us any account of the
situation of this city, which was very remarkable.
" There," says the historian, " burst forth the sources
" of the Meander, and of another stream not less than
" the Meander, whose name is Catarrhactes, which,
" gushing forth from the agora itself of Celænæ, falls
" into the Meander. In which place also, within
" the city, is suspended the skin of the satyr Mar-
" syas, who is said in story to have been flayed
" by Apollo." Xerxes passed through Celænæ on
his way from Cappadocia to Sardes, and was hospit-
ably entertained by Pythius, an individual possessed
of immense wealth, which he liberally offered to his
sovereign. (VII. 26, et seq.) Celænæ was a favourite
residence of the younger Cyrus. Xenophon reports,
" that he had a palace there, and an extensive park,
" full of wild beasts, in which he took the diversion
" of hunting. The Meander had its source close to
" the palace, and flowed through the park and the
" town. There was also a royal fortress, with a
" palace of the king of Persia at the source of the
" Marsyas, below the Acropolis; this, too, flows
" through the town, and falls into the Meander.
" The breadth of the Marsyas is twenty-five feet.
" There Apollo is said to have flayed Marsyas, hav-
" ing vanquished him in a contest for musical skill,
" and to have suspended his skin in the cave whence
" the river flows. Hence the river is called Mar-

" syas. It is said that Xerxes, after his defeat in
" Greece, withdrew to this place, and built these
" palaces and the acropolis of Celænæ." The river
called Catarrhactes by Herodotus, appears to be the
Marsyas of Xenophon and others. Among these
Livy and Pliny assert, that both the Meander and
Marsyas drew their sources from a lake above Celænæ, and named Aulocrene, from the excellence of
the reeds which it produced : a circumstance which
doubtless was connected with the fable of Marsyas.
(Liv. XXXVIII. 13. Plin. V. 29. Strab. XII. p.
578.) Pliny says, the mountain, at the foot of which Signia
Celænæ was placed, bore the name of Signia, and ^{mons.}
that it stood near the junction of the Marsyas, Obrimas, and Orgas, with the Meander. Arrian reports
that Alexander arrived at Celænæ in five days from
Sagalassus. He found the citadel, which was built
on a height precipitous on every side, occupied by
the troops of the Phrygian satrap; but these capi-
tulated on receiving conditions which the strength
of the place induced Alexander to grant. (Anab.
Alex. I. fin.) After the death of this sovereign,
when Asia Minor had passed under the dominion Apamea
of the Seleucidæ, we are told that Antiochus Soter ^{Cibotus.}
removed the inhabitants of Celænæ to a spot situ-
ate above the junction of the Orgas and Meander,
where he founded a city which he named Apamea,
from his mother Apama, daughter of Artabazus,
and espoused to Seleucus Nicator. The new city
soon became a place of great importance, from the
fertility of the surrounding country, the abundance
and beauty of the rivers which flowed around it,
and, above all, its situation on the great road to
Cappadocia and the Euphrates; so that when Strabo

wrote, its traffick yielded only to that of Ephesus, and it was the largest town of Phrygia. (XII. p. 577.) The origin of the term Cibotus, attached to Apamea probably as a distinctive appellation from the Syrian town of the same name, has not been explained. (Plin. V. 29.[b]) Cicero makes frequent mention of Apamea in his letters, particularly during his government in Asia Minor. He held a court of justice there as chief magistrate. (Ep. ad Att. V. 16 et 21. Fam. II. 17. V. 20. Orat. pro Flacc. c. 28.) Pliny states, that it was the capital of a conventus, which included several of the neighbouring towns. (Plin. V. 29.)

We learn from Tacitus that under the reign of Claudius, Apamea, having been much injured by the shock of an earthquake, was exempted from taxes for five years. (Ann. XII. 58.) It must have been on some such catastrophe as this that entire lakes, as Nicolaus of Damascus reported, disappeared in the vicinity of Apamea, while others on the contrary, which had never seen the light, spread themselves over the plains, and rivers and fountains gushed forth[c]. This is said to have happened in the time of Mithridates. (Athen. VIII. p. 332.) Apamea, however, appears to have survived all these disasters, since we find Dio Chrysostom, in one of his orations, extolling the greatness and flourishing condition of the town. (XXXV. p. 432.) The church of Apamea does not figure amongst the earliest in the province of Phry-

---

[b] It appears on the coins of Apamea. ΚΙΒΩΤΟC. ΑΠΑΜΕΩΝ. These monuments also frequently allude to the rivers Marsyas and Meander. Sestini, p. 118.

[c] This circumstance may account for the seeming discrepancy between the accounts of the ancients and the present appearance of the country.

gia [d]. In Hierocles it is ranked with the episcopal cities of Pisidia, to which it then belonged. (p. 673: see Wesseling's note.) I find no mention of Apamea in the Byzantine historians [e]; but it appears in the Table Itinerary, and its bishops are known to have sat in the councils of Nice. The knowledge of this ancient site is of importance for clearing up the topography of this part of Asia Minor. Pococke was the first traveller who communicated any information which led to the idea that it stood at a place called *Dinglare*, or *Deenare*, but he did not visit the site himself, and what he collected was only from report [f]. Mr. Arundell seems to have settled this interesting question. From his account, there can be little doubt that Apamea and Celænæ stood at the present town of *Deenare*. He describes it as situate nearly east, but a little inclined to the north from *Khonas*, and near the junction of three rivers. " We walked behind the town to- " wards the north-west, and saw considerable frag- " ments of walls, which had been covered with soil, " but lately again exposed to view, partly by exca- " vation, and partly from the accidental falling away " of the earth; these were at the base of the hill, " and underneath them issued the sources of a small " river. Ascending the hill, we found nearly at the " summit a theatre, with the subsellia remaining, " but the stones removed. Above this was a large " area covered with pottery, probably the acropo-

[d] I should be led to infer from this fact, that St. Paul had not visited this part of Phrygia in person, or at least had not remained there long enough to found a church.

[e] Nicetas speaks only of Celænæ and the sources of the Meander and Marsyas. Ann. p. 115. D.

[f] Travels, tom. III. p. 2. c. 15.

" lis. Descending again, we saw a river flowing
" down through the valley under the acropolis on
" the south-east side, which, after supplying several
" mills, united in the plain before the town with
" the smaller stream, whose sources we had just be-
" fore remarked, and then fell into the larger river
" which we had crossed last evening; which, being
" much increased in size by these additions, flowed
" down through the plain which lay between the
" two ridges of mountains on the north-west." Mr.
Arundell copied several inscriptions, but none contained the name of Apamea [g]. "Walking along
" the south and south-east sides of the town, we
" met with fragments of cornices and capitals, pe-
" destals and columns. We remarked no ancient
" buildings, probably because our search was not
" sufficiently extended; but above the town, on the
" southern side of the river under the Acropolis, I
" remarked large masses of stone. *Deenare* will
" afford a most ample field for the future traveller;
" the situation is magnificent, and at once bespeaks
" the former importance of Apollonia." (Apamea.)
On inquiry " for a hill in the neighbourhood, which
" had a lake on its top, out of which flowed a river,
" an old Turk instantly said, that is at the source of
" the Meander, four hours from *Deenare* [h]."

[g] One, containing the name of Apollonia, led Mr. Arundell to believe that *Deenare* was not Apamea, but Apollonia in Phrygia; but Col. Leake justly observed that the inscription refers to Apollonia on the Rhyndacus, and concludes there can be no doubt of the identity of Apamea and *Deenare*. Note to Arundell's Visit, &c. p. 109.

[h] Visit to the Seven Churches, &c. p. 107—111. See also Col. Leake's Journal. The chief doubt arising from the description of Mr. Arundell is, that the source of the Marsyas agrees very little with the river called Catarrhactes by Herodotus, which must have fallen over the

To the east of Apamea and Celænæ, and beyond Silbium. the source of the Meander, was the small town of Silbium, named by Ptolemy (p. 120.) and Pliny. (V. 29.) In the Byzantine writers it is not frequently mentioned under the corrupt form, Sybleum or Siblia. It was restored and fortified by Manuel Comnenus, but afterwards dismantled. (Nic. Ann. p. 115. A. p. 124. D.) Cinnamus, who calls it Syblas, says, it was near the first source of the Meander; (p. 174.) so I translate περὶ πρώτας που τοῦ Μαιάνδρου ἰδρυμένον ἐκβολὰς, and not "ad prima Mæandri ostia," as the Latin version renders it. We learn from Hierocles (p. 6.) and the Notices, that it was a bishop's see[1]. Apollonia, as we learn from the Table, was Apollonia, prius Margium. twenty-four miles to the south-east of Apamea, on the road to Antioch of Pisidia. It is mentioned by Strabo as one of the minor towns of the province. (XII. p. 576.) Stephanus Byz. in the large list of towns which bore this name, assigns the eighteenth to Phrygia, and remarks that it was previously called Margium. (v. Ἀπολλωνία.) Col. Leake is inclined to place it at *Ketsi-bourlu*, not far from the lake *Boudour*, where Mr. Arundell observed some remains of antiquity. The Orgas, which receives the waters of the Meander and Marsyas soon after their junction, is a larger river than the former, but nevertheless yields its name to the ascendency of that more

precipice, or at least down a rapid. On the other hand, it is possible that the character of this river may have been completely changed, owing to some earthquake, or other physical cause, just as the Anio in Italy is known to have undergone a similar alteration.

[1] There is but one known coin of Siblium: according to Sestini the legend is CEIBΛIANΩN.

celebrated stream.　It receives itself the Glaucus, and other streams which come from the Peltene plain, and the Obrimas, which flows from the central chain of mountains connected with Taurus, and runs nearly in a straight course from east to west, if at least it is the stream which passes in the valley of *Dombai-ovassi*.　Its modern name appears to be *Nabis;* that of the Orgas, *Tchorouk*[k].　Livy, in his narrative of the expedition of Manlius against the Gallo-Græci, (XXXVIII. 15.) says, that he arrived on his march from Sagalassus in Pisidia at the sources of the Obrimas, and encamped there

Aporidos-come.

near a village called Aporidos-come, but which no other author has named, unless it should be, as I suspect, the same place which the Ecclesiastical No-

Apira.

tices call Apira, and assign to Phrygia Pacatiana[l]. In Lapie's map Aporidos-come is identified with the modern site of *Olou Bourlou*, placed by him at the source of the river *Dombai-ovassi*, I know not on what authority.　Besides the towns hitherto described, and the positions of which are all nearly determined, we have several others whose sites have not yet been ascertained.　These I purpose taking in alphabetical order.

Alia, sive Alii.

Alia, or Alii, is known from the Ecclesiastical Notices, and Hierocles, (p. 668.[m]) and its coins[n].

Appia.

Appia is classed with the episcopal towns of Phrygia Pacatiana by Hierocles; (p. 668.) but it is further deserving of attention from being mentioned

[k] Lapie's Map of Greece and Asia Minor.

[l] Geogr. Sacr. p. 240.

[m] Where the name is written ΑΔΙΟΙ; but Wesseling justly corrects it to ΑΛΙΟΙ.

[n] The epigraph is ΑΛΙΗΝΩΝ. Sestini, p. 117.

by Cicero in a letter to Appius Pulcher, (ad Fam. III. 7.) who it appears took some interest in the place, perhaps as its founder. Pliny says the Appiani belonged to the conventus of Synnada. (V. 29.)

Aristium appears only in Hierocles and the Acts Aristium. of Councils among the towns of Phrygia Pacatiana. (p. 668.)

Attuda comes under the same description, but it Attuda. boasts further of several coins, from which it appears to have been a place of some consequence [o].

Atusia, if a unique coin adduced by Sestini[p] be Atusia. genuine, was situated on the Caprus.

Augustopolis is assigned to Phrygia Salutaris by Augusto-polis. the Notices. (Cf. Suid. Ann. Comn. p. 318. B.)

Blæandrus occurs in Ptolemy (p. 120.) and the Blæandrus. Acts of the Council of Chalcedon[q], but it may be doubted whether this is not the same as Blaundus, which Steph. Byz. assigns to Phrygia, (v. Βλαῦδος,) but others to Lydia.

Briana finds a place in the list of Hierocles under Briana. Phrygia Pacatiana, (p. 667.) and has the further evidence of two coins [r].

Bryzon occurs in Ptolemy, (p. 120.) but under Bryzon. the false reading Dryzon, (Δρύζων,) which must be corrected from the coins of the town [s].

Cercopia is known from Pliny to have formed Cercopia.

___

[o] Sestini, p. 118. Epigraphe, IEPA.BOTΛH.ATTOTΔEΩN. Cultus Mensis Cari. MHN.KAPOT. Imperatorii Augusti, indeque Vespasiani, &c.

[p] Attusia vel Atusia. Autonomus unicus. Epigraphe, ATOT-ΣIEΩN ΠΡΟΣ ΚΑΠΡΟΝ. p. 119.

[q] Geogr. Sacr. p. 241.

[r] Sestini, p. 119. Briana. Autonomus unicus. Epigraphe, BPIANΩN. Imperatorius Domnæ.

[s] Sestini, p. 119. Bruzus. Imperatorii tantum ab Antonino Pio usque ad Gordianum. Epigraphe, BPOTZHNΩN.

part of the conventus of Synnada. (V. 29. Cf. Ptol. p. 120.)

Ceretape.

Ceretape may be classed with the towns of Phrygia Pacatiana, on the authority of Hierocles (p. 666.) and other ecclesiastical documents, besides several coins. These point out a river or fountain named Aulindenus in the vicinity of the town[t].

Aulinde-
nus fons
vel fluvius.
Cidramus.

Cidramus is only known from its coins, a description of which is to be found in Sestini[u].

Crasus.

Crasus, which Hierocles assigns to Phrygia Pacatiana, (p. 666.) is also mentioned by Theophanes, with reference to a victory gained there by the Saracens over the emperor Nicephorus. (Chronogr. p. 406. ap. Wessel. ad Hierocl.)

Debalacia.

Debalacia, or Debalicia, is to be placed in Phrygia Salutaris, on the authority of Hierocles, (p. 677.) if the name is not corrupt.

Dioclia.

Dioclia of the same writer (p. 668.) and the Councils is supposed by Wesseling to be the Docela of Ptolemy. (p. 120.[x])

Diocæsa-
rea.

The latter writer has also a Diocæsarea in Phrygia.

Dionysopo-
lis.

Dionysopolis obtains a place from Pliny, who ascribes it to the conventus of Synnada, (V. 29.) and its coins[y].

Dorieum et
Dareium.

Dorieum and Darieum, which Stephanus Byz. gives to Phrygia, are probably one and the same. (vv. Δαρεῖον, Δορίειον.)

---

[t] Ceretape. ΚΕΡΕΤΑΠΕΩΝ. Mentio situs a fl. vel fonte sacro ΑΥΛΙΝΔΗΝΟC. Sestini, p. 119.

[u] Epigraphe, ΚΙΔΡΑΜΗΝΩΝ. Imperatorii M. Aurelii, Caracallæ, &c. p. 120.

[x] Sestini reads Diococlia, from a coin of Gordianus Pius, with the epigraph ΔΙΟΚΟΚΛΙΕΩΝ; but the legend is dubious. p. 121.

[y] Sestini, p. 121. Epigraphe, ΔΙΟΝΥCΟΠΟΛΕΙΤΩΝ.

Eudocia is only known from Hierocles. (p. 668.) Eudocia.

Gammaüsa, or Gambua, occurs in no other geo-grapher but Ptolemy. (p. 120.) The same may be said of Gazena. Gammaüsa, sive Gambua. Gazena.

Geranea is found in Stephanus Byz. (v. Γεράνεια.) Geranea.

Iluza belonged to Phrygia Pacatiana, as we learn from Hierocles and the Acts of Councils. (p. 667.) Iluza.

Leontocephale is mentioned by Appian as a strong fortress of Phrygia; (Mithrid. c. 20.) perhaps it is the same as the Leontos-come of Athenæus, who speaks of its warm springs. (II. p. 43.) Appian also places near it Alexander's inn, ('Αλεξάνδρου πανδοκεῖον.) Leontocephale. Leontoscome. Alexandri diversorium.

Locozus is said by Xanthus the historian to have been founded by some Thracians, but it was destroyed by inundation. (Steph. Byz. v. Λόκοζος.) Locozus.

Lunda is known from Hierocles and the Councils. (p. 667.) Lunda.

Lycaon should have a place, on the same author-ity, in Phrygia Salutaris, strengthened by that of Pliny, who ranges the Lycaones under the jurisdic-tion of Synnada. (V. 29.) Ptolemy fixes the Lyca-ones of Phrygia with the Themisonii on the borders of Lycia. (Ptol. p. 120.) Lycaon.

Manesium and Mantalus occur in Stephanus, on the authority of Alexander Polyhistor. (vv. Μανήσιον, Μάνταλος.) Manesium. Mantalus.

Merus is classed by Hierocles and the Councils among the sees of Phrygia Salutaris. (Hierocl. p. 677. Cf. Socr. Hist. Eccl. III. 15. Sozom. V. 11.) Merus.

Molpe, or Molte, named by Hierocles as a bishop's see of Phrygia Pacatiana, is perhaps no other than the Moccle of Steph. Byz. (v. Μόκκλη,) to which again we must refer the Moccalesii of Ptolemy, whom he places in the northern part of the province towards Molpe, sive Molte. Moccle.

Moxiani. Bithynia. (p. 120.) The Moxiani are ranged by the same geographer after the Peltini.

Otrus. Hierocles names Ostrus, or Otrus, in Phrygia Salutaris, (p. 676.) and his authority derives confirmation from the Councils, and also from Plutarch, in his life of Lucullus.

Pepuza. Pepuza gave its name to an obscure set of heretics noticed by Epiphanius; but they did not flourish long, since their town was ruined and deserted when he wrote. (XLVIII. 14. Cf. Philost. Hist. Eccl. IV. 8.) Hierocles names it among the sees of Phrygia Pacatiana. (p. 677.)

Pulcheria-nopolis. Pulcherianopolis, probably named after the empress Pulcheria, is only known from Hierocles. (p. 668.)

Pylacæum. Pylacæum rests on the sole authority of Ptolemy. (p. 120.) It is probable that the people whom he calls Phylacesii, a little below, were connected with this town.

Sala. Sala claims a place in Phrygia, on the evidence of Ptolemy and its coins, which are numerous, but chiefly of emperors posterior to the twelve Cæsars [z].

Sebaste. Sebaste is recognised by Hierocles and the Councils in Phrygia Pacatiana, and is further known from its coins [a].

Sibindus. Sibindus, which the Ecclesiastical Notices assign to Phrygia Salutaris, should be written Sibidunda,

Situpolis. from a unique coin of the reign of Caracalla [b]. Situpolis is only known from Hierocles. (p. 666.)

Stectori-um. Stectorium finds a place in the geography of Pto-

---

[z] The epigraph is ΣΑΛΗΝΩΝ. Sestini, p. 126.

[a] Sestini, p. 126. Sebaste. Autonomi. Epigraphe, ΔΗΜΟC CEBACTHNΩN. Imperatorii

Domnæ, Caracallæ, &c.

[b] Sestini, p. 126. Sibidunda corrupte Sibildi in Notitiis. Imperatorius unicus Caracallæ. Epigraphe, CIBIΔΟΥΝΔΕΩΝ.

lemy, according to some MSS.: others read Istorium; but the former orthography is proved by Hierocles, who names it in Phrygia Salutaris; and still further by the coins of the town [c].

Struthia is placed in this province, but on the borders of Lycaonia, by Steph. Byz. (v. Στρούθεια.)

Syassus is assigned to Phrygia by the same geographer; (v. Σύασσος.) it is said to have remained for some time in the hands of the Cimmerians.

Tarandrus is a place in Phrygia, according to the same writer. (v. Τάρανδρος.)

Tiberiopolis, probably founded or restored by the emperor whose name it bore, is assigned to Phrygia by Ptolemy, (p. 120.) the historian Socrates, (VII. 46.) Hierocles, (p. 668.) and the Councils. Its coins also are not uncommon, and prove it to have been a place of some note. On one of them reference is made, as Sestini imagines, to a river or fountain Tilius [d].

Tibium is a mountain of Phrygia, whence the name of Tibii commonly given to slaves. (Steph. Byz. v. Τίβειον, where see the note of Berkelius.)

Trajanopolis would only be known from Ptolemy, its coins [e], and the Council of Constantinople, (II. p. 240.) unless we are allowed to add to these authorities that of Hierocles, who writes the name corruptly Tanupolis. Ptolemy (p. 119.) assigns Trajanopolis

[marginal notes: Struthia. Syassus. Tarandrus. Tiberiopolis. Tibium mons. Trajanopolis.]

[c] Sestini, p. 126. Stectorium Autonomi. Epigraphe, CTEKTO-PHNΩN.

[d] Epigraphe, ΔΗΜΟC or CTN-KΛHTOC ΤΙΒΕΡΙΟΠΟΛΕΙΤΩΝ. Imperatorii Trajani, Hadriani, &c. Mentio situs a fluvio vel a fonte TIΛI. Sestin. p. 127.

[e] Sestini, p. 127. Trajanopolis Autonomi. Epigraphe, ΔΗ-ΜΟC — IEPA. CTNKΛHTOC ΤΡΑΙΑΝΟΠΟΛΙΤΩΝ. Imperatorii Trajani, Hadriani, L. Veri, &c.

to the Trimenothyritæ, or Temenothyritæ, of whom we have already spoken under the head of Mysia, which Pausanias (Attic. c. 35.) and others assigned to Lydia.

Tribanta. Tribanta is only known from Ptolemy, who places it next to Nacolea. (p. 120.)

Trinessa. Trinessa is placed by Stephanus Byz. in Phrygia, on the authority of Theopompus. (v. Τρίνησσα.)

Tymenæum mons. Tymenæum was a mountain of the same province. (Id. v. Τυμεναῖον.)

Pharnacia. Pharnacia is given on the testimony of Alexander Polyhistor. (Id. v. Φαρνακία.)

Charax Alexandri. Charax Alexandri obtained its name from the encampment of that sovereign, near Celænæ. (Id. v. Χάραξ.)

To this list, taken from ancient writers, may be added a few places derived from the more modern authority of the Byzantine historians.

Caria, Tantalus. Caria and Tantalus, towns of Phrygia, taken and razed by the sultan of Iconium. (Nic. Ann. p. 319. C.)

Charax. Charax, between Lampe and Graosgala, in Phrygia. (Nicet. Ann. p. 127. B. p. 159. B.)

Chiliocomon. Chiliocomon, near Doryleum. (Cedren. p. 531.)

Lampe. Lampe, or Lampis, was near Celænæ. (Nicet. Ann. p. 115. D. p. 127. B.)

Limmocheir. Hyelium. Limmocheir and Hyelium, small places on the Meander, where there had once been a bridge. (Nicet. Ann. p. 125. D.)

Luma. Pentachira. Luma and Pentachira, fortresses near the Meander, taken by the Turks.

Myriocephalus. Myriocephalus, a fortress of Phrygia, near which the Greeks under Man. Comnenus were defeated by the Turks. Choma. Choma, a place near it, a defile between continuous mountains called Tzybitza, on the road Tzybitza montes. to Iconium. (Nicet. Ann. p. 115, et seq.)

Paipert, a fortress near Philomelium. (Ann. Comn. Paipert. p. 326.)

LYCAONIA.

When Herodotus wrote his history, the Phrygians, or at least tribes included under that general name, extended as far as the Halys, which divided them from Cappadocia. (I. 72.) He nowhere makes mention of the Lycaonians, who appear to have a place in history for the first time in the Anabasis of Xenophon. (I. 2. 19.) Cyrus marched through their country in five days, and gave it up to plunder, because the inhabitants were hostile. Like the Pisidians, the Lycaonians were a hardy mountain race, who owned no subjection to the Persian king, but lived by plunder and foray. They nominally followed the revolutions which befell Asia Minor; first, in being under the rule of Alexander, then of the Seleucidæ and Antiochus, Eumenes king of Pergamum, and finally of the Romans. (Liv. XXXVII. 54. XXXVIII. 39.) Under this change of rulers the character of the people remained the same:

Ἴδριες ἐν πολέμοισι Λυκάονες ἀγκυλότοξοι.

DION. PERIEG. v. 857.

daring and intractable, they still continued their lawless and marauding habits, till at last the Romans were compelled to send an army against them, and to curb their system of plunder by force of arms. The Isauri, who were a Lycaonian tribe, are said to have offered the greatest resistance, and the consul Publius Servilius, who achieved their subjection, was thought worthy of adding the title of Isauricus

to the trophies he had gained on this occasion.
(Strab. XII. p. 568. Eutrop. VI. 3. Flor. III. 6.
Epit. Liv. XCIII.) The Lycaonians, though originally a small and insignificant people, had acquired
a greater political consistency and extent of territory, under the conduct of Amyntas their chief,
whom Strabo even dignifies with the appellation of
king. This leader had gained by force of arms a
considerable part of Pisidia, and a portion of Lycaonia, previously occupied by another bandit chief,
named Antipater, whom he conquered and slew.
(Strab. XII. p. 569.) The favour of Antony subsequently obtained for Amyntas still greater acqui-
sitions; since he was put in possession of all the
territory which had belonged to Dejotarus, tetrarch
of Galatia, together with a great part of Pamphylia.
(Appian. Bell. Civ. c. 75. Dio Cass. XLIX. c. 32.)
This prosperity was, however, of short duration;
for in his attempt to reduce some of the mountain
tribes on the borders of Cilicia, he fell into a snare
laid for him by the Homonadenses, the principal
clan of these highlanders, and was put to death by
them: after which, the whole of his principality
devolved to the Roman empire. (Strab. XII. p. 569.)
The northern part of Lycaonia is described by Strabo
as a cold and bleak country, especially where it bordered on Galatia, in the vicinity of the great salt
lake Tattæa; there, too, water was so scarce, that
wells were sunk to an unusual depth, and in some
places water was actually sold. The mountain pastures, however, afforded herbage for vast flocks of
sheep, whose wool, though coarse, yielded a considerable profit to the proprietors. Augustus is said
to have fed there more than 300 flocks. (Strab. XII.

p. 568.) Towards the east, the Lycaonians bordered on Cappadocia, from which they were separated by the Halys; while towards the south, they extended themselves from the frontiers of Cilicia to the country of the Pisidians. Between them and the latter people, there seems to have been considerable affinity of character, and probably also of blood; both nations, I conceive, being originally sprung from the ancient Solymi; but subsequently distinguished from each other, from the various increments which each received from the nations in their immediate vicinity. Thus, while the Pisidians were intermixed with the Carians, Lycians, and Phrygians, the Lycaonians received colonists probably from Cappadocia, Cilicia, Pamphylia, Phrygia, and Galatia; at the same time that both, in common with all the nations of Asia Minor, had no small proportion of Greek settlers in their principal towns. It is a curious fact, which we derive from the New Testament, (Acts xiv. 11.) that the Lycaonians had a peculiar dialect, which therefore must have differed from the Pisidian language; but even that, as we know from Strabo, was a distinct tongue from that of the ancient Solymi. (XIII. p. 631.) It is however very probable, that the Lycaonian idiom was only a mixture of these and the Phrygian language[f].

Strabo includes Isauria within the limits of Lycaonia; but Pliny assigns the latter rather to Pamphylia. (V. 27.) I shall here adopt the arrangement of the former geographer, as it accords with that of Hierocles and the Notitiæ.

[f] The reader will find this question elaborately discussed in the learned treatise of Prof. Jablonski de Ling. Lycaon. Opusc. tom. III. p. 8.

Iconium.   The most considerable and celebrated town of
Lycaonia was Iconium, to which we had nearly
arrived in our periegesis of Phrygia, which terminated at Philomelium : that place, as we know from
Cicero, being only one day's journey from the city
of which we are now speaking. (Att. V. 20.) Xenophon, who mentions it for the first time in his Anabasis, ascribes it to Phrygia. (I. 2.) Cicero, however,
certainly places it in Lycaonia; (Ep. Fam. XV. 3.
Cf. III. 6 et 8.) he mentions his army being encamped there for several days previous to entering
on the Cilician campaign. Strabo says, Iconium
was a small, but well inhabited town, situate in a
more fertile tract of country than the northern part
of Lycaonia : this district had once been subject to
Polemo. (XII. p. 568.) Mythological writers asserted, that the name of this city was derived from
the image (εἰκὼν) of the Gorgon, brought there by
Perseus. The grammarian Chœroboscus observes,
however, that the first syllable was pronounced
short by Menander; (Cod. Barocc. 50. f. 134.) he
has been copied by the Etymol. M. and Eustath.
(Dionys. Perieg. 857.) But the most interesting circumstances connected with the history of Iconium,
are those which relate to St. Paul's preaching there,
towards the commencement of his apostolical mis-
sion to the Gentiles. We read in Acts xiii. 51. that
St. Paul and Barnabas, having been expelled from
Antioch in Pisidia, by a persecution of the Jews,
" shook off the dust of their feet against them, and
" came unto Iconium. And the disciples were filled
" with joy, and with the Holy Ghost. And it came
" to pass in Iconium, that they went both together
" into the synagogue of the Jews, and so spake, that

" a great multitude both of the Jews and also of the
" Greeks believed. But the unbelieving Jews stirred
" up the Gentiles, and made their minds evil affected
" against the brethren. Long time therefore abode
" they speaking boldly in the Lord, which gave tes-
" timony unto the word of his grace, and granted
" signs and wonders to be done by their hands. But
" the multitude of the city was divided: and part
" held with the Jews, and part with the apostles.
" And when there was an assault made both of the
" Gentiles, and also of the Jews with their rulers,
" to use them despitefully, and to stone them, they
" were aware of it, and fled unto Lystra and Derbe,
" cities of Lycaonia, and unto the region that lieth
" round about." Even there, however, they were
pursued by their furious enemies, and Paul was only
preserved by divine interposition from the effects of
their blind rage. Nevertheless he and Barnabas returned to Iconium after a time, to confirm and
strengthen the disciples, and to appoint elders over the
church. (v. 21—23.) This city appears from Hierocles, and the Acts of Councils, to have been always
considered the metropolis of Lycaonia[g]. In Pliny's
time Iconium had become a more considerable town
than it was when Strabo wrote, for he says, " Datur
" et tetrarchia ex Lycaonia qua parte Galatiæ con-
" termina est, civitatum XIV. urbe celeberrima Ico-
" nio." (V. 27. Cf. Steph. Byz. v. 'Ικόνιον.) Under the
Byzantine emperors frequent mention is made of this
city, but it had been wrested from them first by the
Saracens, and afterwards by the Turks, who made it
the capital of an empire, the sovereigns of which
took the title of sultans of Iconium. They were

[g] See Wesseling on Hierocles, p. 675.

constantly engaged in hostilities with the Greek emperors and the crusaders, with various success; and they must be considered as having laid the foundation of the Ottoman power in Asia Minor, which commenced under Osman Oglou, and his descendants, on the termination of the Iconian dynasty, towards the beginning of the fourteenth century. *Konia*, as it is now called by the Turks, is a large and populous town, the residence of a Pasha. Col. Leake states, that he saw there several Greek inscriptions, and remains of architecture and sculpture, but they appeared to belong chiefly to the Byzantine Greeks[h].

Strabo mentions two lakes in the neighbourhood of Iconium; the largest of these he names Caralis, the other Trogitis. The former was situated, as we shall see, to the south-west of the town, on the borders of Pisidia and Pamphylia; but Trogitis may have been the lake in the immediate vicinity of Iconium, and occupying, as Col. Leake observes, the centre of the plain in which that town is seated[i]. But on the side of Galatia was a much more extensive lake, named Tattæa, which had originally belonged to Phrygia, but afterwards was annexed to the Lycaonian tetrarchy. Its waters were so impregnated with brine, that if any substance was dipped into the lake, it was presently incrusted with a thick coat of salt; and even birds, when flying

Caralis pa-lus.
Trogitis palus.

Tattæa palus.

[h] Asia Minor, p. 48. The coins of Iconium prove that it had once obtained the distinction of a Roman colony, perhaps under Claudius. Sestini. Epigraphe, ΙΚΟΝΙΕΩΝ. Imperatorii Neronis, Hadriani, &c. p. 97. Epigraphe, ΚΛΑΤΔΕΙΚΟ-ΝΙΕΩΝ. But certainly under Hadrian. Imperat. Gordiani Pii, Valeriani Sen. et Gallieni. Col. ÆL. HAD. ICONIENSI.

[i] Col. Leake is inclined to think that Trogitis was the lake of *Ilgun*, but that would be in Phrygia.

near the surface, had their wings moistened with the saline particles, so as to become incapable of rising into the air, and were easily caught. (Strab. XII. p. 568. Dioscor. V. 126.) Stephanus Byz. speaks of a lake Attæa in Phrygia, which produced salt; near it was the town of Botieum. (v. Βοτίειον.) Botieum. It is probably the Tattæa of Strabo. The Turks call it *Tuzla*, and it still continues to furnish in abundance the substance for which it was anciently famous [k]. Soatra, or Sabatra [l], was a small town Soatra,
sive Saba-
tra. in this direction, but nearer the Cappadocian frontier. The Table Itinerary places it on a road leading apparently from Laodicea Catacecaumene to Iconium, the distance from the former being fifty-five miles, and from the latter forty-four. But there must be some great error in the construction of the Itinerary, as the distance between Laodicea and Iconium, which is omitted, cannot be more than twenty-five miles. Sabatra is also noticed by Ptolemy, (p. 124.) Hierocles, (p. 676.) and the Councils. According to Strabo, water was so scarce at Sabatra as to be an article for sale. On the neighbouring downs were wild asses. (XII. p. 568.) The last place of Lycaonia on the side of Cappadocia was Coropassus, or Coropissus [m], on the great road to Coropissus. that province and the Euphrates. (Artemid. ap. Strab. XIV. p. 663. XII. p. 568.) It is not mentioned, I believe, by other writers, and was appa-

---

[k] Leake's Asia Minor, p. 70.
[l] The real name, according to the coins, is Sabatra; i. e. Σαουάτρα in Greek. Sestini, p. 97. Savatra. Imperatorii tantum Antonini Pii. Epigraphe, ΣΑΟΥΑΤΡΕΩΝ.

[m] Coropissus appears to be the true mode of writing the name, from the coins of this town. Sestini, p. 97. Coropissus. Imperatorii Hadriani. Epigraphe, ΜΗΤΡΟ. ΚΟΡΟΠΙΣ-ΣΕΩΝ.

rently only a small town. It was 120 stadia from
Garsabora on the frontier of Cappadocia. Towards
Cappadocia also, but more to the south, we must
seek for Derbe and Lystra, two towns of Lycaonia,
which derive considerable interest from what befell
St. Paul and Barnabas there on leaving Iconium.
Derbe, as we learn from Strabo, had been the residence and capital of Antipater, the robber chief
of Lycaonia, mentioned above: but he being conquered and slain by Amyntas, Derbe and his other
possessions fell into the hands of the latter. (XII.
p. 569.) Stephanus Byz. reports, that this town was
called by some Delbia, which in the Lycaonian language signified " the juniper." The same lexicographer describes it as a fortress and port of Isauria;
but I agree with the French translators of Strabo in
thinking that for λιμὴν we ought to substitute λίμνη,
which would imply that the town was situated near
some one of the numerous lakes that are to be found
in this part of Asia Minor. Col. Leake is disposed
to identify Derbe with some extensive ruins he heard
of near *Kassaba*. They are called *Binbir-Klissa*,
or 1000 churches, and are situated at the foot of a
lofty insulated mountain named *Karadagh*, to the
south-east of Iconium; but as he did not explore
the site himself, we cannot be certain that it answers to Derbe[n]. Strabo places that town on the
border of Isauria and towards Cappadocia: Ptolemy
assigns it to a particular district, which he calls An-
tiochiana, (p. 124.) distinct from Lycaonia, but contiguous to it to the south-east. Stephanus Byz. (v.
Δέρβη) says it was in Isauria, but St. Luke, in the

Derbe.

[n] Asia Minor, p. 101.

Acts, and Hierocles (p. 675.) place it in Lycaonia.
Cicero states, in one of his letters to Q. Philippus,
that he had been treated with great civility and
kindness by Antipater of Derbe; whence it would
seem that he had passed through or near it, on his way
to Cilicia from Iconium. Philip, on the other hand,
who had also been proconsul in Asia Minor, appears
to have been much displeased with this Lycaonian
chief. (Cic. ad Fam. XIII. 73.) Lystra, as Col.
Leake remarks justly, must have been situated nearer
to Iconium, since St. Paul proceeded there first on
leaving the latter city. It is not noticed by Strabo,
and probably was not so considerable a place. It is
mentioned, however, by Ptolemy (p. 124.) and Hierocles. (p. 675.) What relates to the incidents which
took place at Lystra and Derbe in the history of
St. Paul, will best be collected from the words of
St. Luke. Having been threatened with an assault
on the part of the Gentiles and Jews of Iconium, he
says, " they were ware of it, and fled unto Lystra
" and Derbe, cities of Lycaonia, and unto the region
" that lieth round about: and there they preached
" the Gospel. And there sat a certain man at Lys-
" tra, impotent in his feet, being a cripple from his
" mother's womb, who never had walked : the same
" heard Paul speak : who stedfastly beholding him,
" and perceiving that he had faith to be healed, said
" with a loud voice, Stand upright on thy feet. And
" he leaped and walked. And when the people saw
" what Paul had done, they lifted up their voices,
" saying in the speech of Lycaonia, The gods are come
" down to us in the likeness of men. And they
" called Barnabas, Jupiter ; and Paul, Mercurius,
" because he was the chief speaker. Then the priest

" of Jupiter, which was before their city, brought
" oxen and garlands unto the gates, and would have
" done sacrifice with the people.　Which when the
" apostles, Barnabas and Paul, heard of, they rent
" their clothes, and ran in among the people, crying
" out, and saying, Sirs, why do ye these things?
" We also are men of like passions with you, and
" preach unto you that ye should turn from these
" vanities unto the living God, which made heaven,
" and earth, and the sea, and all things that are
" therein: who in times past suffered all nations to
" walk in their own ways.　Nevertheless he left not
" himself without witness, in that he did good, and
" gave us rain from heaven, and fruitful seasons,
" filling our hearts with food and gladness.　And
" with these sayings scarce restrained they the peo-
" ple, that they had not done sacrifice unto them.
" And there came thither certain Jews from An-
" tioch and Iconium, who persuaded the people, and,
" having stoned Paul, drew him out of the city, sup-
" posing he had been dead.　Howbeit, as the dis-
" ciples stood round about him, he rose up, and
" came into the city: and the next day he departed
" with Barnabas to Derbe.　And when they had
" preached the Gospel to that city, and had taught
" many, they returned again to Lystra, and to Ico-
" nium, and Antioch." Acts xiv. 6—21.　I find no
mention of Derbe or Lystra in the Byzantine writers, but a bishop of the latter see sat in the council of
Chalcedon [n].　Col. Leake is inclined to place Lystra
at *Khatoun Seraï*, about thirty miles to the south-

[n] Wesseling's note to Hierocles, p. 675.　It is somewhat
singular that there should be
no coins extant of these two
towns.

ward of Iconium [o].   Laranda, which according to Laranda.
Strabo belonged originally to Antipater of Derbe,
must have stood at no great distance from the latter
town. (Strab. XII. p. 569.)   Diodorus seems to assign it to Pisidia, (XVIII. 22.) but Stephanus Byz.
(v. Λάρανδα) and Hierocles (p. 675.) to Lycaonia.
(Cf. Ammian. Marcell. XIV. 2.)   Suidas says, Laranda was the birthplace of Nestor, an epic poet,
and father of Pisander, also a poet, and of greater
celebrity [p]. (Cf. Ptol. p. 124. Euseb. Hist. Eccl. VI.
19. M. Duc. p. 123.)   Laranda has been replaced by
the Turkish town of *Karaman*, about three days'
journey to the south of Iconium.   Col. Leake says
the ancient name is still in use among the Christian
inhabitants of the place ; but there are no remains
of any importance [q].   *Illisera*, a small place in the
same vicinity, is thought by the same geographer to
represent Ilistra [r], an obscure town, assigned to this Ilistra.
province by Hierocles and the Notices; its bishops
are also known to have sat in the councils of Ephesus and Chalcedon [s].   Misthea, which Hierocles Misthea.
names after Lystra, is known also from the Councils and Theophanes. (Chron. p. 320.)   Nicephorus,
the Byzantine historian, seems to place it on the
borders of Cilicia. (Niceph. Phoc. c. 20.)

Vasoda, which occurs likewise in the list of Hie- Vasoda.
rocles, must have been near Misthea, as Wesseling
rightly observes from a passage in Basil. (Ep. 118.)
This Lycaonian town is further known from Pto-

---

[o] Asia Minor, p. 102.

[p] The lexicographer says,
Νέστωρ Λαρανδεὺς ἐκ Λυκίας, which
is either a mistake, or else we
must substitute ἐκ Λυκαονίας.

[q] Asia Minor, p. 98—100.
There are no coins of Laranda.

[r] Asia Minor, p. 102.

[s] Wesseling's note to Hierocles.

Barate.

lemy and the Acts of several councils.   Barate, according to the Table Itinerary, was fifty miles from Iconium, and thirty-nine from Tyana in Cappadocia.

Hyde.

Ptolemy and Hierocles likewise notice it.   Hyde stood, as Pliny remarks, on the confines of Galatia

Thebasa.

and Cappadocia. (V. 27. Cf. Hierocl. p. 675.)   Thebasa, according to the Latin geographer, was placed within mount Taurus. (Plin. loc. cit. Cf. Paul. Diacon. XXIV. p. 770, 771.)

Parlais.
Corna.
Canna.
Casbia.
Perta.
Adopissus.

Ptolemy assigns to Lycaonia, Parlais, Corna, Canna, Casbia, Perta, and Adopissus.   Parlais, of which several coins are extant of the reigns of M. Aurelius, Gallienus, and other emperors, appears from these monuments to have been a place of some consequence, and a Roman colony [t].   Corna is also mentioned by Hierocles, (p. 676.) in whose list we find Carna, (read Canna from Ptolemy and the Councils,) and Pterna, (read Perta from the same

Glauama.

authorities,) Glauama, and Rignum.   The latter is

Rignum.

the Riconium of Pliny, according to the reading of the best MSS., not Iconium.   He places it in Cilicia. (V. 27.)

ISAURIA.

The Isauri, though classed by Strabo and other geographers under Lycaonia, are sufficiently celebrated in history to deserve a separate mention in our work.   They appear to have occupied the mountainous country south of Lycaonia, properly so called, and bordering on Cilicia and Pisidia.   Living in a

[t] Sestini, p. 97. Parlais Imperatorii Coloniæ nomine a M. Aurelio ad Maximinum. Epigraphe, PARLAIS. COL—COLON. PARL. vel IVL. AVG.   COL.   PARLAIS.   Gallieni Græci inscripti et absque Coloniæ mentione Epigraphe ΠΑδΛΛΙΩΝ vel ΠΑδΛΛΙΕΩΝ.

wild and rugged tract, the character of this people
partook of the nature of the air and soil in which
they were bred. They descended into the plain
country, and ravaged and plundered wherever they
could overcome the resistance of the inhabitants of
the valleys, whether in Cilicia, Phrygia, or Pisidia.
These marauding habits rendered them so formidable to their neighbours, that the Roman senate was
obliged at length to send a considerable force against
them, under the command of P. Servilius, A.U.C.
674. After several campaigns, and a laborious and
harassing warfare, this general succeeded in conquering most of their fortresses, and reducing them
to submission. These successes were thought sufficiently important to obtain for him the honours of
the triumph, and the surname of Isauricus. (Strab.
XII. p. 568, 569. Eutrop. VI. 3. Liv. Epitom. XCIII.
Dio Cass. XLV. 16. Flor. III. 6.) The Isaurians
were then separate from the Lycaonians, for Cicero
distinguishes between the Forum Lycaonium and
the Isauricum. (Att. V. 21. Cf. ad Fam. XV. 2.)
Subsequently, however, we find that they still continued to infest their neighbours, which induced
Amyntas, the Lycaonian tetrarch, to attempt their
extirpation. In this project, however, he lost his
life; and they continued to defy the power of Rome,
from the difficult nature of their country and the
celerity of their movements. To the Greek emperors
they proved particularly formidable, since whole armies are said to have been cut in pieces and destroyed by these hardy mountaineers; (Suid. vv.
Βρύχιος, Ἡράκλειος.) and they even made inroads into
distant parts of Asia Minor and Syria. (Philostorg.
Hist. Eccl. XI. 8.) They had once the honour of

giving an emperor to the east, Zeno, surnamed the Isaurian; but they were subsequently much reduced by Anastasius, and were no longer formidable in the time of Justinian [u]. We are but little acquainted with the wild and retired district occupied by the Isaurians; but I conceive it answers nearly to that portion of the pashalick of *Konieh*, which the Turks call *Bei-cher*. It consists chiefly of a bason, surrounded by mountains, and occupied partly by some extensive lakes. Taurus was its principal barrier to the west and south, and on the north and east it was separated by a secondary range of hills from the bason of Iconium. The principal town bore the national name of Isaura. Strabo reports that it was ceded by the Romans to Amyntas, who caused the old town to be destroyed, and commenced the foundation of a new city, which he surrounded with walls, but did not live to complete the work. Hence the distinction which the geographer elsewhere makes of Isaura Palæa and Euerces. (XII. p. 568, 569. Cf. Plin. V. 27. Diod. Sic. XVIII. p. 605. Ammian. Marcell. XIV. 8. Steph. Byz. v. Ἴσαυρα. Hierocl. p. 675 [x].) The Table Itinerary leads us to look for this town on a line of road communicating between Iconium and Anemurium in Cilicia, agreeably to Pliny's account, who says that Isauria stretches down towards the sea in that direction; (V. 27.) but the numbers are very defective and incorrect. Taspa, which is placed between Iconium and Isauria, is perhaps the Thebasa of Pliny. At all events

Marginal notes:

Isaura Palæa et Euerces.

Taspa.

---

[u] See Gibbon, t. IX. c. 40. p. 130—33; and the numerous authorities quoted by him.

[x] Sestini, p. 96, Isaurus (Isaura) Imperatorii Getæ et Elagabali. Epigraphe, ΜΗΤΡΟΠΟΛΕΩΣ ΙϹΑΤΡΩΝ.

we must seek for the capital of the Isaurians in the plain country at the foot of Taurus, and where the chain affords some passage into the neighbouring province of Cilicia.

Lalassis [y] was higher up in the mountains, and on the very border of Cilicia, as appears from Pliny. (loc. cit.) This town is probably the Lalisanda of Stephanus Byz. who informs us that, in his time, the name was changed to Dalisanda. (v. Λαλίσανδα.) It occurs, under the latter form, in Hierocles (p. 710.) and Ptolemy. We are informed by Basilius of Seleucia, who is quoted by Wesseling in his notes to Hierocles, that this town stood on a lofty height, but well provided with water, and not destitute of other advantages. It was, however, greatly reduced, and almost deserted. (Mirac. S. Thec. II. 10.) Clibanus, which Pliny assigns to the Isauri, is unknown.

Carallia is another Isaurian city, according to Steph. Byz.; (v. Κάραλλις.) the same, doubtless, which Hierocles and the Councils assign to Pamphylia. (p. 682 [z].) There is little doubt that we must refer to this town, or rather its vicinity, the lake Caralitis, which Strabo mentions as being not far from Iconium; (XII. p. 568.) and accordingly we find, in modern maps, a lake called *Kerali*, to the west of *Konieh*, in the direction of Isauria; and also another, more to the south, which is named after the

Margin notes: Lalassis, sive Lalisanda, et Dalisanda. — Clibanus. — Carallia. — Caralitis palus.

---

[y] This appears to be the true name from the coins of the town. Sestini, p. 96. Lalassis. Autonomi. Epigraphe, ΔΑΛΔ. EK. in nummo argenteo. ΛΑΛΑCCEΩN, vel ΛΑΛΑΣΣ. ENTIM. in æneis.

[z] There are some scarce imperial coins of Karallia with the inscription KAPAΛΛΙΩΤΩΝ. They belong to the reigns of M. Aurelius, Pescennius, and Maximinus. Sestini, p. 96.

town of *Bei-cher*, situate near it; and this may be the Trogitis of Strabo. But the maps express the reverse of his statement; for they make the lake of *Bei-cher* much more extensive than that of *Kerali;* whereas, in the ancient geographer, Caralis is the larger. I have also other reasons for supposing that the representative of the latter is not well described in our maps. I find, in the Byzantine writers, mention made of a very extensive lake in the neighbourhood of Iconium, which I imagine must be Caralis. The circumstances related by these historians are curious. Nicetas, who calls it Pusgusa, says it contained several islands, the inhabitants of which were Christians, but supposed to be ill affected to the Greeks on account of their vicinity to the Turks of Iconium. The emperor John Comnenus determined, in consequence, to get rid of them; but, as they refused to submit, he was obliged to besiege their islands by means of boats and bridges. This proved a work of great difficulty, especially on account of some storms, which raised the waters of the lake, and destroyed several of the besiegers; the emperor was obliged, therefore, to give up the enterprise, and retire into Isauria, which at that time comprised Pamphylia. (Nicet. Ann. p. 25. A.) Cinnamus supplies some further information, in which the narrative of Nicetas is deficient. He calls the lake Pasgusa, and says it was of very great extent. The islands in it had had fortifications raised on them in former times, which added to their natural strength. The emperor Comnenus, being then at war with the Turks, and in the vicinity, apparently, of Iconium, hearing that the enemy were besieging Sozopolis, a town of Pisidia, determined to march to the relief

Pusgusa palus.

of that place, but on his way he heard that the
enemy had retreated. Finding himself then at liberty in this quarter, he resolved on expelling the
inhabitants of the islands on the lake Pasgusa, especially when he learnt that they were able to go from
thence to Iconium, and return the same day. He
goes on then to describe the siege, and its difficulties,
but he asserts that the Greek emperor at last succeeded in his undertaking. (p. 12, 13.) Elsewhere
the same writer speaks of a lake Pungusa, formerly
called Sclerus, which was in some plains not far
from Iconium apparently, which the emperor Manuel Comnenus passed on his retreat from that city.
(p. 32.) Allowing these facts to be correctly stated,
we must expect to find a great lake, with islands,
somewhere between Iconium and Pisidia, but not
more than fifteen miles or so from the former, since
the Christians, who lived on the lake, could go thither and return the same day. Whether the lake
of *Kerali* would answer to this description can only
be ascertained from actual inspection; and I am not
aware that any traveller has explored it. Lucas,
who must have passed between it and the lake of
Bei-cher, only notices the latter, which he describes
as very large and briny. The salt even formed
small hillocks, from which it was collected. There
appear to have been no islands on it, so it cannot
answer to Pasgusa, or Pusgusa; the water of which
besides was probably not salt. With respect to the
name of Sclerus, by which the latter lake, as Cinnamus reports, was formerly known, I am inclined to
look upon it as a corruption of Caralis. Pusgusa
was perhaps a Turkish name. But the aspect of
the country may have undergone great changes, and

it is not improbable that the lakes of *Kerali* and *Bei-cher* may have been united at the time alluded to by the Byzantine writers.

We must add to the towns of Isauria, from Steph. Byz. Busmasdis, (v. Βούσμασδις,) Isbus, (v. Ἴσβος,) Cotrades and Monabæ, noticed in the Isaurica of Capito. (vv. Κοτράδης, Μοναβαί.) Timyra was a town in the vicinity of Isauria. (v. Τίμυρα.) Psimadæ is likewise assigned to that province on the authority of Capito. (v. Ψίμαδα.)

Busmasdis.
Isbus.
Cotrades.
Monabæ.

Psimada.

SECTION VIII.

GALATIA.

Account of the migration of the Gauls into Asia, and their occupation of a large portion of ancient Phrygia—Their division into Tectosages, Tolistoboii, and Trocmi—Conquest of Galatia by the Romans—Conversion to Christianity—Description of the province.

GALATIA being merely a dismembered portion of ancient Phrygia, it will only be necessary, in inquiring into its former history, to account for its being occupied by the Gauls, or Gallo-græci, from whom its new appellation was derived. We collect from Polybius and Livy, who however only copies from the Greek historian, that this Asiatic colony was in fact but a detachment of those vast hordes which had wandered from their native country Gaul, under the conduct of Brennus. On their arrival in Dardania, a dispute arose between some of the chiefs and the principal commander, when the discontented troops, to the number of 20,000, determined to abandon the main body, and seek their fortunes elsewhere, under the direction of Leonorius and Lutarius [a]. They traversed the plains of Thrace, and,

---

[a] Polybius says, that they escaped from the defeat at Delphi, (διαφυγόντες τὸν περὶ Δελφοὺς κίνδυνον,) which perhaps only means, that they avoided the danger, i. e. were not present, at Delphi. (IV. 46. Cf. I. 6, 5.) Pausanias says not one escaped the defeat in Phocis. (Phoc. c. 23. Cf. Posidon. ap. Strab. IV. Justin. XXIV. 8.)

encamping near Byzantium, were for a time the
bane and terror of its citizens, by the devastations
they committed, and the galling tribute they imposed.   At length however, tempted by the beautiful aspect of the shores of Asia, and the reputed
wealth and fertility of that country, they were easily
induced to listen to the offers of Nicomedes, king of
Bithynia, for entering into his service.   They accordingly crossed the Bosphorus[b], and having joined
the troops of Nicomedes, were of great assistance to
him in his wars with Zibœtes.   They now obtained
a firm footing in Asia Minor; and though not more
than 20,000 men, and of these not more than one
half furnished with arms, they spread alarm and
consternation throughout the peninsula, and compelled whole provinces, and even empires, to pay
them tribute.   They even proceeded to divide the
whole of Asia Minor between their three tribes, al-
lotting to each a portion on which it was to levy
impositions.   The Hellespont was assigned to the
Trocmi, Æolis and Ionia to the Tolistoboii, and
the interior of the peninsula to the Tectosages.   The
settled abode, however, of the three tribes was in
the country between the Sangarius and the Halys,
which they had seized, without resistance or difficulty, from the unwarlike Phrygians.   As their
numbers increased, they became more formidable,
and also more imperious in their exactions; so that
at length even the kings of Syria thought it prudent

[b] According to Pausanias,
this took place one year after
the defeat of Brennus, that is,
in the third year of the 125th
Olympiad, when Democles was
archon at Athens. (Phoc. c. 23.)
Polybius places the defeat and
passage of the Gauls in the same
year; that which preceded the
expedition of Pyrrhus into Italy. (I. 6.)

to comply with their demands. Attalus, king of Pergamum, was the only sovereign who had the resolution to refuse at length to submit to this ignominious extortion. He met the barbarians in the field, and, seconded by the bravery of his troops, obtained a victory over these Gallo-græci, as they were now called, from their intermixture with the Greeks of Phrygia and Bithynia. (Liv. XXXVIII. 16.) Prusias, king of Bithynia, not long after, cut to pieces another body of Gauls, and freed the Hellespont from their depredations. (Polyb. V. 111.[c]) These, however, were only partial advantages, and the Gauls remained the terror and tyrants of Asia Minor, so says at least the Roman historian, till the war with Antiochus brought the Roman armies into Asia. The victory of Magnesia having driven that monarch across the Taurus, there remained the Gallo-græci only between the latter and the entire possession of the peninsula. There wanted but a slight pretext to justify an invasion of these barbarian hordes in their own fastnesses. It was asserted that they had assisted Antiochus in the campaign which had just terminated; and on this pretence war was determined on, and command was given to Cn. Manlius, the consul, to advance into their country, and reduce them by force of arms. That general, being joined by Attalus, brother of Eumenes, king of Pergamum, with a select body of troops, did not march at once towards the enemy; but, setting out from Magnesia on the Meander, he crossed that river, traversed part of Caria and Cibyra, Lycia

---

[c] Polybius makes no mention of the victory of Attalus, nor Livy of that of Prusias. Can the Roman historian have confounded the two names?

original tongue, since we are assured by St. Jerome that in his day they spoke the same language as the Treviri of Gaul. Less effeminate also and debased by superstition than the natives of Phrygia, they were more ready to embrace the tidings of salvation brought to them by the great apostle of the Gentiles. Of his stay in their country we have indeed but little information from the Acts of the Apostles, except the general fact of his success in preaching the Gospel throughout the province, which he must have visited soon after it had received a new political form from the Romans: this was his second journey through Asia Minor, and he appears, accompanied by Silas, to have revisited Lycaonia, and to have traversed part of Phrygia, and then come to Galatia. (Acts xvi. 6.) He himself alludes to his success in his epistle addressed to the converts of Galatia, (IV. 15.) and certainly the adhesion of a whole province forms a remarkable feature in the predication of St. Paul[d], when we consider the strong opposition he encountered in single cities; though after he left them, there were not wanting men who endeavoured to turn the Galatians from the true Christian doctrine, and persuade them to hold opinions contrary to what St. Paul had taught them. (Gal. iii. 1.) The apostle revisited the Galatian churches, on his return from Greece to Antioch, when, " after he had " spent some time" in the latter city, " he departed, " and went over all the country of Galatia and Phry- " gia in order, strengthening all the disciples." (Acts xviii. 23.) The Ecclesiastical Notices assign about

[d] Probably there were fewer Jews in Galatia, which would account for the little opposition the apostle met in his tour through Galatia.

of Pergamum, who might be considered as their lieutenant in Asia, and forsaking their former wandering and marauding habits. (Liv. XXXVIII. 40.) Formerly, as Strabo informs us, the whole of Galatia had been divided into four parts, each governed by a separate chief called tetrarch. Each tetrarch had under him a judge and a military commander, who appointed two lieutenants. These collectively had the power of assembling the general council, which met in a spot called Drynemetum, and consisted of 300 members. This assembly decided only in criminal cases: all other business was transacted by the tetrarchs and judges. Subsequently the number of tetrarchs was reduced to three, and finally to one. The latter change was made by the Romans, in favour of Dejotarus, who had rendered their arms essential service in the Mithridatic war, (Appian. Mithr. c. 114.) and is so often mentioned by Cicero in terms of the greatest esteem and friendship. Having been the warm friend and partisan of Pompey, Dejotarus incurred the displeasure of Cæsar, and was stripped of a great part of his dominions. He was even accused by his own grandson of having conspired against the dictator; but he was warmly and successfully defended by Cicero. (Orat. pro Dejotaro.) On his death, which took place at an advanced age, part of his principality, as we have seen, was annexed to Paphlagonia and Pontus, under Polemo; and part to the dominions of Amyntas, chief of Lycaonia. On the demise of the latter, the whole of Galatia came into the possession of the Romans, and formed one province of their vast empire. (Strab. XII. p. 566, 567. Plin. V. 32.) Though intermixed with Greeks, the Galatians retained throughout their

Dindymus mons.

dess Rhea, or Cybele. Strabo says, that mount Dindymus, whence she was surnamed Dindymene, rose
above the town, and we have seen that there was a
mount sacred to Dindymene near the source of the
Hermus. So great was the fame of the shrine and
statue of the goddess, that the Romans, enjoined, as
it is said, by the Sibylline oracles, had caused the
latter to be conveyed to Rome, since the safety of
the state was declared to depend on its removal to
Italy. A special embassy was sent to king Attalus
to request his assistance on this occasion: this sovereign received the Roman deputies with great kindness and hospitality, and having conveyed them to
Pessinus, obtained for them permission to remove
the statue of the mother of the gods, which was
nothing else but a great stone. On its arrival at
Rome, it was received with great pomp and cere-
mony by the Roman senate and people, headed by
Scipio Nasica, selected for this office by the national
voice as the best citizen, according to the injunction
of the Pythian oracle. This took place in the year
547, U. C. near the close of the second Punic war.
(Liv. XXIX. 10—12. Strabo, XII. p. 567.) Stephanus Byz. affirms that Pessinus originally bore
the name of Arabyza, when this district belonged
to the Caucones: he does not mention from what
author he derives this information. (v. Ἀράβυζα.)
Herodian and Ammianus give various derivations
of the name of Pessinus, which are not worth re-
peating. (Herodian. I. 11. Ammian. Marcell. XXII.
22. Cf. Steph. Byz. v. Πεσσινοῦς.) It appears from
Livy that the worship of Cybele was still observed
in this city after its occupation by the Gauls, since
the priests of the goddess are said to have sent a

deputation to the army of Manlius, when on the banks of the Sangarius. (XXXVIII. 18.) Polybius mentions the names of the individuals who then presided over the worship and temple of Cybele. (Polyb. Frag. XX. 4[e].)

Strabo says Pessinus was the most commercial and flourishing town in this part of Asia, in his time, though the worship of Cybele, or Agdistis, as she was called by the Phrygians, had fallen into decay. The temple and its porticoes were of white marble, and surrounded by a beautiful grove: the city was indebted to the kings of Pergamum for these decorations. Formerly the priests of Cybele were high in rank and dignity, and possessed of great privileges and emoluments. (XII. p. 567.) Pausanias states that Pessinus was at the foot of mount Agdis- Agdistis tis, where Atys was said to have been buried; (Attic. c. 4.) this is probably the same mountain which Strabo calls Dindymus. At a later period we find Pessinus the metropolis of Galatia Salutaris. (Hierocl. p. 697[f].) I am not aware that any modern traveller has explored the ruins of this city, so that its site is not precisely ascertained: by the Antonine

[e] I may remark, by the way, that Polybius, with greater appearance of truth, says, the priests and their procession presented themselves before Manlius whilst he was engaged in throwing a bridge over the Sangarius, and encamped on that river, i. e. on the left bank, on which Pessinus also stood. But Livy says, that the procession met the Romans when they were already on the opposite side of the river, consequently it would have had to cross it likewise, unless we suppose, with Col. Leake, that Pessinus was on the right bank, which hypothesis cannot, I imagine, be correct.

[f] See Wesseling's note, and the ecclesiastical documents quoted by him. The coins of Pessinus exhibit a numerous series from Augustus to Caracalla. They generally allude to the worship of Cybele. The epigraph is ΠΕΣΣΙΝΟΥΝΤΙΩΝ, sometimes ΓΑΛ. ΤΟΛΙΣΤΟ. ΠΕΣΣΙΝΟΥ. Sestini, p. 128.

Itinerary we know it was ninety-nine miles from Ancyra, with which it communicated through Germa, Vindia, and Papira. Germa, the first of these stations, is known to answer to *Yerma,* on the modern road leading from *Eski-cher* to Ancyra: the Itinerary would lead us to place it sixteen miles from that site, towards the Sangarius. The Table Itinerary, on the other hand, gives a route from Doryleum to Pessinus, by Midæum and Tricomia, and allows seventy-seven miles for the whole distance, thus distributed: from Doryleum to Midæum XXVIII; to Tricomia XXVIII; to Pessinus XXI. But the road from Doryleum to Ancyra did not pass by Pessinus, but by Archelaium and Germa, as appears from another route in the Antonine Itinerary; (p. 202⁵.) so that it is evident that Pessinus could not have been situated where Col. Leake would place it, beyond Juliopolis, or Gordium, on the right bank of the Sangarius, and near its junction with the Hierus, as it would then have been exactly on the road to Ancyra, and such a route as that by Germa would never have been given in the Antonine Itinerary. On the whole, I should be inclined to look for the ruins of Pessinus not far from the left bank of the Sangarius, somewhere in the great angle it makes between its junction with the *Yerma* and the *Pursek.* It is evident that Pessinus was to the right of the great road leading from Nicæa to Juliopolis, since Julian is said by Ammianus to have turned off from that route near the Bithynian frontier, probably at Dadastana, to visit Pessinus. (XXII. c. 9.)

---

⁵ Col. Leake supposes the numbers in the Antonine to be incorrect, but the two routes, p. 201 and p. 202, very nearly agree.

In Lapie's map I find the ruins of Pessinus laid
down in the direction I have supposed, on a site
called *Kahé*, but I know not on what authority.
This name strongly resembles that of Caue, a large Caue.
and populous place mentioned by Xenophon in the
Hellenics; it was situate in Phrygia, and on the
road apparently leading into Paphlagonia. (Hell.
IV. 1. 10. Cf. III. 4. 26.)

Tricomia, mentioned above as being twenty-eight Tricomia.
miles from Pessinus, according to the Table, is
placed by Ptolemy in Phrygia. (p. 120.) These
towns on the Sangarius are generally alluded to by
the poet Nonnus, but I do not understand what district is referred to in the second line:

Τοῖσι συνεστρατόωντο καὶ οἱ λάχον ἄστεα ναίειν
Γείτονα Σαγγαρίου καὶ Ἐλέσπιδος ἔδρανα γαίης.

DIONYS. XIII. 518.

Germa, which has been already mentioned more Germa.
than once, is stated by Ptolemy to have been a
Roman colony; (p. 120.) and this title is confirmed
by its coins: the earliest are of the reign of Domitian, so that the colony cannot be older than the
time of Vespasian and his sons [h]. From Hierocles,
and the Ecclesiastical Notices, we are led to consider Germa as an episcopal see of Galatia Salutaris;
and a Byzantine writer, quoted by Wesseling, informs us, that at a later period it took the name of
Myriangeli, (Theophan. Chron. p. 203.) There can
be little doubt that *Yerma* represents the ancient
Germa [i]. Vindia, which the Itinerary removes in Vindia.

[h] Sestini, p. 128. Imperato-
rii Domitiani. Epigraphe, COL.
GERM. Commodi COL. GER-
MEN. vel COL. AUG. F. GER-
MENO.
[i] Leake's Asia Minor, p. 70, 1.

one place twenty-four miles from Germa, in another thirty-two, is also found in the list of Ptolemy.

Papira. (p. 120.) Papira, which next follows, at a distance of thirty-two miles, and twenty-seven from Ancyra, is only known from Antonine.

Archelaium. Archelaium, on the confines of Phrygia, thirty miles from Doryleum, and twenty from Germa, is to be met with in no other ancient authority but the above Itinerary; unless, as Wesseling intimates, it may answer to the Demus Auraclea of Hierocles.

Eudoxia. (p. 678.) Eudoxia, assigned by the same authority to Galatia Salutaris, (p. 698.) is known to have stood not far from Germa, on the evidence of a passage in the Life of Theodore Syceota, (c. 8.) quoted by Wesseling.

The Table furnishes a communication between Pessinus and Laodicea Catacecaumene in Phrygia, with two intervening stations, Abrostola and Amo-

Abrostola. rium. Abrostola, according to this Itinerary, was twenty-four miles from Pessinus. It is recognised by Ptolemy, (p. 120.) who assigns it to Phrygia

Amorium. Magna. Amorium was a place of greater consequence, being mentioned by Strabo as a town of Phrygia, (XII. p. 576.) Ptolemy, (p. 120.) and Steph. Byz. (v. 'Αμόριον.) It is probable that in Hierocles we should substitute 'Αμόριον for Αἰώριον. (p. 697. [k]) Amorium increased in importance under the Byzantine emperors, especially through the protection of Zeno, the Isaurian, who is called its founder by Cedrenus. (p. 351.) But in the ninth century it was

---

[k] See Wesseling's note. There are both autonomous and imperial medals of Amorium. The epigraph ΙΕΡΑ ΣΥΝΚΛΗ. or

ΒΟΥΛΗ-ΑΜΟΡΙΑΝΩΝ. Imperatorii ab Augusto ad Gallienum. Sestini, p. 117.

taken and sacked by the Saracens. (Zonar. Ann. XV. 29.) The site still retains the name of *Amoria*. The Table reckons twenty-three miles to Abrostola, and twenty to Laodicea. Another route led from Amorium into Cappadocia, through the southern part of Galatia. The first station is Tolosochorio, implying probably a fortress on the frontiers of the Tolistoboii. Orcistus, an episcopal see of Galatia, Orcistus. according to the Ecclesiastical Notices[1], is placed by Col. Leake, on the authority of an inscription discovered there by Pococke, at *Alekiam*, to the southwest of *Yerma*[m]. The situation of Bloucium, which Bloucium, . Strabo says was the residence of king Dejotarus, is sive Luceium. unknown. (XII. p. 567.) Cicero calls it Castellum Luceium, in the oration he composed for that king. It was here that the enemies of Dejotarus accused him of having designed to murder Cæsar. (Orat. pro Dejot. c. 6.) "Cum in Castellum Luceium venisses, " et domum regis, hospitis tui, divertisses: locus " erat quidam, in quo erant ea composita, quibus " rex te munerare constituerat. Huc te e balneo, " prius quam accumberes, ducere volebat. Ibi enim " erant armati, qui te interficerent, in eo ipso loco " collocati." From another passage in Cicero's Letters, (Fam. II. 12.) this residence of Dejotarus appears to have been in the vicinity of Pessinus. Of Peium, another fortress belonging to the Tolisto- Peium. boii, we know nothing beyond the fact communicated by Strabo, who further states that Dejotarus kept his treasures there. (loc. cit.)

The Tectosages, next in order to the Tolistoboii, Tectosages. occupied the central portion of the province between Paphlagonia on the north, and the Pisidians and

---

[1] Geogr. Sacr. p. 256.   [m] Asia Minor, p. 70, 71.

Lycaonians towards the south. In the former direction they held the great chain of Olympus and its valleys; in the latter, the barren tract which borders on the great salt lake Tattæa.

Their towns were less numerous than those of their fellow tribes; but, on the other hand, they could boast of having for their capital the largest and most celebrated city of the whole province. *Ancyra.* This was Ancyra, which even now still retains some vestiges of its ancient name under that of *Angur,* or *Angorah.* Pausanias has recorded a tradition, which assigned its foundation to Midas: this prince was said to have named it from an anchor he found on the site, and which was exhibited, as Pausanias relates, in the temple of Jupiter. The Ancyræans pointed out also the fountain where Midas is said to have caught Silenus, by mixing wine with its waters. (Att. c. 4 [n].) Apollonius, the historian of Caria, quoted by Stephanus Byz. (v. Ἄγκυρα.) gives a different account of the foundation of Ancyra, and supposes it to have been built by the Gauls; but his narrative is easily disproved by the authority of Arrian, who states that Alexander passed through Ancyra on his way from Gordium, and received there a deputation from Paphlagonia [o]. (Exp. Alex. II. 4. 1.) Livy also informs us that Ancyra was already a large and flourishing town when Manlius occupied it with his army, after defeating the Tolistoboii. (XXXVIII. 24.) There is no evidence of the Gauls having founded any but minor towns

[n] According to Xenophon, the people of Thymbrium, in Phrygia, laid claim to this fountain; (Anab. I. 2. 13.) while others placed it in Pæonia or Macedonia. (Athen. II. p. 45.)

[o] He calls it the Galatian Ancyra, to distinguish it from Ancyra of Phrygia Epictetus.

in this province: they only seized upon those which had been previously built by the Phrygians. (Cf. Memnon. ap. Phot. p. 722. Nonn. Narrat. ap. Creuz. Meletem, p. 75.) It is certainly surprising, as Cellarius observes, that Strabo should have made so little mention of Ancyra, and have dismissed it with the inadequate notice of its being the fortress of the Tectosages. (XII. p. 567.) This is the more remarkable, when we learn that Ancyra had received great improvements and embellishments under the patronage of Augustus, whence the grammarian Tzetzes is led to style him the founder of the city. Connected with the mention of that emperor is the celebrated inscribed monument found at Ancyra, detailing the several actions and public merits of Augustus; and which, besides its general interest, proves in particular that he had been a great patron of the Ancyrani [p]. Other inscriptions give Ancyra the title of metropolis of Galatia [q]; and Libanius, the sophist, styles it, πρώτην καὶ μεγίστην Γαλατῶν πόλιν. (Orat. XXVI. Cf. Plin. V. 32. Ptol. p. 120.) Ancyra continued under the Byzantine emperors to be one of the most important cities of Asia Minor. Having been taken by the Turks, it was retaken by the crusaders. (Nic. Ann. p. 304. D. In. 14.) It was the scene of the great conflict between the two vast armies of Bajazet and Tamerlane, in which the for-

[p] The marmor Ancyranum was first discovered, I believe, by the celebrated Busbequius at *Angorah;* and from a copy that he made then, was published at Antwerp in 1579 by Andreas Schottus, with some remarks and emendations by Lipsius. Since then it has been often reprinted. It unfortunately exhibits many lacunæ.

[q] The coins of Ancyra exhibit the same honourable distinction. ΑΝΚΤΡΑ ΜΗΤΡΟΠΟΛΙC ΤΗC ΓΑΛΑΤΙΑC, or ΑΝΚΤΡΑΝΩΝ. ΜΗΤ. Sestini, p. 128.

mer lost his crown, and fell into the hands of his victorious enemy. (M. Duc. p. 33, et seq.)

Several roads led to Ancyra from different parts of Asia. The principal communication was with Nicæa and Juliopolis of Bithynia. The Jerusalem Itinerary furnishes us with the greatest detail respecting this route, the stations of which, between Juliopolis and Ancyra, are as follows:

M. P.

Civit. Juliop.—Mutatio Hycron potamum [r] ..XIII.
Mansio Agannia (Lagania) ....XI.
Mutatio Ipeto-brogen ....VI.
Mutatio Mnizcs.................................X.
Mutatio Prasmon..............................XII.
Mutatio Cenaxepalidem ....XIII.
Civitas Anchira Galatia.

The Antonine Itinerary does not give so many stations, but increases the distance.

Iuliopolim—Laganeos ....XXIIII.
Minizo ....XXIII.
Manegordo ....XXVIII.
Ancyra ....XXIIII.

The Table differs very much from the two others, and its numbers are not to be relied upon.

Iuliopolim—Valcaton [s] ....XII.
Fines Cilicie (Galatiæ)..........................X.
Lagania ....XXVIII [t].
Mizago [u].....................................XXXVIII.
Ancyra [x].....................................XXVIII [y].

[r] This is evidently the Hierus potamus of Pliny, the Siberis of Procopius. Wesseling's conjecture about the Hypius is inadmissible.

[s] Probably the Hieron potamon of the Jerusalem Itinerary.

[t] This should be XXIIII.

[u] If this is Minizus, the number should be corrected to XXVIII. In the Jerusalem Itinerary the distance from Lagania to Minizus should be XXVI.

[x] The name is omitted in the Table; but there is an indication of a large town, which can be no other but Ancyra.

[y] This number should be XXIIII.

Lagania, which has a place in the three Itinera- Lagania.
ries, is the Reganagalia of Hierocles. (p. 697. Read
Regelagania, the first part of the word is only a corruption of the Latin word Regio.) It was an episcopal see, and afterwards took the name of Anasta-
siopolis. (Vit. Theod. Syc. c. 2.) [z] Minizus (Re- Minizus.
gemnezus in Hierocles, p. 697.) is known also from
the councils in which its bishops are recorded. The
other stations are unknown; but Cenaxepalidem, in Cenaxe
the Jerusalem Itinerary, refers probably to a lake palus.
near Ancyra, mentioned in the Acts of Theodotus
the martyr. (c. 2 [a].) Sebaste, whose inhabitants are
the Sebasteni of Pliny, is known from an inscription, Sebaste.
adduced by Cellarius, to have belonged to the Tectosages. (V. 32 [b].) Beyond Ancyra, and towards Magaba
the Halys, was mount Magaba, where the second mons.
defeat of the Gauls by the army of the Consul Manlius took place, according to Livy. (XXXVIII. 19
—26.) Rufus Festus reports that it was afterwards called Modiacus. (c. 11.) This chain was
probably in the direction of Paphlagonia. Strabo
places on the borders of Phrygia, and not far from
the lake Tattæa, Pitinissus, and the Orcaorci. (XII.
p. 568.) Pitnissus, or Petnissus, is also noticed by Pitnissus.
Ptolemy, p. 120. and Stephanus Byz. (v. Πίτνισσα.)
who assigns it to Lycaonia, but Hierocles to Galatia
Salutaris. (p. 697.)

Strabo appears to be the only writer who has
mentioned the Orcaorici. In one passage he in- Orcaorici.
cludes them within the limits of the Tectosages;

[z] Cited by Wesseling, who
points out the circumstance ad
Hierocl. p. 696, 697.
[a] Wesseling on the Jerusalem Itinerary, p. 575.
[b] This also appears from its
coins. ΣΕΒΑΣΤΗΝΩΝ ΤΕΚΤΟ-
ΣΑΓΩΝ. Sestini, p. 128.

(XII. p. 567.) in another he joins them rather with the Lycaonians, and the country south of the salt lake Tattæa. (XII. p. 568.) This part of Galatia was traversed by a road already alluded to in speaking of Abrostola and Amorium, in the territory of the Tolistoboii. The stations on this route furnished by the Table are—

	M. P.
Amurio—Abrostola	XI.
Tolosochorio	XXIIII.
Bagrum	VII.
Vetisso	XX.
Egdava	XX.
Pegella	XX.
Congusso	XX.
Petra	XV.
Ubinaca	XX.
Comitanasso	XII.
Salaberina	XXIX.

Ecdaumana. Congustus. Egdaua is supposed by Col. Leake, with every appearance of probability, to be the Ecdaumana of Ptolemy, and Congusso the Congustus of the same geographer. At Salaberina, or Salambria, this road fell into the great route from Byzantium to Syria by Nicæa, Ancyra, and Tyana. The stations on this route, from Ancyra to the Cappadocian frontier of Galatia, are as follows in the Jerusalem Itinerary:

	M. P.
Civitas Anchira—Mutatio Delemna	X.
Mansio Curveunta	XI.
Mutatio Rossolodiaco	XII.
Mutatio Aliassum	XIII.
Mutatio Arpona	XVIII.
Mutatio Galea	XIII.
Mutatio Andrapa	IX.

Finis Galatiæ et Cappadociæ.

The Antonine as usual, has fewer stations, but the distances agree.

	M. P.
Ancyra—Corbeunca	XX.
Rosologiacum	X-II.
Aspona..	XXXI.

In these Itineraries the only names which are known from other sources are Corbeunca, Rosolo-giacum, and Aspona. The former is evidently the Corbeus, or Gorbeus, of Strabo, who informs us that Corbeus. it was the residence of Saocondarius, son-in-law of Dejotarus and father of Castor, who accused the latter before Cæsar of plotting against his life. This conduct of his son involved Saocondarius in a quarrel with his father-in-law, who took Corbeus, and put Saocondarius and his daughter to death. This conduct proves Dejotarus to have been such a tyrant as Plutarch represents him, though Cicero, his particular friend, gives him a very different character. (Plut. de Stoic. Repugn. tom. X. p. 337. Reisk.) Corbeus was on this occasion nearly destroyed. (Strab. XII. p. 568.) It is, however, mentioned by Ptolemy as belonging to the Tectosages, (p. 120.) and by all the Itineraries; but in the Table it is strangely misplaced; indeed the whole route is perfectly unintelligible [c]. Corbeus answers, doubtless,

[c] It seems as if the whole route between Ancyra and Archelais in Cappadocia of Antonine was reversed in the Table; for Nitazus, the last station before Archelais in the Ant. Itinerary, is first in the Table; and Corbeus, which in all the other Itineraries occurs first after Ancyra in the Table, stands last. In the latter document the distance between Aspona and the nameless station, which is doubtless meant for Archelais, is nearly the same as the distance between Aspona and Ancyra; so that it certainly looks as if the two extreme points had been transposed by the transcriber.

to the site of *Corbega*, a few miles from the mo-
Rosologia-
cum.
dern road leading from *Angora* to *Kaisarieh*. Ro-
sologiacum is doubtless the Rosologia of Ptolemy.
Aspona.
Aspona, which is named in all the Itineraries, is
termed by Ammianus, (XXV. 10.) " Galatiæ muni-
" cipium breve;" it is found also in Hierocles, (p.
696.) and the ecclesiastical historians Socrates and
Nicephorus. Ptolemy has besides several obscure
Olenus.
towns belonging to the Tectosages : these are Ole-
Agrizala.
Vincela.
Landosia.
Dictis.
Carima.
nus, Agrizala, Vincela, Landosia, Dictis, and Carima. To Dictis we should perhaps refer, as Harduinus imagined, the Didyenses of Pliny, (V. 32.)
in which case we must read Dictyenses. The latter
geographer is the only writer who classes the Teutobodiaci with the Tectosages. The rest of Galatia
Trocmi.
belonged to the Trocmi, who occupied the north-
eastern portion of that country towards Pontus and
Cappadocia, and chiefly, as it should seem, on the
right bank of the river Halys. The territory of
the Trocmi, as we are informed by Strabo, was the
best and most productive of any that had fallen
to the share of the Galatian tribes. (XII. p. 567.)
Their chief town, according to the same geogra-
Tavium,
sive Tavia.
pher and Ptolemy, was Tavium. Pliny, (V. 32.)
Stephanus Byz. (v. Ἄγκυρα,) and Hierocles, (p. 696.)
write Tavia. It was a city of considerable traffick, as Strabo likewise reports ; and this is further confirmed by the number of communications
branching off from thence to different parts of Asia
Minor. It was also celebrated for a bronze statue of Jupiter, of colossal size, placed in a sacred
grove, having the right of an asylum. (Strab. loc.
cit.) It is known to have been an episcopal see,
from the Ecclesiastical Notices and Acts of Coun-

rary reckons between Tavium and Cæsarea, with that of *Jeuzgatt* to *Kaisarieh* on the map, I find in one case 109 miles, in the other about 100, in a straight line, which, with allowance for hills, would make the two reckonings tally with all the accuracy which is required in such matters. On the other hand, whoever will make the corresponding measurements which have been just stated with respect to *Tchorum*, which is nearly forty miles to the north of *Jeuzgatt*, will find that they disagree with the reckoning in the Itineraries in almost every instance; so that it is not without reason that I attribute to the latter the honour of representing the ancient Tavium. It remains now for me to give the detail of the roads considered above, that is, their stations and distances from the Itineraries of antiquity. And first I shall give those of the road from Ancyra to Tavium, according to the Antonine Itinerary.

Iter ab Ancyra Taviam, M. P. CXVI. Sic,

Bolelasgus ....XXIIII.
Sarmalius ....XXIIII.
Ecobrogis ....XX.
Adapera ....XXIIII.
Tavia ....XXIIII.

Among these stations Sarmalium is the only one which finds a name in any ancient writer; it is the Sarmalia of Ptolemy. (p. 120.) Ecobriga oc- Sarmalia. curs also in the Table, but its list in other respects is very different.

M. P.

Ancyra—Acitoriziaco...............XXXVI.
Eccobriga ....XXXIII.
Lassora ......:...................XXV.

H 3

M. P.

Stabiu ....XVII.

Tavio [e].

Androsia.   Of these stations Acitoriziacum answers perhaps
Lascoria.   to Androsia in Ptolemy, and Lassora to Lascoria.
Strabo informs us, that, besides Tavia, there were
two other towns of note belonging to the Trocmi,
Mithrida-   Mithridatium and Danala : the former had been dis-
tium.   membered from the kingdom of Pontus, and given
Danala.   to Bogodiatarus, a Gallic chief, by Pompey [f]. Danala derived some notoriety from its being the spot
where Lucullus and Pompey held a conference on
the subject of the Mithridatic war, previous to the
latter succeeding to the command. (Strab. XII. p.
567.) Plutarch alludes to this meeting, but merely
says it took place in some village of Galatia. (Lucull. c. 36.) Nothing seems to be known respecting
these two sites [g].

The road from Tavium to Neocæsarea by Amasia is arranged in the following manner in the Table
Itinerary :

M. P.

Tavio—Tonea ....XIII.

Garsi [h] ....XXX.

Amasia ....XXX.

Palalce ....XV.

Coloe ....XII.

---

[e] The distance is wanting.

[f] Some of the commentators of Strabo have wished to substitute the well known name of Dejotarus for the more obscure one of Bogodiatarus, but without just cause, since that reading is proved to be nearly the true one by a silver coin of this Gallo-græcian prince. The legend is ΒΑΣΙΛΕΩΣ ΒΡοΓΙΤΑ-ΡοΥ. ΦΙΛοΡΩΜΑΙοΥ. Sestini, p. 129.

[g] The MSS. differ with respect to the name of Danala : see the note to the French Strabo, tom. IV. b. ii. p. 91.

[h] Probably Gazioura. tom. I. p. 305.

M. P.

Pidis ....X.
Mirones.............................XVI.
Neocæsarea ....X.

Route II. to Neocæsarea, by Zela.

Tavio—Rogmor ....XXXVI.
Ægonne ....XXXVI.
Ptemari............................XXVIII.
Zela ....XXVI.
Stabulum ....XXXII.
Seranusa ....XXII.
Neocæsarea ....XV.

Route III. to Comana Pontica.

Tavio—Tomba....................XVI.
Eugoni ....XXII.
....
Ad Stabulum ....
Mesyla ....XXII.
Comana Pontica ....XV.

Ptolemy assigns likewise to the Trocmi Claudio-polis, Carissa, Phuibagina, Dudua, Saralus, Ucena, Rastia. Of these, Phuibagina and Saralus corre-spond with Evagina of the Table, placed sixteen miles from Tavium on the road to Cæsarea, and Sa-ralium twenty-four miles from Evagina. Pliny names besides, as belonging to Galatia, the Atta-lenses, Arasenses, Comenses, Didyenses, Hieronen-ses, or Hierorenses [i], Lystreni, Neapolitani, Œan-denses, Seleucenses, Sebasteni, Timoniacenses, The-baseni ; but many of these are known to have been included in Pisidia and Lycaonia, and, as Mannert judiciously remarks, probably formed part of the dominions of Amyntas, the last tetrarch of Galatia.

(margin notes: Claudio-polis. Carissa. Phuiba-gina. Dudua. Saralus. Ucena. Rastia.)

[i] See Harduinus' Notes and Emendations to Pliny, No. 97.

H 4

(Plin. V. 32.)   To these may be added Mænalia, a town of Galatia. (Steph. Byz. v. Μαίναλος.)   Anar, a river of Galatia, ("Αναρ. Chœrobosc. ap. Bekker. Anecd. Gr. Ind.) probably the Araros of Ptolemy. Cinna, an episcopal see, according to the Acts of Councils and Ecclesiastical Notices, confirmed by Hierocles, (p. 696—698.) together with Heliopolis, Regemauricium, Regetrocnada, Muricium, and Claneus.

SECTION IX.

CAPPADOCIA AND ARMENIA MINOR.

———◆———

Origin of the Leucosyri, or Cappadocians—Sketch of their history under the Assyrian, Median, and Persian empires—Cappadocian dynasty—Roman province of Cappadocia—Its boundaries and geographical features—Description—Armenia Minor—Its several districts and topography.

HERODOTUS has stated that in the days of Crœsus and Cyrus, the people commonly known in history by the name of Cappadocians were termed Syrians by the Greeks, while the Persians employed the more usual appellation. (I. 72. VII. 72.) We have also seen that a portion of this nation, who occupied the coast of Pontus and Paphlagonia about Sinope and Amisus, had long retained the name of Leucosyri to distinguish them from the more swarthy and southern inhabitants of Syria and Palestine. (Strab. XII. p. 544.) The origin of the Cappadocians, unlike that of most of the other nations of Asia Minor, was therefore of Asiatic growth, unmixed with the Thracian hordes which had overrun Phrygia and all the western parts of the peninsula. This would naturally be expected on the one hand from the proximity of Cappadocia to the passes of Cilicia and Amanus, which communicated with Syria, and the natural separation afforded on the

other by the course of the Halys towards the west.
This river, as we learn from Herodotus, formed the
limit of the empires of Media and Lydia before they
were united into one by the Persian Cyrus : but
there is little doubt that this part of Asia Minor, if
not the whole peninsula, had been previously subject to the Assyrian monarchs, and on the dissolu-
tion of their empire devolved to the victorious
Medes.   The great Semiramis had left monuments
of her rule in Cappadocia, by founding Melitene on
the Euphrates, and constructing a road extending
apparently from Tyana on the borders of Cilicia, to
Cómana in Pontus.   The Cappadocian Comana, and
the worship of Men, owed their origin doubtless to
the same people; and, if we were acquainted with
the language of the ancient Cappadocians, we should
find further traces of their connexion with the Assyrians and Chaldees.   The Cilicians, who derived
their origin from-the same stock, had formed one
people and one province with the Cappadocians
under the empires of Assyria and Media; but they
were subsequently divided by the Persians into two
separate governments.   In the time of Herodotus
the Syrians, or Cappadocians, extended from mount
Taurus and the confines of Cilicia to the shore of
the Euxine, between the Halys and Thermodon, and
in the division made by Darius they constituted the
third section of his vast empire. (III. 90.)   The Cilicia of Herodotus, however, certainly comprised a
portion of Cappadocia, since the tribute which that
satrapy paid to the Persian monarch is said to have
consisted in white horses; and we find at a later
period Cappadocia celebrated for a beautiful breed
of these animals.   In a division made subsequently

to the reign of Darius, Cappadocia was formed into two satrapies, one of which comprised the country bordering on the Euxine, and afterwards known by the name of Pontus; the other, the more southern districts, lying towards Taurus and Cilicia, and on the east as far as the Euphrates. It is with the latter, termed Magna Cappadocia by the geographers of antiquity, that we are concerned at present, since the former has been already discussed in the section relating to Pontus. According to Diodorus, in a passage preserved by Photius, (Cod. 244. p. 1157.) the early Cappadocian sovereigns, or rather satraps, were descended from one of the seven conspirators who slew the false Smerdis. This Persian nobleman was named Anaphus, and his grandson Datames was the first sovereign of the Cappadocian dynasty: after him, and his son Ariamnes, we have a long list of princes, all bearing the name of Ariarathes for several generations [a]. Ariarathes I. was on the throne when Alexander invaded the Persian dominions, and he probably fled with Darius, since we learn from Arrian that the Macedonian prince appointed Sabictas governor of Cappadocia before the battle of Issus. (Exp. Alex. II. 4, 2.) After the death of Alexander, Ariarathes, then at the advanced age of eighty-two, attempted to recover his dominions; but he was defeated by Perdiccas, the Macedonian general, and, being taken, was cruelly put to death. (Diod. Sic. Exc. XVIII. 16. Arrian. ap. Phot. Cod. 92. p. 217.)

[a] Cappadocia was probably much on the same footing as Cilicia, whose hereditary chiefs appear in history under the name of Syennesis, from the time of Croesus to that of the younger Cyrus.

Eumenes, the Cardian, one of Alexander's ablest generals, then for a time held the government of Cappadocia; but on his death, by the hands of Antigonus, and the subsequent contests between the latter and the other Macedonian chiefs, a favourable opportunity was afforded to Ariarathes, the nephew, but adopted son of the first Ariarathes, to recover his principality. Assisted by Ardoatus, sovereign of Armenia, this young prince entered Cappadocia with an army, defeated and killed Amyntas the governor in battle, and quickly expelled the Macedonians from the country. (Diod. Exc. ap. Phot. p. 1160.) Ariarathes II. transmitted the crown to his son Ariamnes, and he was succeeded by another Ariarathes, of whom nothing is recorded, except that on his death he left a son of the same name in his infancy. (Diod. Sic. ap. Phot. loc. cit.) This Ariarathes, the fourth of that name, was contemporary with Philip of Macedon, Antiochus the Great, and Ptolemy Philopator. (Polyb. IV. 2.) His marriage with the daughter of Antiochus involved him in a political alliance with that sovereign, and consequent hostilities with the Romans, which would probably have led to his dethronement, after the battle of Magnesia, if he had not deprecated the anger of the victors by a timely and submissive embassy.

The Consul Manlius accepted his apology, and granted him peace, on condition that he should pay 600 talents. (Polyb. Exc. XXII. 24. Liv. XXXVIII. 37.) Soon after, we find this king of Cappadocia allied to Eumenes, king of Pergamum, who married his daughter, and by his means was admitted to the favour and friendship of the Romans. (Liv. XXXVIII. 39.) In conjunction with Eumenes he made war against Pharnaces and the Galatians. (Polyb. Exc. XXV. 2.) Ariarathes survived Antiochus Epiphanes little more than a year; and after a reign of nearly fifty-eight years [b], transmitted the crown to his son Ariarathes V. who for some time was dethroned by Demetrius Soter, king of Syria, and Orophernes, who pretended to be the son of Ariarathes IV.; but he was restored by the Romans. (Polyb. III. 5.) In return for this assistance, he devoted himself to their service, and fell in the war they were carrying on against Aristonicus, the pretender to the throne of Pergamum. (Justin. XXXVII. 1.) He transmitted the crown to his son Ariarathes VI. who had married Laodice, sister of the celebrated Mithridates; and, after reigning thirty-four years, was treacherously put to death by that crafty monarch. (Justin. XXXVIII. 1.) His two sons lost their lives in attempting to recover their paternal dominions; and the royal line becoming extinct, the nation elected, at the instigation of the Roman senate, Ariobarzanes, a man of rank in the country, king of Cappadocia. This new sovereign was, however, repeatedly expelled by Mithridates, and as often replaced by the Roman generals employed against him, till at length the death of that active and implacable enemy of the Roman name, left him in quiet possession of the throne, for which he was indebted to the latter. (Plut. Syll. et Lucull. Ap. Mithrid. c. 15. 60. Justin. XXXVIII. 2.) After three generations, the line of Ariobarzanes again failing on the death of his grandson Aria-

---

[b] For the succession and chronology of the kings of Cappadocia, see the very learned and accurate summary of Mr. Clinton, Fasti Hellen. tom. II. Appendix, p. 429.

rathes, seventh of that name, who was deposed and put to death by Marc Antony, the latter appointed Archelaus to succeed to the throne of Cappadocia. (Strab. XII. p. 540. Dio Cass. XLIX. 32.) This prince, though a creature of Antony, had the art to secure the favour of Augustus also, and obtained from that emperor a considerable accession to his territory, consisting of a part of Cilicia, and some districts of Lycaonia, which had belonged to Antipater. (Strab. XII. p. 535. Dio Cass. LIV. 9.) But he incurred the displeasure of Tiberius for having neglected to pay him his court when in the island of Rhodes. He was therefore summoned to Rome, under some pretended charge; and, though acquitted of the offence imputed to him, chagrin and vexation at the treatment he received from the emperor, joined to old age and bodily infirmity, terminated his life, and with him ended the Cappadocian kingdom, which was converted into a province under the charge of a proconsul. (Tacit. Ann. II. 42. Dio Cass. LVII. 17.) Strabo states that Magna Cappadocia, as it was then called, was divided into ten præfecturæ, of which five lay towards Taurus, namely, Melitene, Cataonia, Cilicia, Tyanitis, and Garsauritis; the five others, further removed from the mountain above mentioned, were Laviniasene, Sargarausene, Saravene, Chammanene, and Morimene; to these was added afterwards an eleventh, which comprised the cantons of Castabala and Cibystra, as far as Derbe in Lycaonia, and in favour of Archelaus, Cilicia Trachea, and the coast formerly infested by pirates. (XII. p. 535.) These divisions are, with some exceptions, unknown to the later geographers. It is to be presumed, therefore, that they made way for other changes in the distribution of the province; and, as Strabo himself has not ventured to define their limits, we must content ourselves with such general indications of their extent and position, as can be collected from his succinct and rapid view of this portion of Asia Minor. Under the Greek emperors, Cappadocia was divided into two sections, one of which was under a consular government, the other was administered by a count, (ἡγεμών). This province, if we include within its limits certain districts, which, under a specific arrangement, are assignable to Armenia Minor, will have for its boundaries the Euphrates and Mount Amanus, to the west and south-west; to the north, a chain of mountains, running obliquely from the head of the Euphrates along the left bank of the Lycus, then passing by the source of the Halys, and following that river till it meets the Cilician, or southern arm, near the ancient Mocissus; towards the west, it bordered on the Galatian Trocmi and Lycaonia; and, finally, towards the south, Taurus interposed its great ridge between it and Cilicia.

Cappadocia was thus surrounded on three sides by great ranges of mountains, besides being intersected by others of as great elevation as any in the peninsula. Hence its mineral productions were various and abundant, and a source of wealth to the country. Strabo specifies the rich mineral colour called Sinople, from its being exported by the merchants of Sinope, but really dug in the mines of Cappadocia: also onyx; crystal; a kind of white agate employed for ornamental purposes; and the lapis specularis: this last was found in large masses, and was a considerable article of the export trade.

The champaign country yielded almost every kind
of fruit and grain, and the wines of some districts
vied with those of Greece in strength and flavour.
Cappadocia was also rich in herds and flocks, but
more particularly celebrated for its breed of horses;
and the onager, or wild ass, abounded in the mountains towards Lycaonia. (Strab. XII. p. 535—540.)
The breadth of the whole province, taken from
Pontus [c] to Mount Taurus, measured, according to
Strabo, 1800 stadia; while its length, from Lycaonia and Phrygia to the Euphrates, was not less
than 3000. (XII. p. 539.) This geographer commences his periegesis of the province from the Euphrates; but as our march is, on the contrary, from
west to east, we shall begin rather from the Halys
and the Lycaonian frontier.

Garsau-
ritis.
Garsaura,
sive Garsa-
bora.

The first district we enter upon in this direction
is Garsauritis, which took its name from Garsaura,
or Garsabora, a small town, mentioned more than
once by Strabo, as situated on the great road from
Ephesus to the Euphrates. (XII. p. 537. Cf. XII.
p. 568. XIV. p. 663.) It was 120 stadia from Coropassus, the last town of Lycaonia. Pliny says
Garsauritis joins on to Phrygia. (VI. 3.) Ptolemy
ascribes to this præfectura Archelais, Diocæsarea, and

Archelais. Tetrapyrgia. (p. 125.) Archelais, as we are informed by Pliny, was situate on the Halys, and had
received a colony in the reign of Claudius. It had its
name from Archelaus, the last sovereign of Cappadocia, but it was then only an inconsiderable place,

[c] This must mean from the
Euxine, otherwise this dimen-
sion would be much exaggerated; and therefore Strabo is
here speaking of Cappadocia as
if including the kingdom of
Pontus. Ptolemy also unites
them in his geographical system, p. 125.

since no notice is taken of it by Strabo. We know
from the Itineraries that Archelais was situate on
the road by which Ancyra communicated with Tyana, or, to speak more generally, on the route leading from Constantinople to Syria and Palestine.
(Anton. Itin. p. 144. Itin. Hieros. p. 576.) As we
find no mention of Archelais in Hierocles nor the
Ecclesiastical Notices, it probably sunk into decay
under the eastern emperors. D'Anville is certainly
mistaken in identifying Archelais with *Erklé*, south-
east of Iconium, as this position is totally incom-
patible with the Itineraries. I should rather agree
with Col. Leake, in supposing it may be represented
by the modern *Ak-serai*, on the right bank of the
Halys, which gives its name to a district probably corresponding with Garsauritis [d]. Diocæsa- Diocæsarea, which Ptolemy places in this vicinity, is often rea.
noticed, as Wesseling has remarked, by Gregory of
Nazianzus, and from his account it was evidently
situated not far from the latter town, with which
his name is always connected. Of Diocæsarea he
says,

Γρηγορίου μνήσαιτο τὸν ἔτρεφε Καππαδόκεσσιν
Ἡ Διοκαισαρέων ὀλίγη πολις.

and again,

Τυτθὸν μὲν πτολίεθρον ἀτὰρ πολὺν ἀνέρα δῶκα
Βήμασιν ἰθυδίκης ἡ Διοκαισαρέων
Αμφίλοχον.

It has been remarked that, as Diocæsarea is neither mentioned in Hierocles nor the Notices, and
other documents, it may have perhaps been united
to Nazianzus, but Gregory himself speaks of the
two as very distinct places.

[d] Asia Minor, p. 75.

Nazianzus itself derives all its celebrity from that great writer and poet; he appears to have been born at Arianzus, a small village in the immediate neighbourhood[d], but to have been principally educated at Nazianzus[e], to the bishopric of which he was afterwards promoted. (Niceph. Call. XIV. 39. Philostorg. ap. Suid. v. Γρηγόριος.) He himself informs us, that his father had built a beautiful church in that town. (Orat. XIX. p. 313.) Nazianzus is assigned by Hierocles to Cappadocia Secunda. The Itineraries remove it twenty-four miles from Archelais. In that of Jerusalem, the name is strangely metamorphosed to Anathiango; (p. 577.) and in Ptolemy to Nea-

nessus, or Nanessus. (p. 126.) Above the town was a hill or mountain, named Athar. (Act. Tergemin.

ap. Wesseling, loc. cit.) Sasima, another spot connected with the biography of Gregory, was twenty-five miles from Nazianzus, towards Tyana. It was the first church to which he was appointed, and he has given us a humorous description of the miseries of the place[f].

Σταθμὸς τίς ἐστιν ἐν μίσῃ λεωφόρῳ
Τῆς Καππαδοκῶν ὃς σχίζετ' εἰς τρισσὴν ὁδὸν,
Ἄνυδρος, ἄχλους, οὐδ' ὅλως ἐλεύθερος,
Δεινῶς ἀπευκτὸν καὶ στενὸν καμύδριον.
Κόνις τὰ πάντα καὶ ψόφοοι σὺν ἅρμασι,
Θρῆνοι, στεναγμοὶ, πράκτορες, στρέβλαι, πέδαι,
Λάος δ' ὅσοι ξένοι τε καὶ πλανώμενοι.
Αὕτη Σασίμων τῶν ἐμῶν ἐκκλησία.

(Cf. Orat. XXV. p. 435.) Gregory's complaint of the want of water in this part of the country agrees with the indication we find in Ptolemy, of a place

d Note to Hierocles, p. 700,　　e Wesseling, ibid.　　f Cited by Wesseling.

called Phreata, or "the Wells," in Garsauritis. Phreata.
(p. 125.) Salambria, which he assigns to the same
district, is doubtless the Salaberina of the Table, Salambria.
from which we learn that it stood to the south of
Archelais, and at the junction of two roads; the one
coming from Ancyra, the other from Pessinus and
Amorium. Tetrapyrgia, another Garsauritic town Tetrapyr-
in the list of Ptolemy, cannot be identified with a gia.
station of the same name occurring in the Table,
between Iconium and Pompeiopolis of Cilicia. The
adjoining præfectura, to the north of the one we have Morimene
just described, is called Morimene by Strabo and præfectura.
Pliny, without any indication of the origin of the
name. Pliny observes, that it was contiguous to
Galatia; the boundary of the two provinces was
formed by the river Cappadox, from which the
country we are now describing took its name. (VI.
3.) This stream answers, I conceive, in modern
geography to that now called *Erkurous*, which,
rising in the mountains of Pontus, flows in a south-
westerly direction, and joins the Halys a little below
Kircher. This being so, Morimene will answer
nearly to the district of *Kircher*. Strabo mentions
no towns in Morimene, but he says it possessed a
celebrated temple of Jupiter, at a place named Ve- Venasi.
nasi. There were no less than 3000 slaves belonging to the establishment, and the high priest enjoyed an annual income of fifteen talents, arising
from the produce of the lands belonging to the temple. The sacerdotal office was held for life, and was
next in dignity to that of Comana. (XII. p. 537.)
If the Muriana of Ptolemy, as Cellarius imagines
with great probability, should be identified with the
Morimene of Strabo and Pliny, we shall have to place

in it, from his indication, some towns, which, however obscure, ought not to be entirely omitted; and
the Itineraries will lend us their aid in settling some
of the positions they occupied. The first Cappadocian town, after passing the Galatian frontier, was
Parnassus, as we learn from the Jerusalem Itinerary, which removes it ninety-nine miles from Ancyra, and forty from Archelais. The Antonine Itinerary reckons only eighty-four from the former
city. It was a place of some antiquity, being mentioned by Polybius in a passage contained in the
Excerpta Legat., wherein the historian, narrating
the war carried on by Eumenes and Ariarathes,
king of Cappadocia, against Pharnaces, king of Pontus, states that Eumenes, finding that his adversary
was about to invade Cappadocia, determined to anti-
cipate him: moving then rapidly through Galatia
in five days, from Calpitum[g], he reached the Halys,
and in one day more he came to Parnassus, where
he was joined by Ariarathes with his forces. (XXV.
4. 8.) It is seen from the above passage that Parnassus was on the right bank of the Halys, and one
day's march from it. Parnassus is assigned by Hierocles to Cappadocia Secunda: (p. 700.) it is also
mentioned by Constantine Porphyrogenetes; and
the Acts of Councils prove its having been a bishop's see[h].

Parnassus.

We learn from Philostorgius, that Sadagothina, a
village situate in the vicinity of Parnassus, was the
birthplace of Ulfilas, bishop of the Goths. (II. p.
480.) From Parnassus, the traveller had the choice
of two roads; the one leading to Archelais and

*Sadagothi-
na.*

g Some unknown place or
river of Phrygia, on the Galatian frontier.

h Geogr. Sacr. p. 255.

Tyana, the other to Cæsarea, the capital of the province. There were two stages between Parnassus and Archelais; Ozzala, or, as it is in the Jerusa-*Ozzala.* lem Itinerary, Iogola, seventeen miles, and Nitazus, eighteen miles. Allusion seems to be made to the former station in Greg. Nazian. (Ep. XII.) Nitazus *Nitazus.* occurs in all the Itineraries, but in the Table it has exchanged places with Corbeus, and in the Hierosolymitanum it is corruptly written Nitalis. The road from Parnassus to Cæsarea presents us with four stations: Nyssa twenty-four miles, Osiana thirty-*Nyssa.* two, Saceasena twenty-eight, Cæsarea thirty. Of these, Nyssa is the only one which possesses any interest, from being associated with the fame of Gregory, brother of Basil, and surnamed Nyssenus, from his long residence there as bishop of its church. (Socr. Hist. Eccl. V. 8. Niceph. Call. XI. 49.) Ptolemy assigns Nyssa to Muriana, (Morimene,) and Hierocles to Cappadocia Prima. (p. 699.) The name of *Nour* is still attached to the site on the Halys, below *Mochiour.* This latter place represents Mocis-*Mocissus.* sus, a town of some size and note in the time of Justinian, who built it on the site of an ancient fortress. (Procop. Æd. V. 4. Steph. Byz. v. Μούκισσος.) Ptolemy has several obscure towns in the same district, which occur in no other writer, and which render it still a matter of doubt whether his Muriana is the Morimene of other geographers. He names Sinzita, or Sindita, Cotæna, Zoro-*Sinzita, vel Sindita.* passus, Arasaxa, Carnalis, Garnace: this last is *Cotæna.* perhaps the Garmias of the Table Itinerary, be-*Zoropassus.* tween Aspona in Galatia, and what should be Ni-*Arasaxa. Carnalis.* tazus. *Garnace.*

The next Cappadocian præfectura bore the name

Cilicia præ-
fectura.

of Cilicia, like the well known province south of Taurus, and perhaps there was some local connexion subsisting between it and this part of Cappadocia, which may have given rise to the appellation; but the reason has not been mentioned by Strabo,

Mazaca,
postea
Cæsarea et
Eusebia.

who merely states the fact. Its chief city, and also the capital of the whole province, was Mazaca, latterly better known by the name of Cæsarea, with the topographical adjunct Ad Argæum, to denote its position at the foot of the high mountain so called. It was a city of great antiquity, and its foundation was even ascribed by some writers to Mesech, the son of Japhet. (Joseph. Ant. Jud. I. c. 6.) Philostorgius says it was first called Maza, from Mosoch, a Cappadocian chief; and afterwards Mazaca. (IX. p. 530.) This city, as Strabo reports, was exposed to great inconveniences, being ill supplied with water, and destitute of fortifications. The surrounding country was also unproductive; consisting of a dry, sandy plain[i], with several volcanic pits for the space of many stadia around the town. Fuel was also scarce, for though mount Argæus was well wooded toward its base, it was somewhat dangerous of access, from the marshes and quagmires with which it was girt: the soil of these forests was likewise volcanic. Mount Argæus is a vast mountain covered with perpetual snow, and so high, that, as Strabo reports, those who had ascended to the summit, and they were very few who could boast of such a feat, affirmed that they were able to dis-

---

[i] It is worthy of remark, however, that Mr. Kinneir was struck with the great quantity of vegetables offered for sale in the market of *Kaisarieh*, and he was told there was no part of Asia Minor which surpassed the neighbourhood for the quality and variety of its fruits. p. 103.

cover from thence both the Euxine, and the Cilician sea. (XII. p. 538.) Mr. Kinneir observes, " it is un- " doubtedly a mountain of prodigious elevation; but " he much questions whether any human being ever " reached its summit; and indeed he was positively " informed that this was quite impossible. It is " covered for some miles below the peak with snow, " which was said to be eight or ten feet in depth in " the month of October, when he was at Cæsarea[k];" he adds, that " two branches of this mountain ad- " vance a short distance into the plain, forming a " small recess, in the centre of which stands Cæ- " sarea, surrounded on three sides by mountains[l]." Elsewhere he states, " that mount *Argish*," as it is now called, " rises in a peak from the plain, and at " this season of the year, when the whole of the sur- " rounding country was parched with drought, the " mountain, halfway from its summit, was enve- " loped in the snows of perpetual winter[m]."

The river Melas had its source in the eternal gla- ciers of this lofty summit, but its bed being lower than the level of Mazaca, the inhabitants derived little benefit from it; on the contrary, it was some- times apt to overflow and stagnate in the surround- ing plain, which bred contagious disorders. Its bed also covered some fine stone quarries, which would have been very valuable for building. Strabo re- lates, that king Ariarathes had once closed up a narrow passage by which the Melas found a vent for its waters in the direction of the Euphrates. By this contrivance the whole of the surrounding plains were inundated, and appeared like a vast sea

[k] Journey through Asia Minor, &c. p. 94, note.
[l] p. 100.   [m] p. 105.

dotted with islands, in which the Cappadocian prince took his pastime: this childish amusement cost him dear, for the accumulated waters at length burst the dyke by which they were withheld, and hastened to the Euphrates with prodigious force. This great river rose in consequence far above its usual level, and inundated not only the plains of Cappadocia, and destroyed many habitations and farms; but this accident caused besides considerable damage to some districts of the Galatians[n]. These laid a formal complaint against Ariarathes before the Roman people, who condemned that monarch to pay a sum of 300 talents to the parties who had suffered. (XII. p. 538, 539.) The Melas is now called *Kara-sou*, or the *Black River*; it flows from west to east, entering the Euphrates at *Malatia*: although an inconsiderable stream in the autumn, it frequently inundates the country during the melting of the snows[o].

Notwithstanding these disadvantages attending its position, the kings of Cappadocia had fixed their residence at Mazaca, from its central situation in the midst of other districts more fertile, and better supplied with every article necessary for the prosperity of a great city; such as stones for building, and timber, and rich pastures required for the subsistence of the numerous herds and flocks which they possessed. Claudian alludes to these when he says,

. . . . . . jam pascua fumant
Cappadocum, volucrumque parens Argæus equorum.

IN RUF. II. 30.

---

[n] Some of the waters probably found their way to the Halys, and caused a rise in that river also, and thus flooded the Galatian territory.

[o] Kinneir's Travels, p. 105.

Mazaca assumed therefore the appearance of a large camp rather than of a regular city, being open and unfortified. The royal property, consisting chiefly in slaves, was kept in different fortresses throughout the country.

Mancipiis locuples, eget æris Cappadocum rex.

Hor. Ep. I. 6. 39.

The whole nation might be said to be addicted to servitude; for when they were offered a free constitution by the Romans, they declined the favour, and preferred receiving a master from the hands of their allies. (Strab. XII. p. 540.) After the conquest of Pontus, Rome and Italy were filled with Cappadocian slaves. (Plut. Lucull. Cf. Athen. I. p. 20.) Many of these were excellent bakers and confectioners. (Athen. III. p. 112, 113.) Their orators were not in such good repute. (Anthol. Pal. XI. p. 539.) Strabo informs us that Mazaca was captured by Tigranes, king of Armenia, in a sudden irruption made into Cappadocia to befriend Mithridates. He caused the town immense loss by carrying away nearly all the inhabitants, whom he afterwards settled at Tigranocerta: but when that city was taken by Lucullus, several individuals were enabled to return to their country. (XII. p. 539. Appian. Mithr. c. 67.) The code of Charondas had been adopted at Mazaca; and it was the business of a magistrate, especially appointed to this office, to explain the laws. (Strab. loc. cit.) This city retained its original name till the death of Archelaus took place, when Tiberius, having reduced Cappadocia to the form of a Roman province, changed also the appellation of its capital. (Eutrop. VII. 6. Suid. v. Τιβέριος.) It is remarkable, however, that

Strabo takes no notice of this name, but says it was sometimes called Eusebia ad Argæum. It probably derived the latter from Ariobarzanes, who took the surname of Εὐσεβής. Pliny is the earliest writer who applies to the Cappadocian capital the imperial title. (VI. 3. Ptol. p. 125. Ammian. Marcell. XX. c. 23.) It appears to have increased in size and consequence under successive emperors, till it was captured, after an obstinate defence, by the Persian Sapor, under the reign of the unfortunate Valerian. It is said to have been betrayed into the hands of the eastern monarch, who devoted thousands of the defenceless inhabitants to the sword. The population of the city at that period was estimated at 400,000 souls. (Zonar. Ann. XII. p. 630. Zosim. I. p. 25.) Cæsarea, nevertheless, recovered from this disaster, being frequently mentioned subsequently by the Byzantine historians, Cedrenus, (p. 575.) and Niceph. Bryennius. The latter annalist reports that it was nearly destroyed by an earthquake. It was once more besieged and taken by the Saracens, and finally fell into the hands of the Turks, by whom it is called *Kaisarieh*. It was the metropolis of Cappadocia, and derived additional celebrity from the life and writings of St. Basil, who was born and educated there, and presided over its church for many years. (Socr. Hist. Eccl. V. 8. Niceph. Call. XI. 49. Cf. Hierocl. p. 698. Steph. Byz. v. Μάζακα P.)

Kaisarieh has a population of about 25,000 souls,

P There are no medals with the name of Mazaca, but those with the title of Eusebia, or Cæsarea, are very abundant, from Tiberius to L. Verus. Epigraphe, ΕΤΣΕΒΕΙΑΣ. ΚΑΙΣΑΡΕΙΑΣ, or ΚΑΙϹ. ΠΡΟϹ ΑΡΓΑΙΩ. Epocha ab anno V. C. 770. Sestini, p. 129.

and is the emporium of an extensive trade, and the
resort of merchants from all parts of Asia Minor
and Syria, who come to purchase cotton, cultivated
here in great quantities [q]. Mr. Kinneir remarks,
that the ancient city appears to have covered a much
larger area than the modern one. The sides of the
hills to the south of the town are strewed with
mouldering piles of rubbish, and the ruins of other
edifices may plainly be discovered towards the north
and east. Those on the south side are about a quarter of a mile from the modern town, and are called
Eskisher, or " the old city," where, on the summit of
a small hill, and close to a perpendicular rock, a modern structure seems to have been erected upon the
foundations of a more noble edifice. Under this
building a number of subterraneous passages have
been hewn out of the rock; and about fifty paces
more in advance you perceive the vestiges of a large
and solid superstructure, which presents a parallelo-
gram of one hundred and seventy paces in length,
and eighty in width. In an adjacent suburb were
ruins still more extensive, presenting the walls and
end of a vast arched hall. The fragments of de-
cayed buildings, mantled with shrubs and ivy, are
to be seen on every side; but there were no columns,
no sculptured marbles, nor even a single Greek or
Latin inscription. A considerable part of the city-
wall is still standing; but this in all probability owes
its origin to the Mahomedans [r]. Mazaca, according
to the reckoning of Strabo, was 800 stadia from the
frontier of Pontus, less than 1600 from the Euphrates, and six days' journey from the Pylæ Cili-

[q] Kinneir, p. 100.   [r] Journey, p. 100, 102.

ciæ. (XII. p. 539.) In the vicinity of this city we
hear of Dacora, a village which gave birth to Eu-
nomius, the Arian heretic, and whither he was
banished by Theodosius. (Sozom. Hist. Eccl. VII.
17. Philostorg. X. 6.) Cedrenus, when relating
the expedition of the emperor Basilius into Cappadocia and Syria, notices several petty fortresses in
the same district; such as Xylocastrum, Phyrocastrum, and Phalacrum. (p. 573.) Also a spot named
Βούκου λίθος, Buci lapis. (p. 687.)

Ptolemy includes in his list of the præfectura Ciliciæ, Mustilia, Siva, Campe, Cyzistra, or Cozistra,
Ebagena, or Sebagena, Archalla, Soroba, or Sobara.
Of these, Siva and Campe can be laid down in the
map from the Table on the road from Mazaca to
Tavium; Campe sixteen miles from the former, and
Siva twenty-two miles further. Archalla cannot be
identified with *Erklé*, or *Eregli*, south of *Nigdé*,
for that would certainly include it in Tyanitis, unless we suppose Ptolemy to have been guilty of a
mistake. North of the Cilician præfectura towards
Pontus was that of Chammanene: it was separated
from the latter province by a chain of mountains
parallel with Taurus. Strabo merely notices in it
the fortress of Dasmenda, placed on a steep and lofty
rock; (XII. p. 540.) but Ptolemy names Zama, Andraca, Gadiana, or Gadusena, Vadata, Sarvena, Odogra, or Odoga. (p. 126.) Zama appears in the Table
on the road from Tavium to Mazaca, and three
stages from the former. I know not the name of
the modern district, which answers properly to that
of Chammanene. Contiguous to it, on the south-
east, and towards Armenia, was that of Sargarau-

Marginal notes:
Dacora.

Mustilia.
Siva.
Campe.
Cyzistra.
Ebagena.
Archalla.
Soroba.

Chamma-
nene præ-
fectura.

Dasmenda.

Zama.
Andraca.
Gadiana.
Vadata.
Sarvena.
Odogra.

sene, which Strabo barely mentions under the head
of Cappadocia. (XII. p. 534.)   Pliny (VI. 3.) seems
to place it next to Phrygia, but the authority of
the Itineraries leads to the conclusion that it was
situate in the direction of Armenia.   Ptolemy is
the only writer who specifies the towns belonging to
this præfectura: they are Phiara, Salagena, or Sa- Phiara.
Sadagena.
dagena, Gaugæna, or Gauræna, Sabalassus, Ariara- Gaugæna.
Sabalassus.
thia, and Masora, or Maroza. (p. 126.)   Of these, Ariarathia.
Maroza.
Ariarathia appears evidently from the Antonine Itinerary to have stood between Nicopolis of Armenia
Minor and the Cappadocian Comana. (p. 212, 213.
Cf. p. 181.)   Stephanus Byz. (v. Ἀριαράθεια) says, it
took its name from Ariarathes, who married the
sister of Antiochus.   It would seem therefore that
the præfectura we are now considering must have
occupied nearly the district of *Diconberg* in the
pachalick of *Siwas*, on both banks of the *Karasou*,
or Melas.

Contiguous to it on the east, and reaching to the
Euphrates, was the præfectura of Laviniasene; for Laviniasene præ-
Strabo, when speaking of Pontus, gives us to under- fectura.
stand it was contiguous to Armenia Minor and the
Pontic districts of Coulopene and Camisene.   Ptolemy extends it quite up to the Euphrates, and this
makes it altogether nearly agree with the canton of
Arabkir also in the pachalick of *Siwas*.   The latter Corna.
geographer places on the Euphrates, Corne, Metita, Metita.
and Claudias, which Cellarius thinks, with reason, Claudias,
sive Clau-
should be identified with the Claudiopolis of Pliny. diopolis.
(V. 24.)   Corne and Metita occur also in the Table.
At a greater distance from the river we have Car- Carpacelis.
Dizoatra.
pacelis, Dizoatra, or Zizoatra, Pasarne, Cizara, Saba- Pasarne.
Cizara.
gena, Nolasene, Langasa, (p. 127.)   Respecting these Sabagena.
Nolasene.
Langasa.

we have no further information than what the Alexandrian geographer affords.

Melitene præfectura. Melitene was situate on the right bank of the Euphrates, which separated it from the Syrian district of Sophene. Towards the south it bordered on the principality of Commagene, on the same side of the river, but also annexed to Syria. The soil was fertile, and yielded fruits of every kind; in this differing from the rest of Cappadocia: the chief produce was oil, and a wine called Monarites, which equalled the best of Grecian growth. (Strab. XII. p. 535. Cf. Plin. VI. 3.) Ptolemy seems to include Melitene in Armenia Minor. (p. 127.) Strabo takes no notice of any town in this præfectura; but subsequent to his time, that is, in the reign of Trajan, what had been only a camp or military station, was **Melitene urbs.** converted by order of the emperor into a town, which became one of the most considerable places in Cappadocia. Justinian again enlarged its circuit, and decorated it with several buildings. At this period it was the capital of Armenia Minor. (Procop. de Æd. III. 4.) Melitene had been the station of the Christian legion, in whose behalf a miracle is said to have been performed for the preservation of the Roman army. (Euseb. Hist. Eccl. V. 5. Xiphil. Marc. Aurel. Cf. Dio Cass. LV. p. 564.) In the time of Hierocles it was the metropolis of Armenia Secunda; (p. 703.) and frequent mention is made of it by the Byzantine writers [r]. It retains some vestiges of its former name under that of *Malatia*. Modern travellers describe it as situate in a fine plain between the Euphrates and Melas, but in

---

[r] See the authorities cited by Wesseling ad Antou. Itin. p. 209.

ruins [s]. Ptolemy places near the Euphrates, together with Melitene, Sinis, which he terms a colony, but no other writer has named it [t]. (p. 127.) Dascusa also in the list of the Alexandrine geographer, is placed by Pliny about seventy-four miles from Melitene, but only fifty by the Itineraries. (Cf. Oros. I. 2. Not. Imper.) At some distance from the Euphrates Ptolemy enumerates several minor towns, such as Zoparistus, Titarissus, Cianica, Phusipara, Eusimara, Jassus, Ciacis, Leugæsa, or Leutæsa, Marcada, or Carmada, Semisus, Lalænesis, or Ladænesis. Ciacis is designated in the Notitia Imperii as the station of a squadron of horse: " Ala prima Augusta Co- " lonorum Chiacæ." The Antonine Itinerary and the Table remove this station, the one eighteen, the other twenty-eight miles from Melitene. The latter probably is more correct, as agreeing better with the distance reckoned by Pliny from Melitene to Dascusa. The præfectura called Saravene (Σαραουήνη) by Strabo, is, I imagine, the same as the Ravene, or Avarene, of Ptolemy: if so, we learn from the latter geographer that it was situate near the Euphrates. He places on the banks of that river Juliopolis and Barzalo, in the interior, Seraspere, Lacriassus, Antelia, and Adatha. Juliopolis appears to have been south of Claudiopolis; and Barsalium, as it is written in the Table, was forty-six miles from the same town. From this it may be inferred that Ravene, or Saravene, was the extreme canton of Cappadocia to the south-east, and that it bordered on Commagene. It answers therefore to the southern portion of the present district of *Malatia*.

Sinis.
Dascusa.

Zoparistus.
Titarissus.
Cianica.
Phusipara.
Eusimara.
Jassus.
Ciacis.
Leugæsa.
Marcada.
Semisus.
Lalænesis.

Saravene præfectura.

Juliopolis.
Barsalium.
Seraspere.
Lacriassus.
Antelia.
Adatha.

[s] Kinneir's Journey, Append. p. 555.　　　[t] Perhaps we should separately Σίνις, Κολωνεία.

Tyanitis
præfectura.

Tyana.

Tyanitis comprised that portion of the province which bordered on the defiles of Taurus and the passes leading into Cilicia. It took its name from Tyana, the principal town, and a place of considerable note and great antiquity. Strabo reports that it was built on what was called the causeway of Semiramis, and well fortified. (XII. p. 537[u].) Cellarius is of opinion that the town called Dana by Xenophon in the Anabasis (I. 2. 20.) should be identified with Tyana[x]; and this supposition has great probability to recommend it, Dana being, according to Xenophon, a town of Cappadocia, four days' march from Iconium, and populous and wealthy; moreover close to the defiles leading into Cilicia. The Greeks, always led by a similarity of name to connect the origin of cities with their fables, pretended, that it owed its foundation to Thoas, the king of the Tauric Scythians, in his pursuit thither of Pylades and Orestes. (Arrian. Peripl. Eux. p. 6.) From him it was called Thoana, and afterwards Tuana. (Steph. Byz. v. Τύανα.) It is probable that Alexander passed through Tyana on his way to the " Cilician Gates," but Arrian has not named it in his narrative. The proximity to so important a pass must have rendered this town a place of considerable traffick and consequence; it was besides situate in an extensive and fertile plain at the foot of mount Taurus, and between the Euphrates and Halys. Strabo does not account for the origin of the name of Eusebia, which it afterwards assumed, (XII. p. 537.) but this was perhaps owing to the peculiar sanctity of the religious rites practised in

[u] Zela, in Pontus, was also said to be built on the cause-way, or mound, of Semiramis.

[x] Geogr. Ant. t. II. p. 291.

honour of Jupiter, whose temple was situate near a sacred lake and source named Asmabæon, at a little distance from the town; whence he was surnamed Asmabæus. This lake, from which a source issued, though always appearing to rise, never overflowed its banks. (Ammian. Marcell. XXIII. 19.) Mannert imagines that this is the same lake which Strabo reports to have been sacred to Jupita Dacius, and the priests of which ranked after those of Comana and Venasi. The lake in question was extensive and brackish, and the banks were so steep, that it was necessary to descend by steps cut in the rock. Its waters were never seen to rise or to diminish. (XII. p. 536.) I should imagine, however, that the lakes are different; that of Asmabæus is also mentioned by Philostratus in his Life of Apollonius. (I. 4.) This celebrated impostor derived his birth from Tyana, and conferred upon it in return a notoriety which was not likely to survive the frauds which he practised. (Cf. Vopisc. Aurelian. c. 22. et 24. Lucian. Pseudom. t. II. p. 213.) At a later period Tyana became the see of a Christian bishop, and the metropolis of Cappadocia Secunda. (Greg. Naz. Epist. 33. Orat. XX. p. 355.) This took place in the reign of Valens. (Cf. Basil. Magn. Ep. 74 et 75. Hierocl. p. 700.) Its capture by the Saracens is recorded by Cedrenus. (p. 477.) The Itineraries place Tyana seventy-five miles south of Archelais, and thirty-four miles from Podandus, where the defile of Taurus was narrowest. On the other hand we know from Strabo that it was three days' journey from Mazaca. (XII. p. 539.) These data and other circumstances and topographical marks agree sufficiently in the position of *Ketch-hissar* between

Nigdé and *Erekli*, and near the foot of the central chain of Taurus and the Cilician pass. Captain Kinneir, in one of his journeys, found there considerable ruins. He mentions particularly a beautiful aqueduct of granite, extending, as he was informed, seven or eight miles to the foot of the mountains. The massy foundations of several large edifices were also to be seen in several parts of the town; shafts, pillars, and pedestals of pillars, lay half buried under ground, and near the vestiges of an old building was a handsome granite column yet standing. The aqueduct, as well as the other buildings, are all attributed to Nimrod by the natives; but they are without doubt the work of the Romans, and are probably the ruins of the ancient town of Tyana[y]. According to the same traveller, *Ketch-hissar* stands south-west by west of *Nigdeh*, and is distant from it twelve miles[z].

Not far from Tyana, but nearer mount Taurus, were the two small towns of Castabala and Cybistra, which belonged properly to an eleventh præfectura, added after the death of king Archelaus. (Strab. XII. p. 537.) Frequent mention is made of the latter place in the epistles of Cicero, during his command in Cilicia. It was at Cybistra that he fixed his head-quarters, in order, as he says, to protect Cappadocia from the Armenians, who were known to favour the Parthians; and to be ready to move forward also into Cilicia, if the latter should make an irruption into that province. He remained fifteen

Cybistra.

[y] We find on the medals of Tyana, the titles of ΙΕΡΑ ΑϹΥΛΟϹ. ΑΥΤΟΝΟΜΟϹ: these are of the reigns of Hadrian and Antoninus Pius. On those of Caracalla, that of ΚΟΛΩΝΙΑ ΤΥΑΝΕΩΝ further appears. Sestini, p. 130.

[z] P. 113—115.

days at Cybistra, and then advanced towards mount Amanus, to threaten the enemy, and clear the country of the robbers which infested it. (Ep. ad Fam. XV. 2 et 4. ad Att. V. 20.) Col. Leake is inclined to place Cybistra at *Karahissar*, near Mazaca, where there are considerable remains of antiquity, and the distance of which from the supposed site of Tyana agrees sufficiently with the sixty-four miles reckoned by the Table Itinerary. It must be contended, however, that this position does not correspond with Strabo's account; who says that both Cybistra and Castabala stood nearer Taurus than Tyana did: and Cicero also clearly states that Cybistra was at the foot of that mountain, whereas *Karahissar* is rather at the foot of mount Argæus. D'Anville had imagined, from a similarity of name, that Cybistra might be represented by *Bustereh*, a small place near the source of one of the branches of the Halys, and several miles to the east of *Nigdé*, towards *Bostan;* this locality would certainly agree better with the information of the ancients as to Cybistra; but it is not stated whether there are any remains of antiquity at *Bustereh*, and besides, Col. Leake affirms that, according to the Arabian geographer Hadjy Khalfa, the true name of the place is *Kostere*[a]. However this may be, I cannot agree with that able antiquary's opinion as to the identity of Cybistra with *Karahissar*, for Ptolemy assigns Cybistra to Cataonia, which could never have included *Karahissar* within its limits. Hierocles gives it to Cappadocia Secunda. (p. 700[b].)

[a] Asia Minor, p. 63, note.
[b] There is but one coin extant belonging to Cybistra; the epigraph is ΚΥΒΙϹΤΡΕΩΝ. Sestini, p. 130.

Castabala. Castabala was remarkable for a temple sacred to Diana Perasia. It was asserted that the priestesses of the goddess could tread with naked feet on burning cinders, without receiving any injury. The statue of Diana was also said to have been the identical one brought by Orestes from Tauris, whence the name of Perasia, " from beyond sea," was thought to be derived. (Strab. XII. p. 538. Cf. Steph. Byz. v. Καστάβαλα.) Pliny also names Castabala among the chief towns of Cappadocia. (VI. 3.) Col. Leake is inclined to identify Castabala with *Nigdé*, where there are several vestiges of antiquity[c]; but D'Anville says, *Nigdé* is Cadyna. Cadyna, a town mentioned by Strabo as the residence of Sisina, a partisan of Antony, by whom he was created king of Cappadocia, after expelling Ariarathes; the latter, however, finally recovered his dominions. (Strab. XII. p. 537. Appian. Civ. Bell. V. 7.) If, as Strabo seems to state, Cadyna was on the borders of Lycaonia, the position of *Nigdé* would not be ill suited in regard to that indication. I may add, with respect to Castabala, that some antiquaries place it at *Kalat Masman*, to the north-east of *Nigdeh*[d]. Not far from the latter site is a ruined fortress, named *Nour*, Nora, sive Neroassus. which recalls to mind Nora, where Eumenes, the general of Alexander, sustained a long and difficult siege against Antigonus. (Strab. XII. p. 537. Diod. Sic. XVIII. 41. Plut. Eumen. c. 10—12.) This castle subsequently belonged to Sisina, who deposited there his treasures; it then bore the name of Neroassus. (Strab. loc. cit.) Mr. Kinneir says, " At the end of the third mile (from *Karahissar*)

[c] Asia Minor, p. 63.
[d] Sestini, p. 131. This city took the title of ΙΕΡΟΠΟΛΙΣ ΚΑΣΤΑΒΑΛ. on its coins.

" we passed under a high and perpendicular rock
" crowned with an ancient fortress, called by the
" natives *Yengi Bar*, or *Nour* :" in a note he adds,
the castle of Nour is stated to have been two stadia
in circumference, and that of *Yengi Bar* exactly
corresponds[e].

Argus was another fortress in this direction; it Argus
was near the foot of mount Taurus, and stood on a castellum.
rock prodigiously elevated. (Strab. loc. cit.) The Itineraries indicate, north of Tyana, at a distance of
sixteen miles, a station named Andabalis, or Andavilis. (Itin. Anton. p. 145.) The Jerusalem Itinerary
has this remark annexed to the specification of the
site and distance : " Mansio Andavilis. (M. XVI.)
" Ibi est villa Pampali, unde veniunt equi curules."
This Pampalus is supposed to be the same as Pal-
matius, a famous breeder and trainer of race-horses
under the emperor Valerian[f].

South of Tyana, towards Cilicia, was Faustino- Faustinopolis, distant twelve miles from that city; it was polis.
named after the empress Faustina, the consort of
Marcus Aurelius, who died there in returning from
Syria. Her husband erected there a town and temple to her memory. (Jul. Capit. M. Aur. c. 26.) It
occurs both in the Antonine and Jerusalem Itineraries, and is assigned by Hierocles to Cappadocia Secunda. (p. 700.) The exact position of this town has not
been recognised, but it must have been close to the
defiles leading to the Cilician gates, and perhaps on
the site called the Camp of Cyrus, from the younger Cyri Cas-
Cyrus having stationed his army there for some tra.
days previous to crossing the mountains. (Xen.

[e] P. 111.   [f] See Wesseling's note to the Jerusalem Itinerary, p. 577.

Anab. I. 2. 20.) Xenophon does not himself give this name to the spot, but it occurs in Arrian, who informs us that it was by the same pass Alexander led his army into the plains of Cilicia. (Exp. Alex. II. 4. Quint. Curt. III. 4.) Strabo also names the Camp of Cyrus, and states that it was six days march from Mazaca, and about half that distance from Tyana. (XII. p. 539.) *Erkle*, a place which stands on the modern road from *Konieh* to the Cilician defiles, is thought by Col. Leake to be Archalla, a town which belonged to the Cilician præfectura of Cappadocia, according to Ptolemy; but the position of *Erkle* does not agree with this idea, as it would rather belong to Tyanitis. I should be inclined to identify this site with a place named Herculis Vicus by Cedrenus, who says it was in the vicinity of Tarsus. (p. 637.) Thirteen miles beyond Faustinopolis, the Jerusalem Itinerary has a post called Cæna, and twelve miles further Podandus, a village often mentioned in the Byzantine writers in connexion with these defiles. It is described by Basil as the most miserable spot on earth. He says, figure to yourself " a Laconian Ceada," (i. e. hole or pit, down which criminals were thrown,) " a Charonium " breathing forth pestilential vapours: you will then " have an idea of the wretchedness of Podandus." (Epist. 74.) Constantine Porphyrogenetes, in his Life of the emperor Basilius, (c. 36.) says it took its name from a small stream, which flowed near it[g]. (Cf. Cedr. p. 575. Jo. Scylitz. Hist. p. 829. p. 844.) It retains the name of *Podend*. Cedrenus speaks of a place called Chrysobullum in this vicinity; (p. 576.)

Cæna.
Podandus.

[g] Wesseling ad Itin. Hieros. p. 578.

and Curopolates of another, named Gytarium. (p.
829. p. 844.) The Pylæ Ciliciæ were, according to
the Jerusalem Itinerary, distant fourteen miles from
Podandus. The passage, as Diodorus describes it,
was formed by steep and lofty mountains, extending
on each side of the road for the space of twenty
stadia; after this, a wall had been brought down to
the road from the mountains on each side, and in
this wall gates had been fixed; beyond, you descended into the beautiful plains of Cilicia. (XIV.
p. 250.) Xenophon merely says that it was a car-
riage road, but very steep, and impracticable for an
army if resistance was offered. (Anab. I. 2. 21.)
Cyrus passed through the defiles without opposition,
as well as Alexander. (Cf. Herodian. III. 3.) The
Byzantine historians usually term them κλεισούρα.
(Jo. Scylitz, p. 829. p. 844.) The following description of this celebrated pass, from Capt. Kinneir, may
not be unacceptable to the reader: " After quitting
" *Tchekisla*, (a place about twenty-four miles from
" *Ketch-hissar*, supposed to be Tyana,) we travelled
" for sixteen miles east-south-east through a nar-
" row vale, with a chain of hills on the left and a
" ramification of mount Taurus on the right; at the
" eighth mile we passed the remains of a Roman
" camp, where troops were probably stationed in for-
" mer times to guard the entrance of the Pylæ Cili-
" ciæ. The *Sehoun*, here a little brook, flowed through
" the valley parallel with the road. At the sixteenth
" mile we ascended a mountain, and again descend-
" ing by a steep and narrow path, found ourselves
" enclosed in an intricate defile, at the bottom of
" which flowed the *Sehoun*. At the twenty-first
" mile we halted at a khan, situate at the con-

" fluence of this and another small stream. The
" next morning we continued our journey through
" a dark and gloomy defile, and along the left bank
" of the *Sehoun*, which was gradually enlarged by
" many tributary torrents that tumbled down the
" sides of the mountains. For the first nine miles
" the breadth of the pass varied from fifty to 200
" yards; the steeps of mount Taurus, covered with
" pine trees, rising vertically on each side of us. At
" the ninth mile we crossed the *Sehoun*, on an old
" stone bridge of one arch, after which the pass be-
" came more open, the mountains retiring on each
" side to a distance of about half a mile. The re-
" mains of an ancient way, in some parts hewn out
" of the rock, and in others built upon the side con-
" tiguous to the river, were visible at times during
" the journey. The khan where we halted stood
" near two roads, one on the left leading to the
" town of Adana, the other on the right to Tarsus;
" we followed the latter, and, entering a narrow glen,
" directed our course along the left bank of a small
" stream, which, flowing from the west, enters the
" *Sehoun* a few yards below the khan. At the end of
" the fifth mile, we turned to the south, and during
" three miles ascended the mountains by a path so
" rough and stony, and at the same time so steep,
" that we were in many places compelled to dis-
" mount from our horses. At the tenth mile, we
" reached the posthouse, a mud building, surrounded
" by stables. The third day we travelled for two
" miles and a half over a tolerably good road, when
" we descended to the left bank of a streamlet, and
" for five miles moved slowly through a roman-
" tic pass, in several places not more than ten or

" twelve paces wide from rock to rock. The cliffs
" and sides of the mountains clothed with the most
" beautiful evergreens and noble pine-trees, hung
" like a vast canopy over the defile, whilst their
" bare and desolate peaks towered above the clouds.
" The road ran along the brow of the precipice,
" sometimes on one side and sometimes on the
" other; it was in so bad a condition that it could
" only be passed during the day, many of the large
" stones, which had been used in the construction of
" the Roman way, having been either removed or
" fallen down; whilst the surfaces of those that still
" remained in their places were so smooth and slip-
" pery, that the horses could not tread upon them
" without the momentary danger of being precipi-
" tated over the rocks. This is undoubtedly the
" part of the pass most capable of defence, and
" where a handful of determined men, advantage-
" ously posted, might bid defiance to the most nu-
" merous armies. At the end of the eighth mile the
" mountains again expanded to the right, shewing
" the ruins of a fortress built on the summit of a
" stupendous cliff; and at the tenth mile we halted
" near the mouth of the defile, which is in all likeli-
" hood the Pylæ, through which the armies of the
" younger Cyrus and Alexander entered Cilicia[h].

Ptolemy places in Tyanitis the unknown towns of
Dratæ, or Dagræ, Bazis, and Siala. (p. 127.)

The remaining præfectura, which concludes our Cataonia
account of Cappadocia, was named Cataonia; and præfectura.
originally, as Strabo imagines, was inhabited by a
different people from the Cappadocians, though the
customs and language of the two countries were the
same. The geographer argues chiefly from their

[h] P. 115—19.

ancient political separation prior to Ariarathes I., who conquered Cataonia and annexed it to his dominions; the Romans afterwards restored it to its original state under the administration of a separate governor. (XII. p. 533, 534.)

Cataonia consisted chiefly of deep and extensive plains, surrounded however on all sides by chains of mountains. On the south by mount Amanus, a branch of the Cilician Taurus, which extends from Cataonia to the coast of Cilicia and Syria, and encloses the bay of Issus. On the north it was bounded by Antitaurus, branching out from the central range of Taurus, and advancing first towards the east, and then northwards towards Armenia and the Moschic chain. (Strab. XII. p. 535.) This district answers chiefly to the modern canton of *Aladeuli* in the pashalick of *Adana*, and it may perhaps have included a small portion of that of *Marasch*. On the side flanked by Antitaurus were several deep valleys, which fed the two principal streams which watered the country: these were the Sarus and Pyramus, both presenting the unusual phenomenon of rivers traversing the central chain of Taurus before reaching the plains of Cilicia, and finally discharging their waters into the sea which washes its shores. The Sarus, now called *Seihoun,* finds a passage through the defiles of Podandus, and falls into the Cilician sea a few miles below Adana. In the upper part of its course it traversed the town and territory of Comana, the principal city of Cataonia, and celebrated, like its Pontic namesake, for the worship of Mâ, the Cappadocian Bellona. The population consisted, in a great degree, of soothsayers, priests, and slaves, belonging to the sacred institution: the latter amounted, in the time of Strabo, to more than

Comana.

6000 of both sexes. These belonged exclusively to the high-priest, who stood next in rank to the king of Cappadocia, and was generally chosen from the royal family. The territory annexed to the temple was very considerable, and furnished a large income for the pontiff. (Cf. Cicer. Ep. ad Fam. XV. 4.) It was asserted that the worship of Bellona, like that of Diana Tauropolos, had been brought from Tauris by Orestes and Iphigenia, and it was even pretended that the former had deposited within the temple his mourning locks, (κόμην,) whence the city was called Comana. (XII. p. 535.) These of course are fables of Greek invention. The Bellona of Comana was probably no other than the Anaitis of the Persians and Armenians, and perhaps the Agdistis and Cybele of the Phrygians. Procopius says that Orestes founded, besides the temple of Diana, another to Iphigenia; both of which buildings were afterwards converted into churches by the Christians of Cappadocia. (Bell. Pers. I. c. 17. Dio Cass. XXXV. Plin. VI. 3.) Ptolemy assigns this town to Cataonia, but in the time of Hierocles it formed part of Armenia. (p. 702.) It was distinguished from its Pontic namesake by the epithet of Χρυσῆ, as we learn from Procopius and Justinian. (Novell. XXXI.[i]) From the medals of Comana which are extant of the reign of Antoninus Pius, we learn that it had received a Roman colony at that period, and perhaps another under Caracalla [k].

[i] Wesseling. ad Itin. Ant. p. 181.

[k] In the former case the epigraph is COL. AUG. COMANA; in the second, COL. IUL. AUG. COMANENORU, or COMAINORU.

It is generally admitted that the Turkish town of *Al-Bostan*, seated on the *Seihoun*, or Sarus, not far from its source, represents the Cappadocian Comana. A modern traveller says, " it is situated in " a noble plain, which supports forty villages depen- " dent on *Al-Bostan*. The city and villages are " surrounded with fine trees, cultivated fields, and " meadows, which are irrigated by numerous streams " of excellent water. Few spots in Asia Minor offer " a sight more agreeable. The population amounts " to eight or nine thousand souls [l]."

According to the Antonine Itinerary, Comana was sixty-four miles from Cæsarea, and sixty-two *Cucusus.* from Cucusus, a place of frequent occurrence in the Itinerary referred to, and noted in ecclesiastical history as the spot to which St. Chrysostom was banished in the reign of Arcadius. This Father has left an interesting account of his journey thither, and his abode in the place, which he describes as a most lonely and miserable spot. (Epist. 30. 87. et 119.) Basiliscus was also banished there by Zeno. (Theodoret. Hist. Eccl. II. 5.) Mountain passes led from thence into Commagene and Syria. (Cedren. p. 352. Curopal. p. 825.) In the time of Hierocles it belonged to Armenia. (p. 704.) The name of *Cocsou* is said to be still attached to the site near the source of the *Gihoun*, or Pyramus, and south-east of *Bostan*, or Comana [m]. The Pyramus traverses the greater part of Cataonia: its source is in the plain, and bursts forth from under ground with such

[l] Mr. Bruce's Itinerary in Kinneir's Travels, Append. p. 560.

[m] D'Anville, Geog. Anc. p. 107. ed. fol.

force that a dart hurled into the stream can scarcely penetrate the water. The bed of the river becomes soon broad and deep, and capable of receiving vessels, but on reaching the central chain of Taurus its channel narrows in a surprising manner, and it forces itself a passage through a chasm in the mountain, which presents a wonderful appearance. The rocks seem to have been rent asunder, for on observing the two opposite sides of the mountain, separated from each other by an interval of two or three plethra, it may be seen that the ruptured parts correspond, and would unite again if brought near to each other. The chasm through which the river forces its way is so narrow below, that a hare or hound could easily bound across it. The river fills entirely this narrow channel, which is however of prodigious depth, and its waters, chafed and impeded in their course, produce a sound loud as thunder, and which may be heard at a considerable distance. Issuing from the mountains it then bursts into the plains of Cilicia, and carries to the sea so much slime and mud, that an oracle had predicted

Ἔσσεται ἐσσομένοις ὅτε Πύραμος εὐρυοδίνης
Ἠϊόνα προχέων ἱερὴν εἰς Κύπρον ἵκηται.

(Strab. XII. p. 536.) Besides the Pyramus there is another river of Cataonia, which, according to Strabo, passes into Cilicia. His account of this river, which he calls Carmalas, it must be allowed is somewhat obscure, since in one passage he seems to assign it to Sargarausene, while in another he distinctly ascribes it to Cataonia: for, speaking of that district, he says that it has no towns, but strong fortresses on the heights, such as Azamora and Dastarcum, round which flows the river Carmalas. It

Carmalas fluvius.

Azamora, Dastarcum.

has a temple sacred to the Cataonian Apollo, who is revered throughout Cappadocia. (XII. p. 537.) A little below he says, " Now of the other præfec-" turæ, in Sargarausene [n] there is the little town of " Herpa, and the river Carmalas, which empties it-" self also (that is, like the Pyramus previously " mentioned) into Cilicia." Mannert -has supposed that Strabo was mistaken respecting the course of this river, and he has attempted to prove that the Car-malas is no other than the Melas, which flows by Cæsarea. His argument rests mainly on the sup-

Herpa. position, that the Herpa above named is the same place which elsewhere the geographer calls Herpha, and places, with Artemidorus, near the Euphrates, on the road to Tomisa, a fortress of Sophene, but, though on the left bank of the river, belonging to the Cappadocians, it having been ceded to them by Lucullus. (XII. p. 535. XIV. p. 664.) This may be easily granted, but it will not therefore follow that the Carmalas is the Melas; nor can it be ad-mitted as at all probable that Strabo is again mis-taken in what he reports concerning the same river. (XII. p. 539.) Speaking of the ill-judged pastimes of Ariarathes in stopping the course of the Melas, he says that this prince did the same also to the Carmalas, near Herpa; and the bursting of the dyke having caused some damage to the lands of Mallus, in Cilicia, the inhabitants of that town com-pelled him to pay them for the loss they sustained. (XII. p. 539.) Mannert does not scruple to disbe-lieve the facts, and to imagine that Strabo has made two inundations, whereas there was only one, and

[n] For Sargarausene, we should perhaps read Saravene.

that one caused by the waters of the Melas [o]. This is much too bold an assertion, and our modern maps fully bear out the ancient geographer in his statement. The Carmalas is there marked under the name of the *Kermel-sou,* as rising in the chain (of Antitaurus) which separates the waters which flow into the *Karasou,* or Melas, from those which fall into the Cilician sea: it runs for some miles from north-east to south-west, and then unites with the *Gihoun,* or Pyramus; consequently it was by its action on the latter that the territory of Mallus, which it waters, received the damage recorded by Strabo. It is evident that the whole of this country, especially as regards the course of its rivers, is extremely curious, and well worthy of being examined by some diligent and inquisitive traveller and artist, who might make us better acquainted with the wild and stupendous scenery of these mountains. The geologist would there also find an ample field for inquiry into those extraordinary convulsions which have burst asunder the vast barrier of Taurus, and opened its rocks to the waters of the Cappadocian rivers.

Ptolemy enables us to add to the list of Cataonian towns (p. 128.) Cabassus, to which some Cabassus. writers applied the passage in which Homer, speaking of Othryoneus, the suitor of Cassandra, describes him as

Καβησόθεν ἔνδον ἐόντα.

Il. N. 363.

Apion the grammarian stated that Cabassus lay between Mazaca and Tarsus. (Steph. Byz. v. Καβασσός.)

Tynna is unknown, as well as Tiralli, unless we Tynna. Tiralli.

.[o] Geogr. tom. VI. p. ii. p. 287, 288.

should suppose it to be the same place which Herodotus calls Critalla. The historian says, that Xerxes
assembled there the whole of his land army destined
for the invasion of Greece. (VII. 26.) Claudiopolis
has been already spoken of. Dalisandus is, by others,
placed in Isauria. Polyandus is thought by Mannert to be a false reading for Podandus. Tanadaris
is evidently the Ptanadari of the Antonine Itinerary, between Comana and Cucusus, twenty-four miles
from the one, and thirty-eight from the other. Leandis, which closes the list of Ptolemy, is perhaps
the Laranda of the same Itinerary, (p. 211.) eighteen
miles south-west of Cucusus, on the road to Anazarba of Cilicia. It must not be confounded, as some
critics have done, with the Laranda of Lycaonia or
Isauria [p]. In Cedrenus we have the narrative of an
expedition, undertaken by the emperor Basilius, into
these parts; which, though it throws but little light
on ancient geography, yet deserves mention here.
The Greek emperor, advancing from Cæsarea, destroyed Casaman, Carba, Ardula, and Eremosgræa,
fortresses belonging to the enemy: crossed the rivers
Onopnictes and Sardus, and came to Cucusus: he
then cleared the roads and difficult passes, and advanced to Callipolis and Padasea, (Pindenissus of
Cicero?) crossed the defiles of Taurus, (Amanus rather,) and came to Germanicia of Commagene: he
besieged Adana, then returned, laden with spoil, over
mount Argæus to Cæsarea. (p. 574, 575.)

Strabo speaks of a Cappadocian district named
Bagadaonia; it was in the southernmost part of
the country, and at the foot of Taurus; but bleak,
and scarcely bore any fruit-trees. (XII. p. 539. Cf.

Margin notes: Critalla. Tanadaris. Leandis, sive Laranda. Bagadao-
nia regio.

[p] Wesseling ad Itin. Ant. p. 211.

Steph. Byz. v. Βαγαδαονία.) Another canton, formerly called Lapara, from its fertility, (as if Λιπαρὰ,) bore afterwards the name of Lycandus, as we learn from Cedrenus. (p. 687. Cf. Niceph. Phoc. p. 157 et p. 162.) The same writer mentions also Charsiana, which took its name apparently from Charsia, a fortress. (p. 692, p. 457.) Again, (p. 547.) he speaks of the Charsian defiles. Pancalea, a plain near the Halys. (p. 693.) Martyropolis and Tyropæum, near Cæsarea. (p. 670.) The latter is also noticed by Curopalates, (p. 843.) who says it was very strong. Camuliani, likewise mentioned by Cedrenus, (p. 390.) is said in some acts of councils to have been also called Justinianopolis [q]. The same documents assign to Cappadocia Prima, Ciscissa and Theodosiopolis; to the Secunda, Justinopolis and Asuna [r]. Dasmenda, or Dasmena, a fortress seated on a steep rock near the frontier of Commagene, (Strab. XII. p. 540.) is, with reason, supposed by D'Anville to correspond with Tzamandus, a place of great strength, noticed by Cedrenus. (p. 688.) Drizium is another Cappadocian castle, which occurs in the same writer. (p. 655.) Elsewhere he speaks of Lalacæum and Ptoson, and the river Gyres; these were near Melitene. (p. 547.) Stephanus assigns a Thebe to Cataonia. (v. Θήβη.) Saricha, a Cappadocian town, according to the same geographer, (v. Σάριχα,) is thought, on the authority of some very scarce medals, to belong to Morimene [s].

The detail of the different routes which traversed Cappadocia in various directions will make us acquainted with a few more places in that province.

Marginal notes: Lapara, postea Lycandus regio. — Charsiana regio. Charsia castellum. — Dasmenda. — Drizium. — Lalacæum. — Ptoson. Gyres fl. Thebe. — Saricha.

[q] Geogr. Sacr. p. 254.
[r] Ibid. p. 254, 255.
[s] The legend is ΣΑΡΙ. ΜΟΡΙ. Sestini, p. 130.

I shall commence with that which led from Galatia to Archelais, Tyana, and the Pylæ Ciliciæ, according to the Jerusalem Itinerary.

M. P.

Mutatio Andrapa—Finis Galatiæ et Cappadociæ.	
Mansio Parnasso	XIII.
Mansio Iogola	XVI.
Mansio Nitalis (Nitazus)	XVIII.
Mutatio Argustana	XIII.
Civitas Colonia (Archelais)	XVI.
Mutatio Momoasson [t]	XII.
Mansio Anathiango (Nazianzus)	XII.
Mutatio Chusa	XII.
Mansio Sasimam	XII.
Mansio Andavilis	XVI.
Civitas Thiana	XVI. [u]
Civitas Faustinopoli	XII.
Mutatio Cæna	XIII.
Mansio Opodanda..............................	XII.
Mutatio Pilas	XIIII.

Finis Cappadociæ et Ciliciæ.

The next route is that which led from Tavium to Cæsarea, which we find thus distributed in the Itinerary of Antoninus:

Iter a Tavia Cæsaream usque, M. P. CIX. Sic,	
Therma......................................	XVIIII.
Soanda	XVIII.
Sacoena	XXXII.
Ochras	XVI.
Cæsarea......................................	XXIIII.

Therma, the first station, is not unfrequently mentioned by ecclesiastical writers as a bishopric of Cappadocia [x]. (Cf. Hierocl. p. 699.) Cedrenus and the

[t] Perhaps this is Mocissus; and at all events the Comitanasson of the Table.

[u] This number, being wanting in the Itinerary, has been supplied from Antonine.

[x] See Wesseling, (Itin. Anton. p. 202.) who quotes an

Notitia of the emperor Leo call it Basilica Therma. Soanda may be the Suenda of Frontinus, (Strat. III. 2. 9.) but I doubt its being the Soandus of Strabo, because this spot, together with Sadacora, are mentioned by that geographer as stations on the great road from Coropassus and Garsabora to Mazaca. (XIV. p. 663.[y]) The Table gives a very different route from Tavium to Cæsarea, at least the stations are entirely dissimilar, and the distance is more considerable, being in all 191 miles. I should imagine that the latter was a much more circuitous route [z].

	M. P.
Tavio—Evagina	XVI.
Saralio	XXIIII.
Zama	XXII.
Aquas Aravenas	XXXV.
Dona	XX.
Sermusa	XX.
Siva	XVI.
Cambe	XXII.
Mazaca Cæsarea	XVI.

From Archelais to Tyana, according to the Table,

Archelais[a]—Salaberina	XX.
Cæna	XVI.
Tracias	XVI.
Tyana	XVI.

From Mazaca to Iconium, by Tyana, in the same Itinerary.

Mazaca Cæsarea—Tetra[b].	
Cibistra	IX.

epistle of Gregory Nazianzen, in which mention is made of the Therma of Xanxaris. (Ep. 77.)

[y] It is singular that none of the Itineraries should have pre-served any account of this route.

[z] Col. Leake imagines however that there is some error in Antonine. (p. 312.)

[a] Name omitted.

[b] Number omitted.

	M. P.
Scolla	XXII.
Addavalis	XV.
Tyana	XXVII.
Baratha [c].	
Iconio	L.

From Tyana to Tarsus, by Podandus [d].

Tyana—Aquis Calidis..............	XXXIX.
Paduando (Podandus)..............	XII.
Coriopio	XXII.
In Monte	XII.
Tarso Ciliciæ	XII.

From Mazaca to Comana.

Mazaca Cæsarea—Sinispora	XXIV.
Arasaxa [e]	XIII.
Larissa [f]	X.
Incilissa..............................	XIII.
Comana Cappadocia.................	XX.

ARMENIA MINOR.

The name of Lesser Armenia was originally applied to that extreme western part of Asia Minor which extends along the left bank of the Euphrates towards the source of that great river, and above the mountains of Trapezus and the territories of the Tibareni and Chaldæi, or Chalybes. The inhabitants of this country were doubtless of the same race as the people of Greater Armenia, and spoke the same language; they had also often been governed by the kings of the larger province, but not unfrequently they had been subject to the dominion of

[c] The number is wanting.

[d] The line of direction only is wanting in the Table to complete this route.

[e] The Artaxata of Antonine.

[f] Perhaps the Lacriassus of Ptolemy.

their own princes. These, at one time, possessed a considerable extent of territory, and ruled over the Tibareni and Chaldæi as far as Trapezus and Pharnacia. Subsequently, however, they yielded to the ascendency of the great Mithridates: and Antipater Sisis[g], the last of these chiefs, surrendered to that monarch the whole of his dominions. Mithridates, having become master of the country, perceived the advantages it afforded from the strength of its positions and the resources it possessed. He is said to have built there no less than seventy-five fortresses, in which he deposited his treasures and valuable effects. The chain of mount Paryadres was particularly favourable for his views, as it was abundantly supplied with timber forests and water, and was everywhere intersected by numerous ravines and rocky precipices. After his defeat and expulsion by Pompey, Armenia Minor was made over to Archelaus, king of Cappadocia. Nero afterwards gave it to Aristobulus, grandson of Herod the Great; but on his death it again reverted to the Romans, who erected it into a separate province. (Strab. XII. p. 555. Dio Cass. XLIX. 12. Tacit. Ann. XIII. 7. Jos. Ant. Jud. XX. 5.) At a still later period we find that it had encroached gradually on the Cappadocian border, so that in the time of Ptolemy the whole of Melitene and Aravene, and a considerable part of Cataonia, were included within its limits. Under the eastern emperors we find it divided into two parts, called Prima and Secunda; the one being under the government of a consul, the other of a count or duke, ('Ηγεμών.) Hierocl. p. 702, 703. Not. Imp. Orient. c. 1, 2.) The latter comprising chiefly

[g] Or son of Sisis; the Greek says, 'Αντιπάτρου·τοῦ Σίσιδος.

the Cappadocian præfectura of Melitene and the districts of Comana and Cucusus, which we have already spoken of under the head of Cataonia in the same province. We shall therefore have now only to do with Armenia Prima; but here again we find places assigned to this division which have been noticed in the description of Pontus. Confining ourselves therefore to Armenia Minor, such as it appears to have been constituted in the time of Strabo, we may say generally, that it comprised at that period the districts of *Arabkir* and *Devriki* in the pashalick of *Siwas*, and those of *Erzinghan* and *Turnberan* in the pashalick of *Erzeroum* along the *Mourad-tchai*, or Euphrates, and north of that river, as far as the mountains of *Baibout*, the Scydisces of the ancients. The Euphrates divided Armenia Minor from the district called Acilisene, which appears to have formed part of the modern *Diarbekir*. (Strab. XII. p. 555.) The northern part of the province comprised, according to Ptolemy, the minor districts of Orbalisene and Ætulana; the centre, Æretice and Orsena; the south, Orbesine.

Nicopolis. The only city of any note or celebrity in this remote part of Asia Minor was Nicopolis, founded, as we learn from Strabo, by Pompey, near the position he had long occupied when blockading Mithridates in his last campaign, and where he obtained the decisive victory which he sought thus to commemorate. (Strab. loc. cit. Appian. Mithr. c. 101. c. 105. Dio Cass. XXXV. 33. Plin. VI. 9.) It is noticed by the writer of the Alexandrian war; (c. 36.) and at a later period we learn from Procopius, that it was restored by Justinian. (de Ædif. III. 4.) It was an episcopal see, as may be collected from the Acts of Councils and Notices. (Cf. Basil. Epist. 227.) Ptolemy places Nicopolis away from the Euphrates and towards the mountains. (p. 127.) The Itinerary of Antoninus reckons ninety-eight miles from Sebastia, or *Siwas*, to that city. It is the opinion of most antiquaries, that Nicopolis is represented by the Turkish town of *Devriki*, seated near a river of the same name, which falls into the *Erzinghan*, a branch of the Euphrates. But if the writer in the Acta Martyrum is correct, in stating that the Lycus flowed only six miles from Nicopolis [h], it would follow that it stood in the valley of *Koulei-hissar*, through which the river of that name, the ancient Lycus, took its course. *Koulei-hissar* I moreover take to be Colonia, a town belonging originally to Pontus, and capital of the small district of Colopene, but afterwards annexed to Armenia. And it is further to be observed, that the letters of Basil, quoted by Wesseling [i], lead to the inference that Colonia and Nicopolis were neighbouring cities. If Nicopolis then stood in the valley of the Lycus, I should be inclined to place it at *Kara-hissar;* at the same time it appears to me that the direction of the several routes indicated by the Itineraries is rather in favour of *Devriki.* D'Anville supposes the Tephrice of the Byzantine writers, of which *Devriki* is evidently a corruption, to be the same as Nicopolis; but he allows that they are mentioned as separate places in one of these historians. Of the seventy-five fortresses built by Mithridates in this country, Strabo has only named three which were more important than the rest: these were Hydara, Basgæ-dariza, and Sinoria; the two former of which are

Hydara.
Basgæda-riza.

[h] Cited by Wesseling on Hierocles, p. 703.   [i] Ibid.

unknown to other geographers. Basgædariza offers some resemblance to a place called *Bakoreg*, to the

Sinoria.

south-east of *Erzinghan*. Sinoria was on the borders of the Greater Armenia; which circumstance gave rise to a pun of the historian Theophanes, who followed Pompey; he writing the word Synhoria, Συνόρια. (Strab. XII. p. 555.) Appian calls this fortress Sinorega, and reports that Mithridates took from thence a very considerable sum of money in his last flight from Pontus. (Mithr. c. 100.) Ptolemy (p. 127.) places it under the name of Sinera, or Sinebra, near the Euphrates; and the Itinerary of Antoninus coincides with the geographer in this proximity to the river. As we find it marked in the route entitled, " Iter a Satala Melitenam per " ripam (Euphratis) Samosata usque." (p. 207.) The name is there written Sinerva. The Sinara of the Table seems to be on a different route, leading from Satala however, but into the Greater Armenia. This place appears, in modern maps, under the name of *Senarvir*, a few miles below the junction of the

Satala.

Mourad-tchai and the *Erzinghan* river. Satala, mentioned above, was a place of some traffick and consequence, as may be inferred from the numerous routes which branched off from thence to different parts of Pontus and Cappadocia. Ptolemy enumerates it among the towns remote from the Euphrates; but the Itinerary of Antoninus, in the route just referred to, shews that it could not have been very distant from it. The same Itinerary allows 122 miles between Nicopolis and Satala, and 135 miles between Satala and Trapezus; the Table only 123. From these data I should be inclined to look for the position of Satala near the junction of the two roads leading from *Trebisond* by *Gumich-kaneh* to *Erzeroum*, and that from *Erzinghan* to *Erzeroum*. D'Anville identifies it with *Erzinghan;* but that town seems to be too much to the south to agree with the Itinerary distances. Mannert places it at *Sukme,* a spot about twenty-three hours' march from the Euphrates, where remains of antiquity have been observed by Tournefort and Tavernier[k]. Satala is mentioned by Dio Cassius; (XLVIII.) and we learn from Procopius that its walls were restored by Justinian. (Ædif. III. 4.) From the Antonine Itinerary and inscriptions we collect that it was the station of the fifteenth Roman legion, surnamed Apollinaris. (Anton. Itin. p. 183[1]. Cf. Basil. Ep. 99. Hier. p. 73. Steph. Byz. v. Σάταλα.) Ptolemy names besides Sinera, or Sinebra, four other towns on the bank of the Euphrates, Aziris, Dalanda, or Ladana, Ismara, or Simara, and Zimara. Mannert thinks Aziris may be *Erzinghan;* but that town is not on the Euphrates, but a stream which joins that river[m] about twenty miles below the town. Zimara stands in the Antonine Itinerary, as well as the Table, on the route leading from Satala to Melitene along the Euphrates; and if it is the same town which Pliny calls Simyra, or Zimira, it was not more than twelve miles from the source of the Euphrates in mount Abus: (V. 24.) but this would ill accord with the Itineraries, which fix Zimara much lower down the river. I should rather imagine the site alluded to by Pliny is the Ismara, or Simara, of Ptolemy, also on the

(marginal notes: Aziris. Dalanda. Simara. Zimara.)

[k] Lettre XXI. Voyages, c. 2. p. 17. This is also the opinion of Major Rennell. Asia Minor, tom. II. p. 219.

[1] See Wesseling's note to Anton. p. 183.

[m] Anc. Geogr. t. VI. P. 2. p. 308.

Euphrates, and apparently higher up than Zimara.

Domana, one of the inland towns of Ptolemy, stood, as we are apprised by the Itineraries, eighteen miles north-east of Satala, on the road to Trapezus. The Notitia Imp. Orient. marks it as the station of the Equites Sagittarii Domanæ. Tapura, Chorsabia, Charax, which follow next in Ptolemy, receive no illustration from other sources; but Dagona is the Dogana of the Table, thirty-eight miles east of Sebastia, and Seleoboreia is perhaps the Oloberda of the same Itinerary, twenty-one miles from Nicopolis. Caleorissa, fifteen miles further on the same route, is written Caltiorissa in Ptolemy. Analiba stands, according to Antoninus, sixteen miles above Zimara: the Table says fifteen. The Notitia Imp. describes it as a military station. Pisingara is unknown. Godasa is the Gundusa of Antoninus, between Arabissus and Nicopolis. Then follow, in Ptolemy, Eudixata, Carape, Marsara, Oromandrus, Ispa, obscure places on which the Itineraries and Notices throw no light: Phuphena may be the Euspœna of Antoninus. (p. 177.) Arane is certainly the Aranis of the same Itinerary, twenty-four miles beyond Euspœna, on a road leading from Sebastia to Melitene. Phuphagena, Mardara [n], Væsapa, or Varsapa, Orsara, or Orsa, which close the list of Ptolemy, are but bare names in ancient geography.

The Itinerary of Antoninus is surprisingly copious in its catalogue of Armenian routes, and it is probable that we must refer these to a period when the line of the Euphrates was of such great importance to the protection of the eastern empire against

[n] Marandara in Antoninus, as below.

the inroads of the Parthians, or Persians. The Table has also some which vary considerably as to the intermediate stations and distances. I shall commence with those which converge to Nicopolis, the principal city of the province. The first is that which leads from Cæsarea of Cappadocia to Satala through Nicopolis, according to Antoninus. (p. 206.)

Iter a Cæsarea Satala, M. P. CCCXXIIII. Sic,
Eulepa ....XVI.
Armaxa ....XXIIII.
Marandara ....XXVIII.
Scanatus ....XXXVIII.
Sebastia ....XXVIII.
Camisa ....XXVII.
Zara ....XXVII.
Dagolasso ....XX.
Nicopoli ....XXIIII.
Olotoedariza ....XXIIII.
Dracontes ....XXVI.
Aza ....XXIIII.
Satala ....XXVI.

The same route, according to the Table.
Mazaca Cæsarea—Sorpara ....XIII.
Foroba ....XIIII.
Armaza ....XIIII.
Eudagina ....XVI.
Magalasso ....XXXII.
Comaralis ....XXXII.
Sebastia ....XXII.
Comassa ....XXIII.
Doganis ....XV.
Megalasso ....XXV.
Mesorome ....XXII.
Nicopoli ....XIII.
Draconis ....XIIII.

	M. P.
Cunissa	XIII.
Hassis	X.
Ziziola	XIII.
Satala	XII.

The total of the Table is 317 miles, only five miles short of Antonine, though the stages are very different. Between Cæsarea and Sebastia, Armaxa is the only station common to the two Itineraries. They differ still more between Sebastia and Nicopolis; but between Nicopolis and Satala, they resemble each other in regard to Dracones and Aza, or Hassa. Aza is assigned to the Lesser Armenia by Pliny (VI. 9.)

In the Table we have a second route connecting Comana Pontica with Nicopolis, and a third drawn from Polemonium to the same city.

Comana Pontica—Gagonda	XVI.
Magabula	V.
Danae	XXV.
Speluncis	XXV.
Nicopolis[o]	P

There appears to be no modern road whatever in this direction, which, generally speaking, is that from *Tokat* to *Devriki*.

Polemonio—Sauronisena[q]	
Matuasco	XVI.
Anniaca	XVIII.
.........[r]	XVIII.
Nicopoli[s].	

[o] This road falls into the former between Mesorome and Nicopolis.

[p] The number is wanting.

[q] The number wanting.

[r] Name omitted.

[s] Number wanting.

In the Antonine we have a variation in the route between Nicopolis and Satala. (p. 215.)

Iter a Nicopoli Satalam, M. P. CXXII. Sic,

Olotoedariza ....XXIIII.
Carsat [t] ....XXIIII.
Arauracos ....XXIIII.
Suissa [u] ....XXIIII.
Satala ....XXVI.

From Nicopolis to Melitene, according to the Table,

	M. P.
Nicopoli—Ole oberda [x]	XXI.
Caltiorissa	XV.
Analiba	XXIIII.
Zimara [y]	XV.
Zenocopi	XVIII.
Vereuso	XVIII.
Saba	XIII.
Dascusa	XVIII.
Hispa	XVIII.
Arangas	XVIII.
Ciaca	VIIII.
Melitene	XXVIII.

From Nicopolis to Arabissus we have two routes in Antonine.

Iter a Nicopoli Arabisso, M. P. CCXXVI. Sic,

Dagalasso ....XXIIII.
Zara ....XX.
Camisa ....XVIII.
Sebastia ....XXIIII.

[t] Elsewhere called Carsagis, p. 208.

[u] Named in the Not. Provinciarum sub dispositione Ducis Armeniæ de Minore laterculo, Ala prima Ulpia Dacorum Suissæ.

[x] This name is evidently corrupt; it should be, I think, Seleoboria.

[y] At Zimara this road meets one from Satala.

	M. P.
In Medio	XXV.
Ariarathia	XXV.
Coduzabala	XX.
Comana	XIIII.
Ptandari	XXIIII.
Arabisso	XXII.

This was a very circuitous route, since it passed by Sebastia and Comana; the second is entitled, " Iter ab Arabisso per compendium Satalam." (p. 181.) Taking it from Nicopolis in an inverted order, we shall have the following stages :

Dagolasso	XXIIII.
Zara	XX.
Eumeis	XVIII.
Gundusa	XXX.
Zoana	XXIII.
Tonosa	XXV.
Arabisso	XXVIII.

The total distance is 168 miles, and therefore less than that of the former route by fifty-eight miles.

The next set of roads to be considered are those which diverge from Satala; but as many of these as pass through Nicopolis will of course be omitted. The first communication is that between Trapezus and Satala, which is given in the Antonine and the Table, but with considerable variations in the stations : the total distance is however very nearly the same. In 'the former it is entitled, " Iter a " Trapezunte Satalam, M. P. CXXXV."

Ad Vicesimum	XX.
Zigana	XXXII.
Thia	XXIIII.

	M. P.
Sedisscapifonti [y]	XVII.
Domana	XXIIII.
Satala	XVIII.

According to the Table the same route stands thus:

Trapezunte—Magnana	XX.
Gihenenica	X.
Bylæ	XVIII.
Frigidarium	VI.
Patara	VIII.
Medocia	XIIII.[z]
Solonenica	XII.
Domana	XVIII.
Satala	XVIII.

The two routes are so very different that it is probable they have no part in common except the first and last stages. I suppose one went by *Gumich Khaneh*, the other by *Tekeh* and *Baybout* [a].

2°. From Satala to Melitene, along the Euphrates, in Antoninus. (p. 207.)

Suissa	XVII.
Arauracos	XVIII.
Carsagis	XXIIII.
Sinervas	XXVIII.
Analiba	XXVIII.
Zimara	XVI.
Teucila	XVI.
Sabus [b]	XXVIII.

[y] The MSS. read Sedissa Fiponti, which should be Sedissa Finis Ponti. Sedissa is probably connected with mount Scydisces, which I take to be the separation of Pontus and Armenia in this direction.

[z] In the original the first I is nearly effaced.

[a] Gihenenica seems to be *Gumich Khaneh*, and Thia, *Tekeh*.

[b] Mentioned in the Not. Imp. Equites Sagittarii Sabu.

M. P.

Dascusa ....XVI.
Ciaca ....XXXII.
Melitena ....XVIII.

The Table differs widely from this arrangement, as far as Zimara.

Satala—Ziziola ....XII.
Hassis ....XIII.
Cunissa ....X.
Draconis ....XIII.
Haris ....XVI.
Elegarsina ....XVII.
Bubalia..............................VIII.
Zimara ....XXVII.

The remainder of the route to Melitene has been already given under the road from Nicopolis to that city. (p. 157.)

Melitene will be the last point, whose communications we shall take notice of; those with Nicopolis and Satala have indeed already been considered. What remains will be chiefly in the direction of Sebastia, Comana, and Cucusus. In Antonine we have a route entitled:

Iter a Sebastia Cocuso, per Melitenam, M. P. CCXCIII.

Blandos ....XXIIII.
Euspœna ....XXVIII.
Aranis ....XXIIII.
Ad Prætorium........................XXVIII.
Pisonos ....XXXII.
Melitena ....XXXII.
Arcas ....XXVI.
Dandaxina ....XXIIII.
Ozdara ....XXIIII.
Ptandari ....XXIIII.
Cocuso ....XXXVIII.

But there was a road from Sebastia to Cucusus, by Cæsarea and Comana, without passing by Melitene. (Ibid. p. 178.)

Iter a Sebastia Cocuso per Cæsaream, M. P. CCLVIII.

Scanatus ....XXVIII.
Malandara ....XXX.
Armaxa ....XXVIII.
Eulepa......................................XXIIII.
Cæsarea ....XVI.
Artaxata ....XXIIII.
Coduzabala ....XVIII.
Comana ....XXIIII.
Ptandari ....XXIIII.
Cocuso.......................................XXXVIII.

But the most direct road of all avoided Cæsarea, which made a saving of fifty-two miles.

Iter a Sebastia Cocuso per Compendium, M. P. CCVI.

Tonosa...L.
Ariarathia ....L.
Coduzabala ....XX.

The remaining stages are the same as the last.

The Table gives a route from Comana to Melitene, by Castabala, which can hardly be Coduzabala, as the distances do not correspond, unless there has been some transposition.

Comana Cappadocia—Asarino ....XXIIII.
Castabala ....XXIIII.
Pagrum ....XX.
Arcilapopoli[c] ....XXX.
Singa ....XXX.
Arega ....XIIII.
Zocotesso ....XII.
Lagalasso....................................XXIIII.

[c] Perhaps Archelaopolis, and the Archalla of Ptolemy.

	M. P.
Sama	XVIII.
Melitene	XIII.

Another route from Cæsarea to Melitene. (Anton. Itin. p. 210.)

Artaxata	XXIIII.
Coduzabala	XXIIII.
Comana	XXVI.
Siricis	XXIIII.
Ptandaris	XVI.
Arabisso	XII.
Osdara	XXVIII.
Dandexena	XXIIII.
Arcas	XXII.
Melitenen......................................	XXVIII.

SECTION X.

CARIA.

Origin and early history of the Carians—Princes of Caria—Brief sketch of the principal events in the annals of the country, from its first conquest by Crœsus to its becoming a part of the Roman empire—Boundaries and geography of the province —Dorian colonies, and other towns on the coast—Interior— Islands of Cos and Rhodes.

THE Carians were not considered by Herodotus, and other early Greek historians, as the aboriginal inhabitants of the country to which they communicated their name. Herodotus himself, a native of Caria, and who must therefore be allowed to have been well acquainted with its traditions, believed that the people who inhabited it had formerly occupied the islands of the Ægæan, under the name of Leleges; but that being reduced by Minos, king of Crete, they were removed by that sovereign to the continent of Asia, where they still however continued to be his vassals, and to serve him more especially in his maritime expeditions. At this period, says the historian, the Carians were by far the most celebrated of the existing nations; they excelled in the manufacture of arms, and the Greeks ascribed to them the invention of crests, and the devices and handles of shields. (I. 171. Cf. Anacr. et Alc. ap. Strab. XIV. p. 661.) The occupation of many of the Cyclades by the Carians, at the earliest

period to which Grecian history, divested of fable,
appears to reach, is satisfactorily confirmed by Thucydides, as well as the fact of their expulsion by
Minos. (I. 4.) In proof of the former, he states, that
when the Athenians, under the direction of Pisis-
tratus, purified Delos, by removing all the sepulchres from that sacred island, they observed that
more than half the graves belonged to the Carian
nation. (I. 8.) The Carians, like the Tyrrheni Pelasgi, who belong to the same period, (Metrod. ap.
Athen. XV. c. 12.) were notorious pirates, and it is
for this reason, doubtless, that Minos expelled them
from the islands; while he was glad, at the same
time, to avail himself of their skill and enterprise
for the aggrandizement of his own empire. (Thuc.
loc. cit.) Their reputation, indeed, for the management of ships was such, that they form one of the
naval epochs recorded by Castor, a Greek writer,
quoted by Syncellus, and other chronographers[a],
who wrote on the nations that in ancient times had
been powerful by sea. Such are the earliest accounts
the Greeks have left us of this people; but the Carians themselves, as Herodotus admits, would not
allow that they had been transplanted to the continent of Asia from the islands of the Ægæan, but
maintained that they were an indigenous and aboriginal people of the peninsula. (I. 171.) From their
own shewing, however, it is clear that they could
not be considered as an autochthonous people, independent of the general argument against the fact;
for they claimed, as appears from Herodotus and
Strabo, a near degree of affinity with two other

[a] See Heyne, Comment. su-   Nov. Comment. Soc. Gotting.
pra Epochis Popul. Θαλαττκρατ.   vol. I. p. 80.

nations of Asia Minor; I mean the Lydians and Mysians. This they expressed, by saying, that Lydus and Mysus were brothers of Car, the patriarch of their race. (Herod. I. 171. Strab. XIV. p. 659.) Now it has been stated that, according to the most accredited opinions, the Mysians and Lydians originally came from Thrace; whence it would follow that the Carians likewise must have migrated to Asia from the same country. We have seen, in speaking of the population of Greece, that Thrace and Macedonia furnished those barbaric hordes, which, under the several names of Leleges, Caucones, and Pelasgi, spread themselves over the shores of the Ægæan, and the islands of that sea; the Carians, therefore, must have belonged to the same great family, since they are confounded by the best authorities with the Leleges. It is difficult to say what nation inhabited Caria before Minos had removed thither the people from whom it took its name; but it is not improbable that the Phœnicians occupied a portion of it. For we know that they had colonized Rhodes, and other islands off this coast; and Athenæus remarks that certain poets applied the name of Phœnice to Caria. (IV. p. 174.) The Carians were already settled in Asia at the time of the Trojan war, since they are expressly mentioned by Homer in his catalogue of the auxiliaries of Priam:

Νάστης αὖ Καρῶν ἡγήσατο βαρβαροφώνων
Οἳ Μίλητον ἔχον, Φθειρῶν τ᾽ ὄρος ἀκριτόφυλλον,
Μαιάνδρου τε ῥοὰς, Μυκάλης τ᾽ αἰπεινὰ κάρηνα.

ΙL. B. 867.

The peculiar epithet of βαρβαρόφωνοι, applied by the poet to this people, has given rise to much dis-

M 3

cussion among his commentators. Apollodorus imagined that it was a term of contempt used by the
Ionians more especially to stigmatize a people with
whom they were frequently at war. Others affirmed, that the reason of the epithet was to be sought
for in the Carian language, which was more harsh
and uncouth than those of other nations. This was
denied again by others, especially by Philip of Theangela, a Carian writer, who had composed a history
of the Carians and Leleges. (Strab. XIV. p. 661.
Cf. Athen. VI. p. 271.) Strabo himself conceives
that the word βάρβαρος was used originally to designate some harshness or defect in pronunciation,
which the Greeks, who were peculiarly alive to such
defects, came afterwards to transfer to all languages
but their own. He further accounts for the term
being peculiarly applied to the Carians by Homer,
from the fact that this people had more intercourse
with the Greeks than the other tribes of Asia; being
often employed by them as mercenaries, and afterwards being still more intermixed with the Ionians
and Dorians, when these had formed their settlements in the Asiatic continent. The Carian language had certainly many words common to the
Hellenic, and so doubtless had the Pelasgic, which
must have formed the basis of this and many other
dialects. Nevertheless, from disuse and want of culti-
vation, the latter was accounted barbarous in the time
of Herodotus. This was also the case with the Carian tongue, since we know from the same writer
that in the time of Xerxes a native of that country
would not have been understood by those of Greece.
(VIII. 135.)

The Carians appear to have offered little resistance to the Greek settlers who successively established themselves on their coast. The Ionians first drove them from Miletus and Priene, and compelled them to retire to the left bank of the Meander. The Dorians next obtained a footing on their shore, and seized upon Halicarnassus and the peninsula of Cnidus; so that the Carians were confined chiefly to the southern coast and the valleys of those streams which are tributary to the Meander, towards the borders of Phrygia and Pisidia. Such being their weakness and inability to resist a foreign invader, it is not surprising that they should have yielded to the superior ascendency of the Lydians, under the direction of Alyattes and Crœsus. (Nic. Damasc. p. 243. Herod. I. 28.) On the overthrow of the Lydian empire they passed under the Persian dominion, together with the Dorians and other Greeks settled in their country; having offered no resistance to the troops of Cyrus, commanded by Harpagus. (Herod. I. 174.) In the division of the Persian dominions, subsequently made by Darius, the Carians were attached to the first section of the empire, which comprehended Æolis, Ionia, Lycia, and Pamphylia; and the governor of this province commonly took the title of satrap of Caria, Miletus being the place of his residence. In the Ionian revolt, the Carians took a more active part than might have been expected from their previous want of energy and love of liberty. They fought two great battles with the Persian troops, who had hastened to repress their insurrection; and though they were defeated on both occasions, they behaved with great bravery, and inflicted a severe loss on their enemies. In a third contest they obtained a signal victory, by means of a night ambuscade, and destroyed the entire force of the Persians, with their generals. (Herod. V. 118—121.) They thus for a time averted the storm which threatened them; but after the fall of Miletus, resistance became hopeless, and the whole province was brought once more under the Persian dominion. (VI. 25.) The policy of the sovereigns of Persia was to establish in each subject or tributary state a government apparently independent of them, but whose despotic authority at home afforded the best guarantee that the people would every where be brought under the control of the court of Susa. This system, which had been observed by them throughout Ionia and Æolis, and the islands, was likewise adopted by them in Caria: and it is to this circumstance that the dynasty of the Carian princes, who fixed their residence at Halicarnassus, owed its origin. There had always indeed been native sovereigns in the country, but their power had been limited to their own barbarous subjects. Under the sanction and protection of Persia, they now exercised indiscriminate authority over Greek and barbarian; a measure which tended at once to humble the pride of the former, and to abolish the distinction which they so fondly cherished. Herodotus has dwelt at length on the conduct and energy of Artemisia, daughter of Lygdamis, tyrant of Halicarnassus, and who herself became afterwards sovereign of that city and Cos, together with other islands. The services she rendered Xerxes, and the zeal she displayed in his behalf, entitled her to his highest commendation and thanks; (Herod. VII. 99. VIII. 87, 88, 93.) and he testified his reliance on her prudence and fidelity by intrusting her with the care of his children. (VIII. 101.) The succession of the Carian princes will be given more at length when we come to examine the history of Halicarnassus, with which it is more particularly connected. When Athens had attained to that degree of maritime power, of which we have no other instance in the annals of Greece, Ionia and Caria became her tributaries. (Thuc. II. 9.) But it was along the coast that her power was alone acknowledged; and if any detachments or parties advanced into the interior to levy contributions, they were either cut off or driven back with loss. (III. 19.) The peace of Antalcidas restored the whole of maritime Asia to the sovereigns of Persia, and Caria continued to form part of their empire till Alexander advanced into this quarter of the peninsula, after the battle of the Granicus, and effected its conquest, though not without considerable resistance, especially from Halicarnassus. At a later period it appears that Caria was for a time annexed to the kingdom of Egypt; and Polybius has given an account of the attempt made by Philip, the son of Demetrius, to wrest it from Ptolemy Philopator. (III. 2. 8.[b] Cf. XVI. 12. 1. XVII. 1. 14.) The Romans insisted afterwards on his restoring the towns he had conquered in this invasion. (XVII. 2, 3.) Caria next fell under the domination of Antiochus; but on his defeat by Scipio, the Roman senate rewarded the services and fidelity of the Rhodians with this part of the conquered monarch's territory, which was so conveniently situated with respect to their

[b] See Prof. Schweighæuser's note on the passage, where he confesses that he ought not to have omitted the words εἰς Καρίαν, which the best MSS. exhibit.

island. (XXII. 27. 8. Liv. XXXIII. 16.)   It was
afterwards overrun and occupied for a short time
by Mithridates, (Appian. Mithr. c. 20.) but finally
remained in the possession of the Romans, who annexed it to the proconsular province of Asia.

Caria was bounded on the north by Ionia and
Lydia, from which it was separated by the course of
the Meander; on the west and south, by the Ægean
and Cretan seas; on the east, by Lycia and Milyas,
and a small portion of Southern Phrygia.   In extent
it is the least considerable of the divisions of Asia
Minor; but from the number of towns and villages
assigned to it by the geographers of antiquity, it
would seem to have been very populous.   The corresponding division of the Turkish provinces in
modern geography is called *Muntesha*.   Our description of the western coast of Caria commences
from the promontory of Posidium, south of Didymi,
and the temple of Apollo, where our periplus of the
Ionian shore terminated.   South of cape Posidium
the coast bends considerably to the east, and forms
the opening of one of those deep gulfs which form
a prominent feature in the hydrography of Caria.
The gulf in question, now called *Assem-kalessi*,

Jassicus
Sinus.
was known to the ancients by the name of Jassicus
Sinus, (Thuc. VIII. 26.) from the town of Jassus,
situate at the head of the bay, nearly in the situation occupied by the modern *Assem*, or *Assan*.

The first town within the bay, on the northern

Tichiussa.
shore, was Tichiussa, a fortress belonging to the
Milesians, as we learn from Thucydides, and which
appears to have possessed a port. (Thuc. VIII. 26—
28.)   A bon-mot of Stratonicus, the musician, with
respect to this place, is recorded by Athenæus: " As

" Tichius (Τειχιοῦς) was inhabited by a mixed popu-
" lation, he observed that most of the tombs were
" those of foreigners ; on which he said to his lad,
" Let us be off, since strangers seem to die here,
" but not one of the natives." (VIII. p. 351.)   The
poet Archestratus commends highly the sprats of
Tichiussa :

Σκάρον ἐξ Ἐφέσου ζήτει, χειμῶνι δὲ τρίγλην
ἔσθι᾽ ἐνὶ ψαφαρῇ ληφθεῖσαν Τειχιοέσσῃ
Μιλήτου κώμῃ, Καρῶν πέλας ἀγκυλοκώλων.

AP. ATHEN. VII. p. 320.

.(Cf. Steph. Byz. v. Τειχιόεις, v. l. Cod. Voss.)   The
remains of this place exist in a bay indenting the
northern shore of the Sinus Jassicus, somewhat to
the east of *Jeronta* and the ruins of Didymi.

Jassus, or Jasus, which gave its name to the gulf Jassus.
in which it was situated, but which, in the age of
Polybius, was more commonly called Bargyliaticus
Sinus, had been founded, as the inhabitants pretended, by a colony from Argos ; but these settlers,
having sustained severe losses during their contests
with the natives of Caria, they obtained a fresh supply of colonists from the sons of Neleus, who had
founded Miletus. (Polyb. XVI. 2.)   It was attacked
in the Peloponnesian war, after the Sicilian expedition, by the Lacedæmonians and their allies ; it being at that time held by Amorges, a Persian chief,
who had revolted from Darius.   Jassus was taken
by assault, and Amorges fell into the hands of the
Greeks, who delivered him up to Tissaphernes.
(Thuc. VIII. 28.) Jassus was situate, as Strabo
describes it, in an island close to the shore, with a
good port.   The soil was poor, but the sea made
the inhabitants some amends by the liberal supply
of fish it yielded for their market.   The geographer

has introduced a humourous story with reference to this commodity, on which the Jassians chiefly depended for their subsistence. (XIV. p. 658.)

Ἦν δέ ποτ' εἰς Ἴασον Καρῶν πόλιν εἰσαφίκηαι
Καριδ' εὐμεγέθη λήψει, σπανία δὲ πρίασθαι.

ARCHESTR. AP. ATHEN. III. p.105.

Athenæus relates a story of a dolphin having formed an attachment for a boy of this town. (XIII. p. 606.) Jasus was besieged and taken by Philip king of Macedon, but he was compelled by the Romans to restore it to Ptolemy. (Liv. XXXII. 33. Polyb. XVII. 2, 3.) The circumference of the town was about ten stadia. (Polyb. XVI. 12. Cf. Ptol. p. 120. Steph. Byz. v. Ἰασσός. Plin. V. 29.) The Ecclesiastical Notices and Hierocles (p. 689.) have also recorded it. The neighbouring mountains supplied a beautiful kind of marble, used by the ancients for ornamental purposes. The colour was blood-red and livid white, striped. (Paul. Silent. Ecphr. S. Soph. P. II. 213.) We are told by Chandler, " that the rocky islet on which the town " was built is now united to the main land by a " small isthmus. The north side of the rock is " abrupt and inaccessible; the summit is occupied " by a mean but extensive fortress: at the foot is " a small portion of flat ground. On that, and on " the acclivities, the houses once stood, within a nar- " row compass, bounded towards the sea by the city " wall, which was regular, solid, and handsome, like " that of Ephesus. This, which has been repaired in " many places, now encloses rubbish, with remnants " of ordinary buildings, and a few pieces of marble. " In the side of the rock is the theatre, with many " rows of seats remaining. On the left wing is an " inscription in very large and well formed charac- " ters, ranging in a long line, and recording certain

" donations to Bacchus and the people. By the
" isthmus is the vaulted substruction of a consider-
" able edifice; and on a jamb of the door-way are
" decrees engraved in a fair character, but damaged,
" and black with smoke. The sepulchres of the Ja-
" sians on the continent are very numerous, rang-
" ing along, above a mile, on the slope of the moun-
" tain [c]."

Bargylia, which next follows, was noted for a Bargylia.
temple and statue of Diana Cindyas, so named from
the village of Cindye. Whenever it rained or snowed, Cindye.
the image of the goddess was observed to be free
from moisture. (Polyb. XVI. 12.) Strabo applies
the miracle to the temple rather than the statue.
(XIV. p. 658.) Stephanus states, that the town
was called Andanus by the Carians, who reported
that it was built by Achilles. Other traditions represented it to have been founded by Bellerophon,
and named after his companion Bargylus. (v. Βάρ-
γυλα.) Bargylia was taken by Philip in his Carian
campaign, and Polybius reports that he wintered
there, though with considerable difficulty with regard to the subsistence of his army. (XVI. 24.) He
was compelled by the Romans to evacuate the place
not long after. (XVII. 2, 3. Liv. XXXII. 33. Cf.
XXXIII. 18. 39. Mel. I. 16. Plin. V. 29.) Cicero
calls the citizens Bargyletæ [d]. (ad Fam. Ep. XIII.
56.) Bargylia, as Strabo informs us, was the birthplace of Protarchus, a celebrated Epicurean philo-

---

[c] Travels in Asia Minor, p.
226—228. There are both autonomous and imperial coins of
Jasus, with the legend ΙΑΣΕΩΝ
ΙΑCCΕΩΝ, in the medals of Hadrian. Sestini, p. 88.

[d] On the coins of Bargylia
we read ΒΑΡΓΤΛΙΗΤΩΝ. They
are both republican and imperial. The latter from Titus to
Geta. Sestini, p. 87.

sopher, whose disciple was Demetrius Lacon. (XIV. p. 658. Diog. Laert. X. 26.) The remains of this town have not been accurately explored, but Chandler conceives that he must have been near the site in a plain surrounded by mountains, about two hours from Jasus. Within the plain, which he supposes to have been formerly a recess of the bay, (Sinus Bargyleticus,) was a hillock, with ruins on it. This he recommends to the notice of future travellers [e].

Portus et insula Caryanda. Next to Bargylia Strabo names the port of Caryanda, of the same name as an island situate near the shore. Scylax, the geographer, was a native of the latter, according to the same authority. (XIV. p. 658.) It is most probable that this is the Scylax who flourished, as Herodotus reports, in the time of Darius. (IV. 44.) But some critics are of opinion that there was a junior Scylax posterior to Polybius, and who compiled the periplus which goes by his name [f]. (Cf. Steph. Byz. v. Καρύανδα. Plin. V. 29.) In Scylax, for Κρυΐνδα, we should read Καρύανδα. Col. Leake is inclined to think that the peninsula of *Pasha Liman* represents the former island of Caryanda, which would be another instance of the change produced by the action of the Meander on the coast of Caria [g]. But *Pasha Liman* seems too much to the south-west to answer to Strabo's topography; and there is an island between *Mentecha* and *Hassar-kalessi*, which would better correspond

[e] Travels in Asia Minor, p. 230, 231.

[f] I am inclined to think that the work in question is founded on the survey of the old Caryandian geographer, with alterations and insertions by later hands.

[g] Asia Minor, p. 227.

with the situation which that geographer assigns to Caryanda.

Mentecha, or *Muntecha*, is probably the Myndus $_{Myndus.}$ of Strabo, (XIV. p. 658.) which Polybius places on the extremity of the gulf of Jassus, opposite to Cape Posidium. (XVI. 12. Cf. XVI. 15.) It was founded, as we learn from Pausanias, by a party of Trœzenians, together with Halicarnassus. (Corinth. c. 30.) Pliny, besides Myndus, speaks of Palæmyndus; (V. 29.) and perhaps his Neapolis is no other than the new town. (Cf. Mel. I. 16.) It was the punishment inflicted on the captain of a Myndian vessel, which produced a rupture between Aristagoras and the Persian admiral who commanded the fleet destined against Naxos, and finally brought on the Ionian revolt, the consequences of which were so important to Greece. (Herod. V. 33.) Frequent mention is made of Myndus, as a neighbouring town to Halicarnassus, in Arrian's account of the siege of that city by Alexander. That prince, conceiving that the possession of Myndus would be advantageous for the prosecution of the siege, endeavoured to surprise that place; but the Myndians, with the aid of some reinforcements sent from Halicarnassus by sea, repulsed his attack with loss. (Arrian. Alex. Exp. I. 20. 8.) Other passages relative to Myndus occur in Livy (XXXVII. 15.) and Steph. Byz. (v. Μύνδος. Schol. Theocr. II. 29.) Athenæus says the wine of this district was good for digestion. (I. p. 32.) In Hierocles the name is corruptly written Amyndus. (p. 697.) The Table reckons fifty-six miles from Miletus, which distance agrees nearly with the interval between *Palatcha* and *Mentesha*. Col. Leake identifies Myndus with *Gumishlu*, a small port, where captain Beaufort discovered some ruins[h]. Palæmyndus may have been situate, as Mannert supposes, near cape Astypalæa of Strabo, which derived its name probably from that circumstance, and which I take to be the peninsula of *Pasha Liman;* but Myndus itself must be *Mentesha.* Cape Zephyrium of the same geographer is the headland between *Pasha Liman* and *Gumishlu.* Naziandus, which Pliny places in this direction, is unknown. The Myndian territory extended as far as cape Termerium, opposite to a headland in the isle of Cos, named Scandarium, and only separated from the continent by a channel of forty stadia. Pliny enumerates Termera, which he terms free, among the maritime towns of Caria. (V. 29.) Steph. Byz. improperly assigns it to Lycia. (vv. Τέρμερα et Τέλμερα.) We find the ethnic Τερμερέα in Herodotus. (V. 37.) It appears from Suidas that this place gave rise to the proverbial expression Τερμέρια κακὰ, it being used as a prison by the sovereigns of Caria[i]. Its site is probably occupied by *Carbaglar,* or *Gumishlu.*

On doubling cape *Carabaglar,* or Termerium, we enter the wide and extensive bay of *Stanco,* or *Boudroun,* anciently called Ceramicus Sinus. It is the deepest of the many bays by which the coast of Caria is indented, and was formerly crowded with numerous towns. Of these, the most extensive, as well as most celebrated, was Halicarnassus, founded, ac-

Marginal notes: Naziandus. Termerium promontorium. Termera. Ceramicus Sinus. Halicarnassus.

[h] Beaufort's Karamania, p. 110. Asia Minor, p. 228. The epigraph on the coins of Myndus is ΜΤΝΔΙ and ΜΤΝΔΙΩΝ; they belong chiefly to the period of the Antonines. Sestini, p. 89.

[i] In Suidas we read further, τὸ δὲ χωρίον ἔρυμνον τυγχάνει κεῖται μεταξὺ Μήλου καὶ Ἁλικαρνάσου. Holstenius would substitute Μύνδου for Μήλου, but Μιλήτω is nearer the reading of the MSS.

cording to Strabo, by Anthes, at the head of a body of Trœzenians. (XIV. p. 656.) These were joined afterwards by some Argives, headed by Melas and Areuanias. (Vitruv. II. 8. Cf. Pausan. Corinth. c. 30. Mel. I. 16.) Herodotus only recognises the former colonists. (VII. 99.) It was at first called Zephyria and Isthmus. (Strab. loc. cit. Steph. Byz. v. Ἁλικαρνασσός.) This famous town, on account of its origin, had naturally been included in the Dorian confederacy, which consisted originally of six states; but Agasicles, a citizen of Halicarnassus, having, contrary to prescribed custom, carried off the tripod adjudged to him in the games celebrated in honour of the Triopian Apollo, instead of dedicating it to the god, the other five cities, in consequence of this offence, determined to exclude Halicarnassus from any participation in these festivities, which amounted in fact to an excommunication from the Dorian confederacy, which from thenceforth was named Pentapolis. (Herod. I. 144.) Not long after this event, Halicarnassus may be supposed to have lost its independence, Lygdamis, one of the principal citizens, having usurped the authority. He was succeeded by his daughter Artemisia, of whom Herodotus has made such honourable mention in his history. From his account it appears that this Carian princess was not only sovereign of Halicarnassus, but also of Cos, of Nisyrus, and Calydna. Her armament in the expedition of Xerxes consisted only of five ships, but they were the best appointed in the whole fleet, next to those of the Sidonians. Artemisia, in all probability, transmitted this principality to her son, named Lygdamis, like his natural grandfather; and it was during his reign that Herodotus, unwilling

to see his native city under the domination of a
despot, abandoned it for Samos, where he completed
his studies. (Suid. vv. Ἡρόδοτος, Πανύασις. Pamphil.
ap. Aul. Gell. XV. 23.)   Subsequent to this period
we have little knowledge of what occurred at Halicarnassus : but from Thucydides we learn that Caria and Doris were tributary to Athens, (II. 9.) and
Halicarnassus itself is mentioned, towards the close
of his history, as being in the hands of her troops.
(VIII. 42.)   Somewhat later we find it subject to
princes of Carian extraction.   The first of these appears to have been Hecatomnus, who is styled king
of the Carians by Strabo. (XIV. p. 656.)   This sovereign had three sons, Mausolus, Hidrieus, and Pixodarus ; and two daughters, Artemisia and Ada, who
were married to the two elder brothers.   Mausolus
succeeded his father on the throne of Caria, and we
find him taking part in the social war with Byzantium, Chios, and Rhodes against Athens, on account
of the restrictions placed by that power on their
commerce. (Diod. Sic. XVI. 21.)   The firmness of
the allies compelled the Athenians, after a contest
of some duration, to relinquish their pretended command of the sea, and to remove the grievances com-
plained of.   But not long after, we find the great
Athenian orator exerting his eloquence to urge the
Athenians to defend the Rhodians, whose independence was threatened by Mausolus, their former ally.
That prince, however, did not live to carry his de-
signs, whether real or supposed, against the Rhodians into execution. (Demosthen. de Rhod. Libert.)
He died without offspring, and left the crown to his
sister and consort Artemisia.   If the merit of men
is to be estimated by the regret they leave behind,

and again if that regret is adequately represented
by external demonstration, the Carian prince must
have been the best of sovereigns, and the most beloved of husbands; since the monument which was
erected to his memory by his sorrowing wife far
surpassed in magnitude, costliness, and beauty, every
thing of the kind erected previously, and came to
be looked upon as one of the seven wonders of the
world, and finally supplied a name for sepulchral
memorials of any magnitude. Pliny, describing this
splendid pile, says it measured, from north to south,
sixty-eight feet; somewhat less in opposite dimen-
sions; and in circuit 411 feet. It measured twenty-
five cubits in height, and was surrounded by thirty-
six columns. The sculptures on the eastern front
were by the hand of Scopas, on the northern side
the artist was Bryaxis, Timotheus towards the south,
and Leochares to the east. Artemisia died of grief
before the work was completed; but the sculptors,
from a love of glory, did not give up the undertaking till it was perfected. A fifth architect added a
pyramid to the first story, having twenty-five steps,
with a truncated vertex: on this was placed a four-
horse chariot by Pythis. The height of the whole
monument was 140 feet. The exterior was entirely
cased with Proconnesian marble. (Plin. XXXVI. 5.
Vitruv. Præf. VII. Strab. XIV. p. 656. Pausan.
Arcad. c. 16. Phil. de Sept. Mirac.) Artemisia was
succeeded by Hidrieus, who, dying without issue,
left the crown to Ada, his wife; but Pixodarus, the
youngest of Hecatomnus' sons, formed a party against
her, and, with the assistance of Orontobates, a Persian satrap, succeeded in expelling her from Halicarnassus. Orontobates, having married the daugh-

ter of Pixodarus, remained, on the death of the latter, in possession of Halicarnassus. It was at this
period that Alexander arrived with his forces in
Caria, and laid siege to that city. It was long and
severe, owing to the natural strength of the place,
and the number and description of the troops which
defended it, under the command of Memnon, the
best general in the Persian service. But the courage
and determination of Alexander prevailed at length
over the resistance of the besieged, and they finally
withdrew from the town, leaving only some troops
in the citadel and forts. Alexander razed Halicarnassus to the ground, and restored Ada to the sove-
reignty of Caria. This princess, soon after, compelled the Persians to surrender the citadel and the
other fortresses. (Arrian. Exp. Alex. I. 23. Strab.
loc. cit.)   Halicarnassus, to compensate the losses it
had sustained, had six towns annexed to it by Alexander, as Pliny reports ; namely, Theangela, Sibde,
Medmasa, Euranium, Pedasum, Telmissum. (VI.
29.)   The citadel was named Salmacis, from the
fountain celebrated in the Metamorphoses of Ovid.
(IV. 11. Cf. Strab. loc. cit. Vitruv. II. 8.)   This
Acropolis was adorned with the palace of Mausolus
and several fine temples and other buildings. (Vitruv. II. 8.)   According to Scylax, there were two
ports at Halicarnassus : they were protected by the
little island named Arconnesus, now *Orakadasi*.

Arconne-
sus insula.

(Strab. loc. cit.)   Halicarnassus could boast of having produced Herodotus, Dionysius, and Heraclitus
the poet. (Strab. loc. cit.)   We find incidental mention of this city occurring in Livy. (XXXIII. 20.
XXXVII. 10. 16.)   Cicero compliments his brother
on having restored Samos and Halicarnassus, when

nearly deserted. This condition was probably the effect of the Mithridatic war; (Ep. ad Q. Frat. I. 8.) but he accuses Verres of having carried off some statues from thence. (I. 19.) The Halicarnassians boasted, as we learn from Tacitus, when they competed for the honour of erecting a temple to Tiberius, that their city had stood for 1200 years without experiencing the shock of an earthquake. (Ann. IV. 55.)

We have evidence of its existence from coins as late as the reign of Gordian[k], and we can trace it still further by means of Hierocles, (p. 687.) Theodoret, (Hist. Eccl. II. p. 577.) the Ecclesiastical Notices, and Acts of Councils[l]. Its ruins have long been known to exist at *Boudroun*, but they had not been explored accurately by any traveller before Capt. Beaufort, to whom we are indebted for a plan of the harbour and the Turkish town, with the adjacent coast. He observes, " that a more inviting or convenient situa-" tion could hardly have been selected for the capital " of the kingdom of Caria; it rises gently from a " deep bay, and commands a view of the island of " Cos, and the southern shore of the Ceramic gulf, " as far as cape *Krio*. In front of the town a broad " square rock projects into the bay, on which stands " the citadel. The walls of the ancient city may be " here and there discerned; and several fragments " of columns, mutilated sculpture, and broken in-" scriptions, are scattered in different parts of the " bazaar and streets. Above the town are the re-

[k] Sestini, Imperatorii ab A-grippina Claudii usque ad Gordianum. Epigraphe, ΑΛΙΚΑΡ-ΝΑCCEΩΝ. p. 88. There are also medals of the Carian dynasts, from Hecatomnus to Pixodarus, p. 90.

[l] Geogr. Sacr. p. 246.

" mains of a theatre ;" but though he searched for some traces of the celebrated Mausoleum, he was unsuccessful.   He is of opinion that it occupied the site of the modern fortress, which seems to have been erected by the knights of Rhodes[m].

Of the six towns which, as Pliny relates, Alexander placed under the jurisdiction of Halicarnassus, Theangela is known as the native place of Philip, the Carian historian, mentioned by Athenæus. (VI. p. 271. Steph. Byz. v. Θεάγγελα.) Sibde and Medmasa are also acknowledged by the Byzantine geographer. (vv. Σίβδα, Μέδμασα[n].) Euranium is unknown to other authors, but Pedasum or Pedasa, as Strabo writes the name, was an ancient city belonging once to the Leleges, and the capital of a district which included no less than eight cities within its limits. These Leleges held the whole of this part of Caria, as far as Myndus and Bargylia, and they even conquered a great part of Pisidia ; but they afterwards became blended with the Carians, and ceased to form a separate body. (XIII. p. 611.) Herodotus also notices Pedasa, on account of a strange phenomenon which was stated to occur there. Whenever the inhabitants of Pedasus were threatened with any calamity, the priestess of Minerva's chin became furnished with a beard : this prodigy was reported to have happened three times. The Pedaseans alone, of all the Carians, resisted the army of Cyrus commanded by Harpagus. They fortified a mountain, called Lide, and gave that general much trouble ; at length, however, they were reduced. (Herod. I.

Side notes: Theangela. Sibde. Medmasa. Euranium. Pedasa. Lide mons.

[m] Beaufort's Karamania, p. 95—98.

[n] Some coins are assigned to Medmasa, with the legend ME. Sestini, p. 88.

175. Cf. VIII. 104.)   The ruins of this town must
be looked for above Halicarnassus, towards the east;
indeed, Strabo leads us to suppose it was not far
from Stratonicea, and I observe in this direction a
place named *Peitchin;* this may represent Pedasa.
Synagela, or Syagela, was another town in this vici- Syagela.
nity, belonging to the Leleges, which, together with
Myndus, was the only town allowed to subsist by
Mausolus[o], of the eight claimed by that people.
(Strab. XIII. p. 611.) Steph. Byz. reports, that the
name of Souagela was derived from the circumstance
of its possessing the tomb of Car.   In the language
of the country, " Soua" meant a " tomb," and " gela,"
a " king." (v. Σουάγελα.) Telmissus, the last of the six Telmissus.
mentioned by Pliny, is not to be confounded with
the more celebrated city of Lycia, whose seers were
so famous throughout Asia Minor at a very early
period. It is likewise acknowledged by Steph. Byz.;
(v. Τελμισσός.) many writers, however, attribute the
faculty of divination to the Carian town. (Cic. de
Div. I. 40. Clem. Alex. Strom. I. p. 334.)   Mela
gives the name of Leuca to a portion of the coast Leuca.
between Halicarnassus and Myndus, (I. 16.) and
some critics connect it with the Leucopolis of Pliny;
but this seems to have been in the Dorian gulf. (V.
29.) Ceramus, from which the bay of Halicarnassus Ceramus.
derived its ancient appellation, was a small town
and fortress on the northern side of the gulf, where
the village of *Keramo* sufficiently indicates the site.
(Strab. loc. cit. Ptol. p. 119. Galen. de Alim. Fac.

o What Strabo says of Mausolus, Pliny attributes to Alexander; it seems probable that
the former is the true version.
It is strange that the French
translators of Strabo should
have Minos, instead of Mausolus, without any notice of this
departure from the usual reading.

p. 517. Hesych. v. Κέραμος. Eustath. in Il. E. 387
Hierocl. p. 687[p].) Bargasa was another town on the
gulf, probably more to the east: it is noticed by
Strabo, (XIV. p. 656. Ptol. p. 119.) and Steph. Byz.

Bargasa. (v. Βάργασα.) According to Apollonius, the Carian
annalist, it derived its name from Bargasus, the son
of Barge and Hercules[q]. The ruins of this town are
to be seen a little above the port of *Giva*, at the
eastern extremity of the gulf of *Boudroun*. We
now enter upon the description of a remarkable
peninsula, situate between the Ceramicus Sinus
and the Dorian bay, now gulf of *Symi*. This was

Doris, sive the celebrated tract of country sometimes called Do-
Triopium. ris, (Plin. V. 28.) at other times termed the Carian
Chersonnese: (Pausan. Attic. c. 1.) by Herodotus
it is denominated Triopium. (I. 174.) The extreme
point towards the west, in the direction of Cos, was

Triopium thence called the Triopian promontory, Τριόπιον ἀκρω-
promonto- τήριον, (Scyl. p. 38.) now cape *Krio*. Near this head-
rium. land, a Lacedæmonian colony, headed by Triopas,

Cnidus. had founded the celebrated city of Cnidus, (Herod.
I. 174. Paus. Phoc. c. 11. Diod. Sic. V. 61.) the
metropolis of the Asiatic Dorians. We have seen,
from Herodotus, that this confederacy, consisting
originally of six cities, had been reduced to five by
the exclusion of Halicarnassus: these were Cnidus,
Cos, and the three Rhodian towns, Lindus, Ialyssus,
and Camirus. Like the Ionian states, they held their
assemblies in a temple erected on the Triopian pro-

---

[p] Sestini adduces a silver me-
dal, with the legend ΚΕΡΑΜΙΗ-
ΠΟΛΙΤΩΝ, which he assigns to
Ceramus; others in brass have
ΚΕΡ. ΚΕΡΑΜΙ. and one of An-
toninus, ΚΕΡΑΜΙΗΤΩΝ.

[q] There are extant coins of
Bargasa, with the epigraph ΒΑΡ-
ΓΑΣΗΝΩΝ. The imperial series
extends from Nero to M. Aurelius. Sestini, p. 87.

montory, and consecrated to Apollo, in whose honour games were also celebrated; these games were called ἀγὼν τοῦ Τριοπίου Ἀπόλλωνος, (Herod. I. 144.) or ἀγὼν Δώριος. (Aristid. ap. Schol. Theocr. Idyll. XVII. 69.) The whole Triopian peninsula belonged to the Cnidians, and when they were threatened with an invasion by the Persian army, commanded by Harpagus, Herodotus relates that they had formed the project of separating it from the mainland, by cutting through the isthmus which connected it with the continent. This neck of land was not broader than five stadia, but it was very rocky, and the workmen suffered so much more than usual from the operation of cutting through the stone, particularly as to their eyes, that it was deemed necessary to consult the oracle on the reason of the impediment. The Pythian priestess answered,

> Ἰσθμὸν δὲ μὴ πυργοῦτε, μηδ' ὀρύσσετε,
> Ζεὺς γὰρ κ' ἔθηκε νῆσον, εἴ κ' ἐβούλετο.

The Cnidians, in consequence of this advice, desisted from their enterprise, and surrendered to the Persian general. (Herod. I. 174.) We have further incidental mention of this city in the same historian. (II. 178. III. 138. IV. 164.) After the battle of Mycale, Cnidus, with the rest of Doris, became tributary to the Athenians; (Thuc. II. 9.) but the inhabitants revolted to the Lacedæmonians when the war against Athens was transferred to the coast of Ionia and Caria; nevertheless the Athenians seized upon the Triopian promontory, and captured the few ships they found stationed there, and very nearly took the city by a *coup de main*. (Thuc. VIII. 35. 43.)

Some years after these events, Conon, the Athenian

admiral, at the head of a Persian and Grecian fleet, gained a signal victory over the Peloponnesian fleet, commanded by Pisander. (Xen. Hell. IV. 3. 6. Pausan. Attic. c. 1.)   This event deprived Lacedæmon of the empire of the sea, and raised Athens from its state of weakness and dependence. (Diod. Sic. XIV. 84.)   At a later period Cnidus appears in history as the ally of Rhodes and friend of Rome; (Liv. XXXVII. 16.) and the defender of Calynda against the Caunians. (Polyb. XXXI. 17.)   Plundered by pirates, (Cic. Manil. c. 12.) it was favoured and patronised by Julius Cæsar, who had a great friendship for Theopompus, one of its principal citizens. (Plut. Cæs. Strab. XIV. p. 656.)   It is termed a free city by Pliny, (V. 28.) and described by Pausanias as a large and handsome town.   Like Mitylene, Cnidus was divided into two parts by a euripus, over which a bridge was thrown; one half being situated towards the Triopian promontory, the other towards the east. (Eliac. I. c. 24. Arcad. c. 30.) Among other remarkable works of art to be seen in this city, the famous statue of Venus, by Praxiteles, was more particularly an object of admiration. (Cic. in Verr. IV. 12.)   Pliny says, " Sed ante omnia, et " non solum Praxitelis, verum et in toto orbe terra- " rum, Venus, quam ut viderent multi navigaverunt " Cnidum."   He adds that Nicomedes, king of Bithynia, wished to purchase this admirable work, and actually offered to liquidate the debt of Cnidus, which was very considerable, if the citizens would cede it to him : but they refused to part with what they esteemed the glory of their city.   There were besides several other works by the most eminent sculptors, such as Scopas and Bryaxis, but they were scarcely noticed in the presence of such a ri-val. (XXXVI. 4. VII. 39.) Venus was the deity principally worshipped by the Cnidians; and she had three temples erected to her, under the several surnames of Doritis, Acræa, and Euplœa: it was in the latter that the statue of Praxiteles was conspi-cuous. (Pausan. Attic. c. 1.)

> . . . .   quæ Cnidon
> Fulgentesque tenet Cycladas, et Paphon
> Junctis visit oloribus.   Hor. Od. III. 28.

> Nunc o cæruleo creata ponto
> Quæ sanctum Idalium, Syrosque apertos,
> Quæque Ancona, Cnidumque arundinosam
> Colis.   Catull. Carm. XXXVI. 11.

The Cnidians, according to the same authority, made various offerings to the temple of Delphi. An equestrian statue of their founder Triopas; and a group of Apollo and Diana piercing Tityus with their shafts. (Phoc. c. 11.)

Besides these, they presented the magnificent paint-ings in the Lesche, by Polygnotus, which are so much dwelt upon and elaborately described by Pau-sanias. (Phoc. c. 25—32.) At Olympia the Cnidians had erected a statue of Pelops, and another of the river Alpheus. (Eliac. I. c. 24.) Strabo states that Cnidus possessed two harbours, one of which was destined for galleys, and a roadstead for thirty tri-remes. An island of seven stadia in circuit, and rising in the form of an amphitheatre, added to their security. This was connected with the mainland by a mole, and formed no-inconsiderable part of the town. This agrees with what Pausanias says of the euripus, which divided Cnidus into two parts,

and had a bridge over it. (Eliac. I. c. 24.) The territory of Cnidus produced wine, corn, oil, and various
vegetables noticed by Athenæus (I. p. 33. II. p. 66.
II. p. 59.) and Pliny. (XIII. 35. XV. 7. XXIII. 45.
XIX. 32.)   Its reeds were particularly esteemed for
writing; (XVI. 64.) whence the epithet of " arun-
" dinosa," applied to the city by Catullus. (Cf. Auson.
Ep. IV.)   Cnidus gave birth to the historian Ctesias, Eudoxus, a celebrated mathematician and disciple of Plato, and Agatharcides, a peripatetic philosopher and historian. (Strab. loc. cit.)   We have
evidence of the existence of this city as late as the
seventh and 'eighth centuries [r] from Hierocles, (p.
687.) the Notices, and Acts of Councils.   According
to Captain Beaufort, " Cape *Krio*," the ancient Triopian promontory, " is a high peninsula, united to
" the mainland by a sandy isthmus.   On each side
" of the isthmus there is an artificial harbour; the
" smallest has a narrow entrance between high
" piers, and was evidently the closed basin for tri-
" remes, which Strabo mentions.   The southern and
" largest port is formed by two transverse moles;
" these noble works were carried into the sea to the
" depth of nearly a hundred feet; one of them is
" almost perfect; the other, which is more exposed
" to the southwest swell, can only be seen under
" water.   Few places bear more incontestable proofs
" of former magnificence than Cnidus; the whole
" area of the city is one promiscuous mass of ruins;
" among which may be traced streets and gateways,
" porticoes and theatres [s]."   Colonel Leake observes,

[r] The coins of Cnidus are not
later than the reign of Caracalla.   The legend is KNI and
KNIΔIΩN. Sestini, p. 88.

[s] Karamania, (p. 81,) where
an enlarged sketch of the harbour of Cnidus is given.

there is hardly any ruined Greek city in existence which contains examples of Greek architecture in so many different branches. There are still to be seen remains of the city walls, of two closed ports, of several temples of stone, of artificial terraces for the public and private buildings, of three theatres, one of which is 400 feet in diameter, and of a great number of sepulchral monuments [t].

Herodotus, speaking of the work undertaken by the Cnidians to separate their territory from the mainland, says, that that part of it which is turned towards the sea is called Triopium, but that it commences from the Bybassian peninsula. It was there-fore in this part that they attempted to cut a canal. Modern maps mark a great contraction in the neck of the Cnidian Chersonesus at a place called *Litho-tronda,* which has perhaps some reference to the cut in the rock. Bybassus, which gave its name to the peninsula, must have been in the same site, or nearly so. Pliny says, " regio Bubassus," (V.28.) and Steph. Byz. (Βύβασσος) says Ephorus called it Bybastus P. Mela speaks only of the Bubassian bay which enclosed the town of Acanthus. (I. 16.) Pliny says it was also called Doulopolis, without accounting for the origin of the name. (V. 28.) Stephanus Byz. enumerates several places so denominated, under the head of Δούλων πόλις, without noticing the one of which we are now speaking ; but he refers to Acanthus, which he places in the peninsula of Cnidus. (v. Ἄκανθος.)

Bybassia cherson-nesus.

Acanthus, sive Doulo-polis.

If Mela is to be depended upon, there were three subordinate bays in what Pliny calls Doridis Sinus : these were, the Bubassius, Thymnias, and Schœnus.

Schœnus Sinus.
Thymnias Sinus.

---

[t] Asia Minor, p. 226, note.

(I. 16.)　But Pliny reckons only the two last; and this agrees better with modern hydrography, which defines only two notable indentures, or arms, in the gulf of *Symi;* one towards the north, which I take to be Schœnus; the other, advancing in an easterly direction, would then be Thymnias: the promon-

Aphrodisi-
as promon-
torium.
Hyda.

tory which divided them was called Aphrodisias. (Mel. I. 16. Plin. V. 28.)　The town of Hyda was seated within Schœnus.　Our information respect-ing these places is very defective[u], as well as the following, which Pliny puts together without much arrangement.　In the Dorian bay, he says, Leu-

Leucopolis.
Hamaxi-
tus.
Elæus.
Euthene.
Pitaium.
Eutane.

copolis, Hamaxitus, Elæus, Euthene.　Then follow the towns of Caria, Pitaium, Eutane, Halicarnassus. Elæus is perhaps the island of Elæussa near Lo-ryma; but Euthene and Eutane can hardly be two different towns.　Mela places Euthane, as he writes the name, between Cnidus and the Ceramic gulf, in a bay. (I. 16. Cf. Steph. Byz. vv. Εὐθη-ναὶ, Πιτάον.)　The promontory, which terminates the southern shore of the Dorian gulf, is called

Cynosse-
ma, sive
Onugna-
thos pro-
montori-
um.

Cynossema by Strabo, (XIV. p. 655.) now cape *Aloupo,* or *Volpe.*　It is opposite to the island of *Symi,* the ancient Syme, and only four miles distant from it.　Cynossema is probably the same headland which Ptolemy calls Onugnathos. (p. 119.)　From this point commences the tract of country which

Peræa re-
gio.

belonged to the Rhodians, and was named Peræa from its being over against their island.　It is men-tioned under this name of ἡ Ῥοδίων χώρα, by Scylax. (p. 38.)　Philip, king of Macedon, having seized upon it, was called upon to restore it to the Rho-

---

[u] Captain Beaufort regrets that he could not explore the gulf of *Symi* and the Cnidian peninsula, p. 82, 83.

dians by the Romans. (Polyb. XVII. 2, 3. Liv.
XXXII. 33.) The Rhodians, however, were obliged
to recover this territory by force of arms. (XXXIII.
18. Cf. Polyb. XVII. 6. 6. XXXI. 25.) Close to
cape Cynossema was Loryma, a small town with a Loryma.
port, (Strab. XIV. p. 652, 655.) distant from Rhodes
somewhat more than twenty miles. (Liv. XLV. 10.
Cf. XXXVII. 17. Plin. V. 28. Ptol. p. 119. Steph.
Byz. v. Λώρυμα.) Constantinus Porphyrogenetes.
(Them. I.) says it was situated in a bay named
Œdimus. To modern navigators it is known as Œdimus
Porto Cavaliere, or *Aplotheka*. Strabo reports that sinus.
a high ridge of mountains runs along this part of the
Carian coast, from cape Cynossema to the Caunian
territory.

The name of this mountain was Phœnix, and a Phœnix
fortress, likewise so called, was placed on the summit. mons et castellum.
(XIV. p. 652. Ptol. p. 119.) I am not acquainted
with the modern name of mount Phœnix. The for-
tress was opposite to the little island of Elæussa, no- Elæussa
ticed previously; it was eight stadia in circuit, and insula.
only four from the land. In modern charts it bears
the name *Barbanicolo*. Pliny and Mela notice, besides, some smaller havens with Loryma. Mela
speaks of Gelos and Tisanusa; (I. 16.) Pliny, Tisa- Gelos por-
nusa only; both mention Larymna. Paridion, or tus. Tisanusa.
Panydon of the latter, is called Pandion by the former, Larymna. Paridion.
and described as a headland advancing into the sea:
it is probably cape *Marmorice*. The Stadiasmus, or
maritime survey of the southern coast of Asia Minor, places, after the island of Elæusa, Phalarus, at Phalarus.
a distance of fifty stadia; then Posidium, at the same Posidium.
distance: this was doubtless a cape; and probably
the Paridion and Pandion of Pliny and Mela are

only corruptions of the same word. At the head of
the beautiful bay of *Marmorice* stood the little town

Physcus portus.

and port of Physcus, noted by Artemidorus and
Strabo as the harbour, or emporium, by which Ephesus communicated with Rhodes. Its distance from
the latter city by land was 1520 stadia. (XIV. p.
663.)   Here was a grove sacred to Latona. (XIV.
p. 652.) Ptolemy calls it Physca. (p. 119. Cf. Steph.
Byz. v. Φύσκος.)   The latter geographer seems to
place one Physcus in Caria, another in the isle of
Rhodes; but they are the same, only Physcus belonged to the Rhodian Peræa.   It is surprising that
Strabo should speak so little of the port of Physcus, which is so well known to modern navigators
as one of the finest in the world for vessels of the
largest size [x], under the name of *Marmorice*. Part
of this noble bay is still called *Physco*.   The site of

Cressa portus.

Physcus itself is occupied by *Castro Marmora*.
Pliny does not speak of Physcus, but mentions the
port Cressa, known also to Ptolemy.   The Stadiasmus omits both Cressa and Physcus, probably as

Samus.

being situated high up the bay, but marks Samus at
a distance of sixty stadia from cape Posidium; then

Rhodussa insula.

the island Rhopusa, which is the Rhodussa of Pliny.
(V. 31.)   It is marked in modern charts under the
name of *Limosa*, or *Karagash*.   It is situated at
the entrance of the great bay or bason of *Karagash*, which I take to be the Cressa of Pliny and
Ptolemy.   Beyond, we find the mouth of a considerable river coming from the northern part of Caria;

Calbis fluvius.

this is the ancient Calbis, which Strabo describes as
navigable near its entrance into the sea, (XIV. p.

---

[x] Lord Nelson's fleet anchored here in 1801, just before the
battle of the Nile.

651.) This river finds a place also in the geographical systems of Mela, (I. 16.) Pliny, (V. 28.) and Ptolemy. (p. 119.) The modern name is *Couindji,* which is that of a small town also, seated at its mouth. This may answer either to the Pisilis, or Pisilis. Pilisis, of Strabo, (XIV. p. 651.) or the Pyrnus Pyrnus. of Pliny (V. 28.) and Steph. Byz., (v. Πύρνος) both situate between the Calbis and Caunus. The latter Caunus. city was of great antiquity, and is frequently mentioned in the page of history. It appears from Herodotus to have been the capital of a people, whom he looked upon as differing from the Carians in some important particulars, and possessing more of the character of an indigenous nation. " The Cau- " nians," says the historian, " are, in my estimation, " autochthonous, but they themselves affirm that " they come from Crete. And either they have " adopted the Carian language, or the Carians the " Caunian; for this I am not able positively to de- " termine. But they use customs differing widely " from those of other nations, as well as the Ca- " rians : for they esteem it most seemly to unite to- " gether in their banquets societies of different ages " and sexes, both men and women, and boys; and " when they had erected temples to foreign gods, " they afterwards changed their mind, and deter- " mined only to worship the deities of their coun- " try. The whole male population, therefore, from " the age of puberty, taking up arms, and striking " the air with their spears, advanced as far as the " borders of the Calyndians, pretending that they " were expelling the foreign gods." (I. 172.) The Caunians did not, like the Carians, tamely submit to Cyrus, but surrendered only to superior force. (I.

176.) They also joined in the Ionian revolt. (V.
103.) The name of Caunus occurs often in the last
book of Thucydides as a port conveniently situated
with regard to Phœnicia, Crete, and Rhodes; and it
is stated that Tissaphernes drew up a treaty while
there with the Peloponnesian confederates. (VIII.
39. 42. 57. Cf. I. 116.) The Caunians at a later
period became subject to Rhodes; but this arrangement seems to have given them little satisfaction,
for they are stated to have afterwards thrown off
their domination. The Romans, however, to whose
arbitration they had committed their cause, decided
against them. (Strab. XIV. p. 652. Liv. XLV. 25.
Cf. XXXIII. 20.) It appears, from a fragment of
Polybius, that the Rhodians had acquired Caunus by
purchase from Ptolemy. (XXXI. 7. 6. Cf. XXX.
5. 9. 19.) Appian relates that the Caunians displayed a peculiar degree of animosity against the
Romans in the massacre ordered by Mithridates.
(Mith. c. 23. Dio Chrys. p. 349.) This city, though
possessing the advantages of a good harbour and a
very fertile territory, was nevertheless reckoned particularly unhealthy during the heat of summer; the
abundance of fruit was also prejudicial to the health
of its inhabitants. The musician Stratonicus, as
Strabo reports, observing the pale and sallow com-
plexion of the Caunians, humourously applied to
them this quotation from Homer: (Il. Z. 146.)

$$\text{Οἴη περ φύλλων γενεὴ, τοιήδε καὶ ἀνδρῶν·}$$

On their complaining of this piece of ridicule, he re-
plied still more sarcastically, " How could I presume
" to stigmatize as unhealthy a town where even the
" dead walk?" (Strab. XIV. p. 651. Cf. Mel. I. 16.
Steph. Byz. v. Καῦνος. Dio Chrysost. Or. XXXII.

p. 390.) Under the Byzantine emperors Caunus formed part of Lycia. (Hierocl. p. 685.) See also the Acts of Councils and the Notitiæ [x]. Diodorus Siculus speaks of two citadels or fortresses, belonging to Caunus, named Heracleum and Persicum. (XX. p. 766.) Strabo mentions the fort Imbrus, on Imbrus. a height above the town. (loc. cit.) The site of Caunus is now occupied by a small town and seaport named *Kaiguez*, or *Kheugez*, about four miles to the south of the entrance of the Calbis into the sea. Mr. Hamilton, who writes the name *Coujek*, says it is situate at the head of a lake, communicating with the sea, and having a considerable fishery [y]. Beyond Caunus the Maritime Itinerary reckons thirty stadia from that town to Pasada, a Pasada. station unknown to other geographers; thence to Cymaria sixty stadia, and from the latter to the Cymaria. haven of the Caunians fifty stadia [z]. This port an- Panormus Caunio-swers to the bay and roadstead of *Kaiguez*. This rum. bay receives, at its north-western extremity, a considerable stream, which takes its modern name from *Kaiguez*, but anciently was known by that of Indus. Pliny says it rises in the mountains of Indus the Cibyratæ, and receives sixty perennial rivers, fluvius. and more than a hundred torrents. (V. 28.) Livy also, in his narrative of the expedition of Manlius against the Gauls, places the Indus near the district of Cibyra, and adds that the name was derived from an Indian who had been thrown into it from an elephant. (XXXVIII. 14.) The river which Pliny

[x] Geogr. Sacr. p. 248. In one of the Notices it is called Acaleia.

[y] Rennell's Geogr. of Asia Minor, tom. II. p. 47.

[z] In the printed copy it is Κουνίων Πάνορμον, but it should evidently be Καυνίων.

Axon fluvius.

calls Axon must fall into the Indus from the east, and the Lycian mountains. Near their junction we

Calynda.

must look for the site of Calynda, a town bordering on the Caunian territory, as we know from Herodotus, (I. 172.) and once subject to them. Polybius, in one of his fragments, states that the Calyndians, having revolted from Caunus, first had recourse to the Cnidians for aid, and afterwards placed themselves under the protection of the Rhodians. (Polyb. XXXI. 17.) Strabo says Calynda was sixty stadia from the coast, where was a grove sacred to Latona. (XIV. p. 651.) It must not be confounded with Calynda, a Carian island under Artemisia. (Herod. VII. 99.) Calynda sent some ships to Salamis, and one of them was sunk by Artemisia during the engagement. (VIII. 87. Plin. V. 28. Steph. Byz. v.

Calyndici montes.

Κάλυνδα.) Ptolemy assigns it to Lycia [a]. The Calyndian mountains, which formed the boundary on the side of Caunus, are probably on the right bank of the Indus. Continuing our course along the

Crya, sive Cryassus.

coast we have to notice Crya, with the singular addition in Pliny of " fugitivorum." (V. 28.) Steph. Byz. assigns it to Lycia, (v. Κρύα) which is the arrangement also of Ptolemy, in whose text it is corrupted to Carya. (p. 119.) It is probable that Cryassus, spoken of by Plutarch, (de Virt. Mul. p. 246. Cf. Polyæn. Strat. VIII. c. 64.) is the same as Crya. Artemidorus, quoted by Steph. Byz., assigned to Crya some islands, among which he men-

Carysis insula.
Alina insula.

tions by name Carysis and Alina. Pliny reckons three, but does not name them. (V. 35.)

---

[a] Sestini assigns to Calynda a very scarce coin, with the legend ΚΑΛΛΙΝΔΕΩΝ. Caput Jovis laur. R.—Aquila alis explicatis fulmini insistens, p. 87.

These islands, which are situate in the gulf of *Macri*, or *Scopea*, guide us to the position occupied by the town of Crya; and we have an additional clue in the little village and port of *Cari*, which has an evident analogy to the ancient name. The port or station of Clydæ is placed, in the Stadias-Clydæ. mus, to the west of Crya. Ptolemy names it Lydæ, or Chydæ. But the Stadiasmus gives us, besides, some other intermediate points between the Panormus of the Caunians and Crya. From the former to Ancon on the Glaucus[b] 120 stadia. This Ancon Ancon. must be the headland which forms the bend of the Glaucian bay, now gulf of *Macri*. Strabo calls the western extremity of this gulf cape Artemisium. It Artemi-appears to have derived this name from a temple of sium pro-monto-Diana erected on the height. (XIV. p. 651.) It is rium. the cape *Bokomadhi* of modern geography. Then follows the headland Pedalium, distant eighty sta-Pedalium dia: this answers probably to cape *Contouri*. From promonto-thence to Clydæ thirty stadia. To Cochlia the dis-Cochlia. tance is omitted; but from that station to Crya we have fifty stadia. From Crya to Callimache sixty Callima-stadia: thence to Dædala fifty. The latter place, che. according to Strabo, was the extreme point of Pe-ræa to the east. (XIV. p. 651.) It is also noticed by Pliny, (V. 28.) Ptolemy, (p. 119.) and Steph. Byz. The two latter assign it to Lycia. The historian Alexander, in his account of Lycia, says it was called after Dædalus, who, being stung by a snake on crossing the river Ninus, died, and was Ninus fl. buried there. (Steph. Byz. v. Δαίδαλα.) This river seems to be the little stream which falls into the centre of the gulf of *Macri*, and divides the *Sand-*

[b] Not on the river Glaucus, but the gulf of the same name.

jack of Mentesha from that of *Tekieh*; and it is very probable that in ancient geography it was the boundary of Caria and Lycia. Dædala was also the name of a mountain on the confines of the latter province. (Strab. XIV. p. 664.) Pliny assigns two small islands off the coast to the Dædalenses. (V. 31.)

Glaucus sinus. Strabo says the gulf Glaucus has some good harbours; and the names of these have been given in detail from the maritime Stadiasmus. Our knowledge of the gulf of *Macri*, which answers to it in modern geography, is chiefly derived from the French hydrographers, as captain Beaufort did not take it in his Caramanian survey. Stephanus men-

Ænus. tions a place called Ænus in the Rhodian Peræa. (v. Αἶνος.)

Having thus completed our circumnavigation of the Carian coast, we must now enter upon the examination of the several towns and sites referred to by ancient authorities in the interior of the province. Commencing from the neighbourhood of Miletus, we have to point out, south of that city, and beyond the

Chalceto-res, sive Chalceto-rium. chain of mount Grius, the towns of Chalcetor and Euromus. (Strab. XIV. p. 635, 658.) The former is an obscure place, noticed only by Strabo, unless we ought to identify it with Chalcetorium, which Steph. Byz. assigns to Crete, and on this supposition improperly. (v. Χαλκητόριον.) Strabo, in the first passage cited above, calls the place Χαλκήτορες, which is in accordance with the authority of Craterus, a

Euromus, quæ et Eu-ropus. writer quoted by Stephanus. Euromus was a town of greater consequence, being founded by Idrieus, son of Car, and having borne formerly the names of Idrias and Chrysaoris. According to some writers, the latter appellation was once applied to the

whole of Caria. (Steph. Byz. vv. Εὔρωμος, Ἰδριὰς, Χρυσαορίς.) Apollonius, in his Carian history, affirmed that this town was of Lycian origin. (Steph. Byz. v. Χρυσαορίς.) Pliny calls it Eurome. (V. 29.) I agree with Berkelius in the opinion that Euromus and Europus are the same town. (Steph. Byz. v. Εὐρωπός.) Herodotus says that Mys, a Carian sent by Mardonius to consult the oracle of Apollo Ismenius, was of Europus. (VIII. 133. Pausan. Bœot. c. 23.) The gentile name is, according to these writers, Εὐρωπεὺς, like Εὐρωμεὺς; and not Εὐρώπιος, as Stephanus and the Etymol. M. have it. (v. Εὔρωπος.) Euromus, as we learn from Polybius, included some other towns within its territory; but these were afterwards taken by the neighbouring city of Mylasa. (XXX. 5. Cf. Liv. XLV. 25.) Philip, king of Macedon, had held Euromus for a short time. (Polyb. XVII. 2. XVIII. 27. Liv. XXXII. 33. XXXIII. 30.) The towns belonging to Euromus were probably Tauropolis, Plarassa, and Chrysaoris, mention- Tauropolis.
ed by Apollonius in his history of Caria; (ap. Steph. Plarassa.
Byz. v. Χρυσαορίς. Cf. eund. vv. Ταυρόπολις, Πλάρασσα.) but Strabo refers Chrysaorium to Stratonicea. Euromus may be placed not far from the head of the gulf of Iasus, or Bargylia, where some ruins were observed by Chandler and Choiseul Gouffier[c]. Amy- Amyzon.
zon, a small place noticed by Strabo, seems to have been in the same vicinity. (XIV. p. 658.) It is also found to occur in Ptolemy (p. 119.) and Hierocles. (p. 688.) The Councils prove that it was latterly an episcopal see.

---

[c] Euromus has both autonomous and imperial coins, with the legend ΕΥΡΩΜΕΩΝ; and in a medal of Caracalla, ΖΕΤΣ ΕΥΡΩΜΕΥΣ. Sestini, p. 88.

Mylasa, which next follows, was one of the most considerable towns of Caria. It had been the residence of the Carian dynasts before Halicarnassus had fallen under their power; (Strab. XIV. p. 659.) and its antiquity is further evinced by the circumstance of its possessing a temple sacred to Jupiter Carius, to which the Lydians and Mysians likewise were admitted, in consequence of their consanguinity with the Carian nation. (Herod. I. 171. Strab. loc. cit.) Mylasa, as Strabo reports, was situate in a fertile plain, and at the foot of a mountain containing veins of a beautiful white marble. This was of great advantage to the city, for the construction of public and other buildings; and the inhabitants were not slow in availing themselves of it; few cities, as Strabo remarks, being so sumptuously embellished with handsome porticos and stately temples. (XIV. p. 659.) Athenæus relates, that Stratonicus, the witty musician, on coming to Mylasa, and observing there many temples, but few inhabitants, placed himself in the middle of the forum, and cried out, " Hear, oh ye temples." (VIII. p. 348.) Mylasa, however, was inconveniently situated in one respect, being built in a hollow at the foot of a precipice; whence a governor of the province, on coming there, was heard to remark, that the founder of the town ought at least to have been ashamed of his blunder, if not frightened. (Strab. loc. cit.) Philip of Macedon, son of Demetrius, had in vain endeavoured to obtain possession of Mylasa; and it was probably to reward their zeal that the Romans declared the citizens free, after the defeat of Antiochus. (Polyb. XVI. 24. XXII. 27. Liv. XXXVIII. 39.) In a petty war with their neighbours the Euromians, they were victorious, and occupied some of their towns; but in turn they were forced to yield to the Rhodians. (Polyb. XXX. 5. Liv. XLV. 25.) In the time of Strabo Mylasa could boast of two distinguished characters, Euthydemus and Hybreas, both eminent orators, and having great influence over their countrymen. The former was of an illustrious and wealthy family, but Hybreas owed his birth to obscure parents, who left him little or no provision. Having shewn some disposition for the law, he studied under Diotrephes of Antiochia, and acquired some reputation in his own city: this increased considerably after the death of Euthydemus, who naturally eclipsed him by his wealth and station. Hybreas then became the leading character at Mylasa, and acquired great fame as an orator and politician; he incurred, however, the enmity of Labienus, the Roman partisan, and vainly endeavouring to urge his countrymen to resist his pretensions, was forced to fly to Rhodes. Labienus, at the head of his troops, seized Mylasa, but finding his adversary had escaped, plundered and destroyed his mansion, which was magnificently furnished, and caused great damage to the rest of the town. On his quitting Asia, Hybreas returned to his country. (XIV. p. 660.) The same geographer states that Physcus was the port of the Mylasians; (p. 659.) but Pausanias affirms that they had a haven, distant eighty stadia from the city; (Arcad. c. 10.) and Steph. Byz. says it was called Passala. (v. Πάσσαλα.) Passala. Mylasa is further noticed by Dio Cass. (XLVIII. p. 373. Plin. V. 29. Ptol. p. 119. Steph. Byz. v. Μύλασα.) It is generally agreed that the site of this ancient city is occupied by *Melasso*, where con-

siderable remains were observed by Pococke[d] and
Chandler[e]. " Our first enquiry," says the latter,
" was for the temple erected about twelve years be-
" fore the Christian era by the people of Mylasa to
" Augustus Cæsar and the goddess Rome, which
" was standing not many years ago. We were
" shewn the basement which remains, and were in-
" formed the ruin had been demolished, and a new
" mosque, which we saw on the mountain side, above
" the town, raised with the marble." Chandler also
quotes an inscription on a pillar erected in honour
of a descendant of Euthydemus, mentioned above:
" Beneath the hill on the east side of the town is
" an arch or gateway of marble, of the Corinthian
" order; also a broad marble pavement, with ves-
" tiges of a theatre: and round the town ranges of
" broken columns, the remnants of porticoes. A large
" portion of the plain is covered with scattered frag-
" ments, besides inscriptions mostly ruined and ille-
" gible. Some altars dedicated to Hecatomnus have
" been discovered[f]."

Labranda. Labranda was a small town, dependent on Mylasa, and distant from it about sixty stadia; it was
especially celebrated for two temples sacred to Jupiter Labrandenus, or Labradeus, and Stratius: the
former title was supposed to be derived from the word
" Labrys," which, in the Carian tongue, signified a
hatchet, and the statue of the god was said to bear
this utensil. (Plut. Quæst. Gr. tom. VII. p. 204.
Reisk.) Others derive the name from Labrandus,

[d] Tom. II. p. ii. c. 6.
[e] Asia Minor, p. 234.
[f] The name of Hybreas appears on the medals of Mylasa,
which offer a series from Augustus to Valerian, with the epigraph, ΜΥΛΑΣΕΩΝ. Sestini, p.
88, 89.

one of the Curetes. (Etym. M. p. 389. Lactant. Fals. Rel. I.) But the temple of Jupiter Stratius was held in great veneration by the Mylasians and the neighbouring people. A paved road, called the sacred way, led to it from Mylasa, reserved for processions and religious ceremonies. The priests were selected from the first families in that city, and their office was for life. The same god was worshipped at Mylasa, under the title of Jupiter Osogo, (Strab. XIV. p. 659.) or Ogoa. (Pausan. Arcad. c. 10.) Herodotus reports that the Carians, after sustaining a defeat from the Persian forces in their revolt from Darius, retired to Labranda, where was a large temple sacred to Jupiter Stratius, and a grove of plane trees. (V. 119.) Chandler was of opinion that the ruins he observed near *Mendelet* were those of Labranda, as the distance and situation agreed with Strabo's account. The chief ruin was that of a Corinthian temple with sixteen columns, and part of the entablature standing. A town has ranged with the temple on the north; the wall beginning near it, makes a circuit on the hill, and descends on the side towards *Mendelet*: it had square towers at intervals, and was of a similar construction with the wall at Ephesus; within it is a theatre cut in the rock, with some seats remaining[g]. Messrs. Choiseul[h] and Barbier du Bocage[i] were inclined, however, to think these ruins were those of Euromus, and they placed Labranda beyond *Mendelet*.

Stratonicea, to the south-east of Mylasa, was also a city of some extent and importance: it appears to

Stratoni-
cea.

---

[g] Asia Minor, p. 245.
[h] Voyage Pittoresque de la Grèce, c. 11.

[i] Notes sur le Voyage de Chandler, tom. II. p. 248.

have been founded by Antiochus Soter, in honour of his queen Stratonice, and the Macedonian kings had adorned it subsequently with sumptuous edifices. (Strab. XIV. p. 660. Steph. Byz. v. Στρατονικεία.) It was ceded to the Rhodians by Seleucus and Antiochus. (XXXI. 7. 6. Liv. XXXIII. 30.) Mithridates, during his residence at Stratonicea, became enamoured of Monima, a young lady, daughter of one of the principal citizens, and married her. (Appian. Mithr. c. 20.) Some years after, it was besieged by Labienus, and the obstinate and successful resistance it then made, entitled it to the thanks of Augustus and the senate. (Tacit. Ann. III. 62. Dio Cass. XLVIII. p. 379.) Hadrian is also said to have taken this city under his protection, and to have called it Hadrianopolis, a name which, however, never appears in use. (Steph. Byz.) Pliny styles it a free city. (V. 29.) Near the town was a celebrated
Chrysao-rium. temple of Jupiter Chrysaorius, and there was a political union of certain Carian towns, which held their meetings here, under the name of Chrysaorium. The states had votes in proportion to the number of towns they possessed. The Stratoniceans, though not of Carian origin, were admitted into the union from their holding certain places, which formed part of it. We must refer to this head what has been already said under the article Euromus. (Strab. XIV. p. 660. Tacit. Ann. III. 62.) Menippus, surnamed Catochas, one of the most distinguished orators of his day in the opinion of Cicero, (Brut. c. 91.) was a native of Stratonicea. (Strab. loc. cit.) " *Eski-* " *hissar,* once Stratonicea," says Chandler, " is a " small village, the houses scattered among woody " hills environed by huge mountains; the site is

" strewed with marble fragments: some shafts of
" columns are standing single. In the side of a hill
" is a theatre, with the seats remaining, and ruins
" of the proscenium or front, among which are pe-
" destals of statues; one inscribed, and recording a
" citizen of great merit and magnificence. Without
" the village, on the opposite side, are broken arches,
" with pieces of massive wall, and marble coffins[k]."

Lagina was a small town dependent on Strato- Lagina.
nicea, where was a temple sacred to Hecate, or Tri-
via, which attracted every year, at a certain time, a
great concourse of people. (Strab. XIV. p. 660. Tacit. Ann. III. 62.) Lagina, according to Artemidorus, was 850 stadia from Physcus; but this distance
is certainly much exaggerated, for *Lakena*, which
evidently corresponds with the ancient site, is by
the map somewhat less than forty miles from *Marmorice*, or Physcus. The whole of the distances
between the latter place and Ephesus are very corrupt in Strabo. Tendeba and Astragon were two Tendeba.
fortresses in the territory of Stratonicea. (Livy, Astragon.
XXXIII. 18. Steph. Byz. v. Τένδηβα.)

Alabanda was 250 stadia to the north of Lagina. Alabanda.
It was situated, as the same geographer reports, at
the foot of two hills, so placed that the town re-
sembled in some sort an ass with a pack-saddle.
Hence Apollonius Malacus, the orator, alluding also
to the number of scorpions with which it was infested, called it in jest " the ass laden with scor-

[k] Asia Minor, p. 240. For several inscriptions belonging to this town, see the notes to Brotier's Tacitus, (Ann. III. 62.) and the Oxford Marbles. (Inscr. Ant. p. 28—30.) On the coins of Stratonicea we find the surname of Indica, as INΔEI, or INΔI. ΣTPATONEI, or ΣTPATONIKEΩN. Sestini, p. 90.

" pions." Mylasa, and the whole chain of mouñ-
tains which intervened, abounded with these noxious
reptiles. The inhabitants of Alabanda were devoted to pleasure, and the number of singing women
was very great. (XIV. p. 660.) Alabanda was also
famous for its quarries of a dark coloured marble,
approaching to purple. (Plin. XXXVI. 8.) The
town was said to derive its name from the hero Ala-
bandus, (Steph. Byz. v. 'Αλάβανδα. Cf. Cic. de Nat.
Deor. III. 19.) or from its having been founded
after an equestrian victory. *Ala*, in the Carian language, signifying " a horse," and *Banda*, " victory."
There was also a proverb, which implied that Alabanda was the most fortunate of the Carian cities.
(Steph. Byz.) Aridolis, tyrant of Alabanda, was
taken, with his ship, by the Greeks before the battle
of Artemisium: (Herod. VII. 195.) elsewhere the
same writer calls Alabanda a town of Phrygia.
(VIII. 136.) The Alabandians and Mylasians waged
war with the Rhodians, but were conquered. (Liv.
XLV. 25. Polyb. XXX. 5.) They erected a temple
to the goddess Rome, and celebrated games in her
honour. (XLIII. 6.) Their city sustained great loss
during the irruption of the Parthians under Labienus. (Dio Cass. XLVIII. p. 425.) Pliny says, Alabanda was the seat of a conventus juridicus. (V.
29.) Juvenal mentions it rather contemptuously.
(Sat. III. 70. Cf. Cic. Ep. Fam. XIII. 56. 64. Ptol.
p. 119. Hierocl. p. 688.) Most antiquaries fix the
site of Alabanda at *Carpuseli*, a village, according
to Chandler, twelve hours north of Mylasa. There
are several ancient remains described by Pococke
and the above named traveller. They are partly in
a plain, and partly on the slope of a mountain.

" They consist of a ruined stadium, part of the city
" wall, and above the plain a terrace wall with a
" square area, and vestiges of a colonnade. Beyond
" these, in the rock, is a theatre, with remnants of the
" front, &c. I was here again disappointed in find-
" ing no inscription to inform us of the ancient name
" of the place, but suppose it to have been Ala-
" banda [1]." Col. Leake, however, has given reasons
for thinking that Alabanda is rather represented by
Arabi-hissar, where Pococke observed the remains
of a considerable town on a site which agrees very
well with Strabo's account; and I am of opinion
that they are satisfactory [m]. The ruins of *Carpuseli*
may belong in that case to Trapezopolis, situated
apparently not far from the Meander. (Plin. V. 29.
Ptol. p. 119.[n]) Orthosia and Coscinia were two
other towns of Caria in the vicinity of Alabanda,
and on the left bank of the Meander. (Strab. XIV.
p. 650.) In going from Coscinia to Alabanda the
traveller crossed the same river several times. (XIII.
p. 587.) This river is probably that of *Tshina*, or
China, mentioned by Pococke and other travellers,
and which Mons. Barbier du Bocage judiciously supposes to be the Carian Marsyas of Herodotus. (V. Marsyas fl.
118.) The historian describes it as flowing from
the district of Idrias, and falling into the Meander.
Idrias was one of the names of Euromus, but it probably included the whole of the Chrysaorian tract,
and consequently Lagina and Stratonicea. It is from

[1] Chandler's Travels in Asia Minor, p. 231.

[m] Asia Minor, p. 233. There are numerous coins of Alabanda with the legend ΑΛΑ. ΑΛΑΒΑ, and ΑΛΑΒΑΝΔΕΩΝ. The em-

perors extend from Augustus to Maximus. Sestini, p. 86.

[n] There are coins of Trapezopolis, ΔΗΜΟC ΤΡΑΠΕΖΟΠΟ-ΛΕΙΤΩΝ. Sest. p. 90.

this direction that modern maps represent the river *China* as flowing. Coscinia, or Coscinus, as Pliny calls it, is probably to be identified with *China*, where Pococke observed some remains indicative of an ancient site [o].

Orthosia is mentioned by Livy, (XLV. 25.) Polybius, (XXX. 5.) Ptolemy, (p. 119.) and Hierocles. (p. 688.) It is also known by the Acts of Councils, which prove its episcopal rank [p], and by its coins [q]. D'Anville places this town at *Ortaki*, without however naming his authority for the existence of such a site, or any ruins marking its coincidence with the previously inhabited locality. In Pliny, for the word Halydienses, I would substitute Alindienses; they are the people of Alinda, a Carian town of some note and strength, held by Ada, queen of Caria, at the time that Alexander undertook the siege of Halicarnassus. (Arrian. Exp. Alex. I. 23. Strab. XIV. p. 657. Ptol. p. 119. Steph. Byz. v. Ἄλινα.) This site has been identified by many antiquaries with *Moglah*, the principal town of modern Caria, but on what authority is not apparent. Another traveller, from the similarity of name, places it at *Aleina*, between *Moglah* and *Tshina* [r]. Advancing along the Meander we have to point out Hieracome, noticed by Livy in his account of the expedition of Manlius. (XXXVIII. 13.) Here was a celebrated temple and oracle of Apollo. Answers were

Coscinia.

Orthosia.

Alinda.

Hieracome.

[o] Travels, vol. II. p. ii. c. 9. Leake's Asia Minor, p. 234.

[p] Geogr. Sacr. p. 245.

[q] Sestini, p. 89. Autonomi. Epigraphe, ΟΡΘΩΣΙΕΩΝ. Imperatorii ab Augusto ad Maximinum.

[r] Rennell's Geogr. of Western Asia, tom. II. p. 53. There are coins of this town, with the epigraph ΑΛΙΝΔΕΩΝ, from Augustus to Faustina. Sestini, p. 86.

delivered in verse. One day's march from thence
led to the river Harpasus. (Liv. loc. cit.) The town
of Harpasa was situated on its banks, as we learn Harpasa.
from Pliny. (V. 39. Cf. Steph. Byz. v. Ἄρπασα.
Ptol. p. 119. Hierocl. 688.) The Notices assign to
it the rank of an episcopal see. Pococke's researches
enable us to fix this site at *Harpaz-Calessi* near
the junction of the Meander with a river now called
Harpas, which is clearly the Harpasus. Continuing along the left bank of the Meander towards its
source, we presently reach the site of Antioch, dis-Antiochia
tinguished from other celebrated cities of that name drum.
by a reference to the river on which it was seated.
(Liv. XXXVIII. 13.) Pliny says it stood near the
junction of the Meander and Orsinus. (V. 29.) The
latter is now called *Gongere*. The same author reports that Antiochia was founded on the sites of
two older towns named Seminethus, or Simmethus,
and Cranaus. Stephanus Byz. states it was founded
by Antiochus, son of Seleucus, in honour of his
mother; it had been previously called Pythopolis.
(v. Ἀντιοχεία.) Its territory extended on both banks
of the river, over which a bridge was built. It
abounded in fruit of every kind, but especially in
the fig, called " triphylla." The town was of no
great extent, and was much subject to earthquakes.
It was the birthplace of Diotrephes, a celebrated
sophist, the instructor of Hybreas. (Strab. XIII. p.
630.) Antiochia of Caria is further mentioned by
Ptolemy (p. 119. Sozomen. Hist. Eccl. VII. 2.
Phlegon. Mirab. c. 6. Hierocles, p. 688.) and the
Notitiæ. It is generally admitted that this ancient
site corresponds with *Jeni-sher*, between the Meander and a small stream named *Gengere*. Here is

an old castle upon a hill, with arched caves or vaults
at the foot; and beyond, thick walls, built with
small stones, and a few fragments of columns[s]. Gor-
diutichos was one day's march from Antioch, as we
learn from Livy in his account of the expedition of
Manlius. (XXXVIII. 13.)   Steph. Byz. says it was
founded by Gordius, son of Midas; it must, in that
case, have once belonged to Phrygia. (v. Γορδίου τεῖχος.)   The site of this obscure town was probably
not far from *Geyra*, which represents the ancient

Aphrodisias; the latter was a considerable place,
and in the time of Hierocles the metropolis of Caria. (p. 688.)   Stephanus states that it was founded
by the Pelasgi Leleges, and was successively called
city of the Leleges, Megalopolis, Ninoe, and Aphrodisias. (vv. Νινόη, Μεγαλόπολις, Ἀφροδισίας.) In Strabo's
time it appears to have belonged to Phrygia. (XII.
p. 576.)   Pliny, however, assigns it to Caria, and
styles it a free city. (V. 29. Cf. Tacit. Ann. III.
62.[t])   The discovery of the site of Aphrodisias at
Geyra, about two hours from Antiochia on the Meander, is to be ascribed to Pococke[u].   It was subsequently visited by Picenini and Dr. Sherard, who
copied there several inscriptions, leaving no doubt
as to the identity of the site with Aphrodisias.
Drawings of the remains of antiquity have been since

[s] Picenini's route in Chandler's Travels in Asia Minor, p.
269. and Pococke, tom. II. p.
ii. c. 11.   The medals of Antiochia are very copious from
the reign of Augustus to Salonina. ΔΗΜΟC, or ΣΤΝΚΛΗΤΟC
ΑΝΤΙΟΧΕΩΝ. Sestini, p. 86.

[t] In Brotier's notes to this
passage will be found an interesting monument relating to

Aphrodisias. It is a decree from
the Roman senate, confirming
the privileges granted to that
town by Julius Cæsar, and the
triumviri who followed him. It
was first published by Chishull
in the Antiq. Asiat. p. 152, but
is emended by Brotier.

[u] Pococke, vol. II. p. ii. c.
12.

made by order of the Dilettanti Society [x]. From
the existing coins of the city, it appears to have
been situated on the Corsymus, or Corsynus river,
which is doubtless the Orsinus, and another named
Timeles. They also prove an alliance between
Aphrodisias and Plarasa, in confirmation of the mo- Plarasa.
nument cited above with reference to a passage in
Tacitus [y]. Plarasa, from that monument, appears
also to have worshipped Venus. It is mentioned
by Stephanus Byz. as a town of Caria. (v. Πλάρασα.)
There are also separate medals of this place [z].

South of Aphrodisias was Tabæ, which Strabo Tabæ.
includes, together with that city, within the limits of
Phrygia, while some writers give it to Lydia, and
others again to Caria. Steph. Byz. makes two different cities of the same name; one in Lydia, the
other in Caria; but it is highly probable that they
are one and the same. It was said to have been
founded by the hero Tabus. Others however derived the name from the word " Taba," which, in
the Carian language, signified a " rock :" it being
built on a height. Strabo informs us, that Tabæ Tabenus
was situated in an extensive plain, to which it com- campus.
municated its name, and which was inhabited by a
mixed population of Phrygians, Pisidians, and other
nations; meaning, probably, the Cibyratæ and Cabalees, of whom we shall have occasion to speak in
the next section. (Strab. XIII. p. 629. XII. p. 576.)
Livy, in his narrative of the operations of Manlius,

---

[x] Chandler's Travels in Asia
Minor, p. 270. Leake's Asia
Minor, p. 250.

[y] Epigraphe, ΔΗΜΟC ΑΦΡΟ-
ΔΙCΙΕΩΝ. Fluvii, vel fontes sa-
cri, ΚΟΡCΥΜΟC, vel ΚΟΡCΥΝΟC-
ΤΙΜΕΛΗC. Concordia cum Pla-
rasa ΠΛΑΡΑΣΩΝ ΚΑΙ ΑΦΡΟΔΙ-
ΣΙΕΩΝ. Sestini, p. 87.

[z] Sestini, p. 89.

states that he marched in three days from Gordiu-
tichos to Tabæ. (XVIII. 13.)   It was a considerable place ; and having provoked the hostility of the
Romans, was compelled to pay twenty talents of silver and 10,000 medimni of wheat. This proves that
it was in a good corn country. The historian remarks that it stood on the borders of Pisidia, towards the shore of the Pamphylian sea.   D'Anville
is no doubt correct in assigning to this ancient site
the position of *Thaous*, or *Davas*, a place of some
note north-east of *Moglah*, and seated on a river
which is a branch of the Calbis.   Col. Leake is inclined to look for Tabæ to the east of Apamea and
Celænæ; but I imagine he takes Strabo's statement
of Tabæ being in Phrygia in too literal a sense[a].
Hierocles enumerates it among the Carian towns[b].
(p. 689.) So do the Notitiæ.   A modern French
traveller says *Davas* is a large and well built town,
the capital of a considerable district. The governor's
residence stands on a height overlooking the town.
The view from thence over the surrounding plain
is most magnificent[c]. Three days' march from Tabæ

Chaus fl. brought the Roman army to the Chaus, which is
probably a branch of the Indus, or *Keughes* river ;

Eriza. beyond it was the town of Eriza, which the Roman
army took at the first onset. (XXXVIII. 14.) Ptolemy places the Erizeli on the borders of Phrygia
and Caria ; and there is little doubt that they are
the people of Eriza ; but we must alter this name
to Erizeni, which is the ethnic of Eriza[d].   This

[a] Asia Minor, p. 153.
[b] Geogr. Sacr. p. 245. There
are autonomous and imperial
coins of Tabæ, with the inscription TABHNΩN.

[c] Itineraire d'une partie de
l'Asie Mineure, Paris, 1816,
8vo. p. 432.
[d] This is apparent from a
very scarce medal of this town

town is the Erezus of Hierocles. (p. 689.) The Acts of Councils, which prove it to have been of episcopal rank, more correctly write the name Eriza[e]. It must have stood not far from the modern town of *Bazarkhan.* Mr. Corancez, the traveller quoted above, says it is situated in a marshy plain at the foot of a chain of mountains which branch from mount Cadmus. He observed several marble sarcophagi, which must have been brought there from Eriza[f]. In Lapie's map the ruins of Eriza are marked a little to the north-east of *Bazarkhan,* and on the left bank of its river, which must be the Caus. Thabusion was a fortress on a height above Thabusion. the river Indus, and apparently the last place of Caria towards the petty state of Cibyra. (Liv. XXXVIII. 14.) Mr. Corancez, coming from Cibyra, observed on the road to *Bazarkhan* a remarkable rock overhanging the valley, near which were several fragments of antiquity: this may have been the site of Thabusion[g].

We have now gone over all the principal places in Caria, whose sites can be determined with any degree of probability and precision; the rest are obscure, and of uncertain position. Pliny names Thy- Thydonos. donos, which is unknown to other writers; he connects it with Pyrrha, Eurome, Heraclea, and Amyzon; so that it must have stood near the western coast between Miletus and Halicarnassus. He assigns to the Forum Alabandicum, Hynidos, Ceramus, Trœzene, Phorontis; of which Ceramus only

described by Sestini. Eriza. Autonomi, epigraphe, EPI.EPIZH-NON. Mentio situs ab amne Cao. KAOC. p. 88.

[e] Geogr. Sacr. p. 245.
[f] Itineraire d'une partie de l'Asie Mineure, p. 429.
[g] Itineraire, &c. p. 427.

comes under the cognizance of history: the others probably were dependent upon it; since we know from Strabo that the Ceramietæ had several votes in the Chrysaorian assembly, from the number of their boroughs. Perhaps also Phorontis is only a distinguishing epithet attached to Trœzene, that it might not be confounded with the mother city in Argolis.

At a greater distance from Alabanda he places the Orthronienses, who must exist upon his sole authority; and the Halydienses, whom the better reading, Alidienses, has enabled us to restore to Alinda; but when he adds, "seu Hippini," I suspect that here also the text requires correction; and looking to the numismatic geography of Caria, I find a town named Euippe, the inhabitants of which are the Euippini, whose name has been corrupted by the transcribers of the Latin geographer [h]. (Cf. Steph. Byz. v. Εὐίππη.) The Xystiani are to be referred to Xystis, assigned to Caria by Steph. Byz. (v. Ξύστις.) The Hydissenses are the people of Hydissa, (Ptol. p. 119.) or Hydissus. (Steph. Byz. v. Ὑδισσός.) Apollonia, surnamed ad Lambanum, according to Ptolemy, will be the city of the Apolloniatæ, mentioned by Pliny; but whether Lambanus is a river, or a mountain, is uncertain. Wesseling, in his notes to Hierocles, who recognises Apollonia in Caria [i], would read Albacus for Lambanus. The reason of this alteration rests on the circumstance that there is another Carian town, called Heraclea, with the surname of Albace, or Salbace; the reader may, if he pleases, con-

Euippe.

Xystis.

Apollonia ad Lambanum.

Heraclea Albace, sive Salbace.

[h] Sestini, p. 88. Euippe. Imperatorii Lucillæ, Domnæ ΕΥΙΠΠΕΩΝ.

[i] There are several coins of the Carian Apollonia, but the epigraph gives the bare name ΑΠΟΛΛΩΝΙΑΤΩΝ. Sestini, p. 87.

sult Wesseling's observations on the subject, and his authorities.

Trallicon had been seated on the Harpasus, but it no longer existed when Pliny wrote. Ptolemy's catalogue contains the unknown towns of Bitoana, Bardissus, Idymus, Thera, and Pystus. (p. 119.) But the Byzantine lexicographer furnishes more names in Caria than any other province, and hence I am inclined to suspect that many a place had more than one appellation. *Trallicon.* *Bitoana.* *Bardissus.* *Idymus.* *Thera,* *Pystus.*

Aba, given on the authority of Herodian. (v. Ἄβαι.) Abacænum, according to the same grammarian. (v. Ἀβακαῖνον.) Agoresus, founded by some Argive colonists. (v. Ἀγορησός.) Athenæ, the third in the list. (v. Ἀθῆναι [k].) Alexandria, near Latmus, where was a temple of Adonis, with a Venus by Praxiteles. (v. Ἀλεξάνδρεια.) Amos, noticed by Alexander in his Carian history, (v. Ἄμος,) and Argila. (v. Ἄργιλα.) Bæbæ. (v. Βαῖβαι.) Bolbæ, a town, and Bolbæotes, a river: this place was also called Heraclea, but which of the two noticed in this section does not appear. Dedmasa, (v. Δέδμασα,) probably the same which Pliny called Medmasa. Delia, (v. Δηλία.) Dia, near Miletus, (v. Δία.) Didymonteichos. (v. Δίδυμον τεῖχος.) Dyndasum, which appears from the passage cited out of the Carica of Alexander, to have been near Calynda. (v. Δύνδασον.) Eunæ, and the river Eunæus. (v. Εὐναί.) Euonymia, (v. Εὐωνυμία.) Edyme, probably the same as the Idymus of Ptolemy. (v. Ἡδύμη.) Thembrimus. (v. Θέμβριμος.) Berkelius thinks it may be Thymbria near Myus. Themissus. (v. Θεμισσός.) Thera, (v. Θήρα,) which we *Aba.* *Abacænum.* *Agoresus.* *Athenæ.* *Alexandria ad Latmum.* *Amos.* *Argila.* *Bæbæ.* *Bolbæ.* *Bolbæotes fluvius.* *Dedmasa.* *Delia.* *Dia.* *Dyndasum.* *Eunæ.* *Eunæus fl.* *Euonymia.* *Edyme.* *Thembrimus.* *Themissus.* *Thera.*

[k] Can this be a false reading for Euthene?

Idyma.
have already noticed from Ptolemy. Idyma, and the river Idymus; (v. Ἴδυμα) see Edyme. Hie-

Hieramæ.
Hippone-
sus.
Callipolis.
ramæ. (v. Ἱεραμαί.) Hipponesus, a town noticed by Hecatæus, in his work on Asia. (v. Ἱππόνησος.) Callipolis. (v. Καλλίπολις.) I observe a place, called *Gallipoli* in modern maps, on the southern shore of the

Candasa.
gulf of *Boudroun*. Candasa, a fortress mentioned in the seventeenth book of Polybius. (v. Κάνδασα.)

Caropolis.
Caropolis, on the authority of Alexander in his his-

Cedreæ.
tory of Caria. (v. Καρόπολις.) Cedreæ, on that of

Curopolis.
Hecatæus on Asia. (v. Κεδρέαι) Curopolis, on that of Apollonius, the historian of Caria. (v. Κουρόπολις.)

Crade.
Cyarda.
Cybassus.
Cylandrus.
Cyon.
Crade, named by Hecatæus. (v. Κράδη.) Cyarda. (v. Κύαρδα.) Cybassus. (v. Κυβασσὸς.) Cylandus, mentioned by Hecatæus. (v. Κύλανδος.) Cyon, before called Canebium, according to Apollonius. (v. Κύον[1].)

Cyrbasa.
Labara.
Laea.
Cyrbasa. (v. Κύρβασα.) Labara, mentioned by Alexander. (v. Λάβαρα.) Laea, by Hecatæus. (v. Λαεία.)

Masano-
rada.
Melia.
Messaba.
Monogissa.
Masanorada. (v. Μασανώραδα.) Melia, cited in the Genealogies of Hecatæus. (v. Μελία.) Messaba, in the Asia of the same author. (v. Μέσσαβα.) Monogissa, whence Diana was surnamed Monogissene, and founded by Dædalus. It is added, that Megissa, in the Carian language, signified a stone. (v. Μινόγισσα.)

Mumastus.
Mumastus, noticed by Alexander. (v. Μούμαστος.)

Mygisi.
Narcasus.
Naxia.
Mygisi, by Hecatæus. (v. Μύγισοι.) Narcasus, (v. Νάρκασος.) Naxia, mentioned by Alexander. (v.

Xylus.
Œcus.
Pedicis.
Pigelasus.
Piginda.
Pisye.
Plamus.
Plistar-
chia.
Ναξία.) Xylus, by Hecatæus. (v. Ξύλος.) Œcus. (v. Οἴκους.) Pedieis. (v. Πεδιεῖς.) Pigelasus. (v. Πειγέλασος.) Piginda. (v. Πίγινδα.) Pisye, or Pitye. (v. Πισύη.) Plamus. (v. Πλάμος.) Plistarchia is given to

[1] Cyon has a place in numismatic geography. Autonomi, ΚΥ. ΚΥΙ. ΚΥΙΤΩΝ. Imperatorius Juliæ Domnæ tantum. Sestini, p. 88.

a town called also Heraclea, but we have seen that there were two Heracleas in Caria. Polyara. (v. Polyara. Πολύαρα.) Prinassus (v. Πρινασσός) is mentioned by Polybius. It was besieged by Philip, king of Macedon, and taken. (XVI. 11.) It is also known from its coins [m]. Pyrinthus. (v. Πύρινθος.) Samylia, founded by one Motylus. (v. Σαμυλία.) Sindessus. (v. Σινδησσός.) Sciritis: the explanation of this word is ἡ δωδεκάπολις τῆς Καρίας, which itself requires a commentary. Syrna, founded by Podalirius. (v. Σύρνα.) Sobala. (v. Σώβαλα.) Telandrus, a town, and Telandria, a promontory. The authority, Alexander Polyhistor. (v. Τήλανδρος.) Tnyssus, Hecatæus on Asia. (v. Τνύσσος.) Tripolis, afterwards called Neapolis. (v. Τρίπολις.) Tymnessus is doubtless the same as Tymnus, though Steph. Byz. makes them two different towns. It is probably the same with the Thymnia of Mela, near the Ceramicus Sinus. (vv. Τυμνισσός, Τύμνος.) Hygassus, and the Hygasseian plain. (v. Ὕγασσος.) Hyllarima, a small town above Stratonicea, of which Hierocles the philosopher was a native. (v. Ὑλλαρίμα.) Hyllyala, a spot where Hyllus is said to have perished, and a temple was erected to Apollo. (v. Ὑλλούαλα.) Cholontichos, on the authority of Apollonius. (v. Χωλὸν τεῖχος.)

To complete this section, it will be necessary to take a view of the different islands off the coast of Caria, some of which, especially Rhodes and Cos, are celebrated and important.

Leros, which yet retains its name, belongs to the Sporades: it is situated in the Icarian sea to the south of Lipsia, and nearly facing the gulf of Jasus.

[m] The epigraph is ΠΡΕΝΑ. or ΠΡΕΝΑΣ. Sestini, p. 89.

The Milesians had colonized it, and on the breaking out of the Ionian revolt, Hecatæus the historian advised the confederates to erect a fortress there, and make it their strong hold and centre of operations, if they should be driven from Miletus. (Herod. V. 125. Strab. XIV. p. 635. Plin. V. 31.) The epigram of Phocylides on the inhabitants of this island is well known:

Καὶ τόδε Φωκυλίδεω. Λέριοι κακοί· οὐχ ὁ μὲν, ὃς δ᾽ οὔ·
Πάντες, πλὴν Προκλέους· καὶ Προκλέης Λέριος.

(Strab. XIV. p. 488.) We learn from Athenæus that there was a temple in Lerus sacred to Diana, where birds, called Meleagrides, supposed to be guinea-fowls, or turkeys, were kept. (XIV. p. 655.)

Calymna insula. Calymna, separated by a narrow channel from Leros, is named by Scylax (p. 38.) and Ovid, who praises its honey. (Metam. VIII. 222.)

Dextra Lebynthos erat, fœcundaque melle Calymne.

Calydnæ insulæ. It is probable that Calymne, together with the adjacent islands, which are numerous, formed the group which Homer calls Calydnæ. (νήσους τε Καλύδνας. Il. B. 676.) We know also, from Herodotus, that the Calydnians were subject to Artemisia, queen of Caria. (VII. 99. Strab. X. p. 488. Steph. Byz. vv. Κάλυδνα, Κάλυμνα. Suid. et Etym. M. v. Κάλυμνος.) Calymna in modern charts is called *Calimno*, and the surrounding group towards Cos and the Carian shore, *Kapperi* and *Carabaghlar*. Pliny assigns three towns to Calydna, Notium, Nisyrus, and Men-

Cos insula. deterus. (V. 36.) Cos, which next follows, is an island of considerable celebrity, which, in ancient times, bore the several names of Merope, Cea, and Nymphæa. (Plin. V. 31.) Thucydides in one place uses the surname of Meropis. (VIII. 41. Cf. Pausan. El. II. 14.) Pliny states that it was fifteen miles from Halicarnassus, and 100 in circumference; but Strabo gives only 550 stadia for its circuit, which is only between sixty and seventy miles, and this is more correct. (Strab. XIV. p. 657.) We are not informed by whom this island was first inhabited, nor when it received a Grecian colony. This event, however, must have been prior to the siege of Troy, since Homer represents it as sending its warriors there.

Καὶ Κῶν, Εὐρυπύλοιο πόλιν, νήσους τε Καλύδνας.

Il. B. 677.

Τὸν σὺ ξὺν Βορέῃ ἀνέμῳ πεπιθοῦσα θυέλλας
Πέμψας ἐπ' ἀτρύγετον πόντον, κακὰ μητιόωσα,
Καί μιν ἔπειτα Κόων δ' εὐναιομένην ἀπένεικας.

Il. O. 26.

At this period it appears to have been held by some descendants of Hercules, who, as Strabo imagines, were Æolians, or Thessalians. Subsequently, however, it was occupied by a party of Dorians from Megara, united with an Argive colony, which, headed by Althæmenes, had settled in Crete, Rhodes, and Halicarnassus. (Strab. XIV. p. 653.) Hence it is always reckoned of Dorian origin, and obtained a place in the Triopian Pentapolis. (Herod. I. 144.) The Coans, as Herodotus further acquaints us, were under the government of hereditary princes, and he instances, as a noble act of justice, the resignation of his authority by Cadmus, sovereign of the island, who afterwards retired to Sicily, and was high in the favour of king Gelon. (VII. 164.) After the Persian war Cos became tributary to Athens, and continued so to the end of the Peloponnesian war,

as may be seen from the attack made upon it by
Alcibiades with a Spartan fleet. (Thuc. VIII. 41.)
At a later period we find the Coans joining the
Rhodians and Byzantines in the defence of their
liberty and commerce, against the overbearing pretensions of the Athenians, and compelling them to
recognise their independence.   In general they followed the side which the Rhodians espoused, and
we therefore find them united with that state against
Antiochus in favour of the Romans. (Liv. XXXVII.
16.)   Some individuals, however, were known to
lean towards Perseus, king of Macedon. (Polyb.
XXX. 7. Cf. XVI. 15.)

Cos civitas.
The city of Cos was anciently named Astypalæa,
and had formerly been seated on the coast towards
the Icarian sea, but it was afterwards removed from
thence, on account of a civil war, to the promontory
Scandarium, opposite to cape Termerium in Caria,
and received its name from the island.   We learn
from Thucydides that when Alcibiades landed there
with a Spartan force he found it unfortified, and
easily captured it, many of the inhabitants having
deserted it on account of a disastrous earthquake
which had shaken it to its foundations. (VIII. 41.)
Strabo remarks that the city was not large, but very
populous, and seen to great advantage by those who
came there by sea.   Without the walls was a celebrated temple of Æsculapius, enriched with many
admirable works of art, and, among others, two famous paintings of Apelles, the Antígonus and Venus
Anadyomene.   The latter painting was so much admired that Augustus removed it to Rome, and consecrated it to Julius Cæsar; and in consideration of
the loss thus inflicted on the Coans, he is said to

have remitted a tribute of 100 talents which had been laid on them. Besides the great painter above mentioned, Cos could boast of ranking among her sons the first physician of antiquity, Hippocrates. This illustrious individual, who claimed descent from Æsculapius himself, was said to have derived the greater part of his aphorisms from the cases recorded in the public documents, or archives of the temple of that god. Strabo mentions besides, among other distinguished natives of this island, Simus, another physician, Philetas, a poet and grammarian, Nicias, tyrant of Cos, and Ariston, a peripatetic. (XIV. p. 657.) Athenæus quotes a history of Cos by a writer named Macareus. (VI. p. 262.) The town of Cos was again nearly destroyed by an earthquake in the reign of Antoninus, and Pausanias records the liberality of that emperor in restoring it to its former condition. (Arcad. c. 43.) The soil of the island was very productive, especially in wine, which vied with those of Lesbos and Chios. (Strab. loc. cit. Athen. I. 32.) It was also celebrated for its purple dye and embroidered work.

> Illa gerat vestes tenues, quas fœmina Coa
> Texuit, auratas disposuitque vias.
> > TIBULL. VI. 35.

> Et tenues Coa veste movere sinus.
> > PROPERT. I. 2.

> Nec Coæ referunt jam tibi purpuræ,
> Nec clari lapides tempora.
> > HOR. OD. IV. 13.

Cos was celebrated for the beauty of its youths. (Athen. I. p. 15.) The scene of one of Theocritus'

Bucolics is laid in this island, (Idyll. VII.) and the Scholiast (v. 5.) states that the poet had sojourned there for some time. If this grammarian is correct, Aleus, which is mentioned in the same Idyl, was a demus of Cos, and Burina a fountain. (v. 6.)

Βούρινναν ὃς ἐκ ποδὸς ἄνυε κράναν,

mentioned also by the Coan poet Philetas. (ap. Schol. ibid.)

Νάσσατο δ᾽ ἐν προχοῇσι μελαμπέτροιο Βυρίνης.

Oromedon is said to have been a mountain in the same island. (v. 46.) Pyxas, a spot sacred to Apollo. (v. 130.)

Laceter promontorium.

Halisarna.

Drecanum promontorium.

Stomalimne.

Nisyros insula.

Towards the south was a promontory named Laceter, facing the isle of Nisyrus, and distant from it about sixty stadia. Halisarna was a fortress, seated near the cape. Another headland, situated towards the west, bore the name of Drecanum. It was 200 stadia from the city of Cos; Laceta, 235. I am not acquainted with the modern names of these points. A harbour called Stomalimne, near Drecanum, is probably *Stafodino*. (Strab. XIV. p. 657.)

Nisyros, which appears in the catalogue of Homer, together with Cos, Carpathus, and other Sporades, (Il. B. 676.)

Οἱ δ᾽ ἄρα Νίσυρόν τ᾽ εἶχον, Κράπαθόν τε, Κάσον τε,
Καὶ Κῶν, Εὐρυπύλοιο πόλιν, νήσους τε Καλύδνας,

is now called *Nisari*, and is about eight miles to the south-west of cape *Crio*. It was pretended that it had been torn from Cos by Neptune, that he might cast it against the giant Polybotes. (Strab. X. p. 488. Apollod. I. 6. 2. Pausan. Att. 2. Steph. Byz. v. Νίσυρος.) We learn from Herodotus that

Nisyros was under the dominion of Artemisia, queen of Caria. (VII. 99.) According to Strabo it was high and rocky, having a town of the same name, a port and temple of Neptune, and some warm baths. (X. p. 488.) There was also another town, named Argos. (Steph. Byz. v. Νίσυρος.)

Telos is to the south-east of Nisyros, and directly south of Cnidos. Strabo is not correct in describing it as a long and narrow island, since it is rather of a circular form. He assigns 140 stadia for the circuit, which is not far from the truth. (X. p. 488.) Herodotus acquaints us, that the family of Gelon, tyrant of Sicily, came originally into that island from Telos. (VII. 153.) Pliny says Telos was noted for a particular ointment. (XIII. 2.) The modern name is *Tilo*, or *Piscopi*. ^{Telos insula.}

At the entrance of the Doridis Sinus is the isle of *Symi*, from which that gulf derives its modern name. The ancients called it Syme; and Homer has conferred some celebrity upon it, as the country of the handsome Nireus. (Il. B. 671.) ^{Syme insula.}

> Νιρεὺς δ' αὖ Σύμηθεν ἄγεν τρεῖς νῆας ἐΐσας,
> Νιρεὺς, Ἀγλαΐης θ' υἱὸς Χαρόποιό τ' ἄνακτος,
> Νιρεὺς, ὃς κάλλιστος ἀνὴρ ὑπὸ Ἴλιον ἦλθε
> Τῶν ἄλλων Δαναῶν, μετ' ἀμύμονα Πηλείωνα.

Herodotus and Thucydides speak of it in connection with Cnidus and Rhodes. (Herod. I. 174.) The Lacedæmonian Astyochus gained a victory off this island, over a small Athenian squadron. (Thucyd. VIII. 42.) In Scylax (p. 38.) Vossius has corrected Συησὸς to Σύμη νῆσος. (Plin. V. 31.) Stephanus says it was called first Metapontis and Ægle; he adds, that it contained a town of the same name. (v. Σύμη.

Cf. Diod. Sic. V. 53. Mnas. ap. Athen. VII. p. 296.) Pliny says it has eight ports.

Dieuchidas, a writer quoted by Athenæus, (VI. p. 262.) speaks of certain islets or rocks, named Arææ, ('Αραιαὶ,) between Cnidus and Syme. Stephanus Byz. calls them 'Αραὶ, and states that they were three in number. *Symi* is surrounded with islets, according to modern charts, but their names are not set down.

Aræ insulæ.

RHODUS INSULA.

Nearly facing Syme and the cape Cynossema, which terminates the ridge of Phœnix, stands, at a distance of not more than eight or ten miles from the latter, the isle of Rhodes, which, from its consequence and celebrity, deserves to hold a separate place in the present section. Rhodes having first borne the names of Ophiussa and Stadia, (Strab. XIV. p. 654.) and others which are to be found in Pliny, (V. 31.) assumed afterwards the appellation of Telchinis, from the Telchines, a people concerning whom many fabulous stories were propagated. Some pretended that they dealt in magical spells, and, being inclined to evil, that they destroyed animals and plants, by sprinkling them with the water of Styx, mingled with sulphur. It was maintained, on the other hand, by more rational and sober writers, that the Telchines were artists, who had made surprising progress, at a very early age, in the working of iron and brass. It was further supposed, that the reports which were spread to their disadvantage arose solely from envy of their superior skill. These people were traced to Crete and Cyprus, from whence they had made their way to

Rhodes. (Diod. Sic. V. 55. Strab. XIV. p. 654.)
According to some writers they were nine in number, and were considered to be the same as the Curetes. (Strab. X. p. 472.)   In fact there seems great
affinity between them and the Idæan and Phrygian
Dactyli and Corybantes. (Cf. Suid. v. Τελχῖνες. Eust.
Il. B. p. 291. Steph. Byz. v. Τελχίς.)   There is
reason to suppose that these people were, in reality,
Phœnicians, who, from their skill and enterprise in
maritime affairs, had formed settlements, first in Cyprus, then in Crete and Rhodes, and other islands.
It was through their means that the barbarous inhabitants of Asia Minor were first made acquainted
with useful arts, which were afterwards imparted
to the Greeks by means of the Pelasgi.   We have
the authority of Ergias, or Erxias, a Rhodian historian cited by Athenæus, for the settlement of the
Phœnicians in the island at a very early period;
and he reports, that they made way for the Greeks
under Iphiclus. (VIII. p. 361. Cf. Conon. ap. Phot.
p. 454.)   But, before we come to this historical period of the annals of Rhodes, it may be right to
speak of the poetical fiction which represented that
island as occupied by the Heliades, or descendants
of the Sun.   Pindar has given a conspicuous place
to this fiction in one of his odes, which is addressed
to the Rhodian Diagoras:

καὶ νυν ἐπ' ἀμφοτέρων
σὺν Διαγόρᾳ κατέβαν, τὰν ποντίαν
ὑμνέων παῖδ' Ἀφροδίτας
ἀελίοιό τε, νύμφαν
Ῥόδον, εὐθυμάχαν
ὄφρα πελώριον ἄνδρα παρ' Ἀλ-
φειῷ στεφανωσάμενον

αἰνέσω πυγμᾶς ἄποινα,
καὶ παρὰ Κασταλίᾳ
πατέρα τε Δαμάγητον ἀδόντα Δίκᾳ
Ἀσίας εὐρυχόρου
Τρίπολιν νᾶσον πέλας
Ἐμβόλῳ ναίοντας Ἀργείᾳ σὺν αἰχμᾷ.

OLYMP. VII. 23—35.

Jove is said to have rained a shower of gold upon the island, when Minerva was born: (v. 61.)

. . . . . . ἔνθα ποτὲ
Βρέχε θεῶν βασιλεὺς ὁ μέγας
χρυσαῖς νιφάδεσσι πόλιν.

The poet then goes on to state how it had risen from the depth of the sea to become the portion of the Sun, who by his union with the nymph Rhodus became the father of the Heliadæ:

Βλάστε μὲν ἐξ ἁλὸς ὑγρᾶς
Νᾶσος· ἔχει τέ μιν ὀ-
ξειᾶν ὁ γενέθλιος ἀκτίνων πατὴρ,
πῦρ πνεόντων ἀρχὸς ἵππων.
ἔνθα Ῥόδῳ ποτὲ μιχθεὶς
τέχεν ἑπτὰ σοφώ-
τατα νοήματ᾽ ἐπὶ προτέρων
ἀνδρῶν παραδεξαμένους
παῖδας· ὧν εἷς μὲν Κάμειρον
πρεσβύτατόν τε Ἰά-
λυσον ἔτεχεν, Λίνδον τ᾽. Ἀπάτερθε δ᾽ ἔχον
Διὰ γαῖαν τρίχα δασ-
σάμενοι, πατρωΐαν
Ἀστέων μοῖραν· κέκληνται δέ σφιν ἕδραι.

Ver. 127—140.

The names of these seven Heliades have been preserved by the Scholiast, and he agrees with Strabo that it was from Cercaphus, the eldest, that the three brothers above named derived their birth. (Strab. XIV. p. 654. Schol. Pind. v. 131.)   After these events, to which it is impossible to assign a date, Rhodes was occupied by a colony of Greeks, or rather Pelasgi, under the command of Tlepolemus, son of Hercules, and perhaps also of Iphiclus, brother of that hero. (Athen. VIII. p. 361.) Pindar, however, names Tlepolemus alone, and says he came from Argolis; (v. 60.) but Strabo imagines that these Heraclidæ set out from Bœotia; and, at all events, he contends that they were not Dorians, but Æolians. Homer, who dwells at some length on the history of Tlepolemus, agrees perfectly with Pindar:

Τληπόλεμος δ' Ἡρακλείδης ἠΰς τε μέγας τε,
Ἐκ 'Ρόδου ἐννέα νῆας ἄγεν 'Ραδίων ἀγερώχων
Οἳ 'Ρόδον ἀμφενέμοντο διάτριχα κοσμηθέντες
Λίνδον, Ἰηλυσσόν τε, καὶ ἀργινόεντα Κάμειρον.

Il. B. 653.

Tlepolemus having unfortunately slain his maternal uncle, Licymnius, was forced to fly from Greece, and arrived in the course of his wanderings at Rhodes: (v. 667.)

Αὐτὰρ ὅγ' ἐς 'Ρόδον ἷξεν ἀλώμενος, ἄλγεα πάσχων·
Τριχθὰ δὲ ᾤκηθεν καταφυλαδὸν, ἠδ' ἐφίληθεν
Ἐκ Διὸς, ὅστε θεοῖσι καὶ ἀνθρώποισιν ἀνάσσει.
Καί σφιν θεσπέσιον πλοῦτον κατέχευε Κρονίων.

The great prosperity and affluence implied in the last line of the passage relates doubtless to the maritime skill and enterprise of the Rhodians, by which they signalized themselves, as Strabo reports, long before the institution of the Olympic games. Not only did they undertake distant voyages for commercial purposes, but they founded colonies in several parts of the Mediterranean. In Sicily they colonized Gela, in common with the Cretans, forty-

five years after the foundation of Syracuse; and 108
years later this city had become so prosperous that
it was enabled to build Agrigentum. (Thuc. VI. 4.)
In Italy the Rhodians are said by Strabo to have
founded Parthenope, but the principal honour of
that establishment is due to the Chalcidians of Eubœa. In Apulia they colonized, together with the
Coans, the town of Salapia, and they also formed
a settlement in the country of the Chones, not far
from Sybaris. In Spain they formed an emporium
at Rhode, now *Rosas*, on the *Catalonian* coast, and
which afterwards came into the possession of the
Massilians. (Strab. XIV. p. 654. Steph. Byz. v.
'Ρόδη.) Notwithstanding this early application to
naval affairs, it does not appear that the Rhodians
were ranked with the leading maritime powers of
Greece, since they neither figure among the confe-
derate states in the Ionian revolt, nor in the Median
war. Herodotus simply mentions them as forming
part of the Dorian confederacy, of which Cos and
Cnidus were the only members besides themselves
after the exclusion of Halicarnassus. (I. 144. II.
178.) Nor is there more frequent mention of their
island in Thucydides; we only collect from his history that they were subject to the Athenians during
the Peloponnesian war, and were reluctantly compelled to serve against the Syracusans and Geloans.
(VII. 57.) The total defeat which the Athenians
sustained in this quarter led however to the eman-
cipation of the Rhodians, which was effected by Astyochus, the Spartan admiral, with great facility.
(VIII. 44.) The Rhodians excelled in the service
of light troops, particularly as darters and slingers.
(Thuc. VI. 43. Xen. Anab. III. 3. 11.) We find,

however, the Rhodian navy rising in strength and
consequence towards the time of Demosthenes. We
hear of them at this period as the principal power
opposed to the Athenians in what is called the Social
war, but afterwards, alarmed at the growing power of
the Carian dynasty, we find them soliciting through
Demosthenes the protection of that people. (Dem. de
Libert. Rhod. p. 190.) It appears from that orator
that Mausolus had contrived to introduce a change
into the constitution of Rhodes which was very favourable to the oligarchical party, and very prejudicial to the democracy. Rhodes furnished Darius,
the last king of Persia, with one of his bravest and
ablest generals in the person of Memnon, and, had
he been intrusted with the sole direction of affairs,
Alexander might have been baffled in his enterprise,
and his unfortunate adversary have remained in
possession of his dominions and his life. The Rhodians, after the death of the Macedonian king, added
to their renown by the memorable siege which they
sustained against Demetrius Poliorcetes, though they
were at length compelled to yield to superior force.
Of this siege we shall speak more at length when
we come to speak of the city of Rhodes, as well as
that which it maintained against Mithridates. Polybius has recorded that such was the esteem and
regard entertained by the sovereigns of Sicily, Asia
Minor, Syria, and Egypt, for the character and in-
stitutions of the Rhodians, that when their island,
and especially their city, had sustained great loss
from a violent earthquake, they vied with each other
in the liberality of the supplies and presents they
sent to assist in repairing the effects of the calamity.
It is surprising, says the historian, how speedily

the state recovered from this blow, and what rapid
progress was thenceforth made both towards affluence and prosperity, by private individuals, as
well as by the commonwealth.   After passing a just
eulogium on the wise and able conduct of the Rhodians in the administration of their affairs, he is led
to form a comparison between the sovereigns of that
period and the age in which he lived, which is little
to the advantage of the latter. (V. 88—90.)   Nor
is Strabo less warm in his praise of their civil insti-
tutions and regulations. Rhodes was distinguished, he
says, for the excellence of its laws, as regarded every
branch of the administration, but more especially of
the navy, which was kept in the most efficient state,
and contributed not a little to the renown and influence it enjoyed among the principal states of the
civilized world at the time of the wars waged by
the Romans against Philip and Antiochus[o].   The
services rendered by the Rhodians to that people
were of the most valuable kind in both these contests, and it is chiefly owing to their exertions that
the naval operations of Livius, the Roman admiral, were so successful, a circumstance which had
a material influence on the final issue of the two
struggles. (Liv. XXXI. 14. 46. XXXII. 16. XXXVI.
45. XXXVII. 9—30.)   In return for these important services the Rhodians received from the Roman senate, after the defeat of Antiochus, a considerable accession to the territory they already possessed on the continent of Asia : it consisted of the
rest of Caria and the whole of Lycia. (Liv. XXXVIII.
39. Polyb. XXII. 7. 7. 27. 8.)   The Lycians, how-

---

[o] Rhodes makes nearly as
great a figure in history at this
period, as Venice does in the
annals of modern Europe.

ever, dissatisfied with this arrangement, refused to
consider the Rhodians as their masters: a war therefore ensued, in which the Lycians, though secretly
assisted by Eumenes, were vanquished. (Polyb.
XXIII. 3. XXV. 5. XXVI. 7. Liv. XLI. 25.) The
Romans, however, here interfered, and declaring that
they had not given Lycia to Rhodes as a subject
country, but as an ally and friend, forbad the latter
power from carrying on hostilities any further. (Polyb. XXVI. 7.) The cause of this change in the disposition of the Roman senate towards their old allies, and which induced them to have recourse to
such a subterfuge in the matter of Lycia, is attributed by Polybius to the offence the Rhodians had
given to that jealous and haughty people in convey-
ing the princess Laodice, espoused to Perseus, king
of Macedon, to the court of that sovereign with great
pomp and display. They were openly accused of
favouring the cause of Perseus, already considered
as the avowed enemy of Rome; and though it certainly appears from Polybius that he had many partisans in the island, it is not reasonable to think that
so prudent a republic would have adopted a line of
policy so contrary to its former conduct, and at the
same time so dangerous. It is true that they undertook the part of mediators between Perseus
and the Romans, and we are told by Livy that the
oration delivered by their ambassador at Rome was
insolent and offensive; (XLIV. 14, 15.) but they
obeyed implicitly the orders of the senate, and furnished the necessary supplies; and they further sent
the most submissive embassies to Rome to deprecate
the anger of that jealous power. The senate for a
long time refused to receive their deputations, and

they were treated with contempt and insult; (Polyb. XXIX. 7. XXX. 4.) a decree was even passed which declared Caria and Lycia independent provinces, and thus deprived the Rhodians of a considerable revenue and power. (XXX. 5. 12. XXXI. 7.) At length, however, when the anger of the Romans had been satisfied by these measures, and by the condemnation of those citizens who had favoured Perseus, the Rhodian embassy was allowed to sue for the honour of being received on the list of the allies of Rome. (Liv. XLV. 10—25. XLVI. 4—13.)

Whatever doubts might have been entertained of their zeal for the Romans in the second Macedonian war, their conduct and courage in defending their city against the repeated attacks of Mithridates, must have secured for them the admiration and esteem of their allies. The king of Pontus, baffled in all his assaults by land and sea, was at length compelled to raise the siege and return to the continent of Asia. (Appian. Mithr. c. 23. Liv. Epit. LXXXVIII. Diod. Sic. Frag.) The conduct of these islanders towards Pompey is less deserving of praise; since, after they had received him with distinguished honours on his return from putting an end to the Mithridatic war, they deserted him in the hour of need, and even forbad his entering their port. (Cic. Ep. Fam. XII. 14. Plut. Pomp.) Their adherence to Cæsar led them to resist, after his death, the arms of Cassius; but that republican general, after defeating them in a naval engagement, entered the town by force, and having caused the principal leaders of the opposite faction to be beheaded, carried off all the public property, and even the offerings and ornaments of the temples. (Appian. Civ. Bell.

IV. 72. Dio Cass.) Tiberius resided for some years at Rhodes before his accession to the throne, in a kind of honourable exile, which Tacitus terms " Rho-" dius secessus." (Ann. I. 4. IV. 15.) Under Vespasian the island lost even the semblance of independence, and was erected into a Roman province. (Suet. Vesp. c. 8. Eutrop. VII. 15. Oros. VII, 9. Cf. Tacit. Ann. XII. 58.) This appears to have been a " Provincia Insularum" from Hierocles, (p. 685, 686.) and Rhodes, standing first on the list, must have been the metropolis of this local government. Rhodes was the last barrier opposed by Christian chivalry to the overwhelming force of the Ottoman power; and when the banners of the cross ceased to float over her ramparts, it must have seemed as if Asia was abandoned to her fate, and consigned to endless servitude and oppression. According to Strabo, the island is 920 stadia in circuit. (XIV. p. 654.) Pliny reckons 125 miles; but Isidorus, as he reports, 103: (V. 28.) it produced wine, and its dried raisins were much esteemed. (Athen. I. p. 31. I. p. 27. XIV. p. 654.) It was also famous for its manufacture of saffron oil. (XV. p. 658. Plin. XXXIV. 11. XXVIII. 17.) The sea, which washed its shores, supplied every kind of fish. (Athen. VIII. p. 360. XIV. p. 647.) No country could boast of having given to the public games of Greece so many successful contenders for the prize. (Pausan. Eliac. II. c. 7.) Other peculiarities relating to the customs, manners, religious rites, and language of the Rhodians, may be extracted from Athenæus.

Rhodus, the capital of the island, was situate at Rhodus ci-
its most northern extremity: it was not so ancient ${}^{\text{vitas.}}$
as the three Dorian cities, Lindus, Ialysus, and

Camirus, having been founded, as Strabo affirms, at the time of the Peloponnesian war. The architect was the same who built the celebrated walls of the Piræus, by name Hippodamus of Miletus. (Strab. XIV. p. 654. Harpocr. v. Ἱπποδάμεια.) It excelled all other cities in the estimation of Strabo for the beauty and convenience of its ports, streets, walls, and public edifices: these were adorned with a profusion of works of art, both in painting and sculpture. Of the former were Ialysus, and a satyr, by Protogenes, respecting which many anecdotes were related. (Plut. Demetr. c. 22. Strab. loc. cit. Plin. XXXV. 10.) The principal statues were in the temple of Bacchus and the gymnasium; but the most extraordinary work was the famous Colossus of the Sun, cast by Chares of Lindus, a pupil of Lysippus: it was seventy cubits, or 105 feet high, and few men could encompass the thumb with their arms; the fingers also were thicker than ordinary statues: it took the artist twelve years to model it, and it cost 300 talents, which sum was chiefly raised from the materials left by Demetrius of Poliorcetes, after the siege. This prodigious statue, which ranked among the seven wonders of the world, stood at the entrance of the port, and it is said that ships would pass between the legs; but it was overthrown by a violent earthquake 506 years after its erection, as Pliny reports, (XXXIV. 18.) or in the second year of the 139th Olympiad, according to Eusebius, but Polybius seems to place it a little later, in the 140th Olympiad. (V. 88.) The same writer adds, that the greater part of the walls and docks were thrown down at the same time. (Cf. Pausan. Corinth. c. 7.) The Colossus was never raised up again, as this had been forbidden by an oracle. (Strab. XIV. p. 652.) Cedrenus affirms that a king of the Saracens sold the fragments to a merchant, who employed upwards of 900 camels to convey them away.

Rhodes was also much admired for the excellence of its legislative system, particularly those regulations which regarded the navy, by means of which it attained to so high a rank among maritime states. Every branch of that service was attended to with the utmost care, whether in the construction of ships and warlike engines, or the depots of arms and stores. The entrance to some of the docks was forbidden under the severest penalty of the law. The legislative enactments respecting the condition of the poorer classes were also very remarkable. The government, though far from being a democracy, had a special regard for the poor. They received an allowance of corn from the public stores; and the rich were taxed for their support. There were likewise certain works and offices which they were called upon by law to undertake, on receiving a certain fixed salary. (Strab. XIV. p. 653ᵖ.) Rhodes produced many distinguished characters in philosophy and literature : among these may be mentioned Panætius, (whom Cicero has so much followed in the Offices,) Stratocles, Andronicus, Eudemus, and Hieronymus. Posidonius the stoic resided for a long time in this island, and gave lectures in rhetoric and philosophy. The poet Pisan-

ᵖ The reader will find some other particulars respecting the Rhodian polity in the work of Meursius. Sestini has the following notice respecting the Rhodian money, p. 91. " Autonomi copiosi. Epigraphe, " PO. POΔION. POΔIΩN. ad- " dito sæpe magistratu, variis- " que in area sigillis. In æneis " TAMIA. Quæstor, vel magis- " tratus sine dignitatis mentio- " ne. Imperatorii a Tiberio us- " que ad Commodum. Cultus " Neptuni Asphalii. ΠΟCΕΙΔΩΝ " ΑCΦΑΛΕΙΟC."

der, author of the Heracleid, as well as Simmias and
Aristides, are likewise found in the list of Rhodian
literati. Dionysius Thrax and the poet Apollonius
obtained the surname of Rhodius from their long
residence there. South of the city of Rhodes, and
Lindus. on the eastern coast of the island, was Lindus, one
of the three Dorian cities, and which contained a
temple of Minerva of the highest antiquity, since it
was reported to have been founded by Danaus.
(Strab. XIV. p. 655. Diod. Sic. V. c. 58.) The statue of the goddess was a shapeless stone. (Callim.
ap. Euseb. Præp. Ev. III. c. 8.)

$$\ldots \ldots \ldots \ldots \; \varkappa \alpha \grave{\iota} \; \gamma \grave{\alpha} \rho \; \text{'} A \theta \acute{\eta} \nu \eta \varsigma$$
$$\text{'} E \nu \; \Lambda \acute{\iota} \nu \delta \varphi \; \Delta \alpha \nu \alpha \grave{o} \varsigma \; \lambda \varepsilon \tilde{\iota} o \nu \; \check{\varepsilon} \theta \eta \varkappa \varepsilon \nu \; \check{\varepsilon} \delta o \varsigma.$$

There was also a temple of Hercules, whose rites
were not celebrated with propitiatory expressions,
but with vituperative and injurious language. (Lactant. Inst. I. 31.) It contained a painting of the god
by Parrhasius. (Athen. XII. p. 543.) There were
several other pictures by the same celebrated master
at Lindus, inscribed with his name. (XV. p. 687.)
This town was also famous for having produced
Cleobulus, one of the seven sages. (Strab. loc. cit.)
Athenæus has preserved a pretty song, sung by the
Lindian boys as they went round collecting money
for the coming of the swallows; this he ascribes to
Cleobulus. (VIII. p. 360.) It was seated on a hill
looking towards Egypt, and was still extant in the
time of Eustathius; (ad Dion. Perieg. v. 505.) even
now it retains the name of *Lindo*. Beyond was a
Ixia. small place named Ixia, according to Strabo. (XIV.
p. 655.) It appears further from Artemidorus, quoted
by Steph. Byz. (v. 'Iξίαι,) that there was also a port
Ixus, and that Apollo derived from thence the epithet

of Ixius. It answers, probably, to the site of *Uxilico*.
Not many miles to the south is cape *Tranquillo*,
the extreme point of the island in this direction,
and which answers perhaps to the Mnasyrium of
Strabo. Mount Atabyris, whence Jove obtained the Atabyris
well-known surname of Atabyrius, was the most mons.
elevated mountain in the island. (Strab. loc. cit.)

. . . 'Αλλ' ὦ Ζεῦ πάτερ νω-
τοισιν 'Αταβυρίου
μεδέων, τίμα μὲν ὕμνου
τεθμὸν, 'Ολυμπιονίκαν
ἄνδρατε, πὺξ ἀρετὰν
εὑρόντα.

(Cf. Schol. ad loc. Steph. Byz. v. 'Ατάβυρον. Apollod.
III. 2.) Camirus, to whose cliffs Homer has applied Camirus.
the epithet of chalky, follows next.

Λίνδον, 'Ιηλύσσον τε, καὶ ἀργινόεντα Κάμειρον.   Il. B. 656.

It derived its name, as we have seen, from a son
of Cercaphus, one of the Heliadæ. We learn from
Diodorus, that Juno Telchinia was worshipped here.
(V. 57.) Pisander, the epic poet, was a native of
Camirus. (Steph. Byz. v. Κάμιρος. Suid. v. Πείσανδρος.)
This town is also mentioned by Thucydides, (VIII.
44.) Herodotus, (I. 144.) Ptolemy: (p.121.) it retains
the name of *Camiro*[o]. The promontory *Candura*, a
little to the south of this site, is perhaps the ancient
Mylantia. (Steph. Byz. v. Μυλαντία.) That part of Mylantia
the coast which was situated between Camirus and promontorium.
Ialysus, considerably to the north of the former, was
named Thoantium; but there was also a promontory Thoantium.
so called. (Strab. XIV. p. 655.) Ialysus, which was Ialysus.

---

[o] There are some very ancient coins of Camirus, without
any epigraph; but some are inscribed, KAMI
PEΩN. Sestini, p. 91.

founded at the same time with Lindus and Camirus, had previously been occupied by the Phœnicians, who called the site at that time Achaia[p]: (Athen. VIII. p. 360. Diod. Sic. V. 57.) or, rather, this was a fortress distant eighty stadia from Ialysus, and Ochyroma. called Ochyroma when Strabo wrote. (XIV. p. 655.) Ialysus, besides the authors already mentioned, is noticed by Herodotus, (I. 144.) Thucydides, (VIII. 44.) and Steph. Byz. (v. Ἰάλυσσος.)

. . . . ἄντα δὲ πέζης
Αἰγυπτίης Ῥόδος ἐστὶν, Ἰηλυσίων πέδον ἀνδρῶν.

DION. PERIEG. 505.

Phœbeamque Rhodon, et Ialysios Telchinas.

OVID. METAM. VII. 365.

Near Ialysus was a spot called Schedias. (Dieuch. ap. Athen. VI. p. 262.

Rhodes is surrounded by numerous islets and rocks, some of which are recorded in history. Of Chalcia these the most considerable is Chalcia, now *Karki*. insula. Strabo says it was situate opposite to Thoantium of Rhodes: (XIV. p. 655.) in modern charts it is placed directly off *Camiro*, about eight miles northwest. It is noticed by Thucydides, (VIII. 44.) Scylax, (p. 38.) and Pliny, (V. 31.)

Cyclopis.   Pliny names besides, Cyclopis, Steganos, Cordy-
Steganos.
Cordylusa. lusa, Diabetæ; these last, we are told by Stephanus
Diabetæ.
   Byz., (v. Διαβῆται,) were a small group round Syme,
Teutlusa. now *Kiskilles*; Hymos, Seutlusa, or, as Thucydides
Narthe-
cusa. calls it, Teutlusa, (VIII. 44.) perhaps *Limonia*, north
Dimastos.
Procne. of Chalce; Nartheeusa, Dimastos, Procne. Off Cni-
Cisserussa.
Therio- dus, Cisserussa, Therionarce. On the Carian coast,
narce.

---

[p] There was an Achaia in Crete, and another in Eubœa, islands equally occupied by the Phœnicians. The word Akka, in their language, expresses an elevated spot.

the Argiæ, twenty in number. Near Halicarnassus, Pidosus. In the Ceramic gulf, Priaponnesus, Hipponesus, Psyra, Mya, Lampsemandus; this must be the same as the Lepsemandus of Steph. Byz., who quotes the authority of Craterus; (v. Λημψήμανδος.) Crusa, Pyrrha, Sepiussa, Melano: and a little further from the land, Cinædopolis, so called from some worthless characters left there by Alexander.

Argiæ.
Pidosus.
Priaponnesus.
Hipponesus.
Psyra.
Mya.
Lepsemandus.
Crusa.
Pyrrhe.
Sepiussa.
Melano.
Cinædopolis.

SECTION XI.

LYCIA.

————◆————

Origin and history of the Lycians—Boundaries and maritime topography—Interior—Milyas and Cabalia districts of the ancient Solymi—Cibyra.

HERODOTUS is of opinion that the Lycians were not an indigenous people, but that they came originally from Crete, under the lead of Sarpedon, brother of Minos. They were at first named Termilæ, and this appellation they retained till the arrival of a Greek colony, led by Lycus, son of Pandion, from whom they took that of Lycians. (Herod. I. 173. VII. 92.) The historian does not inform us whence the word Termilæ was derived, and Strabo seems altogether disposed to reject his account, as being at variance with Homer's authority, who makes mention only of the Lycians under that name. But there can be no doubt that the appellation of Termilæ, or Tremilæ, was once applied to a part, at least, of the nation, as we see from several authorities quoted by Steph. Byz. (v. Τρεμίλαι.) One of these is the poet Panyasis, who derives it from Tremilus, an ancient chief:

Ἔνθα δ' ἔναιε μέγας Τρέμιλος καὶ ἔγημε θύγατρα
Νύμφην Ὠγυγίην, ἣν Πραξιδίκην καλέουσι
Σίβρῳ ἐπ' ἀργυρέῳ ποταμῷ παρὰ δινήεντι.

Hecatæus agreed with Herodotus in writing the word Tremilæ. Alexander, the Lycian historian, reported, that Bellerophon, just before his death, changed the name to Lycians[a]. The adventures of that hero in Lycia have afforded a fine field for the poets; and Homer in particular has introduced them with great effect in the parley of Glaucus and Diomed. It is evident from this episode that Lycia was a country well known to the Greeks at the period in which Homer flourished, and that the memory of Bellerophon and his exploits was still preserved there:

Καὶ μήν οἱ Λύκιοι τέμενος τάμον ἔξοχον ἄλλων,
Καλὸν φυταλιῆς καὶ ἀρούρης, ὄφρα νέμοιτο.   Il. Z. 194.

The Lycians, under the conduct of Sarpedon and Glaucus, are certainly the most distinguished of the allies of Priam. And if the people of the same name, who fought under Pandarus, were a colony from the part of Asia Minor which we are now considering, it must be admitted that they were at that time a nation of greater power and consequence than at any subsequent period of their history. With respect to Sarpedon, it may be observed, though we are here treading on mythological ground, that the hero of that name, mentioned by Herodotus as the founder of the Lycian people, is very different from Homer's chieftain: they only agree in the fabulous circumstance of being both the reputed sons of Jupiter.

The Lycians, as we learn from Herodotus, at a later period became subject to Crœsus; (I. 28.) but after the defeat of that sovereign by Cyrus they re-

---

[a] The passage in Steph. Byz. has not been understood by Berkelius: it should be read as a quotation from Alexander: 'Αλεξάνδρος δὲ '' τελευτήσας τούτους '' δὲ τοὺς Τρεμιλέους, Λυκίους Βελ- '' λεροφόντης ὠνόμασεν.''

fused to submit to the arms of the victorious Persians, until they were compelled by force; differing in this respect from the Carians, their neighbours, who had surrendered without a conflict. (I. 176.) Darius assigned to them a place in the first satrapy of his empire. (III. 90.)　They furnished fifty ships to the Persian armament under Xerxes; their troops, which excelled in the use of the bow as early as the siege of Troy, being armed chiefly after the Grecian manner. (VII. 92.)　The Lycians are not mentioned by Thucydides, as having taken part in the Peloponnesian war; but it is probable that, as Rhodes was tributary to Athens, they would not be exempt from similar contributions: these were levied sometimes as far as Aspendus in Pamphylia.　Alexander traversed a part of the province in his march from Caria into Pisidia and Phrygia, and reduced it under his sway. (Arrian. Exp. Alex. I. 24.)　From him it passed under the dominion of the Ptolemies and the Seleucidæ; but after the defeat of Antiochus was ceded by the Roman senate to the Rhodians. The Lycians, however, refused to be considered as the subjects of these islanders, and, secretly favoured by Eumenes, resisted the Rhodian authorities by force of arms.　In this contest, however, they were worsted; but the Romans, as we have seen, displeased with the Rhodians, interfered, and declared the Lycians free. (Polyb. XXII. 7. XXIII. 3. XXVI. 7. XXX. 5.)　Strabo bestows a just encomium on the political system adopted by the Lycians; owing to which, he thinks, they never fell into the piratical practices of their neighbours, the Pamphylians and Cilicians.　According to this writer, the Lycian confederacy consisted of twenty-three towns, which sent deputies to the general assembly held in one of them. The number of deputies sent was in proportion to the size and importance of the deputing place: the most considerable towns had three votes, the next class two, and the rest one vote. The same proportion was equally observed in the contributions of each to the taxes and other public expenses. The chief towns were six in number, as Artemidorus reported; viz. Xanthus, Patara, Pinara, Olympus, Myra, and Tlos. The deliberative assembly first proceeded to the election of a chief magistrate, called Lyciarch; after which the other officers of the state and judges were chosen. Formerly, the assembly deliberated on war and peace, and alliances; but under the Roman empire this was not permitted, except in some particular instances. In all other respects the Lycians retained their liberty and privileges, a mark of confidence bestowed upon them by the Romans, on account of the wisdom and prudence exhibited in their federal association. (XIV. p. 665.) Pliny says that Lycia possessed once seventy towns, but that when he wrote they had diminished to twenty-six. (V. 28.)

Lycia may be considered as divided into two distinct parts: the one comprehending the maritime portion of the province; the other, the mountainous country called Milyas, and Cabalis, or Cabalia, by the Greek geographers, and on the borders of Phrygia the district of Cibyra, which is by some writers annexed to the latter province. The separation between the two portions of territory, comprehended under the general name of Lycia, is effected by the great natural barrier of mount Taurus, which, commencing on the Carian frontier under the names of

Cragus and Anticragus, and the Solymæan mountains, encloses maritime Lycia, and effectually divides it from Milyas by rejoining the sea again where
Pamphylia begins.   If we take in Milyas and Cibyra within its limits, we may state that Lycia generally is bounded on the west by Caria, on the
north by Phrygia, from which it was separated by
mount Cadmus, on the east by Pisidia and Pamphylia, on the south by the sea.

The first place which presented itself to the navigator who followed the course of the Lycian coast
Telmissus. was Telmissus, a town noted in the history of ancient divination for the skill of its augurs.   From
Herodotus we learn that they were frequently consulted by the early kings of Lydia down to the time
of Crœsus. (I. 78.)   Arrian also says their celebrity
was great before the time of Gordius, father of Midas, first king of Phrygia. (Exp. Alex. II. 3, 4.)   It
is true there was a Telmissus in Caria, which might
seem to dispute with the Lycian town the honour of
having produced these soothsayers, but it was a
much more obscure place than the one of which we
are now speaking [b], this last having given its name
to the gulf whereon it stands, and which appears to
be the same as the Glaucus Sinus of Strabo, now
gulf of *Macri*.   For Livy says that the Telmessi-
Telmessi- cus Sinus separated Lycia from Caria. (XXXVII.
cus Sinus. 16.)   Strabo states that Telmissus was bestowed by
the Roman senate on Eumenes at the conclusion of
the war with Antiochus. (XIV. p. 665.)   This is
confirmed by Livy, who informs us besides that its
territory and fortresses had been under the separate

[b] This is the opinion of Cel-   and Holsten. (ad Steph. Byz.
larius, (Geogr. Ant. III. p. 65.)   v. Τελμισσός.)

jurisdiction of a chief named Ptolemy of Telmissus. (XXXVII. 56. Cf. XXXVIII. 39. Polyb. XXII. 27.) Telmissus of Lycia is also spoken of by Scylax, (p. 3.) Mela, (I. 15.) Pliny, (V. 28.) and Steph. Byz. (v. Τελμισσός.) Hierocl. (p. 684.) Ptol. (p. 121.) From the Acts of Councils we infer its episcopal rank [c]. Some ancient vestiges, and a slight analogy of name, together with the agreement of situation, lead to a well grounded opinion that Telmissus is represented by the town of *Myes*, or *Meis*, in the south-easternmost recess of the gulf of *Macri*.

Beyond Telmissus the coast rises abruptly, and presents the escarpment of a lofty and precipitous mountain, which was known in ancient geography by the name of Anticragus. It is now called *Soum-* Anticragus mons. *bourlou*. Captain Beaufort estimates the height of this summit to be not less than 6000 feet. At the foot of it, and in a recess opening towards the sea, stood the fortress of Carmylessus. (Strab. XIV. p. Carmylessus. 665.) Point Telmissis of Strabo is probably cape Telmissis promontorium. *Iria*. Beyond is a mass of mountains, rising also precipitously from the sea, and which, from the number of detached summits they offer to the spectator in that direction, have been called *Yedi Bouroun*, or the *Seven Capes*, by the Turks. This feature leads to the idea that the chain in question can be no other than the Cragus of antiquity, though Strabo Cragus mons. assigns to it eight summits. (XIV. p. 665.) Scylax calls Cragus a promontory, and makes it the separation of Lycia and Caria. (p. 39. Cf. Plin. V. 28.)

> Nigris aut Erymanthi
> Silvis, aut viridis Cragi.
> Hor. I. Od. 21.

[c] Geogr. Sacr. p. 247.

R 3

Jam Cragon, et Lymiren, Xanthique reliquerat undas.

OVID. METAM. IX. 645.

Cragus urbs. Strabo informs us there was a town of the same name, and this is confirmed by numismatic authority[d]. According to mythologists, Cragus was the son of Tremilus. (Steph. Byz. vv. Τρεμίλη et Κρᾶγος.) There was a cave in mount Cragus consecrated to the gods, called Agrii. (Steph. Byz. v. Κρᾶγος. Eustath. ap. Dionys. Perieg. v. 850.) Plutarch, in his treatise on Isis and Osiris, calls them Σκληροὶ, and says their names were Arsalus, Arytus, and Tosibis. (Cf. Euseb. Præp. Ev. V. p. 188.)

Pinara. At the foot of Cragus, on the north side of the mountain and towards the interior of Lycia, stood Pinara, one of the six principal towns of the province in which divine honours were paid to Pandarus, a Lycian chief, perhaps the same as the celebrated archer of Homer, though Strabo does not decide the question. (XIV. p. 665.) It derived its name from Pinarus, son of Termilus. (Steph. Byz. v. Τερμίλη. Cf. v. Πίναρα.) According to this geographer, who quotes the Lyciaca of Menecrates, the original site was named Artymnesus. It was colonized by the Xanthians and called Pinara, from being seated on a round hill; this being the signification of the name in the Lycian tongue. (v. Ἀρτύμνησος. Ptol. p. 121. Plin. V. 28. Hierocl. p. 684.) The precise site of this town remains yet to be discovered; but Arrian seems to place it beyond the Xanthus, a river of which we are about to speak. (Exp. Alex. I. c. 25.) But we must first mention several small places, or rather stations, along the

[d] Sestini, p. 92. Cragus. Autonomi. Epigraphe, ΛΤΚΙΩΝ ΚΡ. vel ΚΡΑ. vel ΚΡΑΓ. Imperatorii Augustus et Julia.

coast, which are pointed out in the Stadiasmus between Telmissus and the Xanthus. We have in this document an island named Lagusa, five stadia from Telmissus. Pliny also notices this island, and says it was near the river Glaucus. The Glaucus must be the river of *Meis*, which flows near the ruins of Telmissus, and falls into the bay to which it gave its name. (V. 31.) Lagusa answers to *l'Isle des Chevaliers*, in Lapie's map. Besides this, Pliny notices Macris, from which the modern name of *Makri* is probably attached to the bay; Didymæ, Helboscope, or Helioscope, Aspis, (Cf. Steph. Byz. v.'Ασπίς,) and Telandria, which once possessed a town. The Stadiasmus reckons eighty stadia from Lagusa to Cissides: this, as Col. Leake observes, was " a pen- " insular promontory, on the south side of which " is the island and harbour of *St. Nicolas*:" some ruins, which he observed there, " indicate a late pe- " riod of the Roman empire [e]." From Cissides to Perdiciæ, fifty stadia. Steph. Byz. notices also this port. (v. Περδίκια.) To Calabantia, fifty; to cape Hiera, thirty. This promontory is thought by Col. Leake to be one of the points of Cragus. From thence to Pydna we have eighty stadia. This place is unknown to other geographers, unless we suppose, with the able antiquary quoted above, that it is the Cydna of Ptolemy. It may be remarked that this variation of orthography took place also in the Macedonian Pydna. (Steph. Byz. v. Κύδνα.) From Pydna to the mouth of the Xanthus, sixty stadia. This river, the most considerable of the Lycian streams, anciently bore the name of Sirbes, as Strabo

Lagusa insula.

Glaucus fluvius.

Macris.
Didymæ.
Helboscope sive Helioscope.
Aspis.
Telandria insulæ.
Cissides.

Perdiciæ.
Calabantia.
Hiera promontorium.

Xanthus fluvius, prius Sibrus.

---

[e] Asia Minor, p. 182.

R 4

writes it; but Sibrus, according to Panyasis. (Ap.
Steph. Byz. v. Τρεμίλη.)

Σίβρῳ ἐπ' ἀργυρέῳ ποταμῷ παρὰ δινήεντι,
Πρὸς δ' ἅλα κεκλιμένην Λύκιοι χθόνα ναιετάουσι
Ξάνθου ἐπὶ προχοῇσιν εὐῤῥείτου ποταμοῖο,
Ἔνθα βαθυκρήμνοιο φαείνεται οὔρεα Ταύρου.

Dion. Perieg. 847.

It was navigable for small vessels; and at the distance of ten stadia from its mouth was a temple of
Xanthus
urbs. Latona; and sixty stadia further, Xanthus, the principal city of the Lycians.   Pliny says it was fifteen
miles from the sea, but that distance is too considerable, there being no doubt that the Lycian capital
occupied the site of *Aksenide,* which occurs in the
situation described by Strabo. (XIV. p. 666. Cf.
Hecat. ap. Steph. Byz. v. Ξάνθος. Ptol. p. 121.) The
Xanthians have twice been recorded in history for
the dauntless courage and perseverance with which
they defended their city against a hostile army.   The
first occasion occurred in the invasion of Lycia by
the army of Cyrus under Harpagus, after the conquest of Lydia, when they buried themselves under
the ruins of their walls and houses. (Herod. I. 176.)
The second event here alluded to took place many
centuries later, during the civil wars consequent
upon the death of Cæsar.   The Xanthians having
refused to open their gates to the republican army
commanded by Brutus, that general invested the
town, and after repelling every attempt made by the
citizens to break through his lines, finally entered
it by force.   The Xanthians are said to have resisted still, and even to have perished in the flames,
with their wives and children, rather than fall into

the hands of the Roman general, who made many attempts to turn their desperate purpose. (Plut. Brut. Appian. Civ. Bell. IV. 18. Dio Cass. XLVII. 34.) Xanthus finds a place also in Arrian, (Exp. Alex. I. 24. 7.) Ptolemy, (p. 121.) Mela, (I. 15.) and Hierocles, (p. 684.[f]) The ruins of this city have not been explored by any modern traveller.

On the left bank of the Xanthus, and near its mouth, stood the town and harbour of Patara, one of the most celebrated in the province, and adorned with several temples. The most famous of these was that of the Lycian Apollo, surnamed also Pataræus: it was very ancient, and second only to that of Delphi. (Mel. I. 15.) Some derived the name from Patarus, a son of Apollo. (Strab. XIV. p. 666. Cf. Steph. Byz. v. Πάταρα.) Pliny affirms it was more anciently called Sataros. (V. 28.) Herodotus says the oracle was delivered by a priestess, for a certain period; (I. 182.) which, according to Servius, was during the six winter months.

Qualis, ubi hibernam Lyciam, Xanthique fluenta
Deserit; ac Delum maternam invisit Apollo.
Æn. IV. 143.

. . . . mihi Delphica tellus,
Et Claros, et Tenedos, Pataræaque regia servit.
Ovid. Metam. I. 515.

. . . . qui Lyciæ tenet
Dumeta, natalemque silvam,
Delius et Patareus Apollo.
Hor. Od. III. 4. 62.

. . . seu te Lyciæ Pataræa nivosis
Exercent dumeta jugis.   Stat. Theb. I. 696.

---

[f] The coins of Xanthus are extremely scarce: the epigraph, according to Sestini, is ΖΑ. ΛΥ-ΚΙΩΝ. (p. 92.)

We learn from Strabo, that Ptolemy Philadelphus restored Patara, and attempted to change its name to Arsinoe in Lycia; but this alteration does not appear to have succeeded. Livy and other writers always use the former appellation. (XXXVII. 15— 17. XXXVIII. 39. Polyb. XXII. 26.) The common ethnic name is Παταρεὺς, in Latin Patarensis; but Cicero uses Pataranus. (Orat. in Flacc. c. 32.) This town is recorded among the Lycian bishoprics in the Acts of Councils; (cf. Hierocl. p. 684.) and the name of *Patera* is still attached to its ruins. These, according to the accurate survey of Captain Beaufort, are situated on the sea-shore, a little to the eastward of the river Xanthus: they consist " of " a theatre excavated in the northern side of a small " hill, a ruined temple on the side of the same hill, " and a deep circular pit, of singular appearance, " which may have been the seat of the oracle. The " town walls surrounded an area of considerable ex- " tent; they may easily be traced, as well as the " situation of a castle which commanded the har- " bour, and of several towers which flanked the " walls. On the outside of the walls there is a mul- " titude of stone sarcophagi, most of them bearing " inscriptions, but all open and empty; and within " the walls, temples, altars, pedestals, and fragments " of sculpture appear in profusion, but ruined and " mutilated. The situation of the harbour is still " apparent, but at present it is a swamp, choked " up with sand and bushes [g]."

A little to the east of Patara was a harbour named

---

[g] Beaufort's Karamania, p. 2, 6. The coins of Patara are not of common occurrence. The inscription is ΛΥΚΙΩΝ ΠΑ. or ΠΑΤΑΡΕΩΝ. Sestini, p. 92.

Phœnicus, according to Livy, who states that a Ro- Phœnicus portus.
man fleet took up its station there, with a view of
taking Patara, in which project they did not succeed. (XXXVII. 16.) Phœnicus was less than two
miles from Patara, and surrounded on all sides by
high cliffs. Captain Beaufort observes, that this
description answers accurately to the bay of *Kalamaki* [h]. The same navigator states, that the shore
beyond is lined with several barren islands. These, Xenagoræ insulæ.
according to the Stadiasmus, are the isles of Xenagoras, sixty stadia from Patara; then Rhope, 300 Rhope.
stadia; (but this distance is evidently incorrect;)
and Megiste, fifty beyond. Strabo also mentions Megiste.
this last island, and states that it had a town of the
same name; he further adds, that it was also called
Cisthene. (XIV. p. 666.) Scylax says that Megiste
belonged to the Rhodians. (p. 38. Cf. Liv. XXXVII.
22 et 24. Steph. Byz. v. Μεγίστη.) Pliny observes,
that the town of Megiste no longer existed in his
day. (V. 31. Cf. Ptol. p. 121.) Megiste answers to
the modern *Castelorizo,* which Captain Beaufort describes as a large rocky island, with a small harbour
for merchant-ships of any size. On the summit of
the island, which is about 800 feet above the level
of the sea, there is a small ruined fortress, which,
from its situation, must have been impregnable [i].
Col. Leake justly observes, that Rhope and the
islands of Xenagoras answer to Rhoge and Ena-
gora of Pliny. Rhoge is *St. George,* and the others
Volo and *Okendra,* at the mouth of the bay of
Kalamaki [k]. It is doubtful whether the Cisthene

[h] Karamania, p. 7. [i] Ibid. p. 7, 8.
[k] Asia Minor, p. 184.

(Κισθήνη) of Isocrates is to be referred to the island mentioned by Strabo. (Paneg. §. 41. p. 172.)

Sidyma.

On the continent, and not far from Patara, was Sidyma, situate on a hill, as we learn from Pliny. (V. 28.) It is also noticed by Ptolemy, (p. 121.) Steph. Byz., (v. Σίδυμα.) the Ecclesiastical Records, and Acts of Councils. Cedrenus reports, that a prodigy happened there to Marcianus. (p. 344.)

Phellus et Antiphellus.

Nearly opposite to Megiste were two ports, situate near each other, named Phellus and Antiphellus: these Strabo incorrectly places inland. (XIV. p. 666. Steph. Byz. vv. Φελλὸς, Ἀντίφελλος. Ptol. p. 121.) Phellus seems to answer to port *Sevedo*, and Antiphellus to *Vathry*; but Captain Beaufort observes, that the name of *Antiphilo* is still attached to the site. The same able officer observed several indications of an ancient town here, including remains of considerable buildings, a theatre, sepulchral excavations, &c.[1] The Stadiasmus reckons fifty stadia from the isle Megiste to Antiphellus.

Acroterium. Aperlæ.

The same document then names in succession Acroterium, fifty stadia further, and Aperlæ, probably close to this headland. This last place is written Aperræ[m] in Ptolemy, and Apyræ in Pliny; Aprillæ in the Ecclesiastical Notices. (Hierocl. p. 684.) The site of this Lycian town has been fixed by Mr. Cockerell above *Assar bay*, where there are some sepulchral inscriptions and other remains[n]. The

Cyaneæ.

same traveller discovered the vestiges of Cyaneæ,

[1] Karamania, p. 13—16. Col. Leake, Asia Minor, p. 185. There are coins of Antiphellus, with the legend ΑΝΤΙΦΕΛ-ΛΕΙΤΩΝ. They are of the reign of Gordianus Pius.

[m] This reading is countenanced by some coins of Gordian, with the inscription ΑΠΕΡ-ΡΑΙΤΩΝ.

[n] Col. Leake's Asia Minor, p. 188.

or Cyane, mentioned by Pliny (V. 27.) and Hierocles, (p. 684.) near port *Tristomo* [o]. From Aperlæ
to Somena the Maritime Survey counts sixty stadia. Simena.
This, as Col. Leake well observes, is the Simena of
Pliny (V. 27.) and Steph. Byz. (v. Σίμηνα.) Opposite this part of the Lycian coast, and near the
shore, is the island of *Kakava*, whose lengthened
shape induced the ancients to give it the name of
Dolichiste. (Plin. V. 31. Steph. Byz. v. Δολιχή.) Dolichiste
Captain Beaufort describes *Kakava* as a long nar- insula.
row ridge of rock, now deserted, but with some appearance of ancient habitations [p].   From Somena Andriace.
the Stadiasmus reckons four stadia to Andriace;
and Captain Beaufort informs us, that, to the eastward of *Kakava*, he came to the mouth of a small
brackish river, named *Andraki;* at the entrance of
which he observed several ruined houses, sarcophagi,
and tombs, with the remains of a spacious granary,
erected apparently by the emperor Trajan [q].   Andriace, as we learn from Appian, was the port of
Myra, a city of some note, situate higher up the
river. (Civ. Bell. IV. p. 636. Cf. Ptol. p. 122.)   It
must therefore have been at Andriace that St. Paul
and his companions were transferred from the Adra-
myttian ship to that of Alexandria, in which they
suffered shipwreck. The sacred historian states that,
after quitting Sidon and passing by Cyprus, they
" sailed over the sea of Cilicia and Pamphylia, and
" came to Myra, a city of Lycia; and there the
" centurion found a ship of Alexandria sailing
" into Italy; and he put us therein." (Acts xxvii.
5, 6.)   Myra, according to Strabo, was seated on

---

[o] Col. Leake's Asia Minor, p. 188.

[p] Karamania, p. 21, 22.   [q] Ibid. p. 22.

the brow of a lofty hill at the distance of twenty
stadia from the coast. (XIV. p. 666.) Pliny names
it in conjunction with Andriace. Myra was one of
the six chief towns of Lycia. (Artemid. ap. Strab.
XIV. p. 665.) At a late period of the empire it became the metropolis of that province. (Malal. Chron.
XIV. Hierocl. p. 684. Cf. Basil. Seleuc. Vit. Thecl.
I. p. 272. ap. Wesseling.) Nicolas, bishop of Myra,
is celebrated in the ecclesiastical writers of this period. (Const. Porphyr. Them. 14. Cf. Steph. Byz.
v. Μύρα. Athen. II. p. 59.) Mr. Cockerell, who visited the ruins of Myra, found them to be considerable. The remains of the theatre are very perfect;
there are also vestiges of other edifices and numerous inscribed sepulchres, with Lycian characters[r].

Sura. Between Myra and Phellus was a spot named Sura,
where divination was practised by means of fish.
(Plut. de Solert. Anim. c. 23. Polycharm. ap. Steph.
Byz.. v. Σούρα. Cf. Athen. VIII. p. 333.)

Continuing our survey of the coast, we have to
Turris Isia. notice, with the Stadiasmus, the Isian tower, sixty
stadia from Andriace; this is the *Pyrgo* of Captain
Limyrus fl. Beaufort. Then follows the mouth of the river Li-
Arycandus myrus, joined by another stream, named Arycandus.
fluvius. (Plin. V. 27.) Strabo also notices the Limyrus, and
adds, that the town of Limyra was situated at a
distance of twenty stadia from its mouth. (XIV.
Limyra. p. 666. Cf. Steph. Byz. vv. Λάμυρα et Λίμυρα.) Caius
Cæsar, the adopted son of Augustus, is reported by
Velleius Paterculus to have died here. (II. c. 102.)
This town is mentioned by Ptolemy and the Eccle-

[r] Col. Leake's Asia Minor,   epigraph, MTPEΩN. Sestini, p.
p. 183, 321. There are impe-   92.
rial coins of Myra, with the

siastical Notitiæ. Captain Beaufort reports, that there are some considerable ruins inland above cape *Fi-nika*, near which the Limyrus falls into the sea. Arycanda, as we learn from Agatharcides, quoted Arycanda. by Athenæus, was another Lycian town in the vicinity of Limyra: these two places are stated by that writer to have become so heavily burthened with debts, that, as the only means of clearing their affairs, they espoused the party of Mithridates. (XII. p.555.) The scholiast of Pindar speaks of a spot named Embolus, near Arycanda, which may have been Embolus. cape *Finika*. Pliny seems to place Arycanda in Milyas, which is the interior of Lycia[s]. (Cf. Steph. Byz. v. Ἀρύκανδα) The Stadiasmus places, after Limyra, Menalippe, a naval station mentioned by Ste-Menalippe. phanus Byz. as a river of Pamphylia or Lycia. This spot appears to have been sacred to Minerva, from a passage of Q. Calaber.

Ναῖε δ' ὅγ' αἰπεινὸν Μελανίππιον ἱρὸν Ἀθηνῆς.

III. 232.

(v. Μεναλίππιον.) Then Gagæ, which occurs in Scylax Gagæ. (p. 38.) and Pliny. (V. 27. Cf. Steph. Byz. v. Γάγαι. Hierocl. p. 684.) A particular sort of stone, called Gagates, from that circumstance, was found in the vicinity. (Dioscor. V. 14. Cf. Nicandr. Sch. p. 7.) Gagæ appears to have been once named Palæopolis. Col. Leake is of opinion that some ruins laid down in Captain Beaufort's chart at *Alaja-dagh*, above *Finika* bay, may represent this Lycian town[t]. The chain of mountains which encompasses that bay from cape *Finika* seems to belong to Mount Massicytes

[s] There are coins of Limyra and Arycanda: those of the former mention the river Limyrus, and a mole called PH-ΓΜΑ, which probably answers to the curious ridge of gravel mentioned by Capt. Beaufort, p. 32. Sestini, p. 92.

[t] Asia Minor, p. 186.

Massicytes mons. or Massicytus, recorded by Pliny and Ptolemy. (Cf. Qu. Cal. III. 232.) There was also a town or community of the same name, as may be collected from some extant coins[x].

The bay of *Finika* is closed towards the east by the lofty headland now called *Kelidonia*, but which was known to the ancients by the name of the Sacred promontory. This cape obtained greater celebrity from its being commonly looked upon as the commencement of the great chain of Taurus, which was accounted to traverse, under various names, the whole continent of Asia; (Plin. V. 27.) but Strabo observes, that Taurus really began in Caria, opposite to Rhodes; (XIV. p. 666.) and other geographers even supposed it to commence with Mycale. (Arrian. Exp. Alex. V. 5. 2.)

Sacrum prom.

The Sacred promontory derives its modern name from a group of islands situated within a short distance of it. The Chelidonian isles were two in number, according to Scylax, (p. 38.) or three, as Strabo reports: the latter geographer says, that they were six stadia from the land, and five from each other. Capt. Beaufort, however, distinctly counted five of these islands; whence he is led, not without reason, to think that this increase of number has been produced by the shock of an earthquake: two are from four to five hundred feet high, the other three are small and barren[y]. Pliny's remark is, " deinde con-" tra Tauri promontorium pestiferæ navigantibus " Chelidoniæ totidem," (i. e. tres.) (V. 35.)

Chelidoniæ insulæ.

A little beyond these to the east, is an island, whose name, *Grambousa*, clearly points out the Crambusa of Strabo. (XIV. p. 666.) Other geogra-

Crambusa, sive Dionysia insula.

---

[x] The epigraph is ΛΤΚΙΩΝ ΜΑΣ. Sestini, p. 92.
[y] Karamania, p. 37, 38.

phers call it Dionysia. (Scyl. p. 39. Plin. loc. cit.)
An accurate description is given of this rugged islet
by Captain Beaufort[z].

The Stadiasmus places between the Sacred Promontory and Crambusa a spot with water, named
Morum; (Μωρὸν ὑδὼρ;) fifty stadia from the former,
and thirty stadia eastward, Posidarison; (Posida-
rion more probably;) this was thirty stadia from
Crambusa. Beyond, the coast becomes still more
rugged, and the mountains, rising at the back of the
perpendicular cliffs which line the shore, attain the
height of six and seven thousand feet; the highest, as
we learn from Captain Beaufort, bears the name of
Adratchan[a], and appears to answer to the Olympus Olympus,
or Phœnicus of Strabo. The Stadiasmus seems to sive Phœnicus mons.
distinguish between Phœnicus and mount Olympus,
and rather considers the former as a port. But there
was also a town named Olympus, which ranked among Olympus
the six chief communities of Lycia. (Strab. XIV. urbs.
p. 666.) Cicero also bears testimony to its importance and opulence. Having become the residence
and haunt of pirates, it was captured by Servilius
Isauricus, and became afterwards a mere fortress.
(Cic. in Verr. I. 21. Eutrop. VI. 3. Plin. V. 27.
Flor. III. 6.) Strabo reports that it was the strong
hold of the pirate Zenicetus; and the situation was
so elevated that it commanded a view of Lycia,
Pamphylia, and Pisidia. (XIV. p. 671.) There is
little doubt that in Hierocles, for ΟΑΝΑΠΟΣ we
should substitute ΟΛΥΜΠΟΣ. (p. 683.) We are indebted to Captain Beaufort for the discovery of the
ruins of this town, which exist in a small circular

[z] P. 39—41.   [a] Karamania, p. 43.

plain surrounded by the chain of *Adratchan,* and at a little distance from the sea. The only way leading to the site is by a natural aperture in the cliff; it is now called *Deliktash,* or " the perforated " rock." Among the ruins are the remains of a temple with an inscription containing the name of the city[b].

Mount Olympus would appear to be the chain which Homer alludes to in the Odyssey, under the name of the Solymæan mountains; whence he supposes Neptune to have beheld in his wrath Ulysses sailing towards Phœnicia.

Solymo-
rum mon-
tes.

Τὸν δ' ἐξ Αἰθιόπων ἀνιὼν κρείων Ἐνοσίχθων
Τηλόθεν ἐκ Σολύμων ὀρέων ἴδεν· εἴσατο γάρ οἱ
Πόντον ἐπιπλείων.   ODYSS. E. 282.

For though the Solymi inhabited rather, as we shall see, the interior of Lycia, there is a decisive circumstance which fixes the mountains alluded to by the poet on this part of the coast; I mean the existence of the celebrated Chimæra, in the highlands, not far from mount *Adratchan.* Homer, it is well known, affirms that this fabled monster was encountered and slain by Bellerophon.

Chimæra.

Πρῶτον μέν ῥα Χίμαιραν ἀμαιμακέτην ἐκέλευσε
Πεφνέμεν· ἡ δ' ἄρ' ἔην θεῖον γένος, οὐδ' ἀνθρώπων,
Πρόσθε λέων, ὄπιθεν δὲ δράκων, μέσση δὲ χίμαιρα,
Δεινὸν ἀποπνείουσα πυρὸς μένος αἰθομένοιο.
Καὶ τὴν μὲν κατέπεφνε, θεῶν τεράεσσι πιθήσας.

                                    IL. Z. 179.

Hesiod's description is somewhat different.

[b] ΟΛΤΝΠΗΝΩΝ ΒΟΤΛΗ ΚΑΙ Ο ΔΗΜΟC, p. 44, 45. This orthography appeared on all the inscriptions which he observed; but the coins of the town exhibit ΟΛΤΜ. and ΟΛΤΜΠΗ.

Ἡ δὲ Χίμαιραν ἔτικτε, πνέουσαν ἀμαιμάκετον πῦρ,
Τῆς δ' ἦν τρεῖς κεφαλαί· μία μὲν χαροποῖο λέοντος,
Ἡ δὲ χιμαίρης· ἡ δ' ὄφιος, κρατεροῖο δράκοντος.
Τὴν μὲν Πήγασος εἷλε καὶ ἐσθλὸς Βελλεροφόντης.

The Latin poets have imitated, as usual, their Grecian masters:

Prima leo, postrema draco, media ipsa Chimæra.

LUCRET. V. 903.

Quoque Chimæra jugo mediis in partibus ignem,
Pectus et ora leæ, caudam serpentis habebat.

OVID. METAM. IX. 646.

And Virgil. (Æn. VI. 288.)

. . . . . . flammisque armata Chimæra.

Servius's explanation is curious: " This, in truth," says he, " is a mountain of Lycia, the top of which " is on fire at the present day: near it are lions: " but the middle region is occupied by pastures, " which abound in goats. The lower parts of the " mountain swarm with serpents." The geographers agree in adapting this fable to the Lycian mountains; but Strabo seems rather to place the site in mount Cragus; (XIV. p. 665.) while Pliny, on the authority of Ctesias, whose words have been preserved by Photius, (Cod. LXXII.) fixes it near Phaselis, beyond Olympus. The Greek historian says, Ὅτι πῦρ ἐστὶν ἐγγὺς Φασηλίδος ἐν τῷ ὄρει, καὶ πῦρ πολὺ αὐτόματον ἐκ τῆς γῆς καίεται, καὶ οὐδέποτε σφέννυται. Scylax has nearly the same words. (p. 39.) Pliny says, "Flagrat in Phaselitide mons Chimæra, et qui- " dem immortali diebus ac noctibus flamma." (II. 106.) Seneca is still more particular in his account of this natural phenomenon. (Ep. LXXIX.) " In " Lycia regio notissima est, Hephæstion incolæ vo- " cant, perforatum pluribus locis solum, quod sine

S 2 ·

" ullo nascentium damno ignis innoxius circuit.
" Læta itaque regio est et herbida, nil flammis adu-
" rentibus, sed tantum vi remissa ac languida reful-
" gentibus." From this description it is plain that
the fire in question had little of the usual volcanic
character, being perfectly harmless. Instances of
this sort of flame are, however, by no means uncommon: that of *Pietra mala* in the Apennines is
well known, and there are others in Epirus and the
Greek islands. We are indebted to Captain Beaufort for an accurate account of the Chimæra flame,
which, after the lapse of so many centuries, is still
unsubdued. This able navigator and antiquary,
being at the time to the east of Olympus, says,
" We had seen from the ship, the preceding night,
" a small but steady light among the hills: on men-
" tioning the circumstance to the inhabitants, we
" learned that it was a *yanar*, or volcanic flame;
" and they offered to supply us with horses and
" guides to examine it. We rode about two miles
" through a fertile plain, partly cultivated; and
" then, winding up a rocky and thickly wooded
" glen, we arrived at the place. In the inner corner
" of a ruined building the wall is undermined, so as
" to leave an aperture of about three feet diameter,
" and shaped like the mouth of an oven; from
" thence the flame issues, giving out an intense
" heat, yet producing no smoke on the wall; and
" though from the neck of the opening we detached
" some small lumps of caked soot, the walls were
" hardly discoloured. Trees, brushwood, and weeds
" grow close round this little crater; a small stream
" trickles down the hill hard by; and the ground
" does not appear to feel the effect of its heat be-

" yond the distance of a few yards. No volcanic
" productions whatever were perceived in the neigh-
" bourhood. The guide declared, that in the me-
" mory of man there had been but one hole, and
" that it had never changed its present size or ap-
" pearance. It was never accompanied, he said,
" by earthquakes or noises; and it ejected neither
" stones, smoke, nor noxious vapours; nothing but
" a brilliant and perpetual flame, which no quantity
" of water could quench [c]."

Beyond Olympus Strabo states that the line of Corycus. coast bore the name of Corycus. The Stadiasmus makes it a naval station, distant thirty stadia from Olympus.

Port Siderus of Scylax was probably the haven of Olympus, corresponding with the modern *Porto Genovese.*

Phaselis is the last town of Lycia, in the direc- Phaselis. tion of Pamphylia. Livy remarks that it was a conspicuous point for those sailing from Cilicia to Rhodes, since it advanced out towards the sea, and, on the other hand, a fleet could easily be descried from thence. (XXXVII. 23.) Hence the epithet of ἠνεμόεσσα applied to it by Dion. Perieg., (v. 854.) who, it may be observed, ascribes it to Pamphylia:

Ἄλλαι δ' ἑξείης Παμφυλίδες εἰσὶ πόληες
Κώρυκος, Πέργητε, καὶ ἠνεμόεσσα Φασηλίς.

We are informed by Herodotus, that this town was colonized by some Dorians. (II. 178.) Heropythus, a Colophonian writer, affirmed that it was colonized by his native city, under the conduct of Lacius; but Philostephanus asserted that Lacius was an Argive, who accompanied Mopsus; others said that he was

c Karamania, p. 47—49.

s 3

a Lindian, and brother of Antiphemus, who founded Gela. (Athen. VII. p. 297.) Stephanus asserts that it was once named Pityussa. (v. Φασηλίς.) Though united to Lycia, it did not form part of the Lycian confederacy, but was governed by its own laws. (XIV. p. 667.) It is mentioned by Thucydides as a place of some importance to the Athenian commerce, with Phœnicia and Cilicia. (II. 69. Cf. VIII. 88. 99. Polyb. XXX. 9.) Phaselis, at a later period, having become the haunt of pirates, was attacked and taken by Servilius Isauricus. (Flor. III. 6. Eutrop. VI. 3.) Cicero, in his Orations against Verres, explains how, from the opportunity of its situation, it had fallen into the hands of the Cilician pirates. (IV. §. 10.) Lucan speaks of it as nearly deserted when visited by Pompey in his flight after the defeat of Pharsalus:

> . . . . . te primum, parva Phaseli,
> Magnus adit: nam te metui vetat incola rarus,
> Exhaustæque domus populis; majorque carinæ,
> Quam tua, turba fuit.   VIII. 251.

Nevertheless, Strabo states that it was a considerable town, and possessed three ports: he observes also, that it was taken by Alexander, as an advantageous post for the prosecution of his conquests into the interior. (XIV. p. 666. Cf. Arrian. Exp. Alex. I. 24. Plut. Vit. Alex. p. 674.) Phaselis, according to Athenæus, was celebrated for the manufacture of rose-perfume. (XIV. p. 688.) Nicander certainly commends its roses. (Ap. eund. p. 683.) Pausanias reports that the spear of Achilles was pretended to be shewn in the temple of Minerva in that town. (Lacon. c. 3.) In Hierocles, Phaselis appears under the corrupt name Φασῦδης. The Acts of Councils prove it to have been of episcopal rank[d]. Theodectes, a dramatic poet and rhetorician of some note, was a native of Phaselis. (Steph. Byz. v. Φασηλίς.) " On a small peninsula, at the foot of mount *Takh-* " *talu,* (the highest point of the Solymæan moun- " tains,)" says Captain Beaufort, " are the remains " of the city of Phaselis, with its three ports and " lake, as described by Strabo. The lake is now a " mere swamp, occupying the middle of the isth- " mus, and was probably the source of those baneful " exhalations which, according to Livy and Cicero, " rendered Phaselis so unhealthy. The principal " port was formed by a stone pier, at the western " side of the isthmus; it projected about 200 yards " into the sea, by which it has been entirely over- " thrown. The theatre is scooped out of the hill, " and fronting it are the remains of several large " buildings. There are also numerous sarcophagi, " some of them of the whitest marble, and of very " neat workmanship. Several inscriptions were tran- " scribed. The modern name of Phaselis is *Te-* " *krova*[e]."

Beyond Phaselis the mountains press in upon the shore, and leave a very narrow passage along the strand, which at low water is practicable, but when storms prevail, and the sea is high, it is extremely dangerous: in this case travellers must pass the mountains, and proceed into the interior by a long circuit. The defile in question was called Climax[f], Climax. and it obtained celebrity from the fact that Alexan-

[d] Geogr. Sacr. p. 248. The legend on the coins of this city is ΦΑΣ. and ΦΑΣΗΛ.

[e] Karamania, p. 56.

[f] This word was often used to express a narrow and difficult pass, (see Anc. Greece, tom. III. p. 305.) as that of *echelle* in French, and *scula* in Italian.

der led his army along it after the conquest of Caria, under circumstances of great difficulty and danger. For though the wind blew violently, Alexander, impatient of delay, hurried his troops forward along the shore, where they had water up to their middle, and had great difficulty in making their way. (Strab. XIV. p. 666, 667. Arrian. Exp. Alex. I. 26. Plut. Alex.) Captain Beaufort remarks, that " the shore at pre- " sent exhibits a remarkable coincidence with the " account of Alexander's march from Phaselis. The " road along the beach is however interrupted in " some places by projecting cliffs, which would have " been difficult to surmount, but round which the " men could readily pass by wading through the " water[g]."

Diodorus speaks of a fortress built upon a lofty rock on the Lycian frontier, which was taken by Alexander; he calls the people who occupied it, Marmarensium rupis. Μαρμαρεῖς. (XVII. c. 28.) Arrian adverts to this event, but does not name the castle. (Exp. Alex. I.) Scylax assigns to Lycia the town of Idyrus, beyond Phaselis, (p. 39.) but Steph. Byz. places it, together with a river of the same name, in Pamphylia. (v. Ἴδυρος.) Pliny notices in the Lycian sea the islets Illyris, Telendos, Attelebusa, and three Cypriæ. (V. 35.) Illyris, Telendos, Attelebusa insulæ. Attelebusa is also named by Ptolemy. Captain Beaufort identifies it with the isle of *Rashat*, near the pass of Climax[h]. The Cypriæ, according to the same navigator, are to be found between *Deliktash* and *Tekrova*, under the name of *Trinesia*. There yet remain a few Lycian towns to be discussed in the interior of the province.

[g] Karamania, p. 115, 116.   [h] Karamania, p. 117, 118.

Araxa is placed by Ptolemy on the borders of Araxa.
Caria, and it is recognised by Stephanus (v. Ἄραξα)
and the ecclesiastical records[i]. In the same direction
we may notice Comba, known to Ptolemy (Hiero- Comba.
cles, p. 684.) and the Notices. Octapolis stands on Octapolis.
the authority of the Alexandrian geographer only.
Tlos was of greater consequence, being reckoned by Tlos.
Artemidorus among the six principal states. (ap.
Strab. XIV. p. 665. Cf. Plin. V. 28. Ptol. p. 121.
Hierocl. p. 684. Steph. Byz. v. Τλῶς.) Strabo says
it was on the road to Cibyra: D'Anville has placed
it, with some appearance of probability, in the upper
valley of the Xanthus. Cana, noticed by Pliny, is Cana.
said, in the episcopal records, to have been also called
Acalea; but this last should be identified more probably with Acalissus, mentioned by Hierocles (p. Acalissus.
683.) and the Notitiæ. Candyba had near it the Candyba.
forest Œnium. (Plin. V. 28. Ptol. p. 121. Steph. Œnium
Byz. v. Κάνδυβα. Hierocl. p. 684.) Choma was situ- nemus. Choma.
ate near the river Adesa. (Plin. loc. cit. Cf. Ptol. Adesa fl.
p. 121. Hierocl. p. 683.) Around mount Massicytes,
and consequently not far from the coast, we have to
point out Rhodia, or Rhodiopolis, (Steph. Byz. v. Rhodia,
Ῥοδία. Plin. loc. cit.) Corydalla, (Plin. loc. cit. Ptol. sive Rho-diopolis.
p. 121. Steph. Byz. v. Κορύδαλλα[k].) Podalia. (Plin. Corydalla. Podalia.
loc. cit. Ptol. loc. cit. Steph. Byz. v. Ποδαλεῖα[l]. Hierocl. p. 683.) Pliny names alone Ascandalis, which Ascandalis.
however may be Acalissus, Amelas, Noscopium, and Amelas. Noscopi-um.

---

[i] Sestini adduces a very scarce coin, with the legend ΛΤΚΙΩΝ ΑΡΑ. which he attributes to A-raxa, p. 92.

[k] There are some few coins of Corydalla, with the inscrip-tion ΛΤΚΟ; and others of im-perial die, inscribed ΚΟΡΥΔΑΛ-ΛΕΩΝ. Sestin. p. 92.

[l] The coins of Podalia, of autonomous character, are very scarce; the legend ΛΥ. ΠΟΔ. The imperial medals bear the effigy of Tranquillina, with the legend ΠΟΔΑΛΙΩΤΩΝ. Sestin. p. 92.

Telandrus. Amelas has preserved some vestige of its name in that of *Almali*, above Myra. It is the Alimala of Steph. Byz. (v. Ἀλίμαλα.) In the Lexicon of Stephanus, the following places are set down to Lycia: Agathe, an island; (v. Ἀγάθη.) Adramyttis, an island; (v. Ἀδραμύττις.) Acarassus, a town; (v. Ἀκαρασσός.) Apollonia, an island; (v. Ἀπολλωνία[m].) Argaïs, an island. Arna, another name for Xanthus; (v. Ἄρνα.) Arneæ, a small town, on the authority of Capito, the Isaurian historian. Aulæ, a fortress; (v. Αὐλαί.) Glauci Demus, a spot so called from the hero Glaucus; (v. Γλαύκου Δῆμος.) Daphne, a fort; (v. Δάφνη.) Dias, founded by Diades; (v. Διάς.) Drys, a village on the river Arus, or as some read, Pinarus; (v. Δρῦς.) Edebessus, a town, on the authority of Capito; (v. Ἐδεβησσός:) in Hierocles (p. 683.) it is erroneously written Elebessus. Elæitichos; (v. Ἐλαίου τεῖχος.) Elgus, on the authority of Xanthus; (v. Ἔλγος.) Ereuatis; (v. Ἐρευάτις.) Erymnæ, cited from the Lyciaca of Alexander. Thryanda; (v. Θρύανδα.) Ilaris, on the authority of Polycharmus, a Lycian historian. Hippocome; (v. Ἵππου κώμη.) Cadrema, a colony of Olbia; the word denotes the drying or parching of corn; (v. Κάδρεμα.) Carbana; (v. Καρβανίς.) Cochliusa, an island so called from the shells found there; (v. Κοχλίουσα.) Lyrnatia, a peninsula and fortress; (v. Λυρνατία.) Melænæ, noticed by Alexander in the Lyciaca; (v. Μέλαιναι.) Menedemium, from Capito; (v. Μενεδήμιον.) Midea; (v. Μίδεια.) Molyndea, cited from the Lyciaca of Alexander; (v. Μολύνδεια.) Plateis, an island; (v. Πλατηΐς.) Rax, another island; (v. Ῥάγα.) Sidace,

Side notes:
Agathe insula.
Adramyttis insula.
Acarassus.
Apollonia insula.
Argaïs insula.
Arna.
Arneæ.
Aulæ.
Glauci Demus.
Dias.
Drys.
Edebessus.
Elæitichos.
Elgus.
Eruatis.
Erymnæ.
Thryanda.
Ilaris.
Cadrema.
Cochliusa insula.
Lyrnatia.
Melænæ.
Menedemium.
Midea.
Molyndea.
Plateis insula.
Rax insula.

[m] Sestini adduces some coins with the epigraph ΑΠΟΛΛΩΝΙ ΑΤΚΙ. which probably belong to this island.

a town; (v. Σιδάκη.) Sidene, quoted from Xanthus;
(v. Σιδήνη.) Sindia, from Hecatæus; (v. Σινδία.) Scari, Scari.
a town and sacred fountain. Syessa, a hut, so called Syessa.
from Syessa, an old woman, who entertained Latona. Telephi
Telephi fons, a fountain, seven stadia from Patara. fons.
Trabala; (v. Τράβαλα.) Tymenna; (v. Τύμηννα.) Hy- Trabala.
laini, from Alexander Polyhistor; (v. Ύλαμοι.) Hy- Hylami. Hytenna.
tenna, a town of Lycia; (v. Ύτεννα.) If I mistake
not, the name of this place throws some light on an
obscure people mentioned by Herodotus. (III. 90.)
The historian, speaking of the several nations who
composed the second satrapy of Darius, names the
Mysians, Lydians and Lasonians, Cabalians, and
Hygennians. (Ύγεννέων.) Schweighæuser observes
that this reading is suspicious, and some read Αὐτε-
νέων. Comparing these with Steph. Byz., the true
reading appears to be Ύτεννέων.

MILYAS, CABALIA, AND CIBYRA.

There yet remain to be considered in the present
section three petty districts, or rather one, which,
under three successive titles, claims the attention of
the historical student. The intermixture of races,
names, and languages, which seems to have taken
place in this corner of the peninsula is quite astonish-
ing, and the geographical confusion resulting there-
from, requires greater knowledge of the physical
distribution of the localities than we possess, in
order to set the matter in a clear point of view.
Strabo, who was well aware of the intricacies of
this part of his subject, has touched upon, rather
than discussed it, in three several parts of his Asiatic
geography. From these it appears that he considered the Solymi of Homer as the aboriginal in-

habitants of Lycia, and some of the neighbouring
mountainous districts, especially in the direction of
Pisidia.   He moreover contends, on the authority of
Homer, that the Lycians were a distinct race, since
Bellerophon is represented as sent by the king of
Lycia to make war upon the Solymi.

> Δεύτερον αὖ, Σολύμοισι μαχέσσατο κυδαλίμοισι·
> Καρτίστην δὴ τήν γε μάχην φάτο δύμεναι ἀνδρῶν.

IL. Z. 184.

And again, the son of Bellerophon is said to have
fallen in battle against this people.

> Ἴσανδρον δέ οἱ υἱὸν Ἄρης, ἄτος πολέμοιο,
> Μαρνάμενον Σολύμοισι κατέκτανε κυδαλίμοισι.

IL. Z. 204.

These Solymi were probably of Phœnician origin,
but it was a mere fancy of Josephus, reechoed by
Eusebius, to imagine that there was any connexion
between them and the Jews[n].   The passage they
quote in support of their opinion from the poet
Chœrilus, who describes the Solymi as forming part
of the great army of Xerxes, undoubtedly applies
to the Solymi of Asia Minor, as may be seen by
comparing the passage of the Samian poet with
Herodotus' account of the Milyæ, in his catalogue
of the Persian forces. (VI. 77.) The verses of Chœrilus are as follows:

> Τῶν δ᾽ ὄπιθεν διέβαινε γένος θαυμαστὸν ἰδέσθαι
> γλῶσσαν μὲν Φοίνισσαν ἀπὸ στομάτων ἀφιέντες,
> ᾤκουν δ᾽ ἐν Σολύμοις ὄρεσι, πλατέῃ παρὰ λίμνῃ,
> αὐχμαλέοι κεφαλὰς, τροχοκουράδες αὐτὰρ ὕπερθεν,
> ἵππων δαρτὰ πρόσωπ᾽ ἐφόρουν ἐσκληκότα καπνῷ.

AP. EUSEB. PRÆP. EV. IX. c. 9.

---

[n] This was founded on a bare similarity of name between Solymi and Hierosolyma.

The lake here mentioned is supposed by Eusebius to be the Asphaltis, but it is much more probably that of *Bourdour*, or *Egreder*, in ancient Pisidia. Strabo affirms that the Solymi afterwards took the name of Milyæ; (XII. p. 573. XIV. p. 667. cf. Herod. I. 173.) he also speaks of their language as being different from those of Greece, Pisidia, and Lydia. (XIII. p. 631.)

The Cabalees, from whom the tract of Cabalia, or Cabalis, took its name, are allowed by Herodotus to have been of Mæonian origin. Probably they were the only remnant of that ancient race subsisting when the historian composed his work. In his third book he distinguished the Lydians, the Lasonians, and Cabalians, though they all belonged to the same Persian satrapy; (III. 90.) but in the seventh he states that the Mæonian Cabalians were called Lasonii. (VII. 77.) Strabo also affirms that Cabalis was the ancient country of the Solymi, and that it was afterwards colonized by the Lydians. This colony became again intermixed with the neighbouring race of Pisidia, and the name of Cabalis was lost in that of Cibyra, which makes some figure, more especially in the Roman history.

Cibyra seems to have been originally a small town of Cabalis, but on the accession of the Pisidian colony the site was changed, and the town considerably enlarged, the whole circuit, as we learn from Strabo, being not less than 100 stadia. Its prosperity was chiefly owing to the excellence of its laws, though the government was that of an absolute monarchy. Under this government were included the three old Cabalian towns of Bubon, Balbura, and Œnoanda, and these, together with the capital, Cibyra, constituted a tetrapolis. Each of these towns had one vote in the general assembly of the states, except Cibyra, which had two, in consideration of its superior power. This city, as we are told by Strabo, could raise no less than 30,000 foot, and 2000 horse, and its influence and power extended over a part of Pisidia, Milyas, and Lycia, as far as Peræa of the Rhodians. (XIII. p. 631.)

The first mention which is made in history of Cibyra occurs in Livy's narrative of the Gallo-græcian war: a war which furnished the Romans with an occasion for settling several minor points of Asiatic policy, according to their sovereign will and pleasure. We learn from the Roman historian, that the consul Manlius, having crossed the Meander, and advanced through Caria to the Cibyratic frontier, detached C. Helvius, with a small corps, to discover whether Moagetes, tyrant of Cibyra, was disposed to submit. On his threatening to lay waste the territory of this chief, he came to the Roman camp, and was ordered to pay 500 talents. This sum, however, after much parleying, was reduced to 100 talents, with the addition of 10,000 medimni of wheat. (XXXVIII. 14.) This sufficiently proves the opulence and fertility of this district, a circumstance which is also insisted on by Strabo. (XIII. p. 631. Cf. Polyb. Frag. XXII. 17.) The last tyrant of Cibyra bore also the name of Moagetes, and he was probably the grandson of the above-mentioned prince, and son of Pancrates, who is incidentally noticed by Polybius as sovereign of Cibyra about the time of the second Macedonian war. (XXX. 9.) The last Moagetes became involved in hostilities with the Romans, and was conquered by Murena, who di-

vided his territory into two parts; Cibyra was annexed to Phrygia, but Bubon, Balbura, and Œnoanda, to Lycia. (Strab. XIII. p. 631.[s]) From this
time we find Cibyra mentioned as the chief town of
a considerable forum, or conventus, comprising not
less than twenty-five towns. This conventus was
however generally held, as it should seem, at Laodicea in Phrygia, to which province indeed most of
its states belonged. (Cic. Att. Ep. V. 21. Plin. V.
28.) We learn from Tacitus that Cibyra, having
been nearly destroyed by an earthquake, was afterwards restored by Tiberius. (Tacit. Ann. IV. 13.)
In later writers we find Cibyra included within the
limits of Caria. (Hierocl. p. 690.) In Ptolemy, and
some ancient inscriptions, we find the name written
Κίβυρρα. We shall see that there was another Cibyra on the coast of Pamphylia, which is not unfrequently noticed by the Byzantine writers. Strabo
reports that there were four dialects in use at Cibyra: that of the ancient Solymi, the Greek, the Pisidian, and the Lydian; the latter, however, in his
time was quite extinct, even in Lydia. He adds,
that the Cibyratæ excelled in engraving on iron, or
steel. (XIII. p. 631.) Verres employed two brothers, named Tlepolemus and Hiero, artists of this
town. (Cic. Verr. VI. c. 13.) No traces of the site
of Cibyra have as yet been discovered, but it is probable that they are to be found not far from *Denisli*,
or Laodicea, on a river, which is either the Lycus,
or a branch of it. Mons. Corancez, who is the only

[s] There are extant coins of
Moagetes, and two other Cibyratic chiefs, named Amintas
and Chotes. The usual epigraph is KIBΥΡΑ. and KIBΥΡΑ-
TΩN. The title of KAIΣA-
PEΩN, which appears on some
few, is probably in acknowledg-
ment of the benefit conferred
by Tiberius. Sestin. p. 120.

traveller who seems to have explored this valley, did not proceed so low down as the probable site of Cibyra, but he discovered some ruins on either bank of this river, which he supposed, not unreasonably, to belong to the Cabalian towns, Bubon, Balbura, and Œnoanda[t]. These are always mentioned together by ancient geographers. (Cf. Strab. loc. cit. Plin. V. 28. Ptol. p. 122. Hierocl. p. 685. et Not. Eccl. Steph. Byz. Βουβὼν, Βάλβουρα, Οἰνόανδα.) Bubon is said to have been afterwards called Sophianopolis. (Not. Eccl. p. 15.) It may be observed that Livy, who doubtless copies from Polybius, assigns to Cibyra, in the time of Moagetes, Syleum, which Steph. Byz. on the other hand attributes to Phrygia, or Pamphylia; (v. Σύλειον) also Alimne, probably a corrupt reading for Alimala, noticed above; Berkelius thinks it may be the Alychme of Stephanus. Sinda is another town which is noticed by Livy in this direction: (XXXVIII. 15.) and it must not be confounded, as Berkelius has done, with Isionda, or Isinda, since the Roman historian has named them as two different towns in the same chapter. Steph. Byz. places Sinda, or Sindia, in Lycia; (v. Σινδία) Strabo has connected it with Cibyra, Cabalis, and Milyas; (XIII. p. 630.) but elsewhere he seems to assign it to Pisidia. (XII. p. 570.)

Marginal notes: Bubon. Balbura. Œnoanda. Syleum. Alimne. Sinda.

[t] Itineraire de l'Asie Min. p. 418.

SECTION XII.

PAMPHYLIA AND PISIDIA.

Origin of the Pamphylians—Description of their coast and towns —Pisidia—Account of its inhabitants—Boundaries and geographical features of the country—Topography.

THE Greeks, ever prone to those derivations which flattered their national vanity, attached to the word Pamphyli that meaning which the component words πᾶν and φῦλον would in their language naturally convey, " an assemblage of different nations." (Strab. XIV. p. 668.) It was, however, further necessary to account for the importation of Grecian terms among a people as barbarous, as the Carians, Lycians, and other tribes on the same line of coast; and the siege of Troy, so fertile a source of fiction, gave rise to the tale which supposed Calchas and Amphilochus to have settled on the Pamphylian shores, with their dispersed followers. This story, which seems to have obtained general credit, is to be traced in the first instance to the father of history, (VII. 92.) and after him it has been repeated by Strabo, (loc. cit.) Pausanias, (Ach. c. 3.) and others. Of the Grecian origin of several towns on the Pamphylian coast we can indeed have no doubt; but there is no reason for supposing that the main population of the country was of the same race. It is more probable that they derived their origin from the Cilicians, or the ancient Solymi. Other etymologies will be found in Stephanus Byz. (v. Παμφυλία.) Pliny reports that this country was once called Mopsopia, probably from the celebrated Grecian soothsayer Mopsus. (V. 26.)

Pamphylia possesses but little interest in an historical point of view. It became subject in turn to Crœsus, the Persian monarchs, Alexander, the Ptolemies, Antiochus, and the Romans. The latter, however, had considerable difficulty in extirpating the pirates, who swarmed along the whole of the southern coast of Asia Minor, and even dared to insult the galleys of those proud republicans off the shores of Italy, and in sight of Ostia. (Cic. pro Leg. Manil.) Pamphylia was entirely a maritime country: its coast is indented by a deep gulf, commencing soon after the Sacred Promontory of Lycia, and extending to that of Anemurium in Cilicia. This wide bay was known to the ancients by the name of Mare Pamphylium, and in modern geography it bears that of *Gulf of Attalia*. The boundaries of Pamphylia, according to Strabo, were the pass of Climax beyond Phaselis of Lycia on one side, and the fortress of Coracesium, belonging to Cilicia, on the other. This comprised an extent of coast of 640 stadia. (XIV. p. 667.) The Turks call this part of *Karamania, Teké-Ili*.

Olbia.

Strabo, beginning his description of Pamphylia on the side of Lycia, names Olbia as the first town in this province; (XIV. p. 667.) and Pliny, proceeding in an inverse order, places it last. (V. 26.) Ptolemy mentions successively Phaselis, Olbia, and Attaleia. Stephanus censures Philo for ascribing this town to Pamphylia, since, as he asserts, it was situate in the territory of the Solymi, and its real name was Olba. (v. Ὀλβία.) The lexicographer is, however, himself in error, as Holstenius has acutely observed; and he has confounded Olbia with the Pisidian Olbasa. Strabo describes Olbia as a place of great strength, but without entering into any particulars as to its origin, which was probably Grecian. We have seen that Cydrema, a Lycian town, was colonized by the Olbians.

Strabo then proceeds to notice the Catarrhactes, a Catarrhactes fluvius. considerable river so called from its precipitating its waters over a high rock, with a thundering noise. (Cf. Plin. V. 26. P. Mel. I. 14.) Beyond was Attaleia, which owed its name and foundation to Attalus Philadelphus. This statement of the Greek Attaleia. geographer is precise, but it contains considerable difficulties in regard to the present topography of the coast. It seems reasonable to suppose, on the one hand, that the modern *Adalia*, or *Satalia*, which possesses numerous vestiges betokening a large and flourishing city, should represent Attaleia; while, on the other, it is found impracticable to identify the Catarrhactes with any river discharging its waters into the sea westward of Attaleia. This has led the judicious D'Anville, and also Captain Beaufort, who, from his accurate knowledge of the coast, brings great weight along with him, to suppose that *Adalia* occupies, in fact, the site of Olbia; and that the ancient Attaleia stood more to the east, at a place called *Palaia Attalia*, according to the French geographer; but *Laara*, as reported by the English navigator. Captain Beaufort's account of the Catarrhactes is so satisfactory, that I shall insert it

T 2

here in his own words. " The principal difficulty
" is to ascertain the position of the river Cataractes,
" which Strabo places between the cities of Olbia
" and Attalia, and which, he says, precipitates itself
" from a lofty rock, with a tremendous din : he does
" not expressly state that this fall is into the sea,
" but that seems to be implied by the context. Were
" the present *Adalia* and the ancient Attaleia the
" same, this river should therefore be found to the
" westward of the town ; yet on that side of it there
" are only two small rivers, both of which glide qui-
" etly into the sea through the sandy beach, and can
" by no means answer the description of the Cata-
" ractes.   On the eastern side of *Adalia*, however,
" no great river is to be met with till we come to
" the ancient Cestrus ; but it has been already no-
" ticed, that a number of small rivers, which fer-
" tilize the gardens, and turn the mills, near the
" town, rush directly over the cliff into the sea ;
" and if these rivulets had ever been united, they
" must have formed a considerable body of water.
" The water of those streams is so highly impreg-
" nated with calcareous particles, as to be reckoned
" unfit for man or beast ; and near some of the mills
" we observed large masses of stalactites and pe-
" trifactions.   Now the broad and high plain, which
" stretches to the eastward of the city, terminates in
" abrupt cliffs along the shore : these cliffs are above
" 100 feet high, and considerably overhang the sea ;
" not in consequence of their base having crumbled
" away, but from their summit projecting in a lip,
" which consists of parallel laminæ, each jutting out
" beyond its inferior layer ; as if water had been
" continually flowing over them, and continually

" forming fresh accretions. It is therefore not im-
" possible that this accumulation may have gra-
" dually impeded the course of that body of water
" which had once formed here a magnificent fall,
" and may have thus forced it to divide into various
" channels [a]." Col. Leake however, whose opinion
is also entitled to great consideration, is much disposed to think that *Adalia* really occupies the site
of the ancient Attaleia; and he supposes " that Ol-
" bia may be found in some part of the plain, which
" extends for seven miles from the modern *Adalia*
" to the foot of mount Solyma." This opinion, however, seems to rest principally on the erroneous statement of Stephanus Byz.[b]; and though the question
remains still uncertain, I feel rather disposed to ad-
here to the hypothesis of D'Anville and Captain
Beaufort. I would not, however, place Attalia so
far as *Laara*, but suppose it to have stood first on
the left bank of the river, and gradually to have extended itself to the right shore, and finally to have
included also Olbia within its circuit. Of the latter
place there is no distinct mention subsequent to Ptolemy. The Stadiasmus, which appears to be a later
document, takes no notice of it, and places Attaleia
west of the Catarrhactes. Scylax, on the other hand,
who wrote before the foundation of the latter city,
names only Olbia. (p. 39.) It appears, by comparing Strabo with Stephanus, that Attaleia stood on a
spot originally called Corycus, and which must not
be confounded with the Cilician site of the same

[a] Karamania, p. 134—136.
Col. Leake states that, after
heavy rains, the river precipitates itself copiously over the
cliffs, near the most projecting
point of the coast, a little to
the west of *Laara*. Asia Minor,
p. 192.

[b] Asia Minor, p. 190.

name. The appellation of Corycus seems to have belonged to a tract of coast or portion of the gulf. Attaleia was a sea-port town, since we are told in the Acts of the Apostles, that Paul and Barnabas sailed from thence to Antioch. (xiv. 25.) Its church attained to episcopal rank, being recorded as such in the Ecclesiastical Notices [c]. The remains of antiquity, consisting of city walls, triumphal arches, aqueducts, and inscriptions, attest its former consequence [d]. Strabo reports, that the sites of two towns, named Thebes and Lyrnessus, were pointed out between Phaselis and Attaleia; these were founded, as Callisthenes affirmed, by the Cilicians of Troas, who quitted their country, and settled on the Pamphylian coast. (XIV. p. 667.) The Stadiasmus has two places in the above-mentioned interval, named Tenedos and Lyrnas; the latter is probably the Lyrnessus of Strabo and Pliny. It is said to retain the name of *Ernatia* [e].

Magydus.   Proceeding along the coast from Attaleia, we have to notice Magydus, a place mentioned by Ptolemy and the ecclesiastical records, which attest its episcopal rank. (Hierocl. p. 6.) If it is the same place which Scylax calls Μάσηδος, it must lay claim to considerable antiquity. (Peripl. p. 39.) Magydus is probably to be identified with the Mygdala of the Stadiasmus. Col. Leake fixes it at *Laara* [f]. The

Masura.   latter document marks beyond Mygdala, Masura,

[c] Geogr. Sacr. p. 250.

[d] Karamania, p. 126—129. Leake's Asia Minor, p. 193. There are imperial coins of this city from Augustus to Salonina: legend ATTAΛEΩN. Sestini, p. 93.

[e] French Strabo, note, tom. III. part ii. p. 363.

[f] Asia Minor, p. 194. There are numerous imperial coins of Magydus, of Augustus, Nero, Trajan, &c.: legend MAΓΓAEΩN. Sestini, p. 93.

seventy stadia. Then the Catarracts, Ruscopoda, Ruscopoda. and the river Cestrus. Before we quit the Catarrhactes it may be proper to observe, that it answers to the river now called *Duden.* This is a considerable stream which issues from the great lake of *Egreder,* and, after receiving several minor rivers, breaks through the great chain of Taurus, and falls into the gulf of *Satalia.* The Cestrus, a navigable Cestrus fl. river, falls into the same gulf, about eight miles further to the east. At a distance of sixty stadia from its mouth stood inland the city of Perga, renowned Perga. for the worship of Diana Pergæa. The temple of the goddess stood on a hill near the town, and a festival was celebrated annually in her honour.

Νῆσων μὲν Δολίχη, πολίων δέ τοι εὔαδε Πέργη.
CALLIM. HYMN. IN DIAN. v. 187.

(Strab. XIV. p. 667. Scyl. Peripl. p. 39.)

Ἄλλαι δ᾽ ἐξείης Παμφυλίδες εἰσὶ πόλης,
Κώρυκος, Πέργη τε, καὶ ἠνεμόεσσα Φάσηλις.
DION. PER. 854.

Alexander occupied Perga with part of his army after quitting Phaselis; and we are informed by Arrian, that the road between these two towns was long and difficult. (I. 26.) Polybius leads us to suppose Perga belonged rather to Pisidia than Pamphylia. (V. 72. 9. Cf. XXII. 25. Liv. XXXVIII. 37.) We learn from the Acts of the Apostles, that Paul and Barnabas, having " passed throughout Pi- " sidia, came to Pamphylia. And when they had " preached the word in Perga, they went down into " Attalia." (Acts xiv. 24, 25.) This was their second visit to that town, since they had come there from Cyprus. It was here that John, surnamed Mark, departed from them; for which he incurred

T 4

the censure of St. Paul. (Acts xiii. 13.) Perga, in the Ecclesiastical Notices and in Hierocles, (p. 679.) stands as the metropolis of Pamphylia. (Cf. Plin. V. 28. Steph. Byz. v. Πέργη [g].) The ruins of this city are probably those noticed by Gen. Koehler under the name of *Eski Kelesi*, between *Stauros* and *Adalia*, on the left of a large and rapid stream, which must be the Cestrus [h]. On the other side of

Sylleum.

the same river stood Sylleum, or Syllium, at a distance of forty stadia from the sea. Its site was so lofty as to be visible from Perga. (Strab. XIV. p. 667.) Arrian reports that it was very strong, and resisted Alexander. (I. 25.) Scylax places it beyond the Eurymedon. (p. 40.) This town is also indicated by Ptolemy, Hierocles, (p. 679.) and the Ecclesiastical Notices. I am of opinion, however, that it must be distinguished from the Syleum already mentioned under the head of Cibyra.

Capria
lacus.
Euryme-
don fl.

Beyond the Cestrus, Strabo notices a lake of some extent named Capria, and still so called in modern charts. Somewhat further we come to the Eurymedon, a river rendered celebrated in history from the double defeat sustained by land and sea by the Persian fleet, from the Greek forces commanded by Cimon. The Persian ships were drawn up at the mouth of the river to the amount of 350, or, as some affirm, 600; but on the first attack they fled to the shore, and were stranded. Cimon then landed his forces, and after a severe engagement routed the enemy, and took their camp and baggage. (Plut.

[g] There are numerous coins of Perga, with the legend ΠΕΡΓΑ and ΠΕΡΓΑΙΕΩΝ, and sometimes ΠΕΡΓΑΙΑΣ ΑΡΤΕΜΙΔΟΣ. Sestini, p. 93.

[h] In Col. Leake's Asia Minor, p. 132.

Vit. Cim. Thuc. I. 100.) This signal victory anni-
hilated the Persian navy. Many years after this
event, we read in Livy that a considerable Rhodian
fleet anchored off the same river previous to en-
gaging with the ships of Antiochus, commanded by
Hannibal. (XXXVII. 22.) Captain Beaufort observes, with respect to these naval events, that the
state of the river must have undergone a considerable change, since, though it is now 420 feet wide,
the bar at its mouth is so shallow as to be impass-
able to boats that draw more than one foot of water.
I should not imagine, however, that on the above
occasions either fleet advanced far up the river.
The Persian fleet was certainly drawn up within it
at first, but they advanced out to meet the enemy,
and the engagement, if it deserves that name, took
place off the mouth : and as to the Rhodian galleys,
which were of the largest class, it appears that they
only anchored near the coast. The modern name of
the river is *Caprisou.* Aspendus, a town of size Aspendus.
and note founded by the Argives, was seated about
sixty stadia higher up the country. (Strab. XIV. p.
667.) Thucydides seems to speak of Aspendus as a
sea-port, but he meant probably the station at the
mouth of the Eurymedon. (VIII. 81. 87. 108.) It
was here that the Athenian patriot, Thrasybulus,
terminated his life. Being off the coast, he levied
contributions from the Aspendians, who, seizing an
opportunity when he was on shore, surprised him in
his tent at night, and slew him. (Xen. Hell. IV. 8.
Diod. Sic. XIV. 99. Corn. Nep. Thrasyb. c. 4.) Arrian relates that Alexander, having traversed Caria
and Lycia, advanced to the walls of Aspendus, when
the inhabitants having at first consented to pay fifty

talents, and give up the horses which they bred for
the Persian king, afterwards refused to fulfil their
agreement; on which the Macedonian king surrounded the town, situated on a rocky precipice,
at the foot of which flowed the Eurymedon, and
prepared to besiege it.   But they submitted on seeing the attack about to be made. (I. 26, 27.)   They
furnished contributions also at a later period to
the army of the consul Manlius. (Liv. XXXVIII.
15. Cf. Polyb. XXII. 18. 4. V. 73. 3. Scyl. Peripl.
p. 39, 40. Plin. V. 26. Mel. I. 14.)

> Κεῖθι δ᾽ ἂν ἀθρήσειας ὑπειράλιον πτολίεθρον,
> Ἀσπένδου ποταμοῖο παρὰ ῥόον Εὐρυμέδοντος.
> Ἔνθα συοκτονίῃσι Διωναίην ἱλάονται.

DION. PER. 852.

It appears from this last passage that Venus had
a peculiar worship in this town. (Vid. Eustath. ad
loc.)   The site of Aspendus has not yet been explored, but it would be easily discovered by ascending the banks of the Eurymedon.   General Koehler
crossed that river between *Dasha-cher* and *Stauros*, on a bridge built upon the ruins of a magnificent ancient bridge, one arch of which is still standing [i]. Steph. Byz. mentions a mountain, called Castnius, at Aspendus. (v. Κάσταξ.)   Pliny names, between Perga and Aspendus, the promontory Leucolla, and mount Sardemisus: (V. 26.) the latter is
also noticed by Mela. (I. 14.)   It is observed that
Stephanus has in this direction a town called Sardessus. (v. Σάρδησσος.)   The Stadiasmus points out

Castnius mons.

Leucolla promonto-rium. Sardemisus mons.

[i] Col. Leake's Asia Minor,
p. 131, 132. The first medals
of Aspendus betoken considerable antiquity, and the Doric
legend is curious: ΕΣ. ΕΣΤ.
ΕΣΤϜ. ΕΣΤϜΕΔΝΤΣ. In those
of a more recent date the name
of the city is exhibited in its
usual form, ΑΣ. and ΑΣΠΕΝ-
ΔΙΩΝ.

Cynosthrium, a spot between the Eurymedon and Cynos-
Cestrus. The same document reckons 100 stadia thrium.
from the former river to a station named Seleucia. Seleucia.
This place must have been near the mouth of a
nameless river pointed out by Strabo after the Eurymedon, and observed by Captain Beaufort, who
says : "After quitting the Eurymedon we passed se-
" veral streams, and one small river about fifty feet
" wide, which winds round the ruins of a village
" about half a mile from its mouth :" he adds, " that
" the islands, mentioned by Strabo, appear as large
" patches of sunken rocks near the mouth of the
" above mentioned river [k]." Col. Leake thinks Seleucia may have been the port of Sylleum [l]. Eighty
stadia further we find the important town and harbour of Side, founded, as several authors have re- Side.
lated, by the Cumæans of Æolis. (Scyl. Per. p. 40.
Strab. XIV. p. 667.) Arrian relates that the Sidetæ, soon after their settlement, forgot the Greek
language, and spoke a barbarous tongue peculiar to
themselves. It surrendered to Alexander in his
march through Pamphylia. (I. 26.) Side, many
years after, was the scene of a severe naval action
between the fleet of Antiochus, commanded by Hannibal, and that of the Rhodians, in which the former
was defeated. (Liv. XXXVII. 23, 24. Cf. XXXV.
13 et 48.) Polybius intimates there was a great
enmity between the Sidetæ and Aspendians. (V.
73. 3.) When the pirates of Asia Minor had attained to that degree of audacity and power which
rendered them so formidable, we learn from Strabo
that Side became their principal harbour, as well

[k] Karamania, p. 145, 146.   [l] Asia Minor, p. 195.

as the market where they disposed of their prisoners by auction. (XIV. p. 664.)   Side was still a
considerable town under the emperors, and when a
division was made of the provinces into two parts,
it became the metropolis of Pamphylia prima. (Hierocl. p. 682. Concil. Const. II. p. 240.)   Minerva was
the deity principally worshipped here. (Strab. loc.
cit.)   Mention of Side occurs also in Xenophon,
(Anab. I. 2. 12.)   Athenæus, (VIII. p. 350.) Cicero,
(Fam. Ep. III. 6.) Steph. Byz. v. (Σίδη.[m])   An interesting account of its ruins is to be found in Captain Beaufort's valuable work, with an accurate plan.
" It stands on a low peninsula, and was surrounded
" by walls ; that which faces the land was of excel-
" lent workmanship, and much of it is still perfect.
" It was flanked at intervals by square towers.
" There were four gates, one from the country, and
" three from the sea.   The agora, 180 feet in dia-
" meter, was surrounded by a double row of co-
" lumns.   One side of the square is occupied by the
" ruins of a temple and portico.   The theatre ap-
" pears like a lofty acropolis rising from the centre
" of the town, and is by far the largest and best pre-
" served of any that came under our observation in
" Asia Minor.   The harbour consisted of two small
" moles, connected with the quay and principal sea-
" gate.   At the extremity of the peninsula were
" two artificial harbours for larger craft.   Both are
" now almost filled with sand and stones, which
" have been borne in by the swell[n]."   In the middle

[m] The earliest coins of Side are extremely ancient; the in-scriptions are in very barbarous characters, resembling the Phœ-nician.   The imperial medals exhibit the proud titles of ΛΑΜ-ΠΡΟΤΑΤΗ and ΕΝΔΟΞΟΣ. Ses-tini, p. 94.

[n] Karamania, p. 146—162.

ages the site bore the name of *Scandelor*, or *Can-deloro*, but it now is commonly called *Esky Ada-lia.*

Eastward of Side we find the mouth of the *Me-* Melas fluvius. *noughat* river, called Melas by the ancients. (Strab. XIV. p. 667. Mel. I. 14. Zozim. V. 16.) Pausanias says that it was remarkable for the coldness of its waters. (Arcad. p. 659.) The Stadiasmus places it at a distance of fifty stadia from Side. Then follows, according to the same document, a temple of Diana, nine stadia, and Cyberna, fifty stadia. This last place is supposed by Col. Leake, with great probability, to be the Cibyra parva of Strabo, though Cibyra parva. that geographer has inadvertently placed it to the west of the Melas [o]. Ptolemy has annexed this town to Cilicia Trachea. From thence to cape Leu- Leucotheum promontorium. cotheum we have in the Stadiasmus fifty stadia. This headland answers to cape *Karabournou.* Some ruins, which exist on the headland which next follows, are referred by Captain Beaufort to Ptolemais, the last Ptolemais. Pamphylian town in this direction, since Corace-sium, a well known fortress beyond it, appertained to Cilicia. The Stadiasmus does not notice Ptole-mais, but it has, after cape Leucotheum, Augæ, fifty stadia to the east; then Anaxia, seventy stadia; and close to it a spot called Annesis, which Col. Leake thinks may have been the port of the former [p]. Our account of Pamphylia closes with the circumnaviga-tion of its coast; for though it probably possessed some few places at a distance from the sea, it is hardly possible to distinguish which are those that are strictly Pamphylian, and which that ought to be assigned to the conterminous province of Pisidia. The

o Asia Minor, p. 196.   p Asia Minor, p. 197.

following list is derived from Hierocles (p. 279—282.) and Stephanus Byz. The former names Uliambus, Tresena, Canaura, Berbe, or Barbe, according to the Notitiæ. Sindaunda, probably the same as Sindiandus of Pisidia. Palæopolis, Panemotichos, likewise known from ecclesiastical records and ancient coins [q]. Maximianopolis, an episcopal town, as we collect from the Acts of Councils. Regesalamara, and Limobrama, obscure places which occur nowhere else. Codryla is evidently the Cordylus of Steph. Byz., (v. Κόρδυλος) and Cordyla of the Notitiæ. Demusia, Demus Sabæon. Primopolis, which Wesseling is inclined to identify with Aspendus ; Serna, or Senna ; Cotana, perhaps the Catenna of Strabo. Orymna, or, as it is written in the Notitiæ, Erymne.

Stephanus Byz. assigns to Pamphylia, Cyrbe, on the authority of Hecatæus, but this may be only a false reading for Lyrbe ; (v. Κύρβη) also Lirnytea, (v. Λιρνύτεια) but this is likewise a corruption, instead of Lyrnatia. Rhopes, a people of Pamphylia, mentioned by Phavorinus. (v. Ῥοπεῖς. Cf. v. Ἐνότη.) Singya, a town ; (v. Σίγγυα.) Pharsalus, or Phanalius, a town ; (v. Φάρσαλος.)

PISIDIA.

The ancients seem to have known but little respecting the origin of the Pisidians. They generally, however, agreed as to the fact of their having succeeded to a portion of the territory once occupied by the Homeric Solymi. (Plin. V. 24. Steph. Byz. v. Πισιδία.) Strabo states that, according to some

[q] Panemotichos. Imperat. tantum Domnæ, Epigr. ΠΑΝΕΜΟΤΕΙΧΕΙΤΩΝ.

Marginal notes: Uliambus. Tresena, or Canaura. Berbe. Sindaunda. Palæopolis. Panemotichos. Maximianopolis. Regesalamara. Limobrama. Cordylus. Demusia. Demus Sabæon. Primopolis. Serna, vel Senna. Cotana. Orymna, sive Erymne. Cyrbe. Lirnytea. Rhopes. Singya.

accounts, they were intermixed with the Leleges, which is not improbable, considering their proximity to the Carians. (XII. p. 570.) The name of this people was unknown to Herodotus, but it is probable that he included them under that of Milyæ. There is little doubt also that the people, whom the poet Chœrilus described in the catalogue of Xerxes' army as inhabiting the Solymæan mountains and the shores of a broad lake, were no other than the Pisidians.

Occupying a wild and mountainous district around the highest summits of the chain of Taurus, their character and habits naturally partook of the rugged and untractable features of this highland region. As early as the epoch of the Peloponnesian war we hear them spoken of as a marauding race, hostile to the Persian monarchs, and whom it was found necessary to curb and repress by force of arms. The younger Cyrus had more than once led expeditions into their country, and they furnished him with a pretext for collecting the troops intended to overthrow his brother. (Anab. I. 1. 11. I. 9. 9. III. 2. 14.) These turbulent and savage habits had undergone but little change even in the time of Strabo, since he assures us that, like the Cilicians and Pamphylians, they were governed by petty chiefs, and subsisted principally by plundering their more peaceful neighbours. The Romans endeavoured, by establishing colonies in the country, to civilize, or keep in check this rude and lawless people; Christianity, too, lent its softening influence, and many a church was erected throughout the country; but the wars with the Saracens and Turks, and the final ascendency of the latter, have plunged it once more into

its original wild and barbarous state. Our knowledge of the ancient geography of Pisidia is principally derived from Arrian, in his account of Alexander's march through the country; also Livy's narrative of the expedition of Manlius, the consul, together with the details which are found in Polybius, of the hostilities carried on by Garsyeris, general of Achæus, against the Selgians, one of the leading states of Pisidia. Our information, as to the
actual or physical aspect of the country, is very in-
complete. The sites of some of the principal towns
are yet undetermined, and the mountains and lakes
cannot be laid down with any degree of precision.
Some valuable accession to the topographical knowledge of this part of Asia has, however, been derived from Mr. Arundell's journey through that tract
of country which lies contiguous to the ancient provinces of Caria and Phrygia. It will be seen, by a
reference to the map, that Pisidia is an inland country, having around it Caria on the west, Lycia on
the south-west, Phrygia to the north, Lycaonia and
Isauria, east and south-east, and Pamphylia to the
south. The line of demarcation in regard to the latter province, may be generally considered as formed
by the chain of Taurus, though Strabo seems to allow that some Pisidian cantons were situated on the
southern slope of that ridge, towards Side and Aspendus. (XII. p. 570.) Pisidia in general corresponds to that portion of *Anatolia* comprised within
the government of *Isbarteh*.

The most convenient, as well as the most interesting mode of description which we can adopt with respect to this country, will be to take first for our text
Livy's narrative of the expedition of Manlius; illus-

trating it by a constant reference to the geographers; and, secondly, that of Polybius, in regard to the operations of Garsyeris. In our last section we traced the progress of the Roman consul through Cibyra and the dominions of .Moagetes to the Lycian town of Sinda [r]. (XXXVIII. 15.) Proceeding through the territory of the Sindians he crossed the Cau- Caulares fluvius. lares, a small river, named by no other writer, but which is probably a branch of the Lycus. The next day the army passed the lake Caralis, and halted at Caralis palus. Mandropolis. The lake and town are alike un- Mandropolis. known, except that we find a Mandropolis assigned to Phrygia by Steph. Byz.; (v. Μανδρόπολις) but there is some uncertainty, as there was a Mandra in Troas, or Lesser Phrygia. On their next advance to the neighbouring town of Lagon, they found it deserted by the inhabitants, but well provided with stores of every description. This proves that it was a place of some consequence, and situated in a fertile country, but no other author seems to have recorded it; and this part of the narrative is omitted in the fragments of Polybius. The Roman army was at this time near the source of the Lysis, a branch pro- Lysis fluvius. bably of the Catarrhactes. From thence the consul advanced to the river Colobatus, as it is written by Colobatus, Polybius, (XXII. 18.) or Cobalatus, by Livy. This sive Cobalatus fluvius. would seem to be the stream which now takes its name from the modern town of *Estenaz*, and also joins the Catarrháctes, or river of *Duden*. Here the Roman general received a deputation from the neighbouring town of Isionda, the inhabitants of Isionda. which were then besieged by the Termessians, a

[r] P. 272.

powerful people of Pisidia[s], and reduced to great straits. They were shut up within their citadel, and implored the assistance of the consul. Manlius, who was anxious for a fair opportunity of penetrating into Pamphylia, advanced towards Isionda, raised the siege, and granted peace to the Termessians, on condition that they should pay fifty talents. It will be seen from this narrative that the Roman general was at this time on the borders of Pamphylia and Pisidia, or perhaps more correctly he was among the defiles leading from Milyas into Pamphylia; for Strabo says that the name of Milyas was more especially given to that portion of mountainous country which lay between the passes of Termessus, through the chain of Taurus, and Sinda[t]. This mountainous ridge can be no other than that which forms the continuation of mount Climax above Phaselis. (Strab. XIII. p. 631.) It is generally thought that in Ptolemy we should read Isinda for Pisinda. There is also some error in Stephanus, who places Isindus in Ionia. (v. Ἴσινδος.) The Episcopal Notices record Isindus among the sees of Pamphylia. From the light afforded by the historians cited above, we should expect to discover the site of Isionda, or Isinda, on the Pamphylian side of mount Taurus, above Phaselis and Olbia, or Attalia: and it is in

---

[s] There is one circumstance connected with this event which is peculiar to the narrative of Polybius, and which requires to be considered. The Isiondans came, says the historian, δεόμενοι σφίσι βοηθῆσαι· τοὺς γὰρ Τερμησσεῖς ἐπισπασαμένους Φιλόμηλον, τήν τε χώραν ἔφασαν αὐτῶν ἀνάστατον πεποιηκέναι, καὶ τὴν πόλιν διηρπακέναι. This mention of Philomelium, a town of Phrygia, and very remote from the scene of action, seems very suspicious. I should be inclined to substitute Φασήλιν.

[t] Some MSS. read Isinda.

this direction that a modern traveller, Mons. Co-rancez, observed some very considerable ruins as he was journeying from the latter town precisely in the line along which I have supposed the Roman consul to have moved, only in a contrary direction. According to this gentleman, the remains in question are to be seen on some high land about twelve miles north-west of *Adalia*. They are very extensive, covering a space of ground of about a square league, and having the appearance of a city overthrown by an earthquake. Outside the walls were numberless tombs cut out of the rock [u].

Termessus, which has been already alluded to, is supposed by Strabo to have been a fortress of some note as early as the time of the ancient Solymi. (XIII. p. 630.) Its commanding situation at the entrance of the defiles, by which Pisidia communicated with Pamphylia and Lycia, must always have rendered it a place of importance, and in all military transactions we find its occupation considered to be of great consequence. *Termessus.*

Arrian relates that Alexander, after reducing As-pendus, Perga, and other towns of Pamphylia, " set " out on his march into Phrygia. His route was by " the city of Termessus. These men are of the Pi- " sidian nation, and barbarians : they occupy a site " which is very lofty and precipitous on every side, " and the road which passes close to the city is diffi- " cult ; for the mountain reaches down from the city " to the road, and there it terminates. But there is

[u] Itineraire, &c. p. 391—394. There are coins belonging to this town as low down as the reigns of Gordianus and Valerian; the legends vary in ΙΣΙΝ. and ΙΣΙΝΔΕΩΝ. Sestin. p. 93.

" over against it another mountain, not less precipi-
" tous ; and these heights form a gate, as it were, in
" the road ; and it is possible, by occupying these
" mountains with a small force, to render the passage
" impracticable."　On this occasion, the Termessians
having come out with their whole force, had occupied both mountains.　Alexander, however, having
observed that the main body of the barbarians retired at night to the town, leaving a small force to
guard the pass, seized this opportunity of pushing
forward with the light troops ; and having easily
dislodged the enemy, led his army in safety through
the defiles.　Alexander, however, despairing of taking
the town, after receiving a deputation from the people
of Selge, who though Pisidians were at enmity with
the Termessians, continued his march. (I. 27, 28.)
This must also have been the route of the consul
Manlius, after having relieved Isionda, and received
the submission of Termessus ; but we have many topographical details, as we shall presently see, in the
Roman historian, which are wanting in the narrative of Arrian.　To conclude with Termessus, the
description of the latter historian agrees in a remarkable manner with General Koehler's observations on his journey from *Adalia* to *Burdur*.　After
quitting the former city he journeyed to *Bidjikli*,
seven hours due north along the river *Duden*, the
Catarrhactes of antiquity.　" From *Bidjikli* to *Ka-*
" *rabunar Kivi*, nine hours ; the first two hours
" over the same rugged plain, not far from the ri-
" ver.　The two great ranges on the west and north
" of the plains of *Adalia* now approach each other,
" and at length are only divided by the passes through
" which the river finds its way.　The road, how-

" ever, leaves this gorge to the right, and ascends
" the mountain by a paved winding causeway, a
" work of great labour and ingenuity. At the foot
" of it, in the plain, are the ruins of a castle, and of
" many towers and gateways of elegant architecture,
" with cornices, capitals, and fluted columns, lying
" upon the ground. Sarcophagi, with their covers
" beside them, are seen in great numbers, as well in
" the plain, as for a considerable distance up the
" side of the hill: some of them were of large size,
" many with inscriptions. At the top of this for-
" midable pass, which was anciently commanded by
" the city, standing at the foot of it, the road enters
" an elevated level surrounded with mountains, and
" proceeds along a winding valley amidst rocks and
" precipices [x]." There can be no question that the
pass and ruins in question are those of Termessus.
In addition to the ancient authorities already adduced, I would quote the commentary of Eustathius
on Dion. Perieg. (v. 858.) and Steph. Byz. (v. Τερ-
μισσός. Hierocl. p. 680.) It is to be noticed, that at
a late period the see of Termessus had united to it
the churches of two other neighbouring places, called
Jovia ('Ιοβία) and Eudocia; (Hierocl. loc. cit. where
see the commentary of Wesseling [y].) We may now
return to Livy's account of the march of Manlius.
Quitting Pamphylia, we are not told in what direction, but probably by a different route from that by
Termessus, he encamped on the first day near the

[x] Leake's Asia Minor, page 133—135.

[y] The medals of Termessus go down in the series of empe-rors as low as Severus. The epigraph is generally ΤΕΡΜΗΣ-ΣΕΩΝ, sometimes with the distinctive epithet of ΜΕΙΖΟΝΩΝ. Sestin. p. 96.

Taurus
fluvius.

river Taurus, which must be either a branch of the Cestrus, or the Eurymedon; the next he halted at a small place called Xyline-Come, which implies a village composed of wooden houses, and probably situate in the chain of Taurus. This pass is perhaps that which Polybius calls Saporda: that which

Sapordæ
saltus.

he names Climax, I conceive to be the defile of Termessus. (V. 72.) Proceeding from thence, the consul reached, after some days successive marching,

Cormasa.

the town of Cormasa: this Polybius, relating the same events, calls Κύρματα. (XXII. 19.) We have some indication also of the situation of this place in the Table Itinerary, which places it on the road leading from Laodicea on the Lycus to Perga. The distance between the latter city and Cormasa is twelve miles, which, as Col. Leake justly remarks, cannot be correct, since it was several days' march from the Pamphylian frontier, according to Livy, and Ptolemy has placed it in Pisidia: instead therefore of twelve, it is probable we should read forty. The distance from Cormasa to Themisonium in Phrygia is thirty-four miles, according to the Itinerary; but this likewise I should imagine to be defective.

Darsa.

From Cormasa the Roman army proceeded to Darsa, the nearest town, which the inhabitants had deserted, leaving however behind abundant supplies of every kind. The fragments of Polybius omit the mention of this place, nor does it occur in any other writer, unless it be the Dyrzela of Ptolemy; in Hierocles (p. 674.) it is Zorzila, but the Notitiæ write Zarzela. On quitting Darsa the Roman forces passed by some lakes, or marshes, when a deputation was received

Lysinoe.

from the town of Lysinoe, the citizens of which tendered their submission to the general. In Poly-

bius we read that " Cnæus (Manlius) having taken
" the town of Cyrmasa, and a great booty, proceeded
" forward : and as they were marching along the
" lake, there arrived deputies from Lysinoe surren-
" dering themselves." This town is clearly the same
as the Lysinia of Ptolemy, which that geographer
places to the north of Cormasa. The inhabitants
were perhaps the Lasonii (Alysonii var. r.) of
Herodotus. (III. 90. VII. 77.) The best clue
to the discovery of its site would be furnished by
that of the lake near which it stood. Col. Leake
supposes it to be that of *Bourdour*, but this lay beyond Sagalassus, which, as we shall see, the Roman
army had not yet passed. I should rather imagine
that it was the lake of *Igridi*, or *Egreder*, a very
extensive bason, with islands, from which issues the
river *Duden*. It appears to have been called Acrio- Acrioteri
teri in the middle ages [z], a name from which *Egre-* lacus.
der seems derived by corruption. This broad lake is
probably alluded to in a passage already quoted from
the poet Chœrilus, and being well known generally
as the Pisidian lake, would require no more definite
appellation from Polybius, whom Livy closely copies.

The army next entered on the territory of Saga- Sagalassus.
lassus, which Livy describes " as fertile, and abound-
" ing in every species of produce. The Pisidians
" inhabit it, by far the most warlike people of
" that country ; a circumstance which adds to their
" spirit, in conjunction with the fertility of the
" soil, and the thickness of the population, and the
" strength of their town, in regard to which few
" cities could be compared to it." This account

[z] Le Martinière erroneously   Tattæa Palus, under the word
supposes it, on the authority of   Acrioteri.
Delisle, to be the same as the

agrees remarkably with what Arrian reports of the same town; he informs us that Alexander, after traversing the defiles of Termessus, marched on to Sagalassus. " This too," says he, " was no small " city. The Pisidians likewise inhabited it, and " whereas all the Pisidians are a warlike people, " these appeared to be the most warlike part of " them. On this occasion they had occupied a hill " in advance of their town, because it did not appear " less capable of defence than the wall, and awaited " the enemy." Alexander, however, after a sharp conflict, drove the Sagalassians from their position, and took their town by assault; after which, the rest of Pisidia submitted to his arms. (I. 28.) The Roman general did not attack the city, but by ravaging their territory compelled the Sagalassians to come to terms. They submitted to a contribution of fifty talents, 20,000 medimni of wheat, and the same quantity of barley. Strabo states also that Sagalassus was one of the chief towns of Pisidia, and that after passing under the dominion of Amyntas, tetrarch of Lycaonia and Galatia, it was annexed to the Roman province; he adds, that it was only one day's march from Apamea. (XII. p. 569.) It appears, however, from Arrian, that Alexander was five days on the road between the same towns, but this may be reckoned from his first arrival before Sagalassus, and he seems to have halted some time after the capture of the town to receive the submission of the surrounding fortresses. Sagalassus is further noticed by Pliny, (V. 24.) Ptolemy, (p. 121.) Hierocles, (p. 673.) the Ecclesiastical Notices, and Acts of Councils, which prove it to have been a bishoprick. The name was sometimes written Selgessus, as we are told by Strabo. (loc. cit. Cf. Steph. Byz. v. Σαγάλασσος.)

Lucas, the celebrated traveller, had already reported the existence of considerable ruins at *Aglasoun,* a small place south of the Turkish town of *Isbarteh,* and the affinity of names naturally led to the idea that these remains occupied the site of Sagalassus. This has since been satisfactorily confirmed by the researches of Mr. Arundell. He describes them as situate on the long terrace of a lofty mountain, rising above the village of *Aglasoun,* and consisting chiefly of massy walls, heaps of sculptured stones, and innumerable sepulchral vaults in the almost perpendicular side of the mountain. A little lower down the terrace are the considerable remains of a building, and a large paved oblong area, full of fluted columns, pedestals, &c. about 240 feet long; a portico, nearly 300 feet long, and twenty-seven wide; and beyond this, some magnificent remains either of a temple or gymnasium. Above these rises a steep hill, with a few remains on the top, which was probably the Acropolis. There is also a large theatre in a fine state of preservation. Several inscriptions, with the words ΣΑΓΑΛΑΣΣΕΩΝ ΠΟΛΙΣ, left no doubt as to the identity of these noble ruins[a]. Here our examination of the march of Cn. Manlius through Pisidia terminates, since he afterwards quits that province, and enters Phrygia. Of Alexander's route, beyond Sagalassus, we learn thus much from Arrian : " that he proceeded towards " Phrygia by the lake Ascania, in which salt crystal- " lizes naturally, nor do the inhabitants use any

---

[a] A Visit to the Seven Churches of Asia, &c. p. 132—143.

" other." (I. 29.) Pliny also alludes to the same lake, and its natural history. (XXXI. 10.) It is doubtless the modern lake of *Bourdour*, which exhibits the same phenomenon[b]. Before we quit the neighbourhood of Sagalassus, it may be as well to mention certain places, respecting which there is some uncertainty whether they belong to Pisidia, properly so called,

Cressopolis, sive Cretopolis.

or to Milyas. Of these, Cressopolis, or Cretopolis, is assigned by Polybius, in his account of the operations of Garsyeris, to the latter district. That general having entered Milyas, is said to have encamped near the town of the Cretans, (Κρητῶν πόλιν,) close to the passes leading into Pamphylia, and at that time occupied by the Selgians. (V. 72.) Ptolemy, who writes the name Cressopolis, enumerates it among the towns of Cabalia, which in his system seems to include Milyas. (p. 123.) I should be disposed to identify this town with some ancient remains near *Buttakli*, between Termessus and *Bour-*

Pogla.

dour, and south-west of Sagalassus. Pogla, also assigned to Cabalia by Ptolemy, is corruptly written Socla, (Σώκλα,) by Hierocles, who gives it to Pamphylia. (p. 680.) It was a small place at that time, as the word Δῆμος prefixed to the name implies. It nevertheless had an episcopal church[c], and some of its coins are yet extant[d].

Menedemium.

Menedemium, which follows in Ptolemy's list of the Cabalian towns, is also assigned by Hierocles to Pamphylia, (p. 680,) where Wesseling very properly

Uranopolis.

corrects Δήμου Μενεδενέα to Μενεδήμιον. Uranopolis, which the Alexandrian geographer likewise ascribes

[b] Arundell's Visit, &c.

[c] Geogr. Sacr. p. 672.

[d] Of the reigns of Geta and Decius, epigraph, ΠΩΓΛΕΩΝ. Sestini, p. 94.

to Cabalia, is unknown to other authorities. Arias- Ariassus, sive Aarassus is probably the same with Aarassus, or Arassus, sus. one of the Pisidian cities mentioned by Strabo, from Artemidorus; (XII. p. 570.) but Hierocles also writes Ariassus under the head of Pamphylia, (p. 681.) so do the Acts of Councils and medallic monuments[e]. Corbasa, as it is written in Ptolemy and the eccle- Corbasa. siastical records, is the Colbasa of Hierocles. (p. 681.) We find also, from Ptolemy, that there was a town named Milyas, and his authority derives support Milyas from coins[f]; and Hierocles, (p. 680.) who has a urbs. place called Χωριομυλιαδικὰ, in Pamphylia.

The Byzantine historians speak of a town, named Sozopolis. Sozopolis, which must have been situate on the borders of Pisidia and Pamphylia. Nicetas reports, that it was taken from the Turks by John Comnenus, (Ann. p. 9.) but it was retaken by them. (Ann. p. 169. B.) Cinnamus says it was near the lake Pasgusa. (p. 13.) Hierocles assigns it to Pisidia; (p. 672.) and from some ecclesiastical documents quoted by Wesseling, it appears to have been at no great distance from Antioch of Pisidia. (Evagr. Hist. Eccl. III. 33. Act. Zosim. tom. III. Jul.) Lucas observed some remains of antiquity at a site called *Souzou*, south of *Aglasoun* and *Isbarteh*, on the road to *Adalia*, which probably belong to this town.

We have now to enter upon that part of Pisidia which lies to the east, and north of Sagalassus. At the distance of thirty stadia from that city, in a northerly direction, was the important fortress of Cremna, which, as Strabo reports, had long been Cremna.

[e] Sestin, p. 93. Imperatorii tantum Sept. Severi, &c. Epigraphe, ΑΡΙΑΣΣΕΩΝ.

[f] Milyas. Autonomi. Epig. MI. Regii Alexandri Magni, p. 95.

looked upon as impregnable; but it was at length
taken by the tetrarch Amyntas, with some other
places, in his wars against the Pisidians. This port
was considered afterwards by the Romans to be of
such military consequence, that they established a
colony there. (XII. p. 569. Cf. Ptol. p. 124. Hierocl. p. 681. Zozim. I. c. 60[g].) It is generally supposed that this town is represented by the modern
fort of *Kebrinax*, occupying a commanding situation
between *Isbarteh* and the lake *Egreder*. *Isbarteh*,
which is the capital of the government of *Hamed*,
the modern name for Pisidia, has taken the place
Baris.   probably of Baris, which Ptolemy assigns to Phrygian Pisidia. (p. 123.) Hierocles and the episcopal
records also ascribe it to Pisidia[h]. A modern traveller reports the existence of some ruins in and
near *Isbarteh*[i].

Between Cremna and Sagalassus was another
Sandalium. fortress, named Sandalium, which Amyntas did not
attempt to conquer. (Strab. loc. cit. Steph. Byz. v.
Oroanda. Σανδάλιον[k].) The Oroandenses were a people of Pisidia, occupying a considerable tract of country, and
not unfrequently mentioned in history. Though
their town Oroanda did not lie apparently on the
route followed by Manlius, they were summoned to
submit to the Roman power; and their deputation
followed the army to its camp on the borders of
Galatia. The sum of 200 talents imposed on them
as a contribution proves the wealth and consequence

[g] The coins of Cremna are
all imperial. The epigraph is
COL. CRE. or CREMNA. Ses-
tin. p. 95.
    [h] Baris. Imperatorius unicus

Severi Alexandri. Epigraphe,
BAPHNΩN. p. 95.
    [i] Arundell's Visit, &c. p. 131.
    [k] Sandalium. Autonomus u-
nicus. Epigraphe, ΣΑΜΔΑΛΙ.

of the place. They were employed afterwards as
spies, to report the strength and position of the
Gallogræcian armies. (Liv. XXXVIII. 18, 19.) This
service did not, however, exempt them from the payment of the sum at which they had been taxed.
(XXXVIII. 37—39.) It is remarkable that Strabo
should have made no mention of Oroanda, but it is
noticed by Pliny as one of the principal cities of
Pisidia; (V. 24.) and elsewhere he speaks of the
Oroandicus tractus, as a district of the same province,
bordering on Galatia. He also connects it with part
of Milyas and Baris; (V. 42.) and if we have been
right in identifying the latter place with *Isbarteh*,
this would fix Oroanda not far from the lake of
Egreder, on the north side of it. Ptolemy stations
the Oroandici between Isauria and Pisidia, which
would remove them rather more to the south. D'Anville imagined that there was some similarity between the name of Oroanda and that of *Hawiran*,
a fortress on the northern side of lake *Egreder*, a
position which corresponds sufficiently with the data
of ancient geography.

At the north-eastern extremity of the province Antiochia
we must look for the site of the Pisidian Antioch, a ^{in Pisidia.}
city of considerable importance, and interesting from
its historical recollections, especially those connected
with the labours of St. Paul in Asia Minor. We
learn from Strabo that it was founded by a colony
from Magnesia on the Meander ; this probably took
place under the auspices of Antiochus, from whom it
derived its name. On the defeat of that monarch it
was annexed at first to the territory of Eumenes ;
then to the principality of Amyntas, and on his
death it reverted to the Roman people, who sent a

colony there, and made it the capital of a proconsular government.   We find attached to this city
one of those singular pontifical offices of which we
have so many instances in Asia Minor.   The worship of Men Arcæus, with which this priesthood was
connected, had probably been derived from the Mag-
nesians: it was apparently on a great scale, and extensive estates and numerous slaves were annexed
to the service of the temple, but the whole was abo-
lished on the death of Amyntas. (Strab. XII. p. 577.
Cf. XII. p. 557.)   The circumstances connected with
the visit of St. Paul and Barnabas to Antioch of
Pisidia are related in the 13th chapter of the Acts.
We there learn that the apostle and his companion had
proceeded in the first instance to Perga from Cyprus,
and from thence had reached Antioch of Pisidia,
where they entered into a synagogue on the sabbath-
day; and when they had sat down, the rulers of the
synagogue, probably judging from their appearance
that they were strangers, and qualified to give in-
struction to the people, invited them to address the
assembly.   Upon this Paul stood up, and delivered
a short but most admirably comprehensive discourse,
setting forth the promises made to the patriarchs,
and their accomplishment in our Saviour's person;
his crucifixion, passion, and resurrection; and, finally, explaining the great doctrine of the atone-
ment, and warning them of the danger of rejecting
the proffered salvation.   Such was the effect of this
eloquent address, that the Gentiles besought the apostle that the same doctrine might be preached to
them on the following sabbath.   On this occasion it
is said, " that almost the whole city came together
" to hear the word of God.   But when the Jews

" saw the multitudes, they were filled with envy,
" and spake against those things which were spoken
" by Paul, contradicting and blaspheming.   Then
" Paul and Barnabas waxed bold, and said, It was
" necessary that the word of God should first have
" been spoken to you : but seeing ye put it from
" you, and judge yourselves unworthy of everlasting
" life, lo, we turn to the Gentiles."   The effect of this
declaration was very great, for the Gentiles flocked
to the preaching of the apostles.   "And the word
" of the Lord was published throughout all the re-
" gion.   But the Jews stirred up the devout and
" honourable women, and the chief men of the city,
" and raised persecution against Paul and Barnabas,
" and expelled them out of their coasts.   But they
" shook off the dust of their feet against them, and
" came unto Iconium."   It is evident from the whole
narrative that Antioch was then a large and flourishing town, and the resort of a great many Jews.
The sacred historian informs us, that St. Paul and
his companion returned again thither on quitting
Lycaonia, and passed through Pisidia, confirming
the disciples, and appointing elders in every church.
(XIV. 21.)   In Pliny's time we find Antioch digni-
fied with the title of Colonia Cæsarea, (V. 24.) which
is confirmed by the existing coins; these afford reasons for supposing that it dates from the reign of
Tiberius [k].   Antioch seems originally to have been
included in that part of Phrygia named Parorea, as
we collect from Strabo, who terms it Antioch " near

[k] Antiochia.   Epigraphe, ANTIOC. vel ANTIOCH. et COL. ANT. Imperatorii co- piosi a Tiberio usque ad Clau- dium. COL. CÆS. ANTIOCH. S. R. in multis, et constans, Cultus Dei Mensis. MEN. MENSIS. Sestin. p. 95.

" Pisidia," rather than " of Pisidia." The geographer, describing the district above-mentioned, says, " Phry-" gia Parorea stretches from east to west, following " the direction of a chain of mountains, on each side " of which we find an extensive plain, with a city. " On the north is situate Philomelium ; on the other, " or south side, lies Antioch, said to be near to Pisi-" dia ; the former is in the plain, the latter on a " hill." (XII. p. 577.) This passage in Strabo, and the notation of the Table Itinerary, are the only data we have for fixing the locality of this once flourishing town, and yet these have not been sufficient to lead to the discovery of its ruins. D'Anville looked upon *Ak-cher* as the representative of Antioch, but this would be placing that town on the great road from Apamea to Iconium, which does not appear to have been the case. According to the Table, it lay on a cross communication between Apamea and Side in Pamphylia ; the stages being, from Apamea to Apollonia, twenty-four miles ; to Antioch in Pisidia, forty-five ; to Side, eighty. The same road appears to fall in with the great route above-mentioned at Iconium, distant from Antioch sixty miles. Antioch would thus seem to form a triangle with Iconium and Philomelium ; and if we have been right in placing Apamea-Cibotus at *Dinglare*, we must measure sixty-nine miles from thence towards Iconium, taking care to keep south of Philomelium This perhaps will lead to the discovery of this ancient site ; but until this part of Asia is carefully explored, we must remain ignorant of the precise position it occupied. I see that in General Lapie's map it is fixed at a spot called *Fermak*, about twelve miles to the west of *Ak-cher*, and on a little river which falls into the lake called *Aiou-Gheul* in the same map. If there are any considerable ruins at *Fermak*, the localities would agree sufficiently well in point of distance, except that this spot is more than sixty miles from Iconium; but it is certain that we cannot place much reliance on the statements of the Table Itinerary. Antioch would seem from its coins, to have been situated near a small stream called Anteus, which would agree with the *Caxma* of General Lapie.

It appears from Hierocles and the ecclesiastical records that Antioch was the metropolitan see of Pisidia till a late period. Mention, I think, is made of it in Cedrenus in the reign of Basilius. (p. 688.) We learn from Ulpian that the colonial rights of Antioch were of the class denominated jus Italicum. (Dig. Tit. XV. de Cens.) In this part of Pisidia were a few other towns, which at an earlier period belonged to Phrygia Parorea, and in Pliny's time had been annexed to Lycaonia, as he expresses it, " in Asiaticam jurisdictionem versa ;" he then enumerates the Philomelienses, Tymbriani, Leucolithi, Pelteni, Tyrienses. (V. 24.) The former of these have been already discussed under the head of Phrygia. The Tymbriani are probably the people of Tymbrium, or Tymbrias, a place adverted to by Xenophon in the Anabasis. He states that it lay on Cyrus's route to Iconium, and that near it was to be seen the fountain of Midas, where that king caught the satyr, (meaning Silenus,) after intoxicating him with wine. (I. 2. 13.) The Acts of Councils, and other ecclesiastical records, number Timbrias among the episcopal sees of Pisidia, and there is little doubt

Tymbrium, sive Tymbrias.

that we ought to adopt Wesseling's emendation of Strabo, and read Τεμβριάδα for Βριάδα [1]. Steph. Byz. writes the name Tembrium; Charax, Tymbrium; Menander, Tembricum. (v. Τέμβριον.) This town must be sought for near *Isakli*, south of *Bulwudun*.

Tyriæum. Tyriæum, another Pisidian town on this border, was ten parasangs, and two days' march nearer to Iconium. Cyrus halted here three days, and reviewed his troops : whence it appears·that it was situated in a plain, probably near the modern *Aksher*. (Anab. I. 2. 13.) We have the authority of Artemidorus, quoted by Strabo, for knowing that Tyriæum was on the great Phrygian road between Philomelium and Laodicea Combusta. The above-mentioned geographer reckoned 500 stadia, or rather better, from Holmi, the first point in the Parorea to Tyriæum, beyond which Lycaonia commenced. (XIV. p. 663.) We see, however, that Pliny includes the latter town in Pisidia, as does also Hierocles. (p. 672.)

Amblada. The following Pisidian towns seem to have been situate on the same frontier. Amblada, which produced a sort of wine useful for medicinal purposes. (Strab. XII. p. 570. Cf. Steph. Byz. v. Ἄμβλαδα [m].)

Adada. Adada, named by Artemidorus, (ap. Strab. loc. cit.) Ptolemy, (p. 124.) and Hierocles, (p. 674.[n])

Conana. Conana is erroneously written Comana in Ptolemy, (p. 124.) and Hierocles, (p. 680.) as we are

---

[1] Note to Hierocles, p. 674. Timbrias. Imperatorius unicus Hadriani. Epigraphe, TIMBPIA-ΔΕΩΝ. p. 127.

[m] There are imperial coins of Amblada, of M. Aurelius, Commodus, and Caracalla. Epigraph, AMBΛΛΔΕΩΝ. Sestini, p. 94.

[n] Coins of Valerian and Gallienus, AΔΑΔΕΩΝ. p. 94.

authorized to infer from the existing coins of this town[o]. Prostanna is acknowledged by Ptolemy, Prostanna. (p. 124.) and the Acts of Councils. It has also a place in numismatic geography[p]. Seleucia, surnamed Seleucia. Sidera, as appears from Hierocles (p. 673.) and the Sidera. Notitiæ, is assigned by Ptolemy to Phrygian Pisidia. (p. 123.[q]) Ptolemy notices in the same district, Obasa, which is more correctly written Olbasa, Olbasa. and affords proofs of having once been a Roman colony[r]. Dyrzela, we have supposed to be the Darsa Dyrzela. of Livy. Orbanassa and Talbenda are unknown to Orbanassa. Talbenda. other geographers.

We have yet to speak of that southernmost portion of Pisidia which follows the range of Taurus from Termessus to the confines of Isauria, and consequently borders on Pamphylia. This tract of country contained the most celebrated and powerful city of the whole country, I mean Selge, which Selge. boasted of a Grecian origin; having first been founded, as it is reported by Calchas, and subsequently having received a colony of Lacedæmonians. Whatever doubts may arise as to the former of these events, we cannot reasonably refuse to receive the latter, since it is spoken of as an acknowledged fact by authors of the highest credit, such as Polybius and Strabo.

[o] Conane. Autonomus unicus. Epigraphe, ΚΟΝΑΝΕΩΝ. Imperatorii M. Aurelii, &c. Sestin. p. 95.

[p] Prostanna. Autonomus unicus. Epigraphe, ΠΟΛΙC. et in R. ΠΡΟCΤΑΝΝΕΩΝ. Imperatorii cum capite Cl. Gothici. Epigr. ΠΡΟCΤΑΝΝΕΩΝ. Mentio situs a Monte Viaro. ΟΤΙΑΡΟC.

[q] The name of ΚΛΑΤΔΙCCE-ΛΕΤΚΕΩΝ would lead to the idea that it had been restored by Claudius. Sestin. p. 96.

[r] Olbasa. Imperat. Mæsæ. Epigraphe, COL. JUL. AVG. OLBASEN. Gordiani Pii, COL. OLBA.

Τοῖς δ᾽ ἐπὶ Πισιδέων λιπαρὸν πέδον· ἧχι πόληες
Τερμισσὸς Λύρβητε, καὶ ἣν ἐπολίσσατο λαὸς
Πρίν ποτ᾽ Ἀμυκλαίων, μεγαλώνυμος ἐν χθονὶ Σέλγη.

DIONYS. PERIEG. 858.

(Cf. Eustath. ad loc. Steph. Byz. v. Σέλγη.) From
the superiority of its laws and government, and the
bravery of its citizens, Selge soon surpassed all the
neighbouring towns in population and power; the
number of its inhabitants being at one time, as
Strabo reports, not less than 20,000. The nature of
the country in which it was situate, greatly contributed also to the preservation of its independence.
It was difficult of access, being surrounded by precipices and beds of torrents, which joined the Cestrus
and the Eurymedon, and required bridges to make
them passable. Owing to these circumstances, the
Selgians were never subject to foreign sway, but
remained in the quiet enjoyment of their liberty.
When Alexander traversed Pisidia, they deputed an
embassy to that monarch, and conciliated his favour
and friendship. Arrian, who relates this circumstance, reports that their city was large, and the
people brave and warlike; he adds, that they were
at enmity with the Telmissians. (I. 28.) Polybius
has made us acquainted with another interesting,
but subsequent period, in the history of Selge. At
the time when Achæus had subjected the greatest
portion of Asia Minor, and had attained to a degree
of power enjoyed by no sovereign of that country
since the time of Crœsus, we learn from that historian that the people of Pednelissus, a Pisidian town,
on the Pamphylian frontier, were besieged by the
Selgians. Despairing of resisting their powerful ad-
versaries, the Pednelissians earnestly besought A-

chæus to send them succours. The ambitious monarch eagerly seized this opportunity of extending his conquests, and immediately despatched a force of 6000 foot and 500 horse, under the command of Garsyeris, to their aid. The Selgians, having learnt that this succour was approaching, were not slow in occupying the different passes which led into their country, and destroying the roads and approaches. Garsyeris having advanced as far as Cretopolis, in Milyas, found his further progress obstructed by these measures; he therefore had recourse to stratagem, in the hope of deceiving the enemy. He withdrew his forces to the rear of the passes, and appeared to be in full retreat. The Selgians, deceived by this feint, abandoned the strong posts they had seized, and retired to their city. No sooner had they retired, than the general of Achæus marched rapidly forward, passed the mountains without opposition, and descended upon Perga; leaving an officer named Phayllus, to guard the defiles. He then commenced negotiations with the principal towns of Pisidia and Pamphylia, for the purpose of increasing his army, which was too small to effect the conquest of Selge. The Selgians having discovered their error, attempted to dislodge Phayllus from the passes; but they were beaten back with loss, and forced to desist from the attempt. They nevertheless persevered in the siege of Pednelissus, and pressed their attacks with greater vigour. Garsyeris having now succeeded in collecting a large force, advanced toward that town, and pitched his camp at some distance from it, in the hope of compelling the enemy to raise the siege. The Selgians, however, not only intercepted a convoy, which he at-

tempted to introduce into the town, but proceeded
to assault the camp of Garsyeris. Success seemed
for a time to favour their daring enterprise, till at
length Garsyeris leading out the cavalry, charged
them in the rear, whilst the infantry, relieved by
this manœuvre, resumed the offensive in front. The
Pednelissians now seized this opportunity to make a
sally, and assailed the lines of the enemy, who, thus
attacked on every side, gave way at all points, and
fled in disorder to Selge. Garsyeris, following up
his victory, advanced to that city, and prepared to
invest it. The Selgians, greatly dejected by their
late defeat, sent one of their principal citizens,
named Logbasis, in whom they placed great confidence, to negociate with that general. Logbasis,
however, betraying the trust reposed in him by his
countrymen, concerted measures with Garsyeris for
putting Achæus, who was daily expected, in possession of the city.

On the day appointed, Logbasis and his friends
and relatives armed themselves in his house, ready
to cooperate with the enemy. Garsyeris led his
troops against the Cesbedium, (Κεσβέδιον,) or temple
of Jupiter, which was the Acropolis; and Achæus
himself, with the remainder, advanced towards the
city. A shepherd, however, having beheld the troops
in motion, brought the news to the senate, then
assembled. The Selgians, alarmed at this intelli-
gence, ran speedily to occupy the Cesbedium and
other posts; some also proceeded to the house of
Logbasis, and discovering the treason he was plan-
ning, destroyed him, together with his family and
partisans. After this, they granted liberty to all
their slaves, and prepared to defend their walls.

Garsyeris seeing the citadel guarded, did not think it prudent to hazard an attack. But Achæus, attempting to make himself master of the gates, was beaten back with loss. The Selgians, however, ultimately despairing of being able to resist his power, sent deputies to sue for peace, which was granted to them on the following conditions: they agreed to pay immediately 400 talents, to restore the prisoners they had taken from the Pednelissians, and, after a certain time, to pay 300 talents in addition. The Selgians then, says the historian, having been thus brought into danger by the faithlessness of Logbasis, through their own courage, both preserved their country, and did not disgrace their liberty, nor the affinity which subsisted between them and the Lacedæmonians. (V. 72—77.)

The territory of Selge, as Strabo reports, though mountainous, was of an excellent quality, and very productive; it yielded abundance of oil and wine, and afforded pasturage for great numbers of cattle. The forests too supplied a great variety of timber trees; of these, the storax was particularly valuable, from its yielding a strong perfume. Selge was also noted for an ointment prepared from the iris root. (Strab. XII. p. 570, 571. Plin. XXI. 7. XV. 7. XXIII. 4.) It is somewhat remarkable that Pliny should have omitted all mention of Selge in his geography, for we know, from its coins, that it still flourished in the time of Hadrian[s]. It appears also in the System of Ptolemy and the Synecdemus of

[s] Selge. Autonomi. Epigr. ΣΕ. ΣΕΛ. ΣΕΛΓΕΩΝ. Imperatorii ab Hadriano usque ad Saloninam. Concordia cum Lacedæmoniis in num. Decii, ϹΕΛΓΕΩΝ ΛΑΚΕΔΑΙΜΟΝΙΩΝ ΟΜΟΝΟΙΑ.

Hierocles; (p. 681.) but from the term πολίχνη applied to it by Zosimus, (V. 15.) it had evidently much fallen off from its pristine state. The ruins of this once flourishing city are yet undiscovered, for no traveller has explored these solitary and pathless wilds of Taurus. We know generally from Strabo that it was situate near the sources of the Eurymedon and Cestrus; and it is possible that its ruins may be those which Captain Beaufort heard of at *Alaya;* they were described " as extensive remains " of an ancient Greek city, with many temples, about " fifteen hours distance to the northward[t]."

Pednelissus, which has already been brought under our notice in the history of Selge, is placed by Strabo near the Eurymedon, above Aspendus. (XIV. p. 667.) He there seems to ascribe it to Pamphylia, but he distinctly enumerates it elsewhere in the list of Pisidian towns, borrowed from Artemidorus. (XII. p. 570. Cf. Steph. Byz. v. Πεδνιλισσός.) Ptolemy also attaches it to Pisidia, (p. 124,) but Hierocles, who gives great extension to Pamphylia, brings it, together with Selge, under that province. (p. 681.) Pednelissus[u] is also known from the ecclesiastical annals, and its coins[x]. To the east of Selge, and towards the confines of Cilicia and Isauria, were the Etennians, or, as Strabo writes the name, the Catennians; (Κατεννεῖς, XII. p. 570.) the former nomenclature is that of Polybius, (Ἐτεννεῖς) and seems preferable, being confirmed by the Ecclesiastical Notices. (V. 73.) He states, that they inhabited a

Pednelissus.

Etenna.

---

[t] Karamania, p. 168.

[u] Where, instead of Παστι-λημισσός, we ought to read, with Wesseling, Πεδνηλισσός.

[x] Imperatorius unicus Maximi Cæsaris. Epigr. ΠΕΔΝΗ-ΛΙΣΣΕΩΝ. Sest. p. 96.

mountainous tract of Pisidia, above Side, and sent
8000 heavy armed soldiers to reinforce the army of
Garsyeris; a fact which demonstrates that they were
a numerous and warlike people. I am not aware,
however, that any other author has noticed them,
unless the name of their city is disguised in Hierocles under that of Atmenia[x]. We must look in the
same canton for Lyrbe, a town of some note appa- Lyrbe.
rently, since it is mentioned by Dionysius the poet,
(v. 858.) and is known from its coins to have flourished in the reign of Alexander Severus[y]. It is
also ranked among the episcopal towns of Pamphylia by the Not. Eccles., and there is little doubt that
it should be identified with the Lyrope of Ptolemy,
though he places that town in Cilicia Trachea. (p.
124.) Vinzela, of the same geographer, is clearly Vinzela.
the Unzela of the Council of Nicæa[z]. Casa and Colo- Casa.
brassus, which he likewise attributes to Cilicia Tra- Colobros-sus.
chea, are assigned to Pamphylia by the ecclesiastical
records[a].

Hierocles enables us to add the following to our
list of Pisidian towns: (p. 672, 673.) Neapolis and Neapolis.
Limenæ, which occur likewise in the Sacred Geo- Limenæ.
graphy; Sabinæ, Sinethandus, or Siniandus, Ha- Sabinæ.
drianopolis, Tymandrus; the three last are also Sinethan-dus, sive
known to the councils. Eudoxiopolis, Justiniano- Siniandus.
polis, and Mallus; these also find a place in the No- Hadriano-polis.
tices. Tityassus occurs in the list of towns adduced Tyman-drus.
by Strabo from Artemidorus, but it is corruptly Eudoxio-polis. Justinia-nopolis. Tityassus.

[x] There are autonomous and imperial coins of Etenna. Epig. ET. ETEN. ETENNEΩN. Sestin. p. 93.
[y] Lyrbe imperat. ab Alex. Severo usque ad Saloninam, Epigr. ΛΥΡΒΕΙΤΩΝ. Sest. p. 96.
[z] Geogr. Sacr. p. 251.
[a] Geogr. Sacr. p. 249. Some imperial coins, inscribed ΚΑΣΑΤΩΝ, exist in a few collections. Sestin. p. 93.

written, as Wesseling has observed, Pityassus. The reading Tityassus is confirmed by Hierocles, the Tarbassus. Ecclesiastical Notices, and coins[b]. Tarbassus, also in Strabo's list, is unknown to the other geographical authorities. Stephanus places, in the same pro-

Thyessus. vince, Thyessus; (v. Θυεσσός.) Narmalis, mentioned
Narmalis. apparently by Ephorus; (v. Νάρμαλις.) Pera; (v.
Pera.
Pydes urbs Πήρα.) Pydes, a town and river; (v. Πύδης.) Tlos,
et fl. named like the Lycian city; (v. Τλῶς.) Tyrus, perhaps the same as Tyriæum; (v. Τύρος.)

[b] Tityassus. Imperatorii Hadriani, Antonini Pii, Getæ. Epigraphe, ΤΙΤΤΑΣΣΕΩΝ. Sestini, p. 96.

SECTION XIII.

CILICIA.

———◆———

Origin and history of the Cilicians—Boundaries and division of the province into Trachea, or Aspera, and Campestris—Chain of Taurus and mountain passes—Topography.

THE people whom the Greeks called Cilicians, (Κί-λικες,) were, in ancient times, termed Hypachæi, as Herodotus reports. The historian does not account for the origin of the name, which has somewhat of a Grecian air about it; but he adds, that the appellation of Cilicians was subsequently derived from Cilix, the son of Agenor, a Phœnician. (VII. 91.) This passage proves, at least, that there was a general notion among the Greeks that this people were an offset of the Syrian or Phœnician family; and it must be admitted that this opinion is so probable in itself, from the contiguity of the two nations, that it might be received on even less creditable testimony than that of the father of history. I am not aware that any ancient author has positively told us that the language of the Cilicians was the same with that of the Phœnicians; but this is very probable[a]; and at all events history has informed us that some of the most ancient and considerable towns of their country were founded by the Assyrians and Phœnicians[b]. The Cilicians again were from the first a maritime

[a] See Bochart. Geogr. Sacr. I. ch. 5.
[b] Viz. Tarsus, Anchiale, and Celenderis.

people, which strengthens the notion of their connexion with the Phœnicians, since these are allowed on all hands to have first applied themselves to nautical affairs. There is another political feature which seems to distinguish the people, who are the subject of the present section, from the other tribes of Asia Minor, I mean that of being under the government of a king with an hereditary title. We find this prince, named Syennesis, in conjunction with Labynetus, king of Babylon, acting as mediator between Alyattes and Cyaxares, who were at war, and finally reconciling them with each other. (Herod. I. 74.) Another Syennesis is mentioned as king of Cilicia, in the reign of Darius. (V. 118.) Another is said to have been an admiral in the fleet of Xerxes, but he is not styled king, and he is described as the son of Oromedon. (VII. 98.) But we have frequent mention of a Cilician king of this name in the early part of the Anabasis, whence we collect that at this time, Cilicia, though tributary to the Persian king, was nominally under the government of its native princes. The Syennesis, of whom Xenophon writés, had intended opposing Cyrus in his march against his brother, and for that purpose is said to have guarded for a time the defiles of Taurus; but his wife Epyaxa, seduced, it appears, by the Persian prince, prevailed on him to abandon the cause of Artaxerxes, and not only to desist from opposing the progress of Cyrus, but even to supply him with sums of money for the payment of his troops. (I. 2.) It appears, indeed, that Cilicia, more especially that part which consisted of plains, was a wealthy country; since we are informed by Herodotus, that it yielded to Darius a revenue of 500 talents, equal to that of Mysia and

Lydia together, besides 360 white horses. (III. 90.) Xenophon also describes it as a broad and beautiful plain, well watered, and abounding in wine, and all kinds of trees, and yielding barley, millet, and other grain. (Anab. I. 2.) and Ammianus, " Cilicia late " distenta dives omnibus bonis terra." (XIV. 8.) In a military point of view the importance of Cilicia was also very great, since it was surrounded by lofty mountains, presenting only one or two passes, and these easily secured by a small force against the largest armies. Had the Persians known how to defend these, the younger Cyrus would never have reached the Euphrates, nor would Alexander have been able to penetrate to the plains of Issus, which witnessed the overthrow of Darius. (Arrian. II, 4.)

At a later period we learn from Cicero, during his command there, what importance the Romans attached to the province of Cilicia when it became necessary to cover Asia against the growing power of the Parthians. (Att. Ep. V. 20.) Again, the mountain barrier of Cilicia served to protect for a time the tottering empire of the east against the desperate attacks of the Arabs and Turks; and when these had been once fairly forced, the standard of the prophet was soon beheld from the walls of Constantinople. As a maritime country, too, Cilicia makes a considerable figure in history, since it furnished numerous fleets to the Persian monarchs, as well as the Syrian and Egyptian successors of Alexander. But it was more especially from the formidable character of her piratical navy that Cilicia has obtained a name in the seafaring annals of antiquity. Some idea of the alarm inspired by these daring rovers can be formed from the language of

Cicero, however exaggerated we may suppose it to be for a political purpose. "Quis enim toto mari "locus per hos annos, aut tam firmum habuit præ-"sidium ut tutus esset? aut tam abditus fuit, ut la-"teret? Quis navigavit, qui non se aut mortis aut "servitutis periculo committeret cum aut hieme, aut "referto prædonum mari navigaret?—Quam provin-"ciam tenuistis a prædonibus liberam per hosce an-"nos? quod vectigal vobis tutum fuit? quem so-"cium defendistis? cui præsidio, classibus vestris "fuistis? quam multas existimatis insulas esse de-"sertas? quam multas aut metu relictas aut a præ-"donibus captas urbes esse sociorum." (Pro Leg. Man. §. II.)   Allowing the picture to be somewhat highly coloured, there remains enough to shew that the evil was one of considerable magnitude, and which called forth great exertions on the part of the Roman government.   The selection they made of Pompey, the greatest captain of the age, and the unusual powers intrusted to his management, prove this, and the statements of Appian and Plutarch are hardly behind that of Cicero. (Bell. Mithr. c. 92, &c. Plut. Mithr. et Pomp.)   With his name, and the immense means placed at his disposal, he began by restoring confidence to the alarmed provinces and allies, and peace to the seas around Italy.   Afterwards he proceeded to Cilicia, and in less than fifty days he reduced the whole province, either by force of arms or by terror.   More than 20,000 of the pirates are said to have fallen into his hands: these he settled in the interior, or removed to more distant countries, and thus entirely purged the shores of Asia of these nests of robbers.   In the course of the war the Romans are said to have captured 378 ships and burnt 1300, conquered 120 towns and castles, and to have slain 10,000 of the enemy. (Appian. Mithrid. Plut. Pomp. Strab. XIV. p. 665.) The boundaries of Cilicia are easily defined, being marked by the great chain of Taurus, which, skirting round the shores of the Pamphylian gulf, stretches afterwards towards the interior with a wide sweep, and finally closes round again upon the coast of the Issicus Sinus at the Syrian gates. Cilicia is thus enclosed on all sides by the sea and the mountain belt of Taurus, and Amanus, which divides it from Isauria, Lycaonia, Cappadocia, and Syria. But the whole of the space thus girt round does not consist of plain : the most western part is nearly all occupied by the broad ridge of Taurus itself, which leaves scarcely any room for level land towards the sea. The rugged nature of this canton obtained for it the name of Trachea and Tracheotis ; while the larger and more easterly portion of the country was denominated Cilicia Campestris, from its champaign character. Each of these will· be discussed separately in their natural order. And first then,

CILICIA TRACHEA.

This highland tract extended along the shore from Coracesium, the first fortress on the side of Pamphylia, to the river and town of Lamus, comprising an extent of about 1300 stadia. (Strab. XIV. p. 669.) Inland it reached to the higher summits of the central chain, on the confines of Isauria, properly so called. I say properly, because when the fierce banditti, which occupied that country, had rendered themselves so formidable to the weak sovereigns of Constantinople, they found, in the fastnesses of Cilicia Trachea, a congenial soil for extending their system of robbery and plunder ; and in process of time the name of Isauria prevailed over that which had been attached to it in the age of classic geography. The Turks give generally the appellation of *Itshil* to Cilicia, but they divide it also into two pachaliks, those of *Selefkieh* and *Adana :* the former nearly comprises that which was anciently called Trachea.

Corace-
sium.

Coracesium, the first place we come to on passing the boundary of Pamphylia, is described by Strabo as a strong and important fortress, situate on a steep rock. It was held for a long time by Diodotus Tryphon, a patrician who had revolted from the kings of Syria, and maintained himself against their power as an independent chieftain, till he was at length blockaded within one of his castles by Antiochus, and driven to destroy himself, that he might not fall into the hands of that prince. This Tryphon was the first who, taking advantage of the indolence and want of energy of the Syrian monarchs, led the way for that system of piracy for which Cilicia became afterwards so notorious. (XIV. p. 668. Appian. Syr. c. 67. Justin. XXXVI. 1.) Coracesium was taken by Pompey in the piratical war. (Appian. Mithr.) It is also incidentally noticed by Livy. (XXXIII. 20. Cf. Scyl. p. 40. Plin. V. 27. Ptol. p. 124.) In the time of Hierocles it was under the Pamphylian jurisdiction. (p. 682. Cf. Act. Concil[c].) The site of Coracesium corresponds with that of *Alaya,* which Captain Beaufort describes as " a " promontory rising abruptly from a low sandy isth- " mus, separated from the mountains by a broad

[c] There are imperial coins of this place, with the legend ΚΟ-ΡΑΚΗΣΙΩΝ. Sestin. p. 100.

" plain ; two of its sides are cliffs, of great height,
" and absolutely perpendicular ; and the eastern side,
" on which the town is placed, is so steep, that the
" houses seem to rest on each other: in short it
" forms a natural fortress, that might be rendered
" impregnable ; and the numerous walls and towers
" prove how anxiously its former possessors laboured
" to make it so [d]." After Coracesium follows Sye- Syedra.
dra, which occurs in Strabo. (loc. cit. Flor. IV. 2.)

> . . . . . Cilicum per littora tutus
> Parva puppe fugit : sequitur pars magna senatus,
> Ad profugum collecta ducem ; parvisque Syedris,
> Quo portu mittitque rates recipitque Selinus.
>   LUCAN. PHARS. VIII. 257.

(Cf. Ptol. p. 124. Steph. Byz. v. Σύεδρα.) Hierocles
assigns it to Pamphylia. (p. 682.[e]) Captain Beaufort observed some ruins on the summit of a steep
hill, whose rugged ascent from the sea-shore deterred
him from visiting it, which he thinks may be the
site of Syedra [f]. Beyond, Strabo places Amaxia, Amaxia.
seated on a hill, and having a small harbour, where
the timber cut in the woods was brought down to
be shipped. This was mostly cedar, and it grew so
plentifully in the country that Mark Antony made
over the whole of this district to Cleopatra for the
construction of her fleet. (XIV. p. 669. Steph. Byz.
v. Ἀμαξία.) Then follows Laertes, a castle seated on Laertes.
a breast-shaped hill, and having below a small haven. (Strab. XIV. p. 669.) The Stadiasmus reckons 100 stadia between Coracesium and this place,
which was probably not close to the sea, since Pto-

---

[d] Karamania, p. 172.
[e] There are coins belonging
to this town, struck in the reigns
of Nero, Hadrian, &c. Epigr.
ΣΤΕΔΡΕΩΝ.
[f] Karamania, p. 178.

lemy fixes it somewhat inland. (p. 124. Steph. Byz. v. Λαέρτης.) Diogenes, the author of the Lives of the Philosophers, was a native of this town [g]. The ruins of Laertes are possibly those observed by Captain Beaufort after the remains assigned to Syedra, above a little peninsula of rock where there is a cove, and from its head a considerable extent of ruin stretching up the hill. Several inscriptions were found, but none indicating the name of the place [h].

Selinus fl.

Selinus, postea Trajanopolis.

Somewhat further the navigator discovers the mouth of the river *Selenti*, the Selinus of antiquity, with a town and port of the same name. The latter existed in the time of Scylax, (p. 40.) and is noticed by Livy, (XXXIII. 20.) but not by Strabo, who speaks only of the river. (Cf. Ptol. p. 124. Plin. V. 27.) This town became afterwards memorable for the death of Trajan, which suddenly occurred there A. D. 117. (Xiphil. in Traj.) After this event Selinus assumed for a time the name of Trajanopolis, but its bishops were titular of Selinus some centuries later [i]. (Hierocl. p. 709.) Basil of Seleucia, in a passage cited by Wesseling, (Vit. S. Thecl. II. 11.) describes it as reduced to a state of insignificance in his time, though once great and commercial. It was surrounded on almost every side by the sea, and seated on a precipitous rock, by which position it was rendered nearly impregnable. The following description of this ancient locality is supplied by

[g] The ethnic Λαερτιεὺς is used with reference to this author, but Steph. Byz. gives only Λαέρτιος and Λαερτῖνος. We find, besides, Λαερτίτης on coins: they are of the reigns of Hadrian and the Antonines. Sestini, p. 101.

[h] Karamania, p. 178, 179.

[i] The coins of Selinus are chiefly imperial. The epigraph is commonly ΣΕΛΙΝΟΥΣΙΩ. more rarely ΤΡΑΙΑΝΟ. ΣΕΛΙΝΟ. Sestin. p. 103.

Captain Beaufort. " The hill and cape of *Selinty*
" rises steeply from the plain on one side, and breaks
" off into a chain of magnificent cliffs on the other ;
" on the highest point of these are the ruins of a
" castle, which commands the ascent of the hill in
" every direction, and looks perpendicularly down
" on the sea. The whole of this hill was not in-
" cluded in the ancient line of fortification; the
" western side was divided from the rest by a wall,
" which, slanting from the castle on the summit to
" the mouth of the river, was broken into numerous
" flanks, and guarded by towers. Inside of the wall
" there are many traces of houses, but on the out-
" side, and between the foot of the hill and the ri-
" ver, the remains of some large buildings are yet
" standing." They appear to be a mausoleum, perhaps that of Trajan, an agora, a theatre, an aqueduct, and some tombs [k].

The neighbouring tract of country bore the name
of Selenitis, as appears from Ptolemy, and contained Seleniti
regio.
some places of inferior note, such as Iotape, men- Iotape.
tioned also by Pliny, (V. 27.) Hierocles, (p. 709.)
and the Councils [l]. Pliny names with it Arsinoe Arsinoe.
and Dorion ; the former of which is known also to Dorion.
Ptolemy. (Cf. Steph. Byz. v. Ἀρσινόη.) Returning to
the coast we find a headland in the Stadiasmus,
named Nesiazusa, distant 100 stadia from Selinus : Nesiazusa
prom.
then Zephelium, or rather, as Col. Leake justly corrects, Nephelium. Nephelis is stated by Livy to be Nephelis
prom. et
a promontory of Cilicia, rendered famous by an an- urbs.
cient treaty of the Athenians. (XXXIII. 20.) What

[k] Karamania, p. 186—192.
[l] The coins of Iotape belong
to the reigns of the emperors
Philip jun. and Valerian. Epigraph, ΙΩΤΑΠΕΙΤΩΝ. Sestin.
p. 101.

treaty is here alluded to is not very evident. Nephelis, according to Ptolemy, was also a town, and this fact is further confirmed by numismatical evidence [m]. Strabo does not speak of Nephelis, but he

Cragus scopulus. points out, beyond Selinus, Cragus, an abrupt rock rising from the sea; (loc. cit.) and Ptolemy places

Antiochia ad Cragum. near it a town called Antiochia, with the surname of ad Cragum. (p. 124.) There seem also to be some numismatic records of its existence [n]. The Stadiasmus fixes Cragus twenty-five stadia from Nephelis. Captain Beaufort has the following observations on the supposed remains of this place. " We next came " to the ruins of an ancient town, which I appre- " hend must have been the Antiochia ad Cragum of " Ptolemy. Circumstances prevented an attentive " examination of this place, but it seems to have " been formerly of some consequence, though evi- " dently unfitted for a commercial settlement. A " square cliff, the top of which has been carefully " fortified, projects from the town into the sea; " flights of steps cut in the rock lead from the land- " ing-place to the gates; and on the other side there " is a singular arch in the cliffs, with a sloping chan- " nel, as if intended for a slip for boats." Beyond

Charadrus. Cragus was Charadrus, distant, according to the maritime geographer, 100 stadia. (Cf. Scyl. p. 40.) Strabo says it was a fortress, with a small harbour, situated at the foot of a lofty mountain named Andriclus, (the Stadiasmus writes Androclus.) From thence commenced a dangerous navigation, along a

---

[m] These coins are very ancient, and the legend is in a character part Phœnician, and partly Greek. Sestin. p. 102.

[n] Sestin. p. 99. Antiochia In- certa. Autonomus. Epigraphe, ANTIOXEΩN TΩN ΠPO ...... AKΩI, read TΩN ΠPOΣ TΩ KPAΓΩI.

bleak and rugged coast called Platanistus, (Platanus in the Stadiasmus,) as far as cape Anemurium. The brief description of the Greek geographer is most aptly illustrated by Captain Beaufort's survey. " Some miles further to the eastward we came to an " opening through the mountains, with a small ri- " ver, on the banks of which there are a few shep- " herds' huts, and near to its mouth some modern " ruins. The natives call this place *Karadran*, " and both the name and situation accord with " those of Charadrus, a fort and harbour placed by " Strabo between Cragus and Anemurium, on a " rough coast called Platanistus. Rough and dreary " it may well be called, for between the plain of *Se-* " *linty* and the promontory of *Anamour*, a distance " of thirty miles, the ridge of bare rocky hills that " forms the coast is interrupted but twice by narrow " valleys, which conduct the mountain torrents to " the sea. The great arm of mount Taurus, which " proceeds in a direct line from *Alaya* towards cape " *Anamour*, suddenly breaks off abreast of *Kara-* " *dran*, and was probably the mount Andriclus, " which Strabo describes as overhanging Chara- " drus [o]."

Anemurium was the southernmost point of all Asia Minor, being only 350 stadia from cape Crommyon in Cyprus. (Strab. XIV. p. 670. Cf. Livy, XXXIII. 20. Pomp. Mel. I. 13.) There was also a town of the same name, as appears from Scylax, (p. 40.) Pliny, (V. 27.) and Ptolemy. It answers to the modern *Anamour* [p].

Anemurium prom. et urbs.

[o] Karamania, p. 194, 195.

[p] There are numerous medals of Anemurium struck under the emperors. Epigr. ANEMOT-PIEΩN. Sestin. p. 99.

" Cape *Anamour*," says Captain Beaufort, " ter-
" minates in a high bluff knob, one side of which is
" inaccessible ; the other has been well fortified by
" a castle, and outworks placed on the summit, from
" whence a flanked wall, with towers, descends to
" the shore, and separates it from the rest of the
" promontory.   Two aqueducts, that wind along the
" hill for several miles, supplied this fortress with
" water.   Within the walls are the remains of some
" large buildings, and two theatres, and outside a
" vast number of tombs.   The city is now altoge-
" ther deserted [q]."

Beyond *Anamour* a small but rapid stream empties itself into the sea; the modern name is, according to Captain Beaufort, *Direk Ondessy*, and he conceives it to be the Arymagdus of Ptolemy [r].   Some
remains, on a hill near its mouth, may correspond
with Nagidus, a town mentioned by Strabo. (XIV.
p. 670.)   Mela reports that it was colonized by the
Samians. (I. 13.)   Stephanus Byz. (v. Νάγιδος) says
there was also an island named Nagidusa. (Cf. Scyl.
p. 40.)   The latter answers to a little rock about
200 feet long, close to the castle of *Anamour*, with
some remains of buildings [s].

Eastward of Nagidus is the Arsinoe of Strabo,
who observes that it had a small port. (Cf. Steph.
Byz. v. Ἀρσινόη.)   Captain Beaufort identified it
with some ruins which covered a small and high
peninsula near cape *Kizilman ;* on the eastern side
was a small harbour [t].   The cape here mentioned

Margin notes:
Arymag-
dus fl.

Nagidus.

Nagidusa
insula.

Arsinoe.

[q] Karamania, p. 195—201.
[r] P. 204.
[s] P. 206.   The medals of
Nagidus are ancient and rare.

Autonomi Anepigraphi — Inscripti ΝΑΓΙΔΙΚΟΝ — ΝΑΓΙ-
ΔΕΩΝ.
[t] Karamania, p. 206.

answers to the Posidium promontorium of Scylax, Posidium prom.
(p. 40, as corrected by Salmasius) and the Stadiasmus. The latter document furnishes some additional detail of stations in the intervening space between this headland and Anemurium, as follows:
from Anemurium to Rygmana, ('Ρυγμάνοι,) fifty sta- Rygmani.
dia. Col. Leake thinks, with much probability, that
this is the river Arymagdus [u]. To Dionysiophani, Dionysio-phani.
fifty stadia. The same antiquary imagines this to
be the port of Arsinoe [x]. To Mandane, thirty stadia; and from thence seven to cape Posidium. This
place I take to be the Myanda of Pliny, (V. 27.) Myanda, sive Myus.
and Myus of Scylax, whose text therefore stands
clear of error. The Stadiasmus reckons 100 stadia
from thence to Celenderis. Strabo has another place
in this vicinity, called Melania, which is unknown Melania.
to other authorities.

Celenderis, a city of some note, is said to have Celenderis.
been indebted for its foundation to the Phœnicians,
but subsequently to have received a colony from Samos. This circumstance, recorded by P. Mela, (I.
13.) is corroborated by a fragment of the geographer
Scymnus, quoted by Herodian the grammarian. (περὶ
μον. λεξ. p. 19, 5.[y]) We learn from the same passage
several other particulars respecting the topography
of Celenderis: that there was a temple and grove
consecrated to Juno near the town, and that a river
named Is flowed into the sea close to the sacred

[u] Asia Minor, p. 201.
[x] P. 202.
[y] The quotation is as follows: Σκύμνος ἐν τῷ ι τῆς Ἀσίας
περίπλῳ· εὑρέθη ἔχεται Κελενδέρις
πόλις Σαμίων, καὶ ἱερὸν παρὰ τῇ πόλει νήρης καὶ ἄλσος; which should

be read, Σκύμνος ἐν τῷ τῆς Ἀσίας
περίπλῳ.
. . . . εὔθυς δ᾽ ἔχεται Κελένδερις
Πόλις Σαμίων καὶ ἱερὸν παρὰ τῇ πόλει
Καὶ ἄλσος Ἥρης. Ἴς ποταμὸς παρ᾽
αὐτά τ᾽ εἰς
Θάλασσαν ἐξίεισιν.

precincts.   Celenderis is also noticed by Scylax
(p. 40.) and Ptolemy. (p. 124.) Tacitus describes an
attempt made by Piso, the enemy of Germanicus,
to occupy it, but which failed.   He represents it as
a place of great strength, built on a high and craggy
precipice, surrounded by the sea. (Ann. II. 80.)   In
the ecclesiastical documents we find Celenderis ranked among the episcopal towns of Isauria [z].   *Chelin-
dreh*, as it is now called, is, according to Captain
Beaufort, a snug but very small port, from whence
the couriers from Constantinople to Cyprus embark.
There are the ruins of the fortress, some arched
vaults, and a great number of sepulchres and sarcophagi [a].   Artemidorus, as Strabo reports, looked
upon Celenderis as the frontier town of Cilicia, and
not Coracesium.

The Stadiasmus names, to the east of Celenderis,
the bay of Berenice.   That there was a place of this
name in Cilicia we know from Stephanus Byz. (v.
Βερενῖκαι.)   Then follows, after an interval of fifty
stadia, a spot called Pisurgia, (Πισούργια,) probably
where pitch was manufactured, or fir timber cut [b].
Beyond is the isle Crambusa, probably now *Pa-
padoula*, where Captain Beaufort observed some
very old remnants of buildings [c].   Cape Crauni, probably Cruni, (Κρούνοι,) is a promontory near the *Pa-
padoula* islets, forty-five stadia from Pisurgia; and
forty stadia further is the river Melas, which is laid

(marginal notes)
Berenice.
Pisurgia.
Crambusa insula.
Crauni, sive Cruni prom.
Melas fl.

---

[z] Geogr. Sacr. p. 301. There
are coins of the Syrian kings,
and of the later Roman emperors, struck at Celenderis,
with the epigraph, ΚΕΛΕΝΔΕ-
ΡΙΤΩΝ. Sestini, p. 99.
[a] Karamania, p. 209.

[b] Captain Beaufort noticed
in this direction several heaps
of wood and deal boards, which
lay on the beach ready for ex-
portation, p. 211.
[c] P. 210.

down without a name in Captain Beaufort's chart. Thirty-five stadia more brought the navigator to a spot called Ciphisus; and close to it, apparently, was Ciphisus. the town and port of Aphrodisias, which appears Aphrodisias. from Livy to have been of some consequence in the reign of Antiochus Magnus. (XXXIII. 20. Cf. Diod. Sic. XIX. 61. Ptol. p. 124. Steph. Byz. v. Ἀφροδισιάς.) Some ruins which Captain Beaufort noticed at the north-east corner of a bay west of cape *Cavaliere*, near a plain crossed by a small stream, and which he supposed to be those of Holmus, are rather to be assigned to Aphrodisias[d].

The Stadiasmus remarks that Aphrodisias lies nearly in a northerly direction with that part of Cyprus called Aulion, from which it is distant 500 miles. The bay in which Aphrodisias is situate is separated from another more extensive bason, called *Aghaliman*, by a small peninsula, terminated by a headland named in modern charts cape *Cavaliere*. This I conceive to be the cape Zephyrium of the Zephyrium Maritime Survey, but Pliny calls it Promontorium prom. Veneris. The same document is very minute in its detail of the coast between that point and the mouth of the Calycadnus: it points out an island called Pityusa, distant forty-five stadia from the coast near Pityusa Aphrodisias, which seems to agree rather with an insula. islet off point *Cavaliere*, than with *Provencal* island, though the latter is more considerable. Then follows Philæa, a station 130 stadia from Pityusa; the Philæa. port Nesulium; Mylæ, a village near a cape and pe- Nesulium. ninsula, perhaps *Aghaliman;* (Cf. Plin. V. 27.) and Mylæ. forty stadia further Hormi, or Holmi, a town occu- Holmi, pied, as Strabo reports, by the people of Seleucia, sive Hormi.

[d] Karamania, p. 212, 213.

previous to the foundation of that city, but afterwards deserted by them. (XIV. p. 670.) The name of this town is disguised in Scylax under the corrupt reading 'Οάνοι. (p. 40. Cf. Plin. V. 27. Steph. Byz. v. Ὄλμοι.) The ruins of this place must be sought for near *Aghaliman*. Beyond is a long sandy tongue of land, which doubtless answers to

Sarpedon prom.

cape Sarpedon, which, in the treaty made by Antiochus with the Romans, was the boundary set to the navigation of his vessels. It is to be observed that in the extract of Polybius, specifying the con-

Calycadnus prom.

ditions, the cape is called Calycadnus; (XXII. 26.) whereas in Livy (XXXVIII. 38.) and Appian (Syr. c. 39.) both the points, Calycadnus and Sarpedon, are mentioned. At present, however, there seems to ⸱be only one low sandy point, called *Lissan el Capheh*, produced by the alluvium of the neighbouring river, the Calycadnus of antiquity, and therefore evidently subject to great change in the course of time. Scylax mentions Sarpedon rather as a town, but his text is very corrupt. Pliny, on the other hand, notices it as a promontory, and makes no mention of cape Calycadnus. This is also

Calycadnus fluvius.

the case with the Stadiasmus. The Calycadnus, now *Giuk-sou*, is a large and rapid stream, which rises in the central chain of Taurus, and after receiving some minor tributary streams, falls into the sea a little to the east of the above mentioned promontory.

Seleucia.

Seleucia, founded, as Stephanus reports, by Seleucus Nicator, (v. Σελεύκεια,) was situate in a fertile plain, watered by the Calycadnus, a few miles above its mouth. Its foundation, as we have seen from Strabo, was posterior to that of Holmi, which gradually sunk as its more flourishing neighbour rose into consequence and opulence. Under the protection of the Syrian kings Seleucia became à distinguished school of literature and philosophy, and its inhabitants were far more polished and better informed than the natives of Cilicia or Pamphylia. This city gave birth to Athenæus and Xenarchus, two distinguished Peripatetics, who flourished in the reign of Augustus. The latter taught at Alexandria, Athens, and Rome, with great success, and Strabo himself attended his lectures. Seleucia continued to flourish as late as the time of Ammianus Marcellinus. (XIV. 25. Cf. Ptol. p. 124.) Pliny reports that it was surnamed Tracheotis. (V. 27.) The ecclesiastical historians, Socrates and Sozomenus, speaking of a council held there, call it Trachea. (Sozom. IV. 16. Socrat. II. 39.) It is still named *Selefkieh* by the natives. " Its remains," says Captain Beaufort, " are scattered over a large extent of " ground, on the west side of the river. This river, " formerly the Calycadnus, and now called *Giuk-* " *soui*, or Heavenly river, is about 180 feet wide " abreast of the town, where a bridge of six arches " still exists in tolerable repair. The chief remains " are those of a theatre, partly cut out of the side " of a hill; and in front of it, a long line of con- " siderable ruins, with porticoes and other large " buildings: farther on, a temple, which had been " converted into a Christian church, several large " Corinthian columns, about four feet in diameter, " a few of which are still standing." This may have been the temple of the Sarpedonian Apollo, mentioned by Zosimus. (I. 57. Cf. Basil. Seleuc. Vit. Thec. I. p. 275.) Strabo remarks that there was also a temple in Cilicia consecrated to Diana Sarpedonia. (XIV. p. 676.) Near Seleucia was a

Hyria. spot called Hyria, as Stephanus Byz. reports; (v. Τρία.) and higher up the valley of the Calycadnus

Claudiopolis. we may take this opportunity of pointing out Claudiopolis, a town founded by Claudius, as its name imports, and which is assigned by Ammianus and Hierocles to Isauria as well as Seleucia. (Ammian. Marcell. XIV. 25. Hierocl. p. 709.) According to Theophanes, quoted by Wesseling on Hierocles, Claudiopolis was situate in a plain between two summits of Taurus, (Chronogr. p. 119.) and probably also on the Calycadnus, or one of its branches. In

Diocæsarea. the same district we must place, with Ptolemy, Diocæsarea, known also to the ecclesiastical records and

Philadelphia. Hierocles. (p. 709.) Philadelphia, likewise named among the episcopal towns of Isauria. Capt. Beaufort supposes that it may be represented by *Mout,* or *Mood,* a town of some size, situate near the junction of the two principal branches of the Calycadnus, one of which retains the name of *Kalikad*[e]. It is near the source of the western branch, in the Isaurian mountains, that we must seek for the can-

Homonadenses. ton of the Homonadenses, a hardy tribe of mountaineers, bordering, as Strabo reports, on the Pisidians and the Etennenses of Pamphylia. It was in vain that Amyntas, the tetrarch of Galatia and Lycaonia, after conquering a great part of Pisidia, endeavoured to subject these highlanders. For though he succeeded in taking several of their fortresses, and slaying their chief, he himself fell into a snare laid for him by the wife of the deceased leader,

[e] Karamania, p. 223. Col. Leake, however, supposes *Mout* to be Claudiopolis. Asia Minor, p. 17.

assisted by the Cilicians, and was put to death.
Subsequently, Sulpicius Quirinius, the Cyrenius of
St. Luke, undertook to reduce the Homonadenses,
and by surrounding their district, and cutting off all
communications, forced them at last to surrender.
He then removed to the neighbouring towns all the
males capable of bearing arms, leaving none but the
young and infirm. (Strab. XII. p. 569. Cf. Tacit.
Ann. III. 48.) The district occupied by this people
was extremely wild and mountainous, but nevertheless it enclosed some fertile valleys, which the highlanders came down to cultivate, preferring however
to occupy fastnesses and caves on the heights, whence
they could issue forth with impunity to attack and
plunder their lowland neighbours. (Strab. loc. cit.)
D'Anville was of opinion that Homonada, their chief
town, was represented by the fortress of *Ermenak*,
situate near the source of the *Giuk-sou*; and this
locality has been adopted by Gosselin and other
antiquaries [f]; but Col. Leake, in his map, supposes
Ermenak to be Philadelphia, and *Mout*, Claudiopolis. The name of Cetis appears to have been given to Cetis regio.
that part of Cilicia Trachea which comprised the
valley of the eastern branch of the Calycadnus. (Ptol.
p. 124. Basil. Seleuc. Vit. Thecl. I.) The principal
town in this valley was Olba, celebrated for a temple Olba.
of Jupiter, said to have been erected by Ajax, son of
Teucer. The foundation was a considerable one,
and the pontiffs enjoyed great wealth and power,
insomuch that at one time they were lords of the
whole Trachea. But the principality of Olba experienced subsequently different revolutions. When

[f] French Strabo, tom. IV. p. ii. p. 100.

Cilicia was under the dominion of pirates, these chiefs seized upon the sacerdotal revenues, but after their destruction the office was restored by the Romans, who termed it the principality and priesthood of Teucer, and the pontiffs were named after that hero, or Ajax. In the time of Strabo, Aba, daughter of Xenophanes, a chief of the country, had usurped the pontifical domains, under the protection of Mark Antony and Cleopatra, but she was afterwards deposed, and the lineal descendants of the reigning house were reinstated in their rights [f]. (Strab. XIV. p. 671.) It appears, from a coin struck in the reign of Severus, that Olba received a colony under the auspices of that emperor. We observe very generally on the medals of this city the title of chief of the Cennati and Lalassei [g]. Now we know from Ptolemy that Lalassis was a small principality or district of Cilicia Trachea, (p. 129.) and the territory of the Cennati formed another; perhaps it was no other than the Cetis of the same geographer. Ptolemy assigns to Lalassis the town of Necica, mentioned by no other writer, unless it should be the Sice of the anonymous geographer of Ravenna. But this again is to be referred to the Sycea of Athenæus (III. p. 78.) and Stephanus Byz. (v. Συκαί.) The position of Olba has not yet been ascertained; we know generally from Strabo that it stood among the mountains above Soli. (loc. cit.) We must now return to the mouth of the Calycadnus, in order to

Cennati.

Lalassis.

Necica.

Sycea.

f The coins of the pontifical princes of Olba are numerous, and among the number we find Polemo and Augustus. Sestin. p. 102.

g On a coin of Polemo, M. ΑΝΤΩΝΙΟΤ. ΠΟΛΕΜΩΝΟΣ ΑΡ-ΧΙΕΡΕΩΣ. ΚΕΝΝΑΤ. ΔΤΝΑΣ-ΤΟΤ. ΟΛΒΕΩΝ ΤΗΣ ΙΕΡΑΣ ΚΑΙ ΛΑΛΑΣΣΕΩΝ.

complete our periplus of the coast of Cilicia Trachea.
Strabo, beyond this river, points out a rock named
Pœcile, (Ποικίλη,) in which a passage was cut lead- Pœcile
ing to Seleucia. The Stadiasmus reckons forty sta- petra.
dia from thence to the mouth of the Calycadnus.
This spot answers nearly to *Pershendy*, where Captain Beaufort observed some considerable ruins, but,
from an inscription he copied, they appeared to be of
the time of Valentinian and Valens [h].

Beyond Pœcile, Strabo has another cape Anemu- Anemurium, which I take to be the Zephyrium of Ptolemy, Zephyrium
and others. The isle Crambusa, noticed by the first Crambusa
mentioned geographer, (XIV. p. 670.) answers to insula.
an islet near *Korghoz*. The Stadiasmus sets east
of Pœcile seventy stadia the harbour called the Fair Pulchrum
Coracesium. Then follows Corycus, a small town, sium por-
and cape Corycium. The former retains the name Corycus.
of *Korghoz*, and, from Captain Beaufort's account, prom.
exhibits considerable remains of antiquity. It appears to have been a fortress of great strength, and
a mole of vast unhewn rocks is carried across the
bay for about a hundred yards. There are numerous tombs, and other excavations [i]. Twenty stadia
inland from the cape was the Corycian cave, celebrated in mythology as the fabled abode of the giant
Typhœus :

$$\text{Τυφὼς ἑχατονταχάρανος· τόν ποτε}$$
$$\text{Κιλίχιον θρέψεν πολυώ-}$$
$$\text{νυμον ἄντρον·} \qquad \text{PIND. PYTH. I. 31.}$$

and again he is called Τυφὼς Κίλιξ ἑκατόγκρανος. (Pyth.
VIII. 20.). So also Æschylus :

[h] Karamania, p. 238, 239. See also Col. Leake, p. 211.
[i] Karamania, p. 240—247.

Τὸν γηγενῆ τε Κιλικίων οἰκήτορα
Ἄντρων ἰδὼν ᾤκτειρα δάϊον τέρας
Ἑκατοντακάρηνον πρὸς βίαν χειρούμενον
Τυφῶνα θοῦρον.   PROM. VINCT. 350.

In fact many writers, as Strabo reports, placed Arima, or Arimi, the scene of Typhœus's torments, alluded to by Homer, in Cilicia, while others sought it in Lydia, and others in Campania. The description which Strabo has left us of this remarkable spot leads to the idea of its having once been the crater of a volcano. He says it was a deep and broad valley of a circular shape, surrounded on every side by lofty rocks. The lower part of this crater was rugged and strong, but covered nevertheless with shrubs and evergreens, and especially saffron, of which it produced a great quantity. There was also a cavity, from whence gushed a copious stream, which after a short course was again lost, and reappeared near the sea, which it joined. It was called the " bitter water." (XIV. p. 671.) The account of Pomponius Mela, though evidently derived from the same source, perhaps Callisthenes, is yet more minute and elaborate; and as it is written with considerable elegance, I shall insert it below, for the gratification of the Latin reader[k]. I do not believe

[k] " Non longe hinc Corycos " oppidum, portu saloque in- " cingitur, angusto tergore con- " tinenti adnexum. Supra spe- " cus est, nomine Corycius, sin- " gulari ingenio ac supra quam " describi facile sit exiunius. " Grandi namque hiatu patens " montem littori appositum, et " decem stadiorum clivo satis " arduum ex summo statim " vertice aperit. Tunc alte de- " missus, et quantum demitti- " tur amplior, viret lucis pen- " dentibus undique, et totum se " nemoroso laterum orbe com- " plectitur; adeo mirificus ac " pulcher, ut mentes acceden- " tium primo adspectu conster- " nat; ubi contemplati dura- " vere, non satiet. Unus in " eum descensus est, angustus, " asper, quingentorum et mille " passuum, per amœnas um-

that any modern traveller has explored this singular locality. Beyond Corycus was the island of Elæussa, situate close to the mainland. This spot was the favourite residence of Archelaus, king of Cappadocia, to whom likewise the whole of Cilicia Trachea, with the exception of Seleucia, which remained a free town, had been conceded by the Romans. This politic people, wisely preferring to commit the government of a province, so difficult to manage, and offering such temptations and facilities for robbers and pirates, to the direction of a permanent governor, possessed of sufficient power and influence to cause his authority to be respected. (Strab. XIV. p. 671.) The island in question no longer exists, but Captain Beaufort points out " a little peninsula close to " *Ayash,* which is covered with ruins, and connected " with the beach by a low isthmus of drift sand." *Ayash* itself exhibits some extensive ruins, consisting of a temple of the composite order, which appears to have been overthrown by an earthquake;

Elæussa insula.

" bras et opaca silvæ quiddam " agreste resonantis, rivis hinc " atque illinc fluitantibus. Ubi " ad ima perventum est, rur- " sum specus alter aperitur ob " alia dicendus. Terret ingre- " dientes sonitu cymbalorum di- " vinitus et magno fragore cre- " pitantium. Deinde aliquam- " diu perspicuus, mox et quo " magis subitur, obscurior, du- " cit ausos penitus, alteque " quasi cuniculo admittit. Ibi " ingens amnis ingenti fronte " se extollens, tantummodo se " ostendit, et ubi magnum im- " petum brevi alveo traxit, ite- " rum demersus absconditur. " Intra spatium est, magis " quam ut progredi quispiam " ausit horribile, et ideo in- " cognitum. Totus autem au- " gustus et vere sacer, habi- " tarique a diis et dignus et " creditus, nihil non venerabile " et quasi cum aliquo numine " se ostentat. Alius ultra est, " quem Typhoneum vocant, ore " angusto, et multum (ut ex- " perti tradidere) pressus, et ob " id assidua nocte suffusus, ne- " que unquam perspici facilis ; " sed quia aliquando cubile Ty- " phonis fuit, et quia nunc de- " missa in se confestim exani- " mat, natura fabulaque memo- " randus." I. 13.

there is also a theatre, and three aqueducts, one of which conveyed water to the town from a considerable distance. These remains are assigned, by the judicious antiquary who has described them, to Sebaste, a town placed in this direction by Ptolemy, and the foundation of which is probably to be referred to the residence of Archelaus at Elæussa, close to which it is [1]. Sebaste, according to the Stadiasmus, as corrected by Col. Leake, was twenty stadia from Corycus. Elæussa, in the same document, is called Elæus; and 100 stadia further is a small

Lamus fl. place named Calanthia. The river Lamus, now *Lamas,* a few miles beyond *Ayash,* or Sebaste, terminates Cilicia Trachea, since from this point the mountains recede from the coast, which assumes a flat and level character, and the wide plains of Cilicia Campestris open to the sight. (Strab. XIV. p. 671.) The Lamus gave its name to a small district, the principal town of which was Antiochia,

Lamotis regio. Antiochia Lamotis. surnamed Lamotis. (Ptol. p. 129. Cf. Steph. Byz. v. Ἀντιόχεια.) Hierocles names both Lamus and Antiochia; Strabo only Lamus. (loc. cit.) From Theophanes, it appears to have been situated near the sea, (Chronogr. p. 119.) and this topography seems confirmed by the authority of coins[m]. Before we quit this part of Cilicia, it will be necessary to add to our list what few towns yet remain to be noticed from

Cestri. Ptolemy. Of these Caÿstrus, or Clystrus, is doubtless a corrupt reading for Cestri, which Hierocles

Domitiopolis. (p. 709.) and the Councils jointly acknowledge. Domitiopolis seems to have stood in the vicinity of the Arymagdus, and is confirmed by the authority of

[1] Karamania, p. 250—253.
[m] Antiochia Maritima. Epi-graphe, ANTIOXEΩN THC ΠΑΡΑΛΙΟΤ. Sestin. p. 99.

Stephanus Byz. (v. Δομετιούπολις.) Irenopolis, which Neronias, postea Irenopolis.
the Notices assign to Cilicia Secunda, is said to have
been previously called Neronias. (Theodor. Hist.
Eccl. I. 7. II. 8. Socr. II. 26.) Flavias, a town Flavias.
mentioned by Hierocles (p. 709.) and the Notices, is
placed in the Antonine Itinerary, on a route leading
from Cucusus in Cappadocia to Anazarbus in Cilicia
Campestris, whence it appears to have stood on the
confines of the former province. (Itin. Anton. p. 212.
Cf. Ptol. p. 129. Concil. Chalced. p. 660.) Hierocles
names also, in Isauria, (p. 709.) Titiopolis, Juliosebaste, Germanicopolis, Moloe, Darasus, Zede, Neapolis, and Lauzados; most of which are known
from the other Notices, and the Acts of Councils.
The Clitæ are mentioned by Tacitus as a tribe of
Cilician highlanders, who rebelled against Archelaus, and defied his power. (Ann. VI. 41. XII. 55.)

CILICIA CAMPESTRIS.

Champaign Cilicia was accounted to extend from
the river Lamus to the Syrian gates at the extremity
of the gulf of Issus, or *Scanderoon*, as it is now
called. The whole extent of coast comprised within
these limits amounted to about 1000 stadia, (Strab.
XIV. p. 676.) The first maritime town which pre-
sented itself after crossing the Lamus was · Soli, Soli, postea Pompeio-polis.
founded, as we are informed by Strabo, by a mixed
colony of Achæans and Rhodians from Lindus.
(XIV. p. 671.) This consanguinity was acknowledged by the latter in the course of their negotiations with the Romans. (Liv. XXXVII. 56. Pom-
pon. Mel. I. 13.) It is mentioned for the first time
in history by Xenophon in the Anabasis as a maritime town of Cilicia, (I. 2.) and its opulence in the

time of Alexander is evinced by the contribution of
200 talents imposed on it by that prince. (Arrian.
II. 5. Quint. Curt. III. 7.) It was the birthplace of
Chrysippus the philosopher, and of two distinguished
poets, Philemon and Aratus. (Strab. loc. cit.) Many
writers affirmed that the term σολοικισμὸς, which expressed an incorrect and ungrammatical mode of
speaking, was derived from Soli, the inhabitants of
which used a mixed and corrupt language. This
etymology, however, is not fully agreed upon. (Strab.
XIV. p. 671. Eustath. ad Dion. Perieg. v. 875. Suid.
v. Σόλοι.) This town, having been nearly depopu-
lated by an invasion of Tigranes, king of Armenia,
received a new foundation, as it were, under Pompey
the Great, who settled there a colony of the Cilician
pirates, whom he had conquered. In consequence of
this benefit, Soli assumed the name of Pompeiopolis.
(Strab. loc. cit. Dio Cass. XXXVI. p. 18. Pomp.
Mel. I. 13. Plin. V. 27. Steph. Byz. v. Σόλοι. Tacit.
Ann. II. 58. Hierocl. p. 704.) We are indebted to
Captain Beaufort for a detailed account of the topography and remains of this interesting city. "At
"length," says that officer, "the elevated theatre,
"and tall columns of Soli and Pompeiopolis, rose
"above the horizon into view, and appeared to jus-
"tify the representations which the pilots had given
"of its magnificence. We were not altogether dis-
"appointed. The first object that presented itself
"on landing was a beautiful harbour, or basin, with
"parallel sides and circular ends; it is entirely arti-
"ficial, being formed with surrounding walls, or
"moles, which are fifty feet in thickness, and seven
"in height. Opposite to the entrance of the har-
"bour, a portico rises from the surrounding quay,

" and opens to a double row of 200 columns, which,
" crossing the town, communicates with the prin-
" cipal gate towards the country. Of the 200
" columns no more than forty-four are now stand-
" ing; the remainder lie on the spot where they
" fell, intermixed with a vast assemblage of other
" ruined buildings, which were connected with the
" colonnade. The theatre is almost entirely de-
" stroyed. The city walls, strengthened by nume-
" rous towers, entirely surrounded the town. De-
" tached ruins, tombs, and sarcophagi, were found,
" scattered to some distance from the walls, on the
" outside of the town, and it was evident that the
" whole country had been once occupied by a nu-
" merous and industrious people." *Mexetlu* is the
name which most of the natives gave to the modern
site [n].

Pliny mentions some bitumen springs in the vicinity of Soli, (XXXI. 2.) and these were reported to
Captain Beaufort as situated at *Bikhardy*, about six
hours to the north-east of *Mexetlu*[o]. The river of
Soli was named Liparis, from the unctuous nature of
its waters. (Vitruv. VIII. 3. Antigon. Car. c. 150.
Plin. V. 27.)

Strabo places after Soli cape Zephyrium, which the Zephy-
Stadiasmus notices as a spot ($\chi\omega\rho\acute{\iota}o\nu$) between Soli and rium prom.
Tarsus. It answers probably to a ruined castle,
placed on a small round hill a little to the east of

---

[n] Karamania, p. 261—265.
The autonomous coins of Soli are
ancient, but not uncommon; the
epigraph is variously written,
ΣΟΛΙ, ΣΟΛΙΟΝ, and ΣΟΛΙΚΟΝ.
Those of Pompeiopolis come

down from Pompey to the emperor Gallus. ΠΟΜΠΗΙΟΠΟΛΙ-
ΤΩΝ. On one of these appears
the name of a fountain, Sunias.
ΠΗΓΗ ΣΟΥΝΙΑΣ.

[o] Karamania, p. 266.

the former city, observed by Captain Beaufort [p].
Anchiale. Then follows Anchiale, a city of great antiquity,
since it was said to owe its foundation to the Assyrian Sardanapalus. The circumstances connected
with this fact, as they are related by ancient writers,
are very curious and interesting; but it is to be
wished that we had them on more unquestionable
authority than that of Aristobulus, from whom Strabo, Arrian, and Athenæus, have all derived their information. These authors however evidently gave
credence to the story, and Strabo has besides quoted
some lines from the poet Chœrilus, who had thereby
paraphrased the inscription extant on the tomb of
the Assyrian monarch. Aristotle also was well acquainted with the inscription, since, when alluding
to it in one of his treatises, he said that the senti-
ments it records are more worthy to be written on
the grave of an ox than the tomb of a king. (Cicer.
Tusc. Disp. V. 35.) It appears, however, from Athenæus that some historians placed the monument of
Sardanapalus at Nineveh, and the inscription paraphrased by Chœrilus was taken from thence, and
not from Anchiale. The latter, as Aristobulus relates, was engraved on the monument, which was decorated with a statue of the Assyrian monarch. The
figure appeared in the act of snapping its fingers,
and giving utterance to these words, inscribed on
the stone : " Sardanapalus, son of Anacyndaraxes,
" erected in one day the cities of Anchiale and Tar-
" sus. Stranger, eat, drink, and be merry, for all else
" besides is not worth *that*"—meaning the snapping
of the fingers. (Strab. XIV. p. 672. Athen. XII. p.

[p] P. 267.

529.) Arrian relates that Alexander " came in one
" day from Tarsus to Anchialus, which it is reported
" that Sardanapalus, the Assyrian, founded : and it
" appears from the circumference and foundations of
" the walls to have been a great city, and to have at-
" tained to a considerable degree of power." (II. 5.)
I do not apprehend that Arrian speaks of the ruins
of Anchiale as extant in his time, but as they were
described by the Alexandrian historians, whom he
copied. Athenodorus, a writer quoted by Stephanus Byz., (v. Ἀγχιάλη) and a native of that city,
affirmed that it took its name from Anchiale, daughter of Iapetus, and that it was situate near the river
Anchiales. It would seem, from Strabo, that An- Anchiales
chiale was still existing when he wrote ; and from ^{fluvius.}
Dionysius Perieg. (v. 8.)

Πολλαὶ δ' ἐξείης Κιλίκων γεγάασι πόληες
Λύρνησσος, Μαλλός τε καὶ Ἀγχιάλεια, Σόλοιτε.

Pliny also names it, but perhaps as a place which
once flourished ; subsequent writers make no mention of it, and its locality is marked by no apparent
vestiges. They should be sought for near the mouth
of the river *Mersyn*, which probably answers to the
Anchiales of Stephanus Byz. Above Anchiale, towards the mountains, was Cyinda, a fortress, in
which the Macedonians deposited their wealth after
the death of Alexander. Eumenes seized these treasures during his contest with Antigonus. (Strab.
XIV. p. 672.) Returning to the sea, and continuing along the coast, we come to the mouth of the
Cydnus, the celebrated river of Tarsus. Strabo Cydnus ✗
states, that it rises in the central chain of Taurus ^{fluvius.}
above that city, which it traverses, and then falls
into a small lake, or bason, called Rhegma. (XIV.

on account of the zeal with which they had espoused
X his cause, privileges which were subsequently confirmed by Augustus. (Dio Cass. XLVII. p. 342.)
It is to these acts of favour and protection that
St. Paul owed the right of being a free-born citizen
of Tarsus. (Acts xxi. 39.) "But Paul said, I am a
" man which am a Jew of Tarsus, a city in Cilicia,
" a citizen of no mean city." And Acts xxii. 3. " I
" am verily a man which am a Jew, born in Tarsus,
" a city in Cilicia, yet brought up in this city at the
" feet of Gamaliel." Again, v. 27. " Then the chief cap-
" tain came, and said unto him, Tell me, art thou a
" Roman? He said, Yea. And the chief captain an-
" swered, With a great sum obtained I this freedom.
" And Paul said, But I was free born." Respecting the great apostle's early residence in his native
city, we derive little information from the scriptural
narrative; but it is evident, from the whole tenor of
his history, that one important part of his education
was completed there, namely, that part which was
to fit him for becoming the chosen vessel of God to
the Gentiles; by being made thoroughly acquainted
with their philosophy, literature, and even superstitions; and we derive a valuable commentary on this
feature of the apostle's ministry, from Strabo's remarks on the studious character of the Tarsians.
Such was the eagerness with which they cultivated
literature and philosophy, that no other city, not
even excepting Athens and Alexandria, could sur-
pass it in the number and character of its schools.
He adds that the learned however seldom remained
in the city, but generally migrated after a time to
complete their studies elsewhere. St. Paul, after his
conversion, appears to have resided five years at

distinguished a city; and among the many fabulous
accounts recorded, we may select, as most worthy
of notice, the story alluded to by Strabo of some
Argives having arrived there with Triptolemus in
search of Io. (Strab. XIV. p. 673. Steph. Byz. vv.
Ταρσός, Ἀγχιάλη.) Tarsus appears for the first time
in history as the capital of Cilicia and the residence
of its princes, in the Anabasis of Xenophon. He
describes it as a great and opulent city, seated in an
extensive and fertile plain at the foot of the passes
leading into Cappadocia and Lycaonia. These, as
we have before seen, were the defiles of Tyana and
Podandus. On taking possession of Tarsus, (Xenophon writes Ταρσοὶ in the plural,) the city was for a
time given up to plunder, the troops of Cyrus being
enraged at the loss sustained by a detachment in
crossing the mountains. This force appears to have
attempted to force a passage by the mountains of
Isauria with Epyaxa, the Cilician princess. They
set out from Iconium, and, with the exception of
two companies that were cut off by the barbarians
in the mountains, arrived safely at Tarsus five days
before the main body of the army. The route pursued by this detachment was probably by Laranda,
Lalassis, and the valley of the Calycadnus. (Anab.
I. 2.) Cyrus, after making a treaty with Syennesis,
king of Cilicia, remained at Tarsus for twenty days.
Alexander, after crossing the passes of Tyana, occupied also this city without resistance, and was de-
tained there by a dangerous fever for some days.
(Arrian. II. 4.) Tarsus continued to flourish under
the successors of Alexander, and still more under the
empire of the Romans, Julius Cæsar having granted
to the citizens considerable privileges and immunities

into the hands of the Saracens. It was taken from them, after sustaining a memorable siege, by the emperor Nicephorus, (Leo Diacon. p. 37.) but was again restored to them soon after, according to the Arabian historian, Abulpharagius. (Append. ad Leo Diac. p. 381.) Though greatly reduced, it still continues, under the name of *Tersoos*, to be the chief town of this part of *Karamania*. There are, however, few remains of antiquity of any consequence; but the country around is well cultivated, and very productive.

Glaphyræ.   To the west of Tarsus, at a distance of thirty stadia, was a village named Glaphyræ, with a stream which fell from a rock and joined the Cydnus. (Steph.

Tili Castrum. Byz. v. Γλαφυραί. Eustath. ad Iliad. B. p. 327.) Tili Castrum is mentioned as a strong fortress in the vicinity of Tarsus, by Cinnamus. (p. 104.)

Sarus fl.   Resuming the line of the coast, after leaving the Cydnus, we find the Sarus, at a distance of seventy stadia from the mouth of the former river[r]. The Sarus is a large and rapid stream, whose source in the mountains of Cataonia, and its course by the town of Comana, was noticed in our progress through that part of Cappadocia. On quitting that province, it encounters the central chain of Taurus, not far from the defiles of Tyana, and after many a struggle and winding amidst its dark recesses, finally bursts through the rocky barrier, and pours its waters along the Cilician plain into the Mediterranean. Xenophon, in the Anabasis, places the Sarus immediately after the Cydnus, (I. 4.) as well as Ptolemy; (p.

[r] This appears from the Stadiasmus, where we must read Σάρω for Ἄρειον.

129.) but Strabo omits all mention of its course through Cilicia, as well as of the city of Adana, by which it flowed, so that we have reason to suspect some omission in the text of the geographer. But Captain Beaufort thinks it possible that some change may have taken place in the course of the Sarus, and that it may have formerly joined the Pyramus, as Abulfeda, the Arabian geographer, asserts that it did in the fourteenth century. The two rivers, however, are certainly distinctly laid down in the Stadiasmus, which reckons 120 stadia from one to the other. Procopius informs us also that when Justinian repaired a remarkable bridge over the Sarus, above Adana, he turned the course of that river for a time, probably by uniting it with the Pyramus, (Ædif. V. 5.) which proves again the separation. We are informed, by Livy, that the fleet of Antiochus was nearly destroyed near the mouth of this river by a violent storm. (XXXIII. 41.) The expression is remarkable; " ad capita, quæ vocant, Sari " fluminis fœda tempestas oborta," the commentators observe that " ad capita" does not mean the source, but probably some cliffs near the mouth. But in the Stadiasmus we find mention made, not of the " ca- " pita Sari," but the head of the Pyramus, (κεφαλὴ τοῦ Πυράμου,) and it reckons 120 stadia between that point and the Sarus. The latter river is now called *Sihoon.*

Adana, situate on the Sarus, about thirty miles from its mouth, though not mentioned by early writers, appears to have been a town of considerable antiquity, and of Phœnician origin. Stephanus Byz. (v. Ἄδανα) asserts that it was founded by Adanus and Sarus, who made war upon the Tarsians, but were defeated. Adanus is there stated to be the son of Terra and Uranus.

Adana is mentioned by Appian, for the first time, in the Mithridatic war, who states that Pompey established there some of the Cilician pirates. (p. 237.) But if the conjecture of Salmasius, who reads Ἀδάνη for Ἀλάνη in the text of Scylax, (p. 40.) be admitted, we have a much earlier authority for its existence, though the geographer must be allowed to describe it very inaccurately, when he states it to be an emporium and harbour beyond the Pyramus. The emendation, therefore, I think very doubtful. Dio Cassius reports, that its inhabitants had frequent disputes with those of Tarsus. (<u>XLVII. p. 345.</u>) Adana is mentioned by Pliny, (V. 27.) Ptolemy, (p. 129.) Procopius, and several other Byzantine historians, and it is still a large and populous town, capital of a pashalik of the same name[a].

Between the Cydnus and Sarus is a long sandy *Ammodes prom.* tongue, which seems to answer to the **Ammodes** promontorium of Mela.

Pyramus fl. The Pyramus, now *Gihoon*, rose, as we have seen, in the mountains of Cataonia, bordering on Commagene. We there referred to Strabo's description of its source and subterraneous bed, and the deep and narrow channel by which it forces its way through the barrier of Taurus. Such was the quantity of soil it carried with it down to the sea, that an oracle affirmed that the day would come when it would reach the sacred isle of Cyprus.

[a] There are early autonomous coins of Adana, with barbarous characters. Like Tarsus, it assumed the name of Hadrian and other emperors. ΑΔΡΙΑ-ΝΩΝ. ΑΔΑΝΕΩΝ. ΜΑΚΡΕΙΝΙΑ-ΝΩΝ, &c. Sestin. p. 99.

Ἔσσεται ἐσσομένοις ὅτε Πύραμος εὐρυοδίνης
Ἠϊόνα προχέων ἱερὴν εἰς Κύπρον ἵκηται.

(Strab. XII. p. 536.) This, however, has not taken place; but the able navigator, to whose survey we are indebted for an accurate knowledge of this coast, informs us that a remarkable change has occurred with respect to the course of this river, which now finds its way into the sea twenty-three miles more to the east, in the gulf of *Iskenderoon.* Near the mouth of this river, which was navigable, ancient geographers and historians place Mallus, said to Mallus. have been founded by the soothsayers, Amphilochus and Mopsus, after the siege of Troy. The adventures of these heroes in Cilicia formed a favourite subject for poets and mythologists, and their tombs were pointed out at Megarsus, a place situate below Mal- Megarsus. lus, on a height close to the mouth of the Pyramus. (Strab. XIV. p. 676.) We learn from Arrian that Alexander, previous to the battle of Issus, marched along the coast from Soli to Megarsus, where he sacrificed to Minerva Megarsis, and poured libations on the tomb of Amphilochus. He then moved on to Mallus, where he was joined by his cavalry, which had marched across the Aleian plain from Tarsus, under Philotas. (Strab. loc. cit. Arrian. II. 5.) The Pyramus, according to Scylax, might be ascended in ships as far as Mallus. (p. 40. Cf. Mel. I. 13. Plin. V. 27. Ptol. p. 129. Steph. Byz. v. Μάλλος.)

Megarsus, which is known, from Lycophron, to have been seated on a hill close to the shore:

. . . . Πυράμου πρὸς ἐκβολαῖς
. . . .
Αἰπὺς δ' ἁλίβρος ὄχμος ἐν μεταιχμίῳ
Μέγαρσος. CASSAND. v. 439.

(See the Scholiasts.) Captain Beaufort has, with great appearance of probability, placed Megarsus on the height of *Karadash*, a white cliff, about 130 feet high, and twenty-six miles east of the *Syhoon*, or Sarus[t]. The position, however, which he assigns to Mallus, close to the same spot, and his theory with respect to the change in the course of the Pyramus, are not consistent with historical accounts. Megarsus certainly was not on the same side of the Pyramus as Mallus, for Alexander, according to Curtius, entered that town after throwing a bridge across the river. (III. 7.) Mallus, therefore, as Col. Leake justly observes, must have stood on a hill on the eastern bank of the Pyramus, near its mouth. In the middle ages it still retained the name of Malo. (Sanut. Secret. Fid. II. p. iv. c. 26[u].)

Aleius campus.

The Aleian plain, which, as we have seen from Strabo, lay between Tarsus and Mallus, is celebrated in mythology as the scene of Bellerophon's catastrophe:

Ἀλλ' ὅτε δὴ καὶ 'κεῖνος ἀπήχθετο πᾶσι θεοῖσιν,
Ἤτοι ὁ καππεδίον τὸ Ἀλήϊον οἶος ἀλᾶτο,
Ὃν θυμὸν κατέδων, πάτον ἀνθρώπων ἀλεείνων.

Il. Z. 200.

Dionysius, the geographical poet, has connected this tale with the legend of Tarsus. (v. 864—874.)

Κεῖνος τοι Κιλίκων περισύρεται ἔθνεα κόλπος
Μακρὸς ἐπ' ἀντολίην. Ἀσίης δὲ στεινὰ καλῶσι
Καὶ τῷ μὲν πλεόνων ποταμῶν ἐπιμίσγεται ὕδωρ
Τήλοθεν ἐρχομένων Πυράμοιό τε καὶ Πινάροιο,

[t] Karamania, p. 289—293.
[u] Asia Minor, p. 215, 216. There are a few medals both of Mallus and Megarsus. The legend of the former is ΜΑΛΛΩ-ΤΩΝ; of the latter, ΜΕΓΑΡΣΕΩΝ ΠΡΟΣ ΤΩ ΠΥΡΑΜΩ. Sestin. p. 101.

Κύδνου τι σκολιοῖο μέσην διὰ Ταρσὸν ἰόντος
Ταρσὸν ἐϋκτιμένην, ὅθι δή ποτε Πήγασος Ἵππος
Ταρσὸν ἀφεὶς χώρῳ λίπεν οὔνομα, τῆμος ἀφ' Ἵππου
Ἐς Διὸς ἱέμενος πέσεν ἥρως Βελλεροφόντης.
Κεῖθι δὲ καὶ πεδίον τὸ Ἀλήϊον, οὗ κατὰ νῶτα
Ἀνθρώπων ἀπάνευθεν ἀλώμενος ἐνδιάασκε.

These extensive plains appear to occupy the whole tract of country which intervenes between the Sarus and Pyramus. Above Mallus, on the latter river, was the town of Mopsuestia, in Greek Μόψου ἑστία, a name evidently derived from the hero Mopsus. (Steph. Byz. in v.) Strabo, somewhat inaccurately, places this town on the gulf of Issus, (XIV. p. 676.) but Stephanus and other writers distinctly seat it on the Pyramus. Anna Comnena and Cedrenus have, on the other hand, confounded this river with the Sarus. The former speaks of the old and new town. (p. 349. C. Cedren. p. 654.) Procopius says Justinian repaired the bridge over the Pyramus. (Ædif. V. 5.) Leo Diaconus also affirms it was on that river. (p. 32.) We learn from Pliny that it was a free city. (V. 27.) In the middle ages the name of this place was already corrupted to Mamista. (M. Glyc. p. 306. Hier. Itin. p. 580.) and it is now still further distorted to that of *Messis*[x].

Mopsuestia.

Between the Pyramus and Sarus there was another Antiochia, which took a local designation from either river, since the Stadiasmus, which removes it 150 stadia from Mallus, calls it after the former, and so likewise Stephanus Byz.; (v. Ἀντιόχεια.) but,

Antiochia ad Pyramum.

[x] The ethnic of Mopsuestia is Μοψεάτης, as appears from Stephanus, and the medals of the town. Some belong to the kings of the Seleucid dynasty; others are Roman and imperial. The legend in some cases exhibits the titles ΤΗΣ ΙΕΡΑΣ. ΚΑΙ ΑΥΤΟΝΟΜΟΥ ΚΑΙ ΑΣΥΛΟΥ.

there are medals inscribed ΑΝΤΙΟΧΕΩΝ ΤΩΝ ΠΡΟΣ ΤΩΙ ΣΑΡΩΙ, which could hardly be referred to any other town [y].

Anazarba, sive Cæsarea ad Anazarbum.

Above Mopsuestia, and still on the Pyramus, was the town of Anazarba, so called apparently from a mountain of that name, at the foot of which it was situate. (Steph. Byz. v. Ἀναζαρβά.) It afterwards took the appellation of Cæsarea ad Anazarbum, from what emperor is not known, but prior to the time of Pliny. (V. 27. Ptol. p. 129.) The original appellation however finally prevailed, as we find it so designated in Hierocles and the imperial Notitiæ, at which period it had become the chief town of Cilicia Secunda. (Hierocl. p. 705.) It was nearly destroyed by a terrible earthquake under Justinian. (Procop. Hist. Arc. c. 18. Cedren. p. 299.) It was the birthplace of the celebrated physician and naturalist Dioscorides, and the poet Oppian [z]. The Table Itinerary removes Anazarbus eleven miles from Mopsuestia, and the Antonine places it on a road communicating with Cæsarea in Cappadocia by Cucusus and Flavias, or Flaviopolis, from which latter place it was distant eighteen miles. (Itin. Ant. p. 211, 212.)

Issicus sinus.

Returning to the mouth of the Pyramus, we enter upon the periplus of the great gulf of Issus, which begins, in fact, at the cliffs of *Karadash*, the ancient Megarsus, on the western side of the river, and terminates with cape *Hynzir*, the Rossicus Scopulus of ancient navigators. This great bay forms a re-

[y] Sestini imagines this to be another name for Adana, but I see no evidence of that fact. P. 99.

[z] There are numerous medals belonging to this town, both under its appellation of Cæsarea and that of Anazarbus. ΚΑΙΣΑΡ. ΤΠΟ, or ΠΡΟΣ ΤΩ ΑΝΑΖΑΡ. and ΑΝΑΖΑΡΒΕΩΝ.

markable indenture in the angular bend which the
coast of Asia Minor here makes with that of Syria;
the latter commencing immediately after the cape of
Rhosus, which forms the extremity of mount Pieria. Round the gulf was a considerable extent
of plain, enclosed however by two chains of mountains meeting together in one point, and forming,
with their extremities, the two capes above mentioned. And in order to penetrate into the plains
of Issus it was absolutely necessary to cross a chain,
and its defile, whether advancing from the western
parts of Cilicia, or the neighbouring province of Syria on the south-east. The gulf of which we are
now speaking took its name from the town of Issus,
so celebrated for the victory of Alexander over the
army of Darius: it is known to modern navigators
by that of *Iskanderoon*, a town which has taken the
place of Alexandria, once seated near its Syrian extremity. We shall now follow the windings of its
coast from the mouth of the Pyramus and Mallus.
The Maritime Periplus names in succession several
minor stations, respecting which other authorities
are silent. Ionia, afterwards called Cephalus, near Ionia, post-
a headland, at the mouth of the Pyramus. The isles ea Cepha-
called Didymi; the point and village of Januaria; Januaria
Seretile, which is doubtless a corruption of Serre- vicus et
polis, a town placed in this part of Cilicia by Pto- Serrepolis.
lemy. (p. 129.)   Above this place, according to the
Periplus, was a village named Pyramus and mount Pyramus
Parium.   Then follows Ægæ, a seaport town of Parium
greater note, being spoken of by Strabo, (XIV. p. Ægæ.
676.) Ptolemy, (p. 129.) Pliny, (V. 27.) Philostratus, (I. c. 5.) and Lucan.

A a 2

Deseritur Taurique nemus, Perseaque Tarsos,
Coryciumque patens exesis rupibus antrum,
Mallos, et extremæ resonant navalibus Ægæ.

PHARS. III. 225.

(Cf. Steph. Byz. v. Αἰγαί. Hierocl. p. 705. Act. Concil. &c.) This place is now called *Ayas*, a village possessing a small harbour, and a few vestiges of antiquity [a]. Beyond this point the mountains close in upon the shore, and present a narrow passage, or defile, for those who travel on land. This pass was formed by that branch of mount Taurus known to the ancients by the name of Amanus; and hence the term of Amanides, or Amanicæ Pylæ, employed by the Greek historians and geographers to designate the passage in question. These writers have not always however been very clear and explicit in distinguishing between the several defiles by which Cilicia and Syria communicated with each other; hence the difficulties which this point of ancient topography has presented to modern inquirers, particularly with respect to the operations of Alexander and the forces of Darius, which led to the battle of Issus; since, without an accurate knowledge of the surrounding country and mountains, it is impossible to comprehend the movements of the two armies on that memorable occasion. It is to be regretted that Captain Beaufort was prevented by untoward circumstances from completing his survey of the gulf of Issus, as he would then have furnished us, according to his usual accuracy, with a perfect topographical view of the coast and plain, and surrounding mountains.

Amanides. sive Amanicæ Pylæ.

[a] Karamania, p. 299—301.

The Amanides Pylæ then, according to Strabo, who is in harmony with Ptolemy (p. 129.) and the Stadiasmus, began soon after Ægæ, after which occurred the several places to be observed on the shores and plains of Issus; then the mountains closed again on the coast, and formed another defile, called the Cilician gates, on the frontier of Syria. Pliny, however, has reversed the order observed by the abovementioned geographers, and has placed the gates of Amanus nearest Syria, and those of Cilicia close to Ægæ. (V. 27.) The arrangement of Xenophon in the Anabasis is again very different: he represents Cyrus as marching from Tarsus, across the Sarus and Pyramus, to Issus, which he calls the last town of Cilicia; then he describes the Cilician and Syrian gates, two narrow passes between perpendicular rocks and the sea, closed by walls and gates, and distant from each other about three stadia, with a river flowing between. Here there is no mention whatever of the Pylæ Amanides, nor Ægæ, nor any pass in short before Issus. Let us now turn to the historians who relate the actions of Alexander. We shall find that Arrian states that when this prince was at Mallus, he heard that Darius was at Sochi, a spot in Assyria about two days' journey from the Assyrian gates; meaning in both cases Syria and the Syrian gates. Having then consulted his principal officers, Alexander moved rapidly forwards, crossed the defiles, and took up a position at Myriandrus, which, as we know from Xenophon, was a Phœnician town south of Issus and the Syrian gates. Meanwhile Darius, urged by his counsellors, advanced towards Cilicia, and having crossed the mountains by the defiles called the Amanicæ Pylæ, descended upon Issus, and thus found himself interposed between Cilicia and Alexander. (II. 7.) Quintus Curtius agrees in all the principal points with Arrian, and especially in distinctly stating that it was by the Amanicæ Pylæ that Darius advanced to Issus, the same night that Alexander penetrated into Syria. (III. 8.) The Roman historian however speaks of a defile which Alexander had to cross before he could reach Issus, when advancing from Mallus. He is said to have moved in one day from that town to Castabalum, or Castabolum, where he met Parmenio, " quem præmiserat ad explorandum " iter saltus, per quem ad urbem Isson nomine pe- " netrandum erat." (III. 7.) That is, he marched by Ægæ to Castabalum, or Castabala, as Ptolemy calls it, one of the interior towns of Cilicia Propria. In the Jerusalem Itinerary it occurs under the corrupt name of Catavolomis, on the road from Tarsus by Adana and Mopsuestia into Syria; it is stated to be thirty-one miles from the latter town; and the previous station, Tardequia, I take to be another corruption for Turris Ægeæ, *Tor d'Equia.* The Itinerary of Antoninus also places Catabolum beyond Ægeæ. (p. 145, 146. Itin. Hieros. p. 580.) To these authorities we must add that of Callisthenes, the Alexandrian historian quoted by Polybius in one of his fragments. (XII. 17.) He stated, in conformity with Arrian and Quintus Curtius, that Alexander traversed the Cilician gates, whilst Darius penetrated into Cilicia by the Pylæ Amanides. And though Polybius censures and criticises severely the narrative of Callisthenes with respect to the manœuvres of both armies during the battle; he never controverts the truth of the above fact. Cicero also, in his account of the operations in which he was engaged against the Parthians, speaks of having manœuvred against the enemy in the vicinity of Issus, and having cleared the passes of mount Amanus. (Att. Ep. V. 20. Fam. XIV. 4.)

From these several authorities brought together, it will appear that the description given by Strabo of the Pylæ Amanicæ is not correct, or at least that his Pylæ Amanicæ are not those of the Alexandrian historians. It must be charged to a laxity in the geography of that period to extend the name to the narrow way along the coast by Ægæ to Issus, when in fact it must have been originally and properly applied to the pass which led from Syria over the chain of mount Amanus down upon Issus. The maritime pass of Ægæ and Castabolum is clearly that which Parmenio was ordered to clear, and by which Alexander advanced upon Issus ; and though it is probably formed by a root of mount Amanus detaching itself from the main chain, and closing upon the coast near the mouth of the Pyramus, it cannot fairly be called a pass in that mountain. I have thought it necessary to insist upon this point, because it is essential to a correct notion of the topography of the Issic gulf and district, and because, however correct Col. Leake's remarks are on this head, it does not appear to me that he has sufficiently noticed the difference between the geography of Strabo and that of the Alexandrian annalists [b].

Issus itself stood at the foot of the main chain of Issus. Amanus, and nearly at the centre of the head of the gulf to which it gave its name. Xenophon describes

[b] Asia Minor, p. 258.

Issus ("Ισσοι, in the plural) as a considerable town in his time. Cyrus remained there three days, and was joined by his fleet from the Peloponnese. These ships anchored close to the shore where Cyrus had his quarters. (I. 4. Cf. Arrian. II. 7. Diod. Sic. XVII. 32.) In Strabo's time it was only a small place with a port. (XIV. p. 676.) Stephanus says it was called Nicopolis, in consequence of the victory gained by Alexander. (v. "Ισσος.) Strabo however speaks of Nicopolis as a distinct place from Issus. Cicero reports that, during his expedition against the mountaineers of Amanus, he occupied Issus for some days. (Att. Ep. V. 20.) The breadth of plain between the sea and the mountains appears from Callisthenes, quoted by Polybius, not to exceed fourteen stadia, less than two miles, a space very inadequate for the manœuvres of so large an army as that of Darius. The ground was besides broken, and intersected by many ravines and torrents which descended from the mountains. The principal of these, and which is mentioned frequently in the narrative Pinarus fl. of this momentous battle, is the Pinarus. Strabo places it after Issus, and such appears from Arrian, Plutarch, and the other historians, to have been the fact. The two armies were at first drawn up on opposite banks of this stream: Darius on the side of Issus, Alexander towards Syria. It will not be necessary to enter further into the examination of the field of battle, as the narratives of Arrian, Curtius, and Plutarch, with the critical remarks of Polybius on the statement of Callisthenes, give a very clear notion of the whole transaction. I am not aware of the name which now designates this me-

morable site.   The Pinarus is said to be called
Deli sou [c]. Pliny mentions, besides this stream, some
other obscure torrents, such as the Andricus, Lycus, Andricus
fluvius.
and Chlorus. (V. 27.)   The latter may perhaps be Lycus fl.
the same as the Chersus, or Charsus, which Xeno- Chlorus fl.
phon mentions in the Syrian pass.

The defile leading out of Cilicia into Syria, com- Pylæ Cili-
monly termed the Cilician gates, began soon after ciæ.
Issus at a place now called *Bayas*, and which in the
Itineraries appears under the corresponding name of
Baiæ, sixteen miles from Castabolum. (Itin. Anton. Baiæ.
p. 146. Itin. Hierocl. p. 580.)   Here are some ruins
of ancient fortifications, commonly called the " Pil-
" lars of Jonas," which probably mark the site [d].

Sixteen miles beyond Baiæ was the town of Alex- Alexandria
andria, surnamed Catisson, i. e. κατὰ Ἴσσον, which ad Issum.
probably owed its origin to the great victory obtained by Alexander on these shores.   It is mentioned by Strabo as situated on the gulf of Issus.
Pliny includes it in Cilicia, as well as Steph. Byz.
(v. Ἀλεξάνδρεια,) and the Acts of Councils, which
class it among the sees of that province [e].   The modern town is termed by the Franks *Alessandrona*,
or *Alessandretta*, and by the Turks *Iskanderoon;*
and it now communicates these different appellations
to the gulf of Issus.   Above *Iskanderoon* a pass leads
across the chain of mount Amanus by *Beilan* and
Pagras, the ancient Pagræ, to Antioch.   This passage, as Col. Leake observes, is the Syriæ Pylæ of Syriæ
Pylæ.

[c] Gosselin's French Strabo, note, tom. IV. p. ii. p. 384.

[d] See Pococke, Niebuhr, and other travellers, quoted by Col. Leake, Asia Minor, p. 209.

[e] There are Seleucid and imperial medals of Alexandria, with the legend ΑΛΕΞΑΝ-ΔΡΕΩΝ. Sestin. p. 98.

Myrian-
drus.

Ptolemy.   Beyond Alexandria was Myriandrus, a town inhabited by Phœnicians, and which Xenophon (Anab. I. 4.) places in Syria beyond the Pylæ Ciliciæ, but Scylax includes it within the limits of Cilicia, (p. 40.) as well as Strabo, who says that Seleucia of Pieria, near the mouth of the Orontes, was the first Syrian town beyond the gulf of Issus.   The

Rhosus.

last Cilician town therefore was Rhosus, or Rhossus,

Rhosicus
Scopulus.

whose cape, called Rhossicus Scopulus by Ptolemy, forms the southern extremity of the gulf, now cape *Hynzir*. (Cf. Steph. Byz. v. Ῥῶσος. Athen. XIII. p. 586.)   The earthenware of this town was much esteemed. (VI. p. 229.)   It still retains the name of *Rosas*.   The rock of Rhosus forms the termination

Amanus
mons.

of mount Amanus, the great eastern barrier of Cilicia, which stretches to the north as far as Melitene and the Euphrates. (Strab. XI. p. 521.)   It is now called *Al-Lucan*.   Its valleys and recesses were inhabited by wild and fierce tribes, who lived chiefly by plundering their neighbours, though they boasted

Eleuthero-
cilices.

of their freedom under the sounding name of Eleutherocilices.   It was against these mountain robbers that Cicero's Cilician campaign was chiefly directed.   And he has acquainted us, in two of his letters, with the successes he obtained, and the for-

Erana.

tresses he captured.   He mentions particularly Era-

Sepyra.

na, which he terms " Amani caput," and Sepyra,

Commoris.

and Commoris; these he took, with six fortresses not named, besides burning several others.   He then

Aræ Alex-
andri.

encamped for four days near the Aræ Alexandri, at the foot of the mountain; this spot was doubtless close to Issus.   From thence he proceeded to attack

Pindenis-
sus.

Pindenissus, a town of the Eleuthero-Cilicians, and seated on a height of great elevation and strength;

this place he took after a siege of fifty-seven days, and compelled the Tibarani, a neighbouring tribe, to submit likewise. (Ep. Fam. XV. 4. Att. Ep. V. 20.) In another letter he calls the inhabitants of these mountains Amanienses. (Fam. II. 10f.) Strabo observes that Tarcondimotus, a chief of great merit, and who had been a zealous partisan of the Romans, obtained from them a grant of the whole of this mountain district, with the title of king. (XIV. p. 671.) Cicero likewise terms him, " fidelissimus socius " trans Taurum amicissimusque populi Romani g." (Fam. Ep. XV. 1. Cf. Plut. Anton. c. 61.) *[margin: Tibarani gens.]*

Epiphanea, a town which probably took its name from Antiochus Epiphanes, was situate, as we learn from Cicero, a day's march from mount Amanus. (Fam. Ep. XV. 4.) It is also mentioned by Pliny, who reports that it was first called Œniandus. (V. 27.) Appian. (Mithrid. p. 237.) Ammian. Marcell. (XXII. p. 223.) Ptolemy, (p. 129.) Stephanus Byz. (v. Ἐπιφάνεια,) and the ecclesiastical records. The Table Itinerary fixes it between Anazarba and Alexandria, thirty miles from each. Augusta was another Cilician town situate in the interior. (Plin. V. 27.) Ptolemy places it in a small district named Bryelice. (p. 129. Cf. Steph. Byz. v. Αὐγοῦστα.) We have now to close this section with a list of some places, the sites of which are altogether undetermined. Pliny commences his description of the coast from Syria, with the river Diaphanes, which may be the Thapsacus of Scylax; then mount Crocodi- *[margin: Epiphanea. Augusta. Bryelice regio. Diaphanes fluvius. Thapsacus fluvius. Crocodilus mons.]*

---

f The ethnic, Ἀμανῖται, appears on coins which are assigned to these people. Sestin. p. 98.

g The name was not un-common in Cilicia, as we find a bishop of Ægæ subscribing it in the councils of Nice and Antioch.

Cassipolis. lus. After the Aleian plains, Cassipolis, which took its name probably from the celebrated Cassius. Be-

Thynus, sive Tyrus. yond the Pyramus, Thynus, or rather Tyrus, according to the MSS.; and after, Celenderis, Nymphæum.

Nymphæum. Together with Adana, he names Cibyra, Pinara,

Alæ. Pedalia, and Alæ; the latter receives some countenance from Stephanus Byz. (v. Ἄλαι) and a coin of

Bombus fl. Paradisus fluvius. Imbarus mons. Hadrian, with the legend ΑΛΑΙΩΝ ΚΙΛΙΚΩΝ[h]. In the interior he notices the rivers Bombus and Paradisus, and mount Imbarus.

Halice et Halicus. Stephanus enables us to add the following: Halice and Halicus, a district, and place, and mountain, near Augusta; Argos, afterwards called Ar-

Argos, postea Argeopolis. geopolis; (v. Ἄργος.) Asine; (v. Ἀσίνη.) Aulæ, a

Asine. Aulæ. naval station, between Tarsus and Anchiale; (v.

Didymæum. Αὐλαί.) Didymæum, a village; Artemidorus spoke of two islands named Didyma, which are found also

Dryæna, postea Chrysopolis. in the Stadiasmus; Dryæna, afterwards called Chrysopolis; (vv. Δρύαινα, Χρυσόπολις.) Castalia, on the

Pania navale. authority of Theagenes; (v. Κασταλία.) Pania, a

Petrossa insula. port near the Aleian plain; (v. Πανία.) Petrossa, an island; (v. Πέτροσσα.) Rhœxus, a port at the mouth

Rhœxus portus. of the river Sarus; (v. Ῥοῖξος.) Rhogmi, another port, probably the Rhegmi of Strabo; (v. Ῥαγμοί.)

Syagra. Ades. Syagra, a spot said to be near Ades and Laertes, but of Ades we know as little; (v. Σύαγρα.) Chry-

Chrysippa. sippa, a town founded by Chrysippus; (v. Χρύσιππα.)

Pseudocorasium. Pseudocorasium, a tract of coast between Corycus and Seleucia; there was a bay and roadstead; Artemidorus is quoted; (v. Ψευδοκοράσιον.)

The Byzantine historians furnish also a few unimportant sites: Baca, a castle besieged and taken

Baca. by John Comnenus; it was near some river; (Nicet.

[h] Sestin. p. 93.

Ann. p. 15. Cinnam. p. 10.) Cistramum, near Ana- Cistra-
zarba, taken by Alex. Comnenus; (Cinnam. p. 104.) mum.
Corvorum nidi, a lofty mountain with two summits, Corvorum
near which the emperor Jo. Comnenus wounded nidi.
himself mortally in the chase. Herculis Pagus, near Herculis
Tarsus; (Cedr. p. 637.) Longinia, a place mentioned Pagus.
Longinia.
in conjunction with Tarsus; Mamista, or Mopsuestia,
and Adana, taken from the Turks by the Greeks;
(Ann. Comn. p. 340. D. Cinn. p. 104.) Marasia, a Marasia.
place in Cilicia, probably now *Marash*. (Ann. Comn.
p. 334. D.) In Nicephorus Phocas we have some
curious details about the Cilician defiles above Adana; the road leading to that town was called Via Via Mau-
Mauriana; river Cydnus, called Hierax by the na- riana.
tives; pass of Carydius. (p. 157.) The Itinerary Carydius
Table marks a communication which branches off saltus.
from the defiles of Podandus towards Adana; this
is noticed in Captain Kinneir's modern account of
the pass. Papyrii Castrum, a fortress near Tarsus; Papyrii
(Theodor. Hist. Eccl. II. p. 571.) Praca, a town Castrum.
Praca.
near Seleucia, taken from the Turks by Manuel
Comnenus; (Nicet. Ann. p. 35. B.) called Pracana
by Cinnamus. (p. 21.) There was a passage leading
from the valley of Seleucia over the mountains into
the plain of Tarsus, near to Claudiopolis; (Curopal.
p. 833.) and Nicephorus Phocas speaks of the Cli-
suræ or passes of Seleucia; (c. 23. p. 162.) Sisium, Sisium.
a fort of Cilicia. (Cedr. p. 445.)

SECTION XIV.

CYPRUS.

———◆———

Origin of its inhabitants—Sketch of its history from the earliest period to the fall of the eastern empire—Natural history, productions, and principal geographical features of the island—Periplus of the coast—Interior.

THE island of Cyprus, situate at nearly the same distances from the shores of Phœnicia and Cilicia, might with equal facility receive her earliest colonists from either of these two countries; but since we have seen that Cilicia itself was indebted to the former for her population, it is most probable that the island, into whose history we are now briefly inquiring, derived her first settlements from the same primary source; nor is this a conjecture which has only probability to urge in its behalf, since the earliest records and traditions preserved by the Greeks tend to confirm the fact. Herodotus, in his catalogue of the Persian armament assembled by Xerxes, describes the Cyprians as a mixed people, derived from Greece, Phœnicia, and, as they themselves affirmed, from Æthiopia. (VII. 90.) The latter tradition, probably, referred to a colony which may have been imported by Amasis, king of Egypt, when he held Cyprus under his domination. It is generally supposed by the earlier biblical commentators, that the word Chettim, by which the Greeks or Gentiles are designated in the Old Testament, had been derived, in the first instance, from the town of Citium in Cyprus, founded by Belus, king of the Phœnicians. (Joseph. Antiq. Jud. I. 7. Epiphan. Hær. I. 30. §. 25. Hieron. in Esai. V. 23[a].) Other towns are said also to have been founded by Belus, who, in Virgil, is supposed to be the father of Dido:

> . . . . genitor tum Belus opimam
> Vastabat Cyprum, et victor ditione tenebat.
>
> Æn. I. 622.

but we have besides abundant proof of the fact we are seeking to establish, in the whole of the ceremonies and religious rites observed by the Cyprians, with respect to Venus and Adonis, which were, without doubt, borrowed from Phœnicia. Cinyras, whom the Greeks called the father of Adonis, is represented in the Iliad as king of Cyprus, where the ·poet, speaking of Agamemnon, says:

> . . . . θώρηκα περὶ στήθεσσιν ἔδυνε
> Τόν ποτέ οἱ Κινύρης δῶκε, ξεινήϊον εἶναι.
> Πεύθετο γὰρ Κύπρονδε μέγα κλέος.
>
> Iɪ. Λ. 19.

We hear also of Pygmalion, the son of Belus, having reigned in Cyprus. (Porphyr. Abst. Anim. IV. c. 15.) and Elulæus is said, many years after, to have reconquered the Citians, who had revolted from him. ·This Phœnician prince is supposed to be contemporary with Shalmanezer, king of Assyria. (Menand. ap. Joseph. Ant. Jud. IX. 14.) Soon after the siege of Troy, if not before that period, the Greeks began to dispute with the Phœnicians possession of the

---

[a] See other authorities in Meursius. Cypr. c. 10. Bochart. Geogr. Sacr.

island. The colony from Salamis and Athens, under the command of Teucer, was celebrated by poets, (Hor. Od. I. 7.) and acknowledged by historians. (Herod. VII. 90.) Other settlements were formed from Arcadia and Cythnus, (ibid.) and the Telchines were said to have crossed over from Crete.

At first this great island was divided into several petty states, each of which was governed by its own tyrant or independent prince; the number of these is stated by writers of áuthority to have been nine. (Plin. V. 31. Diod. Sic. XVI. P. Mel. II. 7.)

Subsequently, the whole island was brought under subjection, for the first time, by Amasis, king of Egypt, and compelled to become tributary. Amasis was probably assisted in this enterprise by his ally, Polycrates, tyrant of Samos. (Herod. IL 182.) On the invasion of Egypt by Cambyses, the Cyprians surrendered readily to that monarch, and furnished a squadron for the naval part of the expedition. (III. 19.) They continued to form a portion of the Persian empire, and constituted, with Phœnicia and Palestine, the fifth division in the arrangement made by Darius; (III. 91.) but, during the Ionian revolt, the whole island, at the instigation of Onesilus, brother of the tyrant of Salamis, threw off the Persian yoke, and joined the confederates, with the exception of Amathus, which was besieged by Onesilus and his allies. The Persians, however, speedily despatched a large force of infantry and ships to quell the insurrection, and obstinate engagements took place by land and sea, with various success. The Ionians, who formed the naval force of the allies, defeated the Phœnician fleet opposed to them; but the Cyprians, who fought on land, were overcome by the

Persians, and Onesilus their leader was slain. Artybius, the Persian general, fell also in the engagement. After this disaster, the whole of Cyprus again became subject to Darius. (Herod. V. 104—116.) In the expedition of Xerxes, the Cyprians furnished 150 ships. (VII. 90.) After the overthrow of the Persians at Salamis and Mycale, a Grecian fleet invaded the island, and reduced the greater part of it. (Thuc. I. 94.) Another expedition was afterwards undertaken by the Athenians, under the command of Cimon; but a plague having arisen, and that general dying, the undertaking was given up. (I. 112.)

Whilst the enfeebled empire of Persia was scarcely able to resist the attacks of the victorious Greeks, an opportunity was afforded to a wise and politic prince, Evagoras of Salamis, not only to recover his paternal possessions, of which he had been deprived by the Persians, but even to add considerably to their extent, and to raise the name and glory of Cyprus to a much higher pitch than it had ever attained before. He became the patron also of the arts and literature, and entertained at his court distinguished men of all nations. It was in his dominions that Conon, the celebrated Athenian general, sought refuge after the fatal battle of Ægos Potamis, and by his aid was enabled to prepare a fleet, which restored the naval ascendency of his country. (Isocr. Evagor. p. 200. Xenoph. Hell. II. 1. 19. Corn. Nep. Conon. Diod. Sic. XIV. 39.) Judging from the splendid panegyric passed upon his character by Isocrates, Evagoras was certainly a prince of rare and distinguished virtue and merit, and his fortune for a time kept pace with his shining qualities; unfortunately, however, he met with reverses towards the close of his reign, in a war against Artaxerxes, and died by the hand of a domestic assassin, leaving his dominions to his son Nicocles, also favourably known from the writings of Isocrates. Cyprus, however, at this period, must be considered as tributary to the Persian empire, and it remained so till the battle of Issus; when the several states declared for Alexander, and joined the Macedonian fleet with 120 ships at the siege of Tyre. (Arrian, II. 20.) They were afterwards ordered to cruise off the Peloponnese with 100 ships, in conjunction with the Phœnicians. (III. 6.) When the empire of Alexander was dissolved, Cyprus, together with Egypt, fell to the lot of Ptolemy, and remained annexed to that crown under his successors, till, on the death of the last sovereign of the dynasty, it was seized by the Romans, and erected into a province of the empire, under the government of a prætor. It had been ceded for a short time to Cleopatra and her sister Arsinoe, by Mark Antony; but on his overthrow and death the island was once more annexed to the Roman dominions. (Strab. XIV. p. 684. Plut. in Caton. Plin. c. 34. 39. Flor. III. 9.) We find it governed by a proconsul when Paul and Barnabas first preached the Gospel in the island. This officer's name was Sergius Paulus, and he appears to have become a convert on witnessing the judgment of God on Elymas the sorcerer. (Acts xiii. 4 —13.) St. Barnabas is known to have been a native of the island.

Under the Byzantine emperors Cyprus experienced several vicissitudes. It was invaded and ravaged by the Saracens for the first time in the reign of Constans, and repeatedly afterwards. (Const. Porphyr. de Adm. Imp. c. 20. Paul. Diacon. XIX.) Richard Cœur de Lion, having conquered it from Isaac Comnenus, made it over to Lusignan, king of Jerusalem, to which title he added that of this new possession, and both are still retained by the sovereigns of the house of Savoy. Lusignan lost it to Saladin, after which it was taken by the Venetians, and finally wrested from them by the Turks.

This celebrated island, like every other in the Grecian seas, appears to have borne several appellations in remote ages, but many of these are only poetical, and rest on dubious and obscure authority. Those which occur most commonly are Sphecia, Cerastis, and Cryptus, for which fanciful etymologies are adduced by Stephanus, Eustathius, and other authorities compiled by Meursius: that of Cyprus, which finally prevailed over every other, is also uncertain; but the notion which derives it from the shrub cypress, is probably the most correct; and Bochart, whose Phœnician analogies rest here on safer ground, insists strongly on its validity [b].

Cyprus is reckoned by Strabo, or rather Timæus, whom he quotes, the third in extent of the seven Mediterranean isles, which he classes in the following order: Sardinia, Sicily, Cyprus, Crete, Eubœa, Corsica, Lesbos. (XIV. p. 654. Cf. Plin. V. 35.) According to ancient measurements, its circuit amounted to 3,420 stadia, including the sinuosities of the coast. Its greatest length from west to east, between cape Acamas and the little islands called Clides, was reckoned at 1,400 stadia. (Strab. loc. cit. Plin. loc. cit. Agathem. Geogr. I. 5.)

[b] Geogr. Sacr. p. 373.

The interior of Cyprus is mountainous; a ridge being drawn across the entire length of the island from cape Acamas on the west to that of Dinaretum in the opposite direction; it attains the highest elevation near the central region, and was anciently called Olympus. This physical conformation precludes the existence of any considerable rivers. That of *Famagosta* is the largest. There are no lakes, but some salt marshes on the coast.

Cyprus yielded to no other island in fertility, since it produced excellent wine and oil, and abundance of wheat and various fruits. There was also a great supply of timber for building ships. (Strab. XIV. p. 684 [c].) Its mineral productions were likewise very rich, especially copper, found at Tamasus, and supposed to be alluded to in the Odyssey. I am not aware that its mountains have a volcanic character, but we have evidence of its having been frequently exposed to earthquakes. (Senec. Epist. 91.)

That the Cyprians spoke a language different from the Phœnicians, and peculiar to themselves, is evident from the scattered glosses preserved by the lexicographers and grammarians. As might be anticipated from the religious worship and rites of the goddess so universally established amongst them, they were a sensual and licentious people. Prostitution was sanctioned by the laws, (Herod. I. 199. Athen. XII. p. 516.) and hired flatterers and professed sycophants attended on the luxurious princes of the land. (Clearch. ap. Athen. VI. p. 255, 256.) Nevertheless, literature and the arts flourished here

[c] Numerous passages from Athenæus, Pliny, and other writers, have been industriously collected by Meursius, on the productions of Cyprus.

to a considerable extent, even at an early period, as the name of the Cypria Carmina, ascribed by some to Homer, (Herod. II. 118. Athen. XV. p. 682.) sufficiently attests. Several writers appear to have treated of the history and topography of Cyprus, and a list of these, as well as of the distinguished men whom that island produced, will be found in Meursius.

Strabo commences his description at the western extremity from cape Acamas, which he states to be *Acamas prom.* a thickly wooded headland divided into two summits rising towards the north. (XIV. p. 682.) The modern name is cape *Salizano.* (Sext. Empir. in Math. I. 12. Lucian. Salt. c. 40. Ptol. p. 136.) Hence Venus, I imagine, was called Acamantis. (Steph. Byz. v. Ἀκαμάντιον.) The chain, of which this headland is the extremity, bore the name of Acamantis, and was connected with the central ridge of the island. Advancing along the coast in a southerly direction, we meet with cape *Trapano*, evidently the Drepanum of Ptolemy; (p. 136.) then the *Drepanum prom.* roadstead and harbour of Paphos, the most celebrated city perhaps in the whole island: the ancient town, called Palæpaphos, was said to have been *Palæpaphos.* founded by Cinyras, the reputed father of Adonis; (Apollod. III. 14.) it was seated on a height, at a distance of ten stadia from the sea, and near the little river Bocarus, which flowed from mount Acamas. *Bocarus fl.* (Hesych. v. Βώκαρος.) It is very uncertain to what river Euripides alludes in connexion with Cyprus and Paphos:

Ἱκοίμαν ποτὶ τὰν Κύπρον,
νᾶσον τᾶς Ἀφροδίτας,

B b 3

Ἵν' οἱ θελξίφρονες νέμον-
ται θνατοῖσιν Ἔρωτες·
Πάφον θ', ἂν ἑκατόστομοι
βαρβάρου ποταμοῦ ῥοαὶ
καρπίζουσιν ἄνομβροι.

BACCH. v. 400.

The best critics conceive that he refers to the Nile; in that case it is difficult to imagine how that river can be said to fertilize Cyprus. It was reported that Venus had first landed on this part of the island. (Tacit. II. Hist. II. 2. P. Mel. II. 7.)

Tunc Cilicum liquere solum, Cyproque citatas
Immisere rates, nullas cui prætulit aras
Undæ diva memor Paphiæ, si numina nasci
Credimus, aut quemquam fas est cœpisse deorum.

LUCAN. PHARS. VIII. 456.

We are told by Pausanias that the worship of Venus was introduced into the island from Assyria. (Att. c. 14.) It appears to have been established at Paphos before the age of Homer.

Ἡ δ' ἄρα Κύπρον ἵκανε φιλομμειδὴς Ἀφροδίτη,
Ἐς Πάφον· ἔνθα δέ οἱ τέμενος βωμός τε θυήεις.

ODYSS. Θ. 362.

Ipsa Paphum sublimis abit, sedesque revisit
Læta suas: ubi templum illi, centumque Sabæo
Thure calent aræ, sertisque recentibus halant.

VIRG. ÆN. I. 415.

O Venus, regina Cnidi Paphique,
Sperne dilectam Cypron, et vocantis
Thure te multo Glyceræ decoram
Transfer in ædem.

HOR. OD. I. 30.

Paphos. A new town subsequently was founded nearer the sea, at a distance of sixty stadia from the former, by Agapenor, an Arcadian chief, who commanded at Troy, and after the siege, was driven to Cyprus by a storm. This new colony became in time very flourishing, and possessed many magnificent temples sacred to Venus; but Palæpaphos always seems to have retained its preeminence in sanctity; and in the annual festival of the goddess, the road to it, as Strabo reports, was crowded with her votaries, who resorted here from the other towns. (Strab. XIV. p. 683. Pausan. Arcad. c. 5.) This colony from Arcadia is alluded to by Herodotus. (VII. 91.) Having been nearly overthrown by an earthquake, (Senec. Ep. 91. Nat. Quæst. VI. 26.) it was restored by Augustus, and named Augusta; (Dio Cass. LIV.) it was the seat of government when visited by St. Paul, for we read in the Acts, (XIII. 6.) that when the apostle, accompanied by Barnabas and John, surnamed Mark, "had " gone through the isle unto Paphos, they found a cer- " tain sorcerer, a false prophet, a Jew, whose name was " Bar-jesus : which was with the deputy of the coun- " try, Sergius Paulus, a prudent man; who called for " Barnabas and Saul, and desired to hear the word " of God. But Elymas the sorcerer, (for so is his " name by interpretation,) withstood them, seeking " to turn away the deputy from the faith. Then " Saul, (who also is called Paul,) filled with the " Holy Ghost, set his eyes on him, and said, O full " of all subtilty and all mischief, thou child of the " devil, thou enemy of all righteousness, wilt thou " not cease to pervert the right ways of the Lord? " And now, behold, the hand of the Lord is upon " thee, and thou shalt be blind, not seeing the sun " for a season. And immediately there fell on him " a mist and a darkness; and he went about seeking

" some to lead him by the hand.   Then the deputy,
" when he saw what was done, believed, being asto-
" nished at the doctrine of the Lord." It appears,
from Tacitus, that the worship of the heathen deity
was yet remaining in the reign of Titus, who visited Paphos, and made many inquiries respecting
the customs and sacred rites of the place. (Hist. II.
2. Ann. III. 62. Suet. Tit. c. 5.)   Paphos appears
in later writings, both civil and ecclesiastical, as an
episcopal town, and one of the most noted in the
island : the site is yet marked by some ruins, and
the name of *Baffo* serves sufficiently to attest their
identity. The cape which closes the bay of *Baffo* to
Zephyrium the west, must answer to the Zephyrium promonto-
prom. rium of Strabo. (XIV. p. 683.)   The coast presents
Arsinoe to the south-east another headland, named Arsinoe,
prom. which afforded an anchorage to vessels, and possessed
a grove, and temple.   At a little distance further in-
Hierocepia. land was Hierocepis, or Hierocepia, a name which
denotes a sacred enclosure, or pleasure-ground, probably dedicated to the Paphian goddess. (Strab. loc.
cit.)   Pliny names Hierocepia, as a small island, situate off New Paphos. (V. 35.)

    Palæpaphos is said to correspond with the site of
Boosura. *Conclia;* then follow in succession Boosura, (Βοὸς
οὐρὰ,) " the Ox's tail," noticed by Strabo and Pto-
Treta. lemy, (p. 136.) and Treta, only by the former. The
Curium. next town of consequence is Curium, said to have been
founded by an Argive colony ; (Herod. V. 113. Strab.
XIV. p. 683.) it was one of the nine regal cities,
and Stesenor, its sovereign, is stigmatized in history
as having betrayed his country's cause during the
fight waged by the Cyprians against the Persians,
towards the close of the Ionian revolt. (Herod. loc.

cit.) It is also noticed by Ptolemy, (p. 136.) Stephanus Byz. (v. Κούριον) and Pliny. (V. 35.) The site seems to correspond with that now called *Episcopia*, implying the existence of a bishop's see, a circumstance which applies to Curium in the middle ages. (Act. Concil. Ephes. p. 779. Hierocl. p. 706.) Ancient writers report that the hills of Curium contained rich veins of copper ore. (Theophr. de Vent. Aristot. de Mirab. Serv. Æn. III. 111.) Near the town was a cape, whence sacrilegious offenders, who had dared to touch the altar of Apollo, were hurled into the sea. (Strab. XIV. p. 683.) The editor of the French Strabo supposes this may be the cape Phrurium of Ptolemy, and Phrurium cape *Bianco*, of modern geography[c]. prom.

The point, named Curias, was more to the south- Curias east, and was rather a peninsula than a promontory: prom. it answers to what is now called cape *Gatto*, forming a low and rounded excrescence which terminates the island towards the south. At a little distance inland are some salt marshes, which receive an arm of a river corresponding apparently with the Lycus Lycus fl. of Ptolemy. (p. 136.) The main branch joins the sea close to the site of Curium.

Amathus, which next follows, was a town of great Amathus. antiquity. Adonis, who was supposed to be the same as Osiris, was worshipped here, as well as Venus. (Steph. Byz. v. Ἀμαθοῦς. Cf. Paus. Bœot. c. 41.) Scylax affirms that the Amathusians were autochthonous; (Peripl. p. 41. Cf. Theopomp. ap. Phot. Bibl.) and it appears from Hesychius that they had a peculiar dialect. (vv. Ἐτθλαί, Κυβάβδα, Μάλικα.)

c Tom. III. p. ii. p. 401.

Amathus was celebrated as a favourite residence of Venus:

> Est Amathus, est celsa mihi Paphos.
>
> Æn. X. 51.

> Nunc o cœruleo creata ponto
> Quæ sanctum Idalium, Syrosque apertos,
> Quæque Ancona, Cnidumque arundinosam
> Colis, quæque Amathunta, quæque Golgos.
>
> CATULL. Ep. XXXVI.

The goddess, as an author who wrote a history of Amathus, and is quoted by Hesychius, (v. 'Αφρόδιτος,) reported, was represented with a beard. (Cf. Macrob. Sat. III. 8. Serv. Æn. II.)

Some particulars connected with the history of Amathus are related by Herodotus. He informs us that it was the only town in the island which refused to join Onesilus in his revolt against Darius. That chief in consequence laid siege to the place, but a Persian army having advanced to its succour, he was defeated and slain, and the Amathusians after the engagement cut off his head, and fixed it over one of their gates. A swarm of bees having subsequently lodged in the skull, the Amathusians, in compliance with an oracle, buried the head, and paid divine honours to the memory of the Cyprian chief. (V. 114—116.) Other superstitions practised at Amathus are specified by Plutarch in the life of Theseus, and Ovid in his Metamorphoses. (X. 220.) Athenæus relates that Pasicyprus, king of Citium, having sold his patrimony, retired to Amathus and died there. (IV. 7.) We also learn from Hesychius, on the authority of Eratosthenes, that Rhœcus, king of Amathus, having on one occasion been captured by the Athenians, and being afterwards released, acknow-

ledged the obligation by sending them annually a
present of barley. (v. Ῥοίκου κριθοπομπία.) Hipponax,
who is quoted by Strabo, (VIII. p. 340.) affirmed
that Amathus was famous for its wheat; and Ovid
has, in more than one passage, alluded to its mineral
productions.

> At si forte roges fœcundam Amathunta metalli.
> METAM. X. 220.

> Piscosamque Cnidon, gravidamve Amathunta metalli.
> IBID. X. 531.

Amathus is mentioned by Strabo, (XIV. p. 683.)
Pliny, (V. 35.) and Ptolemy, (p. 136.) and it is
known to have been the see of a Christian bishop
under the Byzantine emperors. (Hierocl. p. 706.
Eccl. Not.)   Its ruins are to be seen near the little
town of *Limeson,* or *Limasol,* somewhat to the north-
east of cape *Gatto.*

Beyond was situate the little town of Palæa, at the Palæa.
foot of a mountain shaped like a breast, and named
Olympus, (Strab. XIV. p. 683.) now *Monte Sᵃ. Croce.* Olympus
mons.
Then follows Citium, one of the most ancient cities of Citium.
the island, and whence the name of Chetim or Chit-
tim is not unreasonably supposed to have been derived. (Joseph. Antiq. Jud. I. 7. Epiphan. Hær.
I. 30. Hieron. in Jes. V. 23.[e])   Diogenes Laertius,
in his life of Zeno, reports that this town had been
colonized by the Phœnicians; a circumstance which
is confirmed by Cicero, (de Fin. IV. 20.) and Suidas. (v. Ζήνων.)   It was even said that it owed its
foundation to Belus:

> Βήλου δ' αὖ Κίτιόν τε καὶ ἱμερόεσσα Λάπηθος.

(Alexand. Ephes. ap. Steph. Byz. v. Λάπηθος.)

[e] See Bochart, Geogr. Sacr. 373. and Meurs. Cypr. I. 10.

. Citium was besieged at the close of the Persian war by the Athenian forces under the command of Cimon. (Thuc. I. 112.) According to Diodorus, the place surrendered; (XII. 3.) but it was the last exploit of that distinguished general, for he was soon after taken ill, and died on board his ship in the harbour. (Cf. Plut. et Corn. Nep. Vit. Cim.) Pliny mentions some salt marshes near Citium. (XXI. 7. Antig. Caryst. c. 173.) This town was further celebrated for having given birth to Zeno, the founder of the Stoical sect, and the physician Apollonius. (Strab. XII. p. 682.) It appears to have been a bishoprick under the Byzantine empire [f], and still retains the name of *Chiti*.

Malum. Not far from Citium was a town named Malum, which surrendered likewise to Cimon the Athenian. (Diod. Sic. XII. 3.) The same historian reports that Ptolemy, son of Lagus, having deposed Stasiœcus, prince of Malum, destroyed the town, and removed the inhabitants to Paphos. (XIX. 79.) Ptolemy places, to the west of Citium, the little river Tetius fl. Tetius; and to the east the promontory Dades, Dades prom. which answers to *Capo Chiti*. Then follows a rugged line of coast for several miles, along a bay which lies between the headland just mentioned and that of Pedalium prom. Pedalium: above the latter, according to Strabo, rose a hill, with a temple consecrated to Venus. (XIV. p. 682.) Meursius was of opinion that the word Pedalium was corrupt, and proposed substituting Idalium, a well known spot, beloved by Venus; but such a change does not derive any support from manuscript authority; and, besides, Ptolemy recognises this cape to the east of Citium.

[f] Geogr. Sacr. p. 306.

With respect to Idalium, or Idalia, we have no Idalium, sive Idalia. precise indication of its locality in all the numerous passages of the Greek and Latin poets, which connect it with the worship of Venus.

Est Amathus, est celsa mihi Paphos, atque Cythera,
Idaliæque domus.   Æn. X. 51.

Aut super Idalium sacrata sede recondam.
        Æn. I. 681.

. . . fotum gremio dea tollit in altos
Idaliæ lucos.   Æn. I. 692.

Δέσποιν' ἁ Γολγώς τε καὶ Ἰδάλιον ἐφίλασας.
       Theocr. Id. XV. 100.

Quæque regis Golgos, quæque Idalium frondosum.
      Catull. Pel. et Thet. 96.

. . . . . . percussit Adonem
Venántem Idalio vertice durus aper.
      Propert. II. 13.

Lucan would seem to place it on the sea-shore:

. . ab Idalio Cinyreæ litore Cypri.
     Phars. VIII. 716.

The Scholiast of Theocritus and Stephanus Byz. speak of a small town of the same name as the hill, or mountain. (v. Ἰδάλιον.) Beyond cape Pedalium, Strabo points out the port of Leucolla, which seems Leucolla portus. to answer to that of *Armida*, near *Capo Grego*. This headland is probably to be identified with the sandy promontory called Ammochostos by Ptolemy. Ammochostos prom. The name of this cape seems to have been transmitted by corruption to the neighbouring town of *Famagosta*, which figures in the modern annals of the island. In this vicinity must have stood Arsi- Arsinoe. noe, mentioned by Strabo. It possessed a harbour.

Throni
urbs et
prom.

(XIV. p. 682.) Throni is a spot noticed by the same geographer, as being distant 700 stadia from Curium. Ptolemy mentions both a town and promontory of the name, between capes Ammochostos and Dades.

Salamis.

Further north by east was Salamis, a city of note and considerable antiquity, said to have been founded by Teucer, the son of Telamon. This fact indeed stands on the authority of so many writers of weighty testimony, that we cannot consider it as a mere mythological fiction. Isocrates, in his address to Nicocles, son of Evagoras, dwells much on the descent of that prince and the royal house of Salamis from Teucer. (Evagor. p. 192, 193. Nicocl. p. 33.) Herodotus also admits that Cyprus had received a colony from the Athenian Salamis, though he makes no mention of Teucer. (VII. 90.) Æschylus likewise bears witness to the truth of this tradition:

Κυπρίας τε πόλεις,
Πάφον, ἠδὲ Σόλους,
Σαλαμῖνά τε, τᾶς
Νῦν ματρόπολις
Τῶνδ' αἰτία στεναγμάτων.

PERS. 907.

and Horace has made it a conspicuous feature in one of his odes, where he represents Teucer as addressing the companions of his voyage.

Quo nos cunque feret melior fortuna parente,
   Ibimus, o socii comitesque.
Nil desperandum Teucro duce, et auspice Teucro.
   Certus enim promisit Apollo,
Ambiguam tellure nova Salamina futuram.

OD. I. 7.

(Cf. Tacit. Ann. III. 62.)

Previous to the arrival of Teucer the site had borne the name of Coronis. Porphyrius, who is our authority for this circumstance, records that human sacrifices were offered up to Jupiter and Venus, the tutelary deities of the place; and that this practice continued till the time of Hadrian. (Abst. II. Euseb. Præp. Ev. IV. 16. Lactant. I. 21.)

We learn from Herodotus that Salamis was one of the leading cities of Cyprus in the reign of Cambyses. At that time it was governed by Evethon, a prince who is said to have made some rich offerings to the shrine of Delphi, and to have received at his court Pheretime, mother of Arcesilaus, the ex-king of Cyrene, but to have declined assisting her with an army in reinstating her son. (IV. 162.) In the time of Darius we find Salamis ruled by Gorgus, great grandson of Evethon, whose brother Onesilus caused the whole island to revolt. (V. 104.) The battle which crushed this revolution, and brought back the Cyprians under the Persian yoke, was fought under the walls of Salamis. (V. 110.) It was afterwards besieged by Cimon, but peace being made with Persia, the siege was not persisted in. (Diod. Sic. XII. 3.) Several years after, it was again assailed by Demetrius Poliorcetes, but he retired on the approach of Ptolemy with a fleet. (Diod. Sic. XX. 48—50. Polyæn. IV. 7.) During the reign of Evagoras it might be considered as the principal city of the island, since it was the rendezvous of distinguished men from Greece, and other countries. Cicero speaks of having freed the Salaminians from the vexations to which they were exposed on the part of Scaptius, a Roman knight, and his satellites. (Ep. Att. V. 21. VI. 1 et 2.) It was taken and destroyed by a band of seditious Jews in the reign of Trajan. (Euseb. Chron. Paul. Diacon. IX. Oros. VII. 12.) Overwhelmed by an earthquake in that of Constantine, and being restored, it took the name of Constantia, which it still preserves under the modern form of *Constanza*. It was then the metropolitan see of the island, and derived some lustre from being held by Epiphanius. (Sozom. VII. 26.)

Salamis possessed a very ancient temple of Jupiter, founded by Teucer; and another of Venus, alluded to in the hymn ascribed to Homer:

Χαῖρε θεὰ, Σαλαμῖνος ἐϋκτιμένης μεδέουσα.

This city is casually noticed by Thucydides, (I. 112. Scylax. (Peripl. p. 41.) Pliny, (V. 31.) and Mela. (II. 7.) We learn from Athenæus that it was celebrated for its manufactures of embroidered stuffs. (II. 48. B.) It possessed also salt-works. (Plin. XXXI. 7. Dioscor. V. 126.) Hesychius has preserved some words of the Salaminian dialect; Εὔχους. Θέαγον. Κάγρα, &c. Beyond Salamis, Ptolemy notices a promontory called Elea, which is still known to modern navigators under that name. The north-eastern extremity of the island is formed by a long narrow neck of land, stretching out towards the mouth of the gulf of Issus. The cape by which it was terminated seems to have borne different appellations; for Pliny calls it Dinaretum, but Ptolemy, Οὐρὰ βοὸς, or "the Ox-tail," and in one MS. the reading is Κλεῖδες ἄκρα. The latter variation is easily accounted for, from the existence of some small islands off the cape in question, which were called Clides, and are often mentioned in ancient history and geography. (Strab. XIV. p. 682. Plin. V. 31.) Herodotus has

Elea prom.

Dinaretum, sive Clides prom.

Clides insulæ.

also transferred the name of these islands to the cape. (V. 108.) Strabo does not name this headland, but observes that above it was a mountain named Olympus, with a temple consecrated to Ve- Olympus nus Acræa, from which women were excluded. mons. (XIV. p. 682.) Cape Dinaretum, or Clides, now bears the name of *Sant' Andrea*. Having turned this promontory, we now direct our course towards the west, along that side of the island which faces Cilicia. Here we find the town and port of Carpasia, Carpasia. named by Scylax, (p. 41.) Strabo, (loc. cit.) Ptolemy, and Stephanus Byz. who states that it was founded by Pygmalion. (v. Κάρπασια.) Diodorus reports that it was taken by Demetrius Poliorcetes, together with a neighbouring place called Urania, or Erania; perhaps the temple of Venus Urania, or Acræa, mentioned by Strabo. (Diod. Sic. XX. 48.)

. . . . . καὶ Οὐρανίης πέδον ὄρης
Αἰθερίου κενέωνος ἐπώνυμον, ὅττι πολίτας
Ἔτρεφεν ἀστράπτοντας ἐπουρανίων τύπον ἄστρων.
Οἳ τ' εἶχον Κραπάσειαν ἁλιστεφὲς οὖδας ἀρούρης.

NONN. DIONYS. XIII.

Carpasia has preserved the name of *Carpas*.

A little to the west of Carpasia and near the coast, was a group of islands called Carpasiæ. Strabo Carpasiæ seems to place them to the south of the Clides, but insulæ. the passage is obscure, and probably not free from error; and I cannot agree with the French translators in supposing two towns, and two groups of islands of this name [g]. (Strab. XIV. p. 682. Ptol. p. 136.) The Carpasian islets are known by the name of *Chiro*. Westward of the town of Carpasia was a spot called the shore of the Greeks; ('Αχαιῶν ἀκτὴ) Achivo-rum littus.

[g] Tom. III. p. ii. p. 399.

it being reported that Teucer and his colonists had landed there on their arrival. (Strab. XIV. p. 682.) Beyond was Aphrodisium, situated in the narrowest part of the island, being only seventy stadia from Salamis. (Strab. loc. cit.) Beyond Carpasia, Scylax places Cerynea, (Per. p. 41.) which appears to be called Ceronia by Ptolemy, (p. 136.) and Cyrenia by Constantine Porphyrogenetes. (Them. I. 15. Cf. Diod. Sic. XIX.) This town is known to have been an episcopal see from ecclesiastical records. The name of *Tzerina* is still attached to the spot, and there are a few remains of antiquity. Col. Leake, who landed there from Cilicia, says it is six hours from *Lefkosia,* or *Nicosia,* the modern capital of the island [g]. Meursius thinks that Cerynia ought to be identified with Cinyrea, noticed by Pliny (V. 31.) and Nonnus:

Οἶτε πόλιν Κινύρειαν ἐπώνυμον εἴσετι πετρῶν
Ἀρχεγόνου Κινύραο. DIONYS. XIII.

Lapathus, sive Lapethus. but this is somewhat doubtful. Then follows Lapathus, or Lapethus, a town of considerable antiquity, and the foundation of which was assigned to the Phœnicians, headed by Belus:

Βήλου δ' αὖ Κίτιόν τε καὶ ἱμερόεσσα Λάπηθος.

(Steph. Byz. v. Λάπηθος. Cf. Scyl. Per. p. 41.) Nonnus states that it derived its name from Lapethus, a follower of Bacchus.

. . . . ἐκ δὲ Λαπήθων
Ὕστερον ἣν ἐκάλεσσαν ἐπώνυμον ἡγεμονῆος
Ὅς τοτε λαὸν ἄγειρεν· ἐν εὐθύρσῳ δὲ κυδοιμῷ
Κάτθανε καὶ κτερέϊστο, καὶ οὔνομα λεῖπε πολίταις.
DIONYS. XIII. 447.

[g] Travels in Asia Minor, p. 118, 119.

We learn from Strabo that Lapethus subsequently received a Spartan colony, headed by Praxander. He adds that it was placed opposite to the town of Nagidus in Cilicia, and possessed a harbour and docks. (XIV. p. 682.) Diodorus Siculus mentions a king of this city, named Praxippus. (XIX. p. 715.)

Cape Crommyon, now *Cormachiti*, to the north-west of Lapethus, was the most northern point of the island. It lay opposite to cape Anemurium of Cilicia, from which it was distant 350 stadia. (Strab. XIV. p. 682.)

Crom-myon prom.

Soli, the most important town on the northern coast of Cyprus, was founded, as Plutarch reports in his life of Theseus, by Demophon, son of that hero. But Strabo ascribes its origin to two Athenian leaders named Phalerus and Acamas. (XIV. p. 683.) It derives celebrity from the circumstance of Solon having resided there for some years at the court of Philocyprus, the reigning prince. (Herod. V. 113. Diog. Laert. Solon.) Some writers affirmed that the Athenian philosopher ended his days at Soli. (Suid. v. Σόλων.) Aristocyprus, who succeeded his father Philocyprus, was one of the leaders in the revolt excited by Onesilus against the Persians, and fell in the battle fought near Amathus. Notwith-standing his death, the Solians made a vigorous de-fence when besieged by the enemy, and surrendered only after their walls had been undermined. (Herod. V. 115.) At a later period however they joined the Persians, together with the Amathusians and Chy-trians, against Evagoras. (Diod. Sic.)

Soli.

Stasanor, a distinguished officer in Alexander's service, was a native of Soli. (Strab. XIV. p. 683.) Soli possessed a port at the mouth of a river which is not named, and a temple consecrated to Venus and Isis. (Cf. Plin. V. 35. Ptol. p. 136.) The ecclesiastical records name Soli among the bishoprics of the island. (Cf. Hierocl. p. 707.) The inhabitants were called Σόλιοι, while those of Soli in Cilicia were named Σολεῖς. The town of which we have been speaking has the name of *Solea* still attached to the site. Near Soli was a spot named Gerandrus, whence Gerandrus. a particular sort of marble was derived. (Apoll. Dysc. Hist. c. 36.) Galen speaks also of some mines near the same city. (Simpl. Rem. IX. p. 125.) Strabo places above Soli, and at some distance from the Limenia. coast, a small town named Limenia; it appears from some ecclesiastical documents, cited by Wesseling in a note to Hierocles, to have been four miles from Soli.

Continuing along the northern part of the island Arsinoe. towards the west, we find a town named Arsinoe, but differing apparently from the one situate not far from Paphos. Strabo, who mentions both, speaks Lucus of a grove sacred to Jupiter in the vicinity of the Jovis. former. (XIV. p. 683.) A little beyond we come to cape Acamas, the point from whence our periplus commenced.

There are few places of note to be considered in the interior of Cyprus. The chief of these was Tamasus, celebrated for its rich mines of copper, and the metallic composition prepared on the spot called calcanthum. (Strab. XIV. p. 683.) These mines appear to have been known as early as the days of Homer, for he refers to them in the Odyssey:

Πλέων ἐπὶ οἴνοπα πόντον ἐπ' ἀλλοθρόους ἀνθρώπους,
Ἐς Τεμέσην μετὰ χαλκόν.

Od. A. 183.

It has been disputed, however, among commentators, whether the poet in these lines alluded to the Cyprian Tamasus, or the Italian Temesa, or Tempsa, also famous for its copper mines [h]. (Cf. Steph. Byz. v. Ταμάσεος. Ptol. p. 137. Nonn. Dionys. XIII. 445. Plin. V. 31.)

Ovid, in his Metamorphoses, alludes to it as the spot where the golden apples grew, by which Hippomenes won Atalanta.

> Est ager, indigenæ Tamasenum nomine dicunt;
> Telluris Cypriæ pars optima: quem mihi prisci
> Sacravere senes: templisque accedere dotem
> Hanc jussere meis. Medio nitet arbor in arvo;
> Fulva comam, fulvo ramis crepitantibus auro.
> Hinc tria forte mea veniens decerpta ferebam
> Aurea poma manu: nullique videnda, nisi ipsi,
> Hippomenen adii; docuique, quis usus in illis.
>
> X. 644.

Chytrium was a town of some note also in the interior, but at no great distance from the northern coast of the island. It was once governed by sovereign princes, as we learn from Alexander, whose work on Cyprus is quoted by Stephanus Byz. (v. Χύτροι.) The honey supplied by its territory was much esteemed. (Diophan. Geopon. XV[i].) Ptolemy calls it Chytrus, and the Ecclesiastical Notices, from which we learn that it became an episcopal see, Chytria. _{Chytrium.}

Tremithus, or Trimethus, is also placed in the interior by Ptolemy. (p. 137.) The Byzantine historians mention it as a place of some note. (Constant. Porphyr. Them. I. 15. Niceph. Callist. VIII. 14. Socrat. I. 12.) The ecclesiastical records rank it among the episcopal towns of the island. (Hierocl. _{Tremithus.}

[h] Ancient Italy, tom. II. p. 417.　　[i] Quoted by Meursius.

p. 707.)   The name of *Trimiti* is still attached to the site.

To these must be added the following places, whose positions are less defined. Æpea, was a town in the vicinity of Soli, and existed before that city. The river Clarius ran near it. (Plut. Vit. Solon. Steph. Byz. v. Αἴπεια.)

Æpea.

Amamassus, a maritime town, as appears from a verse of the Bassarica of Dionysius, quoted by Stephanus Byz. (v. Ἀμάμασσος.)

Amamassus.

Τέμβρον, Ἐρύσθειάν τε καὶ εἰναλίην Ἀμάμασσον.

Stephanus reports that Apollo Hylates was also worshipped there.

Argus, a town of Cyprus, according to Ptolemy Hephæstion, quoted by Photius in his Bibliotheca. He speaks of a temple of Apollo Erithius there.

Argus.

Asine, mentioned by Stephanus Byz.; (v. Ἀσίνη.) Callinusa, a promontory, named by Ptolemy; (p. 136.) Cresium; (ap. eund. v. Κρήσιον.) Dionia; (Theopomp. ap. eund. v. Διωνία.

Asine.
Callinusa prom.
Cresium. Dionia.

Elmæum, a river or mountain noticed by Apollonius Dyscolus; (Mir. c. 36.) Epidarus, a town mentioned by Pliny; (V. 31.) Erysthea, where Apollo Hylates was worshipped. (Steph. Byz. v. Ἐρυσθεία.)

Elmæum.
Epidarus.
Erysthea.

Οἵτ' ἔχον Ὑλάταο θεοῦ ἔδος, Ἀπόλλωνος,
Τέμβρον, Ἐρυσθειάν τε καὶ εἰναλίην Ἀμάμασσον.

Golgi, celebrated for the worship of Venus, was said to have been more ancient than Paphos. (Pausan. Arcad. c. 5.) Stephanus Byz. reports that it was colonised by a party of Sicyonians, headed by Golgus. (v. Γολγοί.)

Golgi.

Δέσποιν' ἁ Γολγώς τε καὶ Ἰδάλιον ἐφίλασας.

THEOCR. ID. XV.

Πέμπτοι τέταρτοι γαῖαν ἵξονται θεᾶς
Γόλγων ἀνάσσης.　　　LYCOPHR. 589.

Quæ sanctum Idalium, Syrosque apertos
Colis, quæque Amathunta, quæque Golgos.
　　　　CATULL. EP. XXXVI. 14.

Quæque regis Golgos, quæque Idalium frondosum.
　　　　ID. EPITHAL. PEL. ET THET. v. 96.

Hyle, whence Apollo obtained the surname of Hylates. (Steph. Byz. v. "Υλη.) Tzetzes, in his commentary on Lycophron, says this place was near Carium; (Κάριον) but I imagine we ought to read Κούριον, or Μάριον. Hyle.

Lacedæmon, a place so called in Cyprus, according to Steph. Byz. (v. Λακεδαίμων.) Lacedæmon.

Ledrum, mentioned by ecclesiastical writers as a bishop's see. (Sozom. v. 10. Niceph. Callis. VIII. 42.) Ledrum.

Macaria, mentioned by Pliny (V. 31.) and Ptolemy. (p. 136.) The latter geographer places it on the north side of the island. Macaria.

Marium is said by Steph. Byz. to have been afterwards called Arsinoe. (v. Ἀρσινόη.) It is noticed by Scylax; (Per. p. 41.) but no longer existed in Pliny's time. (V. 31 k.) Marium.

Otia is given by Steph. Byz. (v. Ὠτιεῖς) on the authority of Ephorus. Otia.

Panacra, a mountainous and woody tract. (Steph. Byz. v. Πάνακρα.) Panacra.

Καὶ τέμενος βαθύδενδρον ὀρεσσαύλοιο Πανάκρου.
　　　　NONN. DIONYS. XIII. 447.

Satrachus, a town and river. Satrachus, urbs et fl.

k There are coins of this town with the epigraph MAPl. Sestini, p. 105. Coins of Paphos, Salamis, and Idalium, are also to be met with.

Καὶ Σατράχου βλώξαντες Ὑλάτου τε γήν.
LYCOPHR. 448.

Ἧχι θαλασσίγονου Παφίης νύμφηϊον ὕδωρ
Σάτραχος ἱμερόεις, ὅθι πολλάκις οἶδμα λαβοῦσα
Κύπρις ἀνεχλαίνωσε λελουμένον υἱέα Μύρρης.
NONN. DIONYS. XIII. 458.

Tegessus, urbs et prom. Tegessus, a town and promontory. (Dionys. Bassar. ap. Steph. Byz. v. Τεγησσός. Hesych. ead. v.)

Tembrus. Tembrus, a place where Apollo Hylates was worshipped.

Τέμβρον, Ἐρύσθειάν τε, καὶ εἰναλίην Ἀμαμασσόν.

(Dionys. Bassar. ap. Steph. Byz. v. Ἐρύσθεια. Id. v. Τέμβρος.)

Sestus. Sestus, which Nonnus mentions in conjunction with it, and Tamasus is less known.

Οἵ τ' ἔχον Ὑλάταο πέδον καὶ ἐδέθλια Σηστοῦ
Καὶ Τάμασον καὶ Τέμβρον, Ἐρυσθειάν τε πολίχνην.
XIII. 444.

Chabyris. Chabyris, a spot mentioned by Sozomenus. (Eccl. Hist. V. 9.)

GEOGRAPHICAL INDEX.

ABA, ii. 215.
Ἄβα, Ἀβεύς.
Abacænum, ii. 215.
Abarnis promontorium, i. 68.
Abassus, sive Ambasus, ii. 35.
Ἄμβασος, Ἀμβασίτης.
Abbaites Mysi, ii. 11.
Abbaitis regio, ii. 11.
Ablata, i. 321.
Abonitichos, i. 226.
Ἀβώνου Τεῖχος, Ἀβωνοτειχίτης.
Abrettene regio, i. 54.
Abrinatæ gens, i. 321.
Abrostola, ii. 90.
Absarum, sive Apsarum, i. 293.
Abydos, i. 71.
Ἄβυδος, Ἀβυδηνός.
Acalea, ii. 265.
Acalissus, ii. 265.
Acamantis, ii. 373.
Acamas promontorium, ii. 373.
Acampsis fluvius, i. 293.
Acanthus insula, i. 49.
————— Car. quæ et Doulopolis, ii. 189.
Ἄκανθος, Ἀκάνθιος.
Acarassus, ii. 266.
Ἀκαρασσός, Ἀκαρασσεύς.
Achæium, i. 113.
Achæorum littus, ii. 385.
Achaia Rhod. ii. 238.
Acharaca, i. 468.
Acherusia chersonesus, i. 206.
Achillea insula, i. 412.
Achilleum, i. 110.

Achilleum, Lyd. i. 463.
Acitoriazum, ii. 102.
Acmonia, ii. 18.
Ἀκμόνια, Ἀκμονιεύς.
Aconæ, i. 206.
Ἀκόναι, Ἀκονίτης.
Acrasus, i. 471.
Ἀκρασός, Ἀκρασιώτης.
Acrioteri lacus, ii. 295.
Acritas promontorium, i. 186.
Acrocon, i. 61.
Acroterium, ii. 252.
Acrunum, i. 178.
Acte Mitylenæorum, i. 132.
Adada, ii. 306.
Ἄδαδα, Ἀδαδεύς.
Adæ, i. 150.
Adana, ii. 349.
Ἄδανα, Ἀδανεύς.
Adapera, ii. 101.
Adatha, ii. 127.
Adesa fluvius, ii. 265.
Adienus fluvius, i. 292.
Adopissus, ii. 72.
Adoreus mons, ii. 36.
Ad Prætorium, ii. 160.
Adramyttenus sinus, i. 121.
Adramyttis insula, ii. 266.
Adramyttium, i. 127.
Ἀδραμύττειον, Ἀδραμυττηνός.
Adrastea regio, i. 35.
————— urbs, i. 64.
Ἀδράστεια, Ἀδραστεύς, et Ἀδραστηνός.
Ad Vicesimum, ii. 158.

Æanteum, i. 83.
Ægæ Æolid. i. 153.
———— Cilic. ii. 355.
Αἰγαὶ, Αἰγαῖος, et Αἰγεάτης.
Ægan prom. i. 135.
Ægialus, i. 224.
Æginetes, i. 226.
———————— fluvius, i. 226.
Ægireus, i. 161.
Ægiroessa i. 153.
Ægyllus, i. 187.
Ænea, i. 88.
Ænius fluvius, i. 89.
Ænus, ii. 198.
Æolis, i. 142.
Æpea, ii. 389.
Æretice ii. 150.
Æsepus fluvius, i. 36.
Æsius fluvius, i. 184.
Æsyros fluvius, i. 184.
Æthaloeis fluvius, i. 131.
Aetorynchus, i. 194.
Ætulana, ii. 150.
Agamede, i. 163.
Agamia, i. 111.
Agathe insula, ii. 266.
Agdistis mons. ii. 87.
Agoresus, ii. 215.
Ἀγορησὸς, Ἀγορησεύς.
Agrilium, i. 183.
Agrippenses, i. 214.
Agrizala, ii. 97.
Alabanda, ii. 206.
Ἀλάβανδα, Ἀλαβανδεύς.
Alabastius fluvius, i. 129.
Alæ, ii. 364.
Alander fluvius ii. 35.
Alazia, i. 172.
Alazones, i. 172.
Aleius Campus, ii. 352.
Aleos fluvius, i. 349.
Aleus, ii. 222.
Alexandra mons, i. 126.
Alexandri diversorium, ii. 57.
Alexandria Troas, i. 114.
———————— ad Latmum, ii. 215.
———————— ad Issum, ii. 361.
Ἀλεξάνδρεια, Ἀλεξανδρεύς.
Algiza, i. 414.

Alia, sive Alii, ii. 54.
Ἅλιοι, Ἁλιηρὸς.
Aliassus, ii. 96.
Aligomon fons, i. 474.
Alimala, ii. 266.
Alimne, ii. 272.
Alina insula, ii. 196.
Alinda, ii. 208.
Ἄλινδα, Ἀλινδεύς.
Alisarna, i. 141.
Alyatta, i. 215.
Alyatti, ii. 35.
Alyattis tumulus, i. 432.
Alybe, i. 275.
Ἀλύβη, Ἀλυβεύς.
Alychme, ii. 272.
Alydda, ii. 18.
Amamassus, ii. 389.
Amanides, sive Amanicæ Pylæ, ii. 356.
Amanus mons, ii. 362.
Amasia, i. 303.
Ἀμάσεια, Ἀμασεύς.
Amastris, i. 222.
Ἄμαστρις, Ἀμαστριανός.
Amathus, ii. 377.
Ἀμαθοῦς, Ἀμαθούσιος.
Amaxa, i. 215.
Amaxia, ii. 321.
Ἀμαξία, Ἀμαξιεύς.
Ambiturii, ii. 85.
Amblada, ii. 306.
Ἄμβλαδα, Ἀμβλαδεύς.
Amelas, ii. 65.
Ameletum, i. 272.
Ameria, i. 314.
Amisus, i. 264.
Ἀμισὸς, Ἀμισηνός.
Ammochostos prom. ii. 381.
Ammodes prom. ii. 350.
Amnias fluvius, i. 235.
Amorium, ii. 90.
Ἀμόριον, Ἀμοριεύς.
Amos, ii. 215.
Ἄμος, Ἄμιος.
Ampelus prom. i. 409.
Amphilysus fluvius, i. 410.
Anabura, ii. 35.
Anactoria, i. 383.

Anadynata, i. 240.
Anæa, i. 462.
'Αναία, 'Αναίτης, et 'Αναῖος.
Anagome, i. 474.
Anagurdes, i. 182.
Analiba, ii. 154.
Anaplus, i. 194.
Anar fluvius, ii. 104.
Anava urbs, ii. 46.
—— lacus, ii. 46.
Anaxia, ii. 285.
Anazarba, ii. 354.
'Αναζαρβὰ, 'Αναζαρβεύς.
Anchiali Regia, i. 292.
Anchiale, ii. 342.
Anchiales fluvius, ii. 343.
Ancon, i. 265.
—— Glauci, ii. 197.
Ancyra Phryg. ii. 12.
—— Galat. ii. 92.
"Αγκυρα, 'Αγκυρανός.
Ancyreum prom. i. 195.
Ancyron, i. 186.
Andabalis, sive Andavilis, ii. 133.
Andeira, i. 125.
"Ανδειρα, 'Ανδειρηνός.
Andraca, ii. 124.
Andrapa, postea Neoclaudiopolis, i. 238. ii. 96.
Andriace, ii. 253.
Andriclus, sive Androclus mons, ii. 324.
Andrius fluvius, i. 120.
Andricus fluvius, ii. 351.
Androsia, ii. 102.
Anemurium promontorium et urbs, ii. 324, 335.
'Ανεμούριον, 'Ανεμουριεύς.
Angelocome, i. 182.
Angelocometes, fluvius, i. 37.
Anhydros, i. 345.
—— insula, i. 402.
Aninetum, sive Aninesium, i. 469.
'Ανινήσιον, 'Ανινήσιος.
Annesis, ii. 285.
Anniaca, ii. 156.
Anolus, i. 471.

Antandrus, i. 125.
"Αντανδρος, 'Αντάνδριος.
Antelia, ii. 127.
Anteus fluvius, ii. 305.
Anthine, i. 402.
Anticinolis, i. 227.
Anticragus mons, ii. 245.
Antigonea, i. 49.
'Αντιγόνεια, 'Αντιγόνευς.
Antiochia ad Meandrum, ii. 209.
—— in Pisidia, ii. 301.
—— Lamotis, ii. 338.
—— ad Cragum, ii. 324.
—— ad Pyramum, ii. 353.
'Αντιοχεία, 'Αντιοχεύς.
Antiphellus, ii. 251.
'Αντίφελλος, 'Αντιφελλίτης.
Antitaurus mons, i. 7.
Antissa, i. 162.
"Αντισσα, 'Αντισσαῖος.
Antoniopolis, i. 240.
—— Lyd. i. 469.
Aorata saltus, i. 56.
Apæsus, i. 65.
'Απαισὸς, 'Απαισηνός.
Apaïtæ gens, i. 295.
Apamea Bithyn. i. 173.
—— Cibotus, ii. 49.
'Απάμεια, 'Απαμεύς.
Aperlæ, sive Aperræ, ii. 252.
Aphneium, i. 471.
Aphnitis palus, i. 471.
Aphrodisias Car. ii. 210.
—— Cilic. ii. 329.
'Αφροδισιὰς, 'Αφροδισιεύς.
—— regio Mys. i. 132.
—— prom. ii. 190.
Aphrodisium, ii. 386.
Apiæ Campus, i. 55.
Apira, ii. 54.
Apobathra, i. 72.
Apocremnus, sive Hypocremnus promontorium i. 346.
Apollonia ad Rhyndacum, i. 52.
—— Pergam, i. 141.
—— Lyd. i. 427.
—— Phryg. ii. 53.
—— ad Lambanum, ii. 214.

Apollonia insula, quæ et Thyneas, i. 199.
———— Lyc. ii. 266.
'Απολλωνία, 'Απολλωνιάτης.
Apolloniatis palus, i. 50.
Apollonis, i. 427.
Apollonoshieron, i. 455.
Aporidos come, ii. 54.
Appia, ii. 55.
'Απτία, 'Απτιανός.
Apsarus, qui et Acampsis fluvius, i. 293.
Aquæ Aravenæ, ii. 147.
Arabissus, ii. 157, 158.
Arabyza, ii. 86.
Aræ Alexandri, ii. 362.
Aræ insulæ, ii. 224.
Arane, ii. 154.
Arangas, ii. 157.
Araros, ii. 104.
Arasaxa, ii. 117.
Arasenses, ii. 103.
Arassus, sive Aarassus, ii. 299.
Arauracos, ii. 157.
Araxa, ii. 265.
'Άραξα, 'Αραξεύς.
Arazus, i. 321.
Arbanium, i. 321.
Arca, ii. 160.
Arcadiopolis, i. 469.
Archabis fluvius, i. 292.
Archalla, ii. 124.
Archæopolis, i. 438.
Archelais, ii. 112.
Archelaium, ii. 90.
Arcilapopoli, ii. 161.
Arconnesus insula, i. 355.
———— Car. ii. 180.
Arcton mons, i. 41.
Ardula, ii. 144.
Arega, ii. 161.
Aretias insula, i. 282.
Areus fluvius, i. 184.
Argæus mons, ii. 118.
Argaïs insula, ii. 266.
Arganthonius mons, i. 176.
Argennon prom. i. 379.
Argiæ insula, ii. 239.
Argila, ii. 215.

'Άργιλα, 'Αργιλίτης.
Arginusæ insulæ i. 166.
Argiza, i. 58.
Argos, sive Argeopolis, ii. 364.
Argus castellum, ii. 133.
———— Cypri ii. 390.
Argustana, ii. 146.
Argyna, i. 283.
Argyronium, i. 194.
Ariacos, i. 50. probably the Artæi-tichos ('Αρταίου τεῖχος) of Steph. Byz. (v. 'Αρταῖα.)
Arianzus, ii. 114.
Ariarathia, ii. 125.
Ariassus, ii. 299.
Arion fluvius, i. 295.
Arisbe Troad, i. 70.
————Lesb. i. 164.
'Αρίσβη, 'Αρισβαῖος.
Aristium, ii. 55.
Ariusia, i. 400.
Armaxa, ii. 155.
Armene Paph. i. 227.
———— Pont. i. 292.
Armenia Minor, ii. 148.
———— Prima et Secunda, ii. 149.
Armeno castrum, i. 183.
Arna, ii. 266.
Arneæ, ii. 266.
Aromata, i. 468.
Arsinoe Cilic. ii. 323.
———— Cypr. ii. 381. 388.
———— promontorium, ii. 376.
Artace, i. 47.
'Αρτάκη, 'Αρτακηνός, et 'Αρτακεύς.
Artacie fons, i. 42.
Artanes fluvius, i. 198.
Artemisium prom. ii. 197.
Artymnesus, ii. 246.
Artynia lacus, i. 50.
Arus fluvius, ii. 266.
Arycanda, ii. 255.
'Αρύκανδα, 'Αρικανδεύς.
Arycandus fluvius, ii. 254.
Arymagdus fluvius, ii. 326.
Asarino, ii. 161.
Ascandalis, ii. 265.
Ascania pagus, i. 180.

Ascania regio, i. 179.
Ascanius lacus Bithyn. I. 179.
———— Phryg. ii. 297.
Asia Minor, i. 3.
—— Lyd. i. 471.
—— Palus, i. 361.
—— Propria, i. 3.
Asiana, i. 4.
Asias tribus, i. 1.
Asiba, i. 321.
Asiue Cilic. ii. 363.
—— Cypr. ii. 390.
Asmabæon lacus, ii. 129.
Asopus fluvius, ii. 39.
Aspendus, ii. 281.
Ἄσπενδος, Ἀσπένδιος.
Aspis, sive Arconnesus insula,
   i. 355.
———— Lyc. ii. 247.
Aspona, ii. 98.
Assessus, i. 394.
Ἀσσησὸς, Ἀσσήσιος.
Assorum, i. 410.
Assus, i. 122.
—— campus Lyd. i. 471.
Ἄσσος, Ἄσσιος.
Astacenus Sinus, i. 185.
Astacus, i. 185.
Ἀστακὸς, Ἀστακηνός.
Astragon, ii. 205.
Astron fluvius, i. 129.
Astypalæa arx Sami, i. 408.
———— prom. Car. ii. 176.
Astyra Abyd. i. 175.
—— Antandr. i. 128.
Ἄστυρα, Ἀστυρηνός.
Asuna, ii. 145.
Atabyris mons, ii. 237.
Atarneus, i. 132.
———— sub Pitane, i. 134.
Ἀταρνεὺς, Ἀταρνείτης.
Athar mons, ii. 114.
Athenæ Pont. i. 292.
—— Car. ii. 215.
Athymbra, i. 467.
Ἄθυμβρα, Ἀθυμβρεύς.
Atmenia, ii. 313.
Attæa, i. 132.
—— palus, ii. 67.

Attalenses, ii. 103.
Attalia Agroira, i. 153, 435.
—— Pamphyl. ii. 275.
Ἀττάλεια, Ἀτταλεύς.
Attalyda, i. 471.
Attelebusa insula, ii. 264.
Attuda, ii. 55.
Ἄττουδα, Ἀττουδεύς.
Atusia, ii. 55.
Ἀτούσια, Ἀτουσιεύς.
Augæ, ii. 285.
Augusta, ii. 360.
Αὔγουστα, Αὐγουστανός.
Augustopolis, ii. 55.
Aulæ, ii. 266.
—— Cilic. ii. 364.
Aulindenus fluvius, ii. 56.
Auliucome, i. 474.
Aulocrene, ii. 49.
Auraclea, ii. 90.
Aureliopolis, i. 454.
Axon fluvius, ii. 196.
Axylos regio, ii. 35.
Aza, i. 321. ii. 155.
Azala, i. 182.
Azamora, ii. 141.
Azani, sive Æzani, ii. 12.
Ἀζανοὶ, Ἀζανείτης.
Azaritia fons, i. 193.
Aziris, ii. 152.
Babanomus, i. 305.
Babras, sive Babrantium, i. 401.
Baca, ii. 364.
Bæbæ, ii. 215.
Βαῖβαι, Βαιβαῖος.
Bagadaonia regio, ii. 144.
Bagæ, i. 435.
Βαγαὶ, Βαγηνός.
Bagrum, ii. 96.
Baiæ, ii. 361.
Balbura, ii. 272.
Βάλβουρα, Βαλβουρεύς.
Balcea, i. 141.
Barate, ii. 72.
Bardissus, ii. 215.
Barenus, sive Varenus fl. i. 37.
Bares, i. 71.
Baretta, i. 474.
Bargasa, ii. 184.

Bargylia, ii. 173.
Βαργύλια, Βαργυλήτης.
Bargyliaticus Sinus, ii. 171.
Baris, ii. 300.
Barsalium, ii. 127.
Basgædariza, ii. 151.
Basilia, sive Basilionopolis, i. 182.
Bathys fluvius, ii. 20.
Bazis, ii. 137.
Bebryces, i. 215. ii. 7.
Bechires, i. 291.
Bechireus portus, i. 292.
Belocome, i. 182.
Benna, ii. 17.
Βέννα, Βεννίτης,
Bennamia, i. 363.
Berbe, sive Barbe, ii. 286.
Berecyntii, ii. 24.
Berenice, ii. 328.
Beris fluvius, i. 272.
Berissa, i. 318.
Besbicus insula, i. 53.
Beudos Vetus, ii. 34.
Biblis fons, i. 394.
Billæus fluvius, i. 208.
Bithyni, i. 168.
Bithynia, i. 167.
Bithynium, i. 209.
Βιθύνιον, Βιθυνεύς, et Βιθυνεάτης.
Bitoana, ii. 215.
Blabe insula, i. 194.
Blandos, ii. 160,
Blæandrus, ii. 55.
Blaene regio, i. 236.
Blucium, sive Luceium, ii. 91.
Boane lacus, i. 19.
Boas fluvius, i. 294.
Bocarus fluvius, ii. 373.
Bœnasa, i. 320.
Bolbæ, ii. 215.
Bolbæotes fluvius, ii. 215.
Bolbulæ insula, i. 402.
Bolelasgus, ii. 101.
Bolissus, i. 400.
Βολισσός, Βολίσσιος, et Βαλισσεύς.
Bombus fluvius, ii. 364.
Boona, i. 278.
Booscœte, i. 173.

Boosura, ii. 376.
Briana, ii. 55.
Βρίανα, Βριανός.
Borissus, i. 319.
Boryza, i. 319.
Bos promontorium, i. 193.
Bosphorus Thracius, i. 192.
Botieum, ii. 67.
Branchidæ, i. 390.
Bregmenteni, i. 153.
Brisa, i. 165.
Briula i. 468.
Brunga, i. 185.
Bryazon fl. et locus, i. 184.
Bryges, sive Briges, ii. 2.
Bryllis regio, i. 176.
Bryllium, i. 176.
Bryzon, ii. 55.
Βρυζών, Βρυζηνός.
Bubalia, ii. 160.
Bubon, ii. 272.
Βουβών, Βουβωνεύς.
Buci lapis, ii. 124.
Budea, ii. 34.
Burinna fons, ii. 222.
Busmasdis, ii. 78.
Buthia, i. 395.
Bybassia Chersonesus, ii. 189.
Bybassus, ii. 189.
Βύβασσος, Βυβάσσιος.
Bybassius Sinus, ii. 189.
Bylæ, i. 300.
Bysnæi gens, i. 215.
Byzeres gens, i. 291.
Cabalees, ii. 269.
Cabalia, sive Cabalis, ii. 269.
Cabassus, ii. 143.
Cabira, i. 310.
Cadi, i. 14.
Καδοὶ, Καδοηνός.
Cadmus mons, 239.
———— fluvius, ii. 39.
Cadrema, ii. 266.
Κάδρεμα, Καδρεμεύς.
Cadyna, ii. 132.
Cæna, ii. 134.
Cæsarea Bithyn. i. 173.
———— Cappad. quæ et Maza-
ca, ii. 118.

Καισάρεια, Καισαρεύς.
Caicus fluvius, i. 135.
Calabantia, ii. 247.
Calami, i. 409.
Calanthia, ii. 338.
Calbis fluvius, ii. 192.
Cale, i. 141.
—— Parembole, i. 291.
Cales fl. et emporium, i. 202.
Callatebus, i. 470.
Callica, i. 214.
Callichorus fluvius, i. 207.
Callicolone, i. 102.
Callimache, ii. 197.
Callinusa prom. ii. 390.
Callipolis Bithyn. i. 186.
—— Cariæ, ii. 216.
—— Cappad. ii. 144.
Callistratia, i. 226.
Callydium, sive Calydnium, i. 457.
Caloe, i. 451.
Calogræa, i. 178.
Calos fluvius, i. 290.
Calpe portus, et fluvius, i. 198.
Calpitum, ii. 116.
Caltiorissa, ii. 154.
Calycadnus fluvius, ii. 330.
—— prom. ii. 330.
Calydnæ insulæ, Troad. i. 112.
—— Cariæ, ii. 218.
Calymna insula, ii. 218.
Calynda, ii. 196.
Κάλυνδα, Καλύνδιος.
Calyndici montes, ii. 196.
Camelides insulæ, i. 412.
Camirus, ii. 237.
Κάμιρος, Καμιρεύς.
Camisa Pont. marit. i. 273.
—— mediter. i. 316.
Camisene, i. 316.
Campe, ii. 124.
Camuliani, ii. 145.
Camuresarbum, i. 321.
Cana, ii. 265.
Canæ, i. 135.
Κάναι, Καναῖος.
Canaius fluvius, i. 134.
Canaura, ii. 286.

Candara, i. 241.
Κάνδαρα, Κανδαρηνός.
Candasa, ii. 216.
Κάνδασα, Κανδασεύς.
Candyba, ii. 265.
Κάνδυβα, Κανδυβεύς.
Cane prom. et mons, i. 134.
Canna, ii. 72,
Cantharium prom. i. 410.
Cappadoces, ii. 105.
Cappadocia, ii. 105.
Cappadox fluvius, ii. 115.
Capria palus, ii. 280.
Caprus fluvius, ii. 39.
Caralis palus Isaur. ii. 66, 75.
—— Pisid. ii. 28.
Carallia, ii. 75.
Carambis, prom. i. 225.
—— urbs, i. 226.
Carana, i. 317.
Caranitis, i. 317.
Carape, ii. 154.
Carba, ii. 144.
Carbana, ii. 266.
Κάρβανα, Καρβανεύς.
Cardamyle, i. 401.
Caresene regio, i. 88.
Caresus fluvius, i. 88.
—— urbs, i. 88.
Cares, ii. 163.
Caria Phryg. urbs, ii. 60.
Caria, ii. 163.
Carima, ii. 97.
Carine, i. 133.
Carissa, ii. 103.
Carius mons, i. 474.
Carmalas fluvius, ii. 141.
Carmylessus, ii. 245.
Carnalis, ii. 117.
Carnia, i. 395.
Caropolis, ii. 216.
Carpacelis, ii. 125.
Carpasia, ii. 385.
Carpasiæ insula, ii. 385.
Carsagis, sive Carsat, ii. 157, 159.
Carseæ, i. 55.
Carura, ii. 43.
Carusa, i. 234.

Carus vicus, i. 214.
Carydius saltus, ii. 365.
Caryanda portus, ii. 174.
———————insula, ii. 174.
Καρύανδα, Καρυανδεύς.
Carysis insula, ii. 196.
Casa, ii. 313.
Κάσα, Κασάτης.
Casaman, ii. 144.
Casbia, ii. 72.
Cassiopolis, ii. 364.
Castabala, ii. 132.
Castabolum, ii. 356.
Castalia, ii. 364.
Castamon, i. 239.
Castoli Campus, i. 472.
Castnius, mons, ii. 282.
Casystes portus, i. 350.
Catacecaumene regio, i. 452.
Cataonia, ii. 137.
Catenna, ii. 310.
Catœcia, i. 182.
Catangium, (Κατάγγειον,) i. 194.
Catarrhactes fluvius, ii. 275.
Caucasa Chior. portus Herod.V.
    33.
Caucones, i. 298.
Caue, ii. 89.
Caulares fluvius, ii. 289.
Caunii, ii. 193.
Caunus, ii. 193.
Καῦνος, Καύνιος.
Caystrus fluvius, i. 361.
Cebren fluvius, i. 119.
Cebrene, i. 119.
Κεβρήνη, Κεβρήνιος.
Cebrenia regio, i. 119.
Cedreæ, ii. 216.
Κεδρέαι, Κεδρεάτης.
Celænæ Troad. i. 131.
——— Phryg. ii. 48.
Κελαιναὶ Κελαινεύς.
Celenderis, ii. 327.
Κελένδερις, Κελενδερείτης.
Cenaxe palus, ii. 95.
Cenchreæ, i. 118.
Cenchrius fluvius, i. 376.
Cennati, ii. 334.
Cephalus, ii. 355.

Ceramicus Sinus, ii. 176.
Ceramus, ii. 183.
Κέραμος, Κεραμιήτης.
Ceramorum forum, ii. 26.
Ceranæ, ii. 26.
Cerasæ, i. 455.
Cerasus, i. 280, 283.
Κερασοῦς, Κερασούντιος.
Cerbesia fossa, ii. 25.
Cerbesii, ii. 25.
Cercetæ gens, i. 295.
Cercetius mons, i. 410.
Cercopia, ii. 55.
Ceretape, ii. 56.
Κερετάπη, Κερεταπεύς.
Certonium, i. 133.
Cerynea, ii. 386.
Cesbedium arx Selges, ii. 310.
Cestri, ii. 338.
Cestrus fluvius, ii. 279.
Ceteii gens, i. 136.
Cetis regio, ii. 333.
Cetius fluvius, i. 140
Chabyris, ii. 392.
Chadisia, i. 269.
Chadisius fluvius, i. 265.
Chalcedon, i. 189.
Χαλκηδών, Χαλκηδόνιος.
Chalcertores, sive Chalcetorium,
    ii. 198.
Χαλκήτορες, Χαλκητόριος, Χαλκητο-
ρεύς.
Chalcis insula, ii. 238.
Chalcis Erythr. i. 352.
Chalcitis, i. 352.
——— insula Prop. i. 192.
Chaldæi, sive Chaldi gens, i.
    276.
Chalybes gens, i. 273.
Chammanene, ii. 124.
Characometes fluvius, i. 466.
Charadrus, ii. 324.
Charax Bithyn. i. 215.
——— Phryg. ii. 60.
——— Alexandri, ii. 60.
——— Lyd. i. 465.
——— Armen. ii. 154.
Charimatæ gens, i. 322.
Charonium, i. 468.

Charsia, ii. 145.
Charsiana regio, ii. 145.
Charsianus saltus, ii. 145.
Chaus fluvius, ii. 212.
Chelæ Bosph. i. 195.
—— Thyn. i. 199.
Chelidonia, ii. 30.
Chelidoniæ insulæ, ii. 256.
Chersus sive Charsus, fl. ii. 361.
Chesium promontorium, i. 408.
Chesius fluvius, i. 408.
Chiliocomon campus, i. 305.
———— Phryg. ii. 60.
Chimæra, ii. 258.
Chios insula, i. 395.
—— urbs, i. 399.
Chliara, i. 440.
Chlorus fluvius, ii. 361.
Chœrides, i. 282.
Cholontichos, ii. 217.
Χωλὸν τεῖχος, Χωλοτειχίτης.
Choma, ii. 60.
Chonæ, ii. 44.
Χωναὶ, Χωνιάτης.
Chorsabia, ii. 154.
Chrysa, quæ et Dia, i. 115.
—— Adramytt. i. 130.
Chrysaoris, ii. 199.
Chrysaorium, ii. 199. 204.
Chrysippa, ii. 364.
Chrysobullum, ii. 134.
Chrysopolis, i. 191.
Χρυσόπολις, Χρυσοπολίτης.
Chrysorrhoas fluvius, i. 468.
Chusa, ii. 146.
Chytrium Ion. i. 343.
———— Cypr. ii. 389.
Χύτριον, Χυτριεύς.
Chytus portus Cyzic. i. 42.
Ciacis, ii. 127.
Cianica, ii. 127.
Cianus Sinus, i. 174.
Cibyra Magna, ii. 269.
—— Parva, ii. 285.
Κίβυρα, Κιβυραῖος.
Ciconium, i. 194.
Cidramus ii. 56.
Κίδραμος, Κιδραμηνός.
Cidyssus, ii. 18.

Κιδυσσὸς, Κιδυσσεύς.
Cilbiani Cetei, i. 451.
———— Inferiores, i. 451.
———— Nicæenses, i. 451.
———— Pergameni, i. 451.
———— Superiores, i. 451.
Cilbianus Campus, i. 451.
Cilices, ii. 314.
———— Troad. i. 129.
CILICIA, ii. 314.
————————Trachea, ii. 319.
———————— Campestris, ii. 339.
———————— Cappad. Præfect. ii. 118.
Cilicum insulæ, i. 273.
Cilla Troad. i. 130.
—— sive Cylla Phryg. ii. 30.
Cillanius campus, ii. 30.
Cillæum mons, i. 127.
Cillæus fluvius, i. 130.
Cimiata, i. 235.
Cimiatene, i. 235.
Cimpsus fluvius, i. 473.
Cinædopolis, ii. 239.
Cindye, ii. 173.
Κινδύη, Κινδυεύς. Herod. V. 110.
Cingularium, ii. 32.
Cinna, ii. 104.
Cinolis, i. 227.
Ciphisus, ii. 329.
Ciscissa, ii. 145.
Cissa, i. 295.
Cisserusa insula, ii. 238.
Cissides insulæ, ii. 247.
Cissus locus, i. 295.
Cissus fluvius, i. 295.
Cisthene, i. 132.
————insula, ii. 251.
Cistramum, ii. 365.
Citium, ii. 379.
Κίτιον, Κιτιεύς.
Cius, i. 174.
Κιὸς, Κιανός.
—— fluvius, i. 175.
Cizara, ii. 125.
Claneus, ii. 104.
Clanudda, i. 457.
Clarius fluvius, ii. 389.
Claros, i. 359.

Κλάρος, Κλάριος.
Claudiopolis, prius Bithynium,
i. 209.
——————— Galat. ii. 103.
——————— Cappad. ii. 125.
——————— Cilic. ii. 332.
Clazomenæ, i. 342.
Κλαζομεναὶ, Κλαζομένιος.
Cleandria, i. 131.
Clibanus, ii. 75.
Clides promontorium, ii. 384.
—— insulæ, ii. 384.
Climax Paphlag. i. 225.
——————— Lyciæ, ii. 263.
——————— Pisid. ii. 294.
Clitæ, i. 214.
—— gens Cil. ii. 339.
Clite fons, i. 42.
Cludrus fluvius, ii. 24.
Clydæ, ii. 197.
Clystrus, ii. 338.
Cnidus, ii. 184.
Κνίδος, Κνίδιος.
Cnopupolis, i. 348.
Cochlia, ii. 197.
Cochliusa insula, ii. 266.
Cocylia sive Cocylium, i. 118.
Κοκύλιον, Κοκυλίτης.
Coddini scopulus, i. 439.
Codryla, sive Codrylus, ii. 286.
Coduzabala, ii. 158.
Cœna, i. 272.
Cœnon Chorion, i. 313.
——————— Gallicanon, i. 214.
Cœti, i. 296.
Cogamus fluvius, i. 456.
Collusa, i. 227.
Colobatus, sive Cobalatus flu-
vius, ii. 289.
Colobrassus, ii. 313.
Coloe, i. 319.
Κολόη, Κολοηνός.
Colonæ Troad, i. 113.
——————— Lampsac. i. 68.
Colonia, ii. 151.
Colope, i. 316.
Colopene, i. 316.
Colossæ, ii. 43.
Κολοσσαὶ, Κολοσσηνός.

Colpe, i. 438; should probably
be Coloe.
Colophon, i. 357.
Κολοφὼν, Κολοφώνιος.
Comana Pont. i. 307.
——————— Cappad. ii. 138.
Κόμανα, Κομανηνός.
Comania, i. 141.
Comaralis, ii. 155.
Comassa, ii. 155.
Comba, ii. 265.
Comenses, ii. 103.
Comitanasson, ii. 146.
Commoris, ii. 362.
Conana, sive Comana, ii. 306.
Κόνανα, Κονανεύς.
Congustus, ii. 96.
Conica, i. 238.
Conisium, i. 141.
Conni, ii. 25.
Conopeium, i. 263.
Constantia, ii. 384.
Coracesium, ii. 320.
Coracium promontorium, i. 195.
Coralla, i. 283.
Corassiæ, sive Corseæ insulæ, i.
411.
Corax, sive Coracium mons, i.
359.
Corbasa, sive Colbasa, ii. 299.
Corbeus, ii. 97.
Cordyle, i. 286.
Cordylusa insula, ii. 238.
Coressus mons, i. 374.
Coriopium, ii. 148.
Cormalus fluvius, i. 129.
Cormasa, ii. 294.
Corna Galat. ii. 72.
—— Cappad. ii. 125.
Corone, i. 215.
Coropassus, sive Coropissus, ii.
67.
Κοροπισσὸς, Κοροπισσεύς.
Corsymus, sive Corsynus fluvius,
ii. 210.
Corvorum nidi, ii. 365.
Corybantium, i. 131.
Corybissa, i. 131.
Coryceon promontorium

Corycium antrum, ii. 3
——————promont. ii. 335.
Corycus mons, i. 351.
—————— Lyc. ii. 261.
—————— Cilic. ii. 335.
Corydalla, ii. 265.
Κορυδαλλα, Κορυδαλλεύς.
Coryleum, i. 241.
Coryne promontorium, i. 350.
Coryphas Troad. i. 132.
—————————— Bithyn. i. 214.
Cos insula, ii. 218.
— urbs, ii. 220.
Κᾶς, Κόος, et Κόως.
Coscinia, ii. 207.
Cossus mons, i. 215.
Cotæna, ii. 117.
Cotana, ii. 286.
Cotrades, ii. 78.
Cotyæum, ii. 17.
Κοτυάειον, Κοτυαεύς.
Cotylus mons, i. 37, 121.
Cotyora, i. 278.
Κοτύωρα, Κοτυωρίτης.
Crade ii. 216.
Κράδη, Κραδίτης.
Cragus mons, ii. 245.
—————— urbs, ii. 246.
—————— scopulus, ii. 324.
Crambusa ins. Lyc. ii. 256.
——————————Cilic. ii. 328.
—————————————— ii. 335.
Cranaus, ii. 209.
Craspedites Sinus, i. 186.
Crasus, ii. 56.
Cratia, postea Flaviopolis, i. 210.
Cremaste, i. 75.
Creme, i. 322.
Κρέμη, Κρεμήσιος.
Cremna, ii. 299.
Crenides, i. 207.
Crentius vicus, Anton. Itin. p. 201.
Creon mons, i. 161.
Cresium, ii. 390.
Κρήσιον, Κρησιεύς.
Cressa, i. 241.
—————— port. Car. ii. 192.
Cressopolis, s. Cretopolis, ii. 298.

Crobialus, i. 225.
Κρωβίαλος, Κρωβιαλεύς.
Crocodilus mons, ii. 363.
Cromna, i. 223.
Κρώμνα, Κρωμνίτης, et Κρωμναῖος.
Crommyon prom. ii. 387.
Crossa, i. 322.
Crulla, i. 182.
Cruni promontorium, ii. 328.
Crusa, ii. 239.
Crya, sive Cryassus, ii. 196.
Crynis fluvius, i. 215.
Cryon fluvius, i. 440.
Cuballus, ii. 35.
Cucusus, ii. 140.
Cunissa, ii. 156.
Curias promontorium, ii. 377.
Curium, ii. 376.
Κούριον, Κουριεύς.
Curopolis, ii. 216.
Cyalus, i. 473.
Cyaneæ Lyc. ii. 252.
—————— insula, i. 195.
Cyarda, ii. 216.
Κύαρδα, Κυαρδεύς.
Cybassus, ii. 216.
Cybellia, i. 347.
Cybistra, ii. 130.
Κύβιστρα, Κυβιστρεύς.
Cyclopis insula, ii. 238.
Cydna, ii. 247.
Cydnus fluvius, ii. 343.
Cydonea insula, ii. 216.
Cyinda, ii. 343.
Cylandus, ii. 216.
Cymaria, ii. 195.
Cyme, i. 147.
Κύμη, Κυμαῖος.
Cyne, i. 473.
Cynossema promontorium, ii. 190.
Cyon, ii. 216.
Cypriæ insulæ, ii. 264.
Cyprus, ii. 366.
Cyptasia, i. 234.
Cyrbasa, ii. 216.
Κύρβασα, Κυρβασεύς.
Cyrbe, ii. 286.
Κύρβη, Κυρβαῖος.

Cyri Campus, ii. 22.
——Castra, ii. 133.
Cyssus portus, i. 353.
Cytonium, i. 133.
Cytorum, i. 224.
Κύτωρον, Κυτωρίτης, et Κυτώριος.
Cytorus mons, i. 224.
Cyzicus, i. 29.
Κύζικος, Κυζικηνός.
Cyzistra, sive Cozistra, ii. 124.
Dablæ, i. 211.
Dacora, ii. 124.
Dadastana, i. 211.
Dadaucana, i. 214.
Dades promontorium, ii. 380.
Dadibra, i. 238.
Dædala, ii. 197.
—————— mons, ii. 198.
Dædalensium insulæ, ii. 198.
Dagolassus, ii. 155.
Dagona, ii. 154.
Dalanda, sive Ladana, ii. 153.
Daldes, sive Daldia, i. 454.
Dalisanda, ii. 75.
Danae, sive Danati, i. 320. ii. 156.
Danala, ii. 102.
Dandaxina, ii. 160.
Daphne, i. 194.
—————— Lyc. ii. 206.
Daphni portus, i. 289.
Daphnus, i. 345.
Δαφνοῦς, Δαφνούσιος.
Daphnusia, i. 202.
Daphnusis palus, i. 202.
Daraanon, i. 294.
Darazus, ii. 339.
Dardani, i. 80.
Dardania, i. 76.
Dardanis, sive Dardanium promontorium, i. 81.
Dardanus, i. 81.
Δάρδανος, Δαρδάνιος, et Δαρδανεύς.
Daridna, i. 240.
Δάριδνα, Δαριδναῖος.
Darium, ii. 56.
Δαρεῖον, Δαρειεύς.
Darsa, ii. 294.
Dascylitis palus, i. 171.

Dascylium Bithyn. i. 171.
—————— Ephes. Steph. Byz.
Δασκύλιον, Δασκύλιος, et Δασκυλίτης.
Dasmenda, ii. 124, 145.
Dastarcum, ii. 141.
Daximonitis, i. 306.
Debalacia, ii. 56.
Dedmasa, ii. 96.
Δεδμασα, Δεδμασεύς.
Delemna, ii. 96.
Delia, ii. 215.
Δηλία, Δηλιεύς.
Delphacia insula, i. 49.
Delphinium, i. 401.
Demetrium, i. 211.
Demonesi, i. 192.
Demas Sabæon, ii. 286.
Demusia, ii. 286.
Derbe, ii. 68.
Δέρβη, Δερβήτης.
Dia Bithyn. i. 202.
——Car, ii. 215.
Δία, Διεύς.
Diabetæ insulæ, ii. 238.
Diacopene regio, i. 305.
Diaphanes fluvius, ii. 363.
Diarrheusa insula, i. 402.
Dias, ii. 266.
Dicte mons, i. 121.
Dictys, ii. 97.
Didyenses, ii. 97. 103.
Didyma, i. 390.
Δίδυμα, Διδυμαῖος.
Didymæ insulæ, ii. 247.
Didymæum, ii. 364.
Didymi tiche, i. 36.
Didymon tichos, ii. 215.
Dimastos, ii. 238.
Dinaretum promontorium, ii. 384.
Dindymene mons, ii. 15.
Dindymus mons Cyzic. i. 41.
—————— Pessin. ii. 87.
Diniæ, ii. 30.
Diobulium, i. 321.
Diocæsarea Phryg. ii. 56.
—————— Cappad. ii. 113.
—————— Cilic. ii. 332.

Διοκαισάρεια, Διοκαισαρεύς.
Dioclia, ii. 56.
Dionia, ii. 390.
Dionysia insula, ii. 256.
Dionysopolis, ii. 56.
Dionysiophanæ, ii. 327.
Dioshieron Ion. i. 357.
——————— Lyd. i. 236.
Diospolis, i. 471.
Discus, i. 194.
Dizoatra, sive Zizoatra, ii. 125.
Docimia, ii. 27.
Δοκιμία, Δοκιμεὺς, et Δοκιμίτης.
Dœantius campus Pont. i. 269,
——————————— Phryg. ii. 35.
Dogana, ii. 154.
Dolichiste insula, ii. 253.
Doliones gens, i. 39.
Domana, ii. 154.
Domanitis regio.
Domitiopolis, ii. 338.
Dona, ii. 147.
Doranon, i. 311.
Doridis Sinus, ii. 389.
Dorieum, ii. 56.
Doris, ii. 184.
Dorion, ii. 323.
Doryleum, ii. 19.
Δορυλάειον, Δορυλαεύς.
Doulopolis, ii. 189.
Dracanum prom. et mons, i. 410.
————— urbs, i. 411.
Draco fluvius, i. 184.
——— mons, i. 440.
Dracontes, ii. 155.
Dratræ, sive Dagræ, ii. 137.
Drecanum prom. ii. 222.
Drepane, i. 184.
Drepanum prom. ii. 373.
Dresia, ii. 34.
Δρεσία, Δρεσιεύς.
Drilæ gens, i. 286.
Drizium, ii. 145.
Dryæna, ii. 364.
Drymusa insula, i. 345.
Drynemetum, ii. 83.
Drys, ii. 266.
Dusis pros Olympum, i. 211.
Dyndasum, ii. 215.

Δύνδασον, Δυνδασεύς.
Dyrzela, ii. 294.
Ebagena, sive Sebagena, ii. 124.
Ecdaumana, ii. 96.
Ecdaua, ii. 96.
Ecechiries gens, i. 291.
Echæa, i. 194.
Ecobriga, ii. 101.
Edebessus, ii. 266.
Ἐδεβησσὸς, Ἐδεβησσεύς.
Edyme, ii. 215.
Ἡδύμη, Ἡδυμεύς.
Elaphitis insula, i. 402.
Elaphonnesus, i. 49.
Elæa, i. 145.
Ἐλαία, Ἐλαιίτης.
——— insula Bithyn. i. 192.
Elæaticus Sinus, i. 145.
Elæitichos, ii. 266.
Elæum emporium, i. 202.
Elæus, ii. 190.
Elæussa insula, Mys. i. 134.
——————— Car. ii. 191.
——————— Cil. ii. 337.
Elea promontorium, ii. 384.
Elæus fluvius, i. 202.
Elegarsina, ii. 160.
Elespis regio, ii. 89.
Eleutherocilices, ii. 362.
Elgus, ii. 266.
Ἔλγος, Ἔλγιος.
Elmæum, ii. 390.
Elvia, i. 238.
Embatum Ion. i. 350.
Embolus, ii. 255.
Empelus fluvius, i. 37.
Enara, i. 469.
Epetobrogium, ii. 94.
Ephesus, i. 363.
Ἔφεσος, Ἐφέσιος.
Epidarus, ii. 390.
Epiphanea Bithyn. 215.
——————— Cilic. ii. 363.
Ἐπιφάνεια, Ἐπιφανεύς.
Eræ, sive Geræ, i. 352.
Erana, ii. 362.
Erania, ii. 385.
Erebinthodes insula, i. 192.
Eremosgræa, ii. 144.

Eressus, i. 162.

Ἔρεσσος, Ἐρέσσιος.

Ereuatis, ii. 266.

Erezii, i. 59.

Ergasterion, i. 58.

Eribolum, sive Eribœa, i. 187.

Eriza, ii. 212.

Ἐρίζα, Ἐριζηνός.

Eryannis fluvius, i. 129.

Erymnæ, ii. 266.

Ἐρυμναὶ, Ἐρυμναῖος.

Erysthea, ii. 390.

Erythini, i. 223.

Erythræ Dardan. i. 84.

———— Ion. i. 347.

Ἐρυθραὶ, Ἐρυθραῖος.

Estiæ promontorium, i. 195.

Etenna, ii. 310.

Ἔτεννα, Ἐτεννεύς.

Etheleus fluvius, i. 131.

Evagina, ii. 103.

Evarchus fluvius, i. 234.

Eucarpia, ii. 25.

Εὐκαρπία, Εὐκαρπεύς.

Evenus fluvius, i. 129, 134.

Eudagina, ii. 155.

Eudiphus, i. 321.

Eudixata, ii. 154.

Eudon fluvius, i. 465.

Eudocia, ii. 57.

———— Pisid. ii. 293.

Eudoxia, ii. 90.

Eudoxiopolis, ii. 313.

Euippe, ii. 214.

Εὐΐππη, Εὐϊππεύς.

Eulepa, i. 321. ii. 155.

Eumenia, ii. 24.

Εὐμενεία, Εὐμενεύς.

Eunæ, ii. 215.

Εὐναὶ, Εὐναῖος.

Eunæus fluvius, ii. 215.

Euonymia, ii. 215.

Eupatoria, postea Magnopolis, i. 309.

Eupatria, i. 471.

Euphorbium, ii. 28.

Euphrates, ii. 150.

Euranium, ii. 182.

Eureis fluvius et vicus, i. 131.

Euromus, sive Europus, ii. 198.

Εὔρωμος, sive Εὔρωπος, Εὐρωμεὺς et Εὐρωπεύς.

Eurymedon fluvius, ii. 280.

Eurynassa, i. 402.

Eusebia ad Argæum, ii. 122.

Eusene, i. 263.

Eusimara, ii. 127.

Euspœna, ii. 160.

Eutane, ii. 190.

Euthene, ii. 190.

Εὐθῆναι, Εὐθηναῖος, Εὐθηνεὺς, et Εὐθηνίτης.

Faustinopolis, ii. 133.

Flavias, ii. 339.

Foroba, ii. 155.

Frigidarium, i. 300.

Gadiana, sive Gadusena, ii. 124.

Gadilonitis, sive Gazelonitis, i. 263.

Gadilon, sive Gazelon, i. 264. 300.

Gæson fluvius, i. 381.

Gæsonis palus, i. 381.

Gagæ, ii. 255.

Γάγαι, Γαγαῖος.

Galatia, ii. 79.

———— Consularis, ii. 85.

———— Salutaris, ii. 85.

Galea, ii. 96.

Gallesus mons, i. 359.

Gallogræci, ii. 79.

Gallus fluvius Bithyn. i. 183.

———————— Phryg. ii. 32.

Gambrium, i. 395.

Γαμβρεῖον, Γαμβρειεύς.

Gammaüsa, sive Gambua, ii. 57.

Gangra, i. 237.

Γάγγρα, Γαγγρηνός.

Gargara mons, i. 121.

———— urbs, i. 124.

Γάργαρα, Γαργαρεύς.

Garium, i. 226.

Garmias, ii. 117.

Garnace, ii. 117.

Garsaura, sive Garsabora, ii.112.

Garsauritis, ii. 112.

Gaugæna, sive Gauræna, ii.125.

Gazacena, i. 305.

Gazena, ii. 57.
Gazioura, i. 305.
Gazorum, i. 234.
Gebes, sive Gelbes fluvius, i. 173.
Gelos, ii. 191.
Gendos fluvius, i. 184.
Genetes prom. et fluvius, i. 278.
Georgii castellum, i. 182.
Geræ, i. 352.
Geræsticus portus, i. 352.
Gerandrus, ii. 388.
Geranea, ii. 57.
Geren, i. 164.
Gergis, sive Gergitha, i. 84.
Γεργὶς, et Γέργιθα, Γεργίθιος.
Gergithium, i. 68.
Germanicopolis Bithyn. i. 173.
——————— Paphlag. i. 238.
——————— Cil. ii. 339.
Germe, sive Hiera Germe, i. 60.
Germa Lyd. i. 430.
———— Gal. ii. 89.
Γέρμη, Γερμηνός.
Germiani colles, i. 60.
Gerrhæidæ, i. 352.
Gigartho, i. 410.
Gihenenica, i. 299. ii. 159.
Glauama, ii. 72.
Glauce, sive Glaucia, i. 380.
Glauci demus, ii. 266.
Glaucus Pont. fluvius, i. 294.
———— Phryg. ii. 24.
———— Lyc. ii. 247.
Glaucus Sinus, ii. 198.
Godasa, sive Gundusa, ii. 154.
Golgi, ii. 390.
Gordium, postea Juliopolis, i. 212.
Γορδίειον, Γορδιεύς.
Gordiu tichos, ii. 210.
Γορδίου τεῖχος, Γορδιουτειχίτης.
Gordus, sive Juliagordus, i. 431.
———— Troad. i. 131.
Gorgyia, i. 410.
Granicus fluvius, i. 36.
Graosgala, ii. 60.
Grius mons, i. 394.

Gronychia, i. 194.
Grylius fluvius, i. 132.
Grynium, sive Grynea, i. 146.
Γρύνειον, Γρύνειος, et Γρυνεύς.
Gunaria campus, i. 240.
Gurzubanthon, i. 234.
Gygæa palus, i. 432.
Gymnias, i. 297.
Gyres fluvius, ii. 145.
Gytarium, ii. 135.
Hadriani, i. 179.
Hadrianopolis Bithyn. i. 210.
——————— Pisid. ii. 313.
Hadrianotheræ, i. 142.
'Αδριανοθηραὶ, 'Αδριανοθηρίτης.
Hales fluvius, i. 359.
Halesium, i. 116.
Halicarnassus, ii. 176.
'Αλικαρνασσὸς, 'Αλικαρνάσσιος.
Halice, et Halicus, ii. 364.
Halisarna, ii. 222.
Halizones, i. 172.
Halizonium, i. 88.
Halone insula, i. 402.
Halonnesus, i. 351.
Hamaxitus Troad. i. 116.
———— Car. ii. 199.
'Αμαξιτὸς, 'Αμαξιτεύς.
Haris, ii. 160.
Harmatus prom. i. 145.
Harpagium, sive Harpagia, i. 35.
Harpasa, ii. 209.
Ἅρπασα, Ἁρπασεύς.
Harpasus fluvius Armen. i. 296.
———— Car. ii. 209.
Hassis, ii. 156.
Hecatonnesi, i. 165.
Helboscope, sive Helioscope insula, ii. 247.
Helenopolis, i. 184.
Helgas, i. 173.
Heliopolis, ii. 104.
Hellespontus, i. 60.
Heneti gens, i. 218.
Heniochi gens, i. 295.
Heptacometæ gens, i. 291.
Heptaporus, sive Polyporus fluvius, i. 131.

Heraclea Mys. i. 132.
———— Pontica, i. 203.
———— Latmi, i. 393.
———— Magnes. i. 472.
———— Albase, sive Salbace, ii. 214.
Ἡράκλεια, Ἡρακλεώτης.
Heracleum, i. 182.
———————— Caun. ii. 195.
———————— promont. et portus Ponti, i. 266.
Herculis Vicus, ii. 134.
Hermagoræ fons, i. 193.
Hermæum, i. 69.
Hermesia, i. 438.
Hermius Sinus, i. 342.
Hermocapelia, i. 434.
Hermonassa, i. 287.
Ἑρμώνασσα, Ἑρμωνασσαῖος, et Ἑρμωνάσσιος.
Hermopolis, i. 434.
Hermus fluvius, i. 336.
Herpa, sive Herpha, ii. 142.
Hiera, i. 164.
———— prom. ii. 247.
Hieracæsarea, i. 431.
Hieracome, ii. 208.
Hieracometæ, i. 153.
Hieramæ, ii. 216.
Ἱεραμαὶ, Ἱεραμεύς.
Hierapolis, ii. 371.
Ἱεράπολις, Ἱεραπολίτης.
Hierocepia, sive Hierocepis, ii. 376.
Hierolophienses, i. 154.
Hieron, sive Templum Jovis Urii, i. 194.
———— Oros. i. 285.
Hieronenses, sive Hierorenses, ii. 103.
Hierus fluvius Troad. i. 129.
———————— Bithyn. i. 213.
Hippi insula, i. 350.
Hippocome, ii. 266.
Hipponesus, ii. 216, 239.
Hispa, ii. 157.
Hodiopolis, i. 315.
Ὁδιούπολις, Ὁδιουπολίτης.
Holmi Phryg. ii. 31.

Holmi Cilic. ii. 329.
Homonadenses, ii. 332.
Homonada, ii. 333.
Ὁμόναδα, Ὁμοναδεύς.
Horisius fluvius, i. 173.
Hydara, ii. 151.
Hyde Lyd. i. 434.
———— Lycaon. ii. 72.
———— Car. ii. 190.
Hydra prom. i. 150.
Hydissus, ii. 214.
Ὑδισσὸς, Ὑδισσεύς.
Hyelium, ii. 60.
Hyettusa insula, i. 412.
Hygassus, ii. 217.
Ὑγασσὸς, Ὑγάσσιος.
Hygenna, ii. 267.
Ὑγεννα, Ὑγεννεύς.
Hylami, ii. 266.
Hyllarima, ii. 217.
Ὑλλάριμα, Ὑλλαριμεύς.
Hylas fluvius, i. 176.
Hyle, ii. 391.
Hylluala, ii. 217.
Hyllus, sive Phrygius fluvius, i. 427.
Hynidos, ii. 213.
Hypachæi, ii. 315.
Hypæpa, i. 450.
Ὕπαιπα, Ὑπαιπηνός.
Hyperdexion, i. 165.
Hypii montes, i. 202,
Hypius fluvius, i. 201.
Hyrcanius campus, i. 428.
Hyria, ii. 332.
Hyris prom. i. 188.
Hysbe, i. 472.
Ὕσβη, Ὑσβαῖος, et Ὑσβίτης.
Hyssus portus, i. 290.
Hytenna, ii. 267.
Ὕτεννα, Ὑτεννεύς.
Ialysus, ii. 237.
Ἰάλυσος, Ἰαλύσιος.
Januaria, ii. 355.
Iaonitæ, i. 473.
Jasonium prom. i. 273.
Iassicus Sinus, ii. 170.
Iassus Cappad. ii. 127.
———— Car. ii. 170.

Ἰασσὸς, Ἰάσσιος.
Ibeni, i. 473.
Ibettes fluvius, i. 408.
Ibibus mons, i. 37.
Icaria insula, i. 410.
Iconium, ii. 62.
Ἰκόνιον, Ἰκονιεύς.
Ida mons, i. 120.
Idalium, sive Idalia, ii. 381.
Idea, i. 437.
Idyma, sive Idymus, ii. 215.
Idymus fluvius, ii. 216.
Ilaris, ii. 266.
Ἰλάρις, Ἰλαρεύς.
Iliocolone, i. 65.
Ilistra, ii. 71.
Ilium vetus, i. 100.
—— novum, i. 104.
Illyris insula, ii. 264.
Iluza, ii. 57.
Imbarus mons, ii. 364.
Imbrasus fluvius, i. 408.
Imbrus, ii. 195.
Incilissa, ii. 148.
Indus fluvius, ii. 195.
In Medio, ii. 158.
In Monte, ii. 148.
Iones, i. 324.
Ionia, i. 323.
—— Cilic. loc. ii. 355.
Iotape, ii. 323.
Ἰωτάπη, Ἰωταπείτης.
Iovia, ii. 293.
Ipnus, i. 410.
Ipsus, ii. 33.
Irenopolis, ii. 339.
Iris fluvius, i. 266.
Is fluvius, ii. 328.
Isaura Palæa, ii. 74.
—— Euerces, ii. 74.
Isauri, ii. 72.
Isauria, ii. 72.
Isbus, ii. 78.
Ischopolis, i. 283.
Isinda, sive Isionda, ii. 289.
Ἴσινδα, et Ἰσίονδα, Ἰσινδεύς, et
Ἰσιανδεύς.
Ismara, sive Simara, ii. 153.
Ispa, ii. 154.

Issa, i. 164.
Issicus Sinus, ii. 354.
Issus, ii. 360.
Ἴσσος, Ἰσσαῖος.
Isti promontorium, i. 410.
Itone, i. 473.
Itonia, i. 320.
Ixiæ, ii. 2.
Julia, ii. 32.
Julianopolis, i. 454.
Juliopolis, prius Gordium, i.
212.
—————— Cappad. ii. 127.
Juliagordus, i. 431.
Juliosebaste, ii. 339.
Justinianopolis, ii. 313.
Justinopolis, ii. 145.
Labara, ii. 116.
Λάβαρα, Λαβαρεύς.
Labranda, ii. 202.
Λάβρανδα, Λαβρανδεύς.
Laceter prom. ii. 222.
Lacriassus, ii. 127.
Lacus Jovis Dacii, ii. 129.
Lade insula, i. 389.
Ladepsi gens, i. 215.
Læa, ii. 216.
Λαεία, Λαΐτης.
Laertes, ii. 321.
Λαέρτης, Λαερτιεὺς, Λαερτίτης, et
Λαέρτιος.
Lagalassus, ii. 161.
Lagania, ii. 95.
Lagina, ii. 205.
Laginea, i. 214.
Lagon, ii. 289.
Lagusa insula, ii. 247.
Lagussæ insula, i. 111.
Laius portus, i. 400.
Lalacæum, ii. 145.
Lalassis, sive Lalisanda, ii. 75.
ii. 334.
Lalænesis, sive Ladænesis, ii.
127.
Lamotis regio, ii. 338.
Lampe, ii. 60.
Lampes fluvius, Mys. i. 53.
Lamponia, sive Lamponium, i.
125.

Λαμπώνιον, Λαμπωνιεύς.
Lampsacus, i. 65.
Λάμψακος, Λαμψακηνός.
Lampsus, i. 345.
Lamus fluvius, ii. 338.
Landosia, ii. 97.
Langasa, ii. 125.
Laodicea Catacecaumene, ii. 33.
———— ad Lycum, ii. 38.
Λαοδίκεια, Λαοδικεύς.
Lapara, ii. 145.
Lapathus, sive Lapethus, ii. 386.
Λάπηθος, Λαπήθιος, et Λαπηθεύς.
Lapsias fluvius, i. 215.
Laranda Lycaon, ii. 71.
Λάρανδα, Λαρανδεύς.
Larissa Troad. i. 113.
———— Phriconis, i. 150.
———— Ephes. i. 458.
———— Cappad. ii. 148.
Λάρισσα, Λαρισσαῖος.
Larymna, ii. 191.
Lascoria, ii. 102.
Lasonii, ii. 295.
Latania, i. 211.
Latmicus Sinus, i. 389, 393.
Latmus mons, i. 394.
Lauzados, ii. 339.
Laviniasene, ii. 125.
Leandis, ii. 144.
Lebade, i. 438.
Lebedos, i. 355.
Λέβεδος, Λεβέδιος.
Lectum promontorium, i. 116.
Ledrum, ii. 391.
Leleges, i. 20. ii. 165, 182.
Lembus, i. 194.
Lentiana regio, i. 56.
Lentiani colles, i. 56.
Leontocephale, ii. 57.
Leontoscome, ii. 57.
Leopodium, i. 350.
Lepetymnus mons, i. 161.
Lepria insula, i. 402.
Lepsemandus insula, ii. 239.
Lepsia insula, i. 412.
Lepte prom. i. 227.
Leros, ii. 217.
Λέρος, Λέριος.

Lesbos insula, i. 154.
Lethæus fluvius, i. 461.
Leuca Bithyn. i. 182.
———— Car. prom. ii. 183.
Leucæ insulæ, i. 166.
———— Ioniæ, i. 335.
Leucatas prom. i. 166.
Leucolla prom. ii. 282.
———— portus, ii. 381.
Leuconium, i. 401.
Leucophrys, i. 461.
Leucopolis, ii. 190.
Leucothea, i. 410.
Leucotheum prom. ii. 285.
Leucosyri, i. 186, 261.
Leugæsa, sive Leutæsa, ii. 127.
Liba, sive Libum, i. 187.
Libyssa, i. 187.
Λίβυσσα, Λιβυσσαῖος.
Libyssus fluvius, i. 187.
Lide mons, ii. 182.
Lilium emporium, i. 202.
Lilius fluvius, i. 202.
Limenæ, ii. 313.
Limenia, ii. 388.
Limeneium, i. 392.
Limobrama, ii. 286.
Limmocheir, ii. 60.
Limne, i. 292.
Limon, i. 468.
Limyra, ii. 254.
Λίμυρα, Λιμυρεύς.
Limyrus fluvius, ii. 254.
Lindus, ii. 236.
Λίνδος, Λίνδιος.
Liparis fluvius, ii. 341.
Lirnytea, ii. 286.
Lithrus mons, i. 310.
Liviopolis, i. 287.
Locozus, ii. 57.
Λόκοζος, Λοκόζιος, et Λοκοξίτης.
Longinia, ii. 365.
Lopadium, i. 53.
Loryma, ii. 191.
Λόρυμα, Λωρυμαῖος.
Luma, ii. 60.
Lunda, ii. 57.
Lycadium, sive Cycladium, i. 194.

Lycæus campus, i. 203.
Lycandus, ii. 145.
Lycaon, ii. 57.
Lycaones, ii. 61.
Lycaonia, ii. 61.
Lycapsus, i. 473.
Λύκαψος, Λυκάψιος.
Lycastus, i. 265.
————fluvius, i. 265.
Λύκαστος, Λυκάστιος.
Lycia, ii. 240.
Lycii, ii. 240.
·Lycide, i. 142.
Lycosthene, i. 473.
Λυκοσθένη, Λυκοσθενεὺς, et Λυκοσθε-
νίτης.
Lycus fluvius Mys. i. 55.
———— Bithyn. i. 203.
———— Pont. i. 294.
————i. 309.
———— Phryg. ii. 39.
———— Cypr. ii. 377.
Lydia, i. 413.
Lydi, i. 414.
Lygdamum, i. 142.
Lyperus mons, i. 215.
Lyrbe, ii. 313.
Λύρβη, Λυρβείτης.
Lyrope, ii. 313.
Lyrnatia, ii. 266.
Lyrnessus Troad. i. 129.
———— Pamph. ii. 278.
Λυρνησσὸς, Λυρνήσσιος.
Lysias, ii. 24.
Λυσιὰς, Λυσιάδης.
Lysinoe, ii. 296.
Lysis fluvius, ii. 289.
Lystra, ii. 69.
Λύστρα, Λυστρηνός.
Macaria, ii. 391.
Macedones Hyrcani, i. 429.
Macistus fluvius, i.
———— mons, i. 161.
Machelones gens, i. 295.
Macria prom. i. 355.
Macris insula Ion. i. 355.
———— Lyc. ii. 247.
Macrocephali, i. 285.
Macrones, i. 285.

Mænalia, ii. 104.
Mænomenus Campus, i. 464.
Mæones, i. 21, 416.
Mæonia, i. 416.
———— urbs, i. 453.
Magaba mons, ii. 95.
Magalassus, ii. 155.
Magnana, i. 299. ii. 159.
Magnesia ad Sipylum, i. 436.
————————Mæandrum, i. 459.
Μαγνησία, Μάγνης.
Magnopolis, i. 309.
Magydus, ii. 278.
Μάγυδος, Μαγυδεύς.
Malea, i. 164.
Malene, i. 133.
Mallus Troad. i. 88.
—·—— Pisid. ii. 3.
———— Cilic. ii. 351.
Μάλλος, Μαλλώτης.
Malum, ii. 380.
Mandane, ii. 327.
Mandra, i. 55.
Mandropolis, ii. 289.
Manegordus, ii. 95.
Manesium, ii. 57.
Manoris, i. 240.
Mantalus, ii. 57.
Μάνταλος, Μανταληνός.
Mantinium, i. 239.
Marasia, ii. 365.
Marathesia, i. 377.
Marathusa, i. 345.
Marcada, sive Carmada, ii. 127.
Marcæum mons, i. 85.
Mardara, sive Marandara, i.
    321. ii. 154.
Mare Pamphylium, ii. 274.
Mares gens, i. 322.
Mariandyni gens, i. 200.
Marium, ii. 391.
Μάριον, Μάριος.
Marmarensium rupis, ii. 264.
Marmolitis, i. 235.
Maroscus mons, i. 189.
Marsara, ii. 154.
Marsyas fluvius Phryg. ii.
———————— Car. ii. 207.
Marthyla, i. 295.

Martyropolis, ii. 145.
Martyrum Lacus, ii. 32.
Masanorada, ii. 216.
Μασανώραδα, Μασανωραδεύς.
Masedus, ii. 278.
Massicytes mons, ii. 256.
Mastaura, i. 468.
Mastusia mons, i. 440.
Mastya, i. 239.
Masura, ii. 278.
Matuasco, ii. 156.
Mausoleum, ii. 179.
Maximianopolis, ii. 286.
Mazaca, ii. 118.
Mazæum, i. 215.
Mazora, sive Maroza, ii. 125.
Meander fluvius, i. 282.
Meandrius Campus, i. 463.
Medeæ turris, i. 195.
Medmasa, ii. 182.
Μέδμασα, Μεδμασεύς.
Medocia, i. 300. ii. 159.
Megabula, ii. 156.
Megalassus, ii. 155.
Megale insula, i. 192.
Megalopolis, ii. 210.
Megaricum, i. 183.
Megarsus, ii. 351.
Μέγαρσος, Μεγαρσεύς.
Megiste insula, ii. 251.
Melæna prom. Bithyn. i. 198.
————————Ion. i. 346.
————————Chior. i. 401.
Melænæ, ii. 266.
Melampea, i. 473.
Melane insula, i. 402.
Melangia, i. 178.
Melania, ii. 327.
Melanippe et Melanippium, ii. 255.
Melano insula, ii. 239.
Melanos prom. i. 48.
Melanudium, i. 392.
Melanthius fluvius, i. 279.
Melantii scopuli, i. 411.
Melas fluvius Cappad. ii. 118.
———————— Pamphyl. ii. 283.
———————— Cilic. ii. 329.
Meles fluvius, i. 338, 342.

Melia, ii. 216.
Μελία, Μελιεύς.
Melisse, sive Melitæa, ii. 29.
Melitene Præfect. ii. 126.
———————— urbs, ii. 126.
Μελιτηνή, Μελιτηνός.
Memnonis tumulus et vicus, i. 38.
Men Carus, ii. 43.
Menedeterus, ii. 218.
Menedemium, ii. 298.
Mermessus, sive Myrmissus, i. 68.
Merus, ii. 57.
Mesate promontorium, i. 350.
Mesonacte, ii. 32.
Mesorome, ii. 155.
Mesotmolus, i. 443.
Messaba, ii. 216.
Μέσσαβα, Μεσσαβεύς.
Messogis mons, i. 459.
Metabole, i. 189.
Metadula, sive Megabula, i. 320.
Metalassus, sive Megalassus, ii. 155.
Metaum, i. 165.
Methymna, i. 160.
Metita, ii. 125.
Metorome, sive Mesorome, i. 320.
Metroum, i. 207.
Metropolis Lyd. i. 451.
———————— Phryg. ii. 29.
Μητρόπολις, Μητροπολίτης.
Midæum, ii. 20.
Μιδάειον, Μιδαεύς.
Midea, ii. 266.
Miletopolis, i. 52.
Miletopolitis palus, i. 50.
Miletus Paphl. i. 38.
———————— Ion. i. 383.
Milyas, ii. 267.
————————urbs, ii. 299.
Milyæ, ii. 268.
Mimas mons, i. 346.
Minizus, ii. 95.
Mirones, ii. 103.
Misthea, ii. 71.
Mithridatium, ii. 102.

Mitylene, i. 157.
Μυτιλήνη, Μυτιληναῖος.
Mnasyrium prom. ii. 237.
Mocata, i. 215.
Moccle, ii. 57.
Mocissus, ii. 117.
Modia, i. 183.
Mogarissus, i. 321.
Mogaron, i. 311.
Molpe, sive Molte, ii. 57.
Moloe, ii. 339.
Molyndea, ii. 266.
Μολύνδεια, Μολυνδεύς.
Momoasson, ii. 146.
Monabæ, ii. 78.
Monarites, ii. 126.
Monastia, i. 182.
Monogissa, ii. 216.
Μονόγισσα, Μονογισσηνός.
Mopsuestia, ii. 353.
Μόψου ἑστία, Μοψεάτης.
Morene regio, i. 54.
Morimene, ii. 115.
Moson, i. 238.
Mossine, i. 474.
Mostene, i. 429.
Mosynœci gens, i. 279.
Moxiani, ii. 58.
Mumastus, ii. 216.
Μούμαστος, Μουμαστίτης.
Muriana, ii. 115.
Muricium, ii. 104.
Mya, ii. 239.
Myanda, sive Myus, ii. 327.
Mycale mons, i. 378.
Mycaporis Sinus, i. 194.
Myes, i. 395.
Mygdones, i. 7.
Mygisi, ii. 216.
Mylæ, ii. 329.
Mylantia prom. ii. 237.
Mylasa, ii. 200.
Μύλασα, Μυλασεύς.
Myndus, ii. 175.
Μύνδος, Μύνδιος.
Myonnesus, i. 354.
Μυόνησος, Μυονήσιος.
Myra, ii. 253.
Μύρα, Μυρεύς.

Myriandrus, ii. 362.
Μυρίανδρος, Μυριανδρηνός.
Myrina, i. 146.
Μύρινα, Μυριναῖος.
Myriocephalus, ii. 60.
Myrlea, i. 173.
Μύρλεια, Μυρλεανός.
Myrleanus Sinus, i. 174.
Myrmeces scopuli, i. 336.
Myrmissus, i. 68.
Μυρμισσός, Μυρμίσσιος.
Mysi, i. 30.
Mysia, i. 32.
—— Major, i. 31.
—— Minor, i. 31.
Mysius fluvius, i. 135.
Myso Macedones, i. 60.
Mythopolis, i. 181.
Myus, i. 392.
Μυοῦς, Μυούσιος.
Nacolia, ii. 21.
Νακολία, Νακολεύς.
Nacrasa, i. 430.
Νάκρασα, Νακρασείτης.
Nagidus, ii. 326.
Νάγιδος, Ναγιδεύς.
Nagidusa insula, ii. 326.
Nape, i. 165.
Narcasus, ii. 216.
Ναρκασός, Ναρκασεύς.
Narmalis, ii. 314.
Νάρμαλις, Ναρμαλεύς.
Narthecusa insula, ii. 238.
Nausiclea, i. 194.
Nausimachium, i. 194.
Naxia, ii. 216.
Ναξία, Ναξιεύς.
Naziandus, ii. 176.
Nazianzus, ii. 114.
Ναζιανζός, Ναζιανζηνός.
Neacome, i. 88.
Neandria, i. 117.
Neanessus, ii. 114.
Neapolis Pont. i. 301.
———— Galat. ii. 103.
———— Ion. i. 377.
———— Pisid. ii. 313.
———— Cilic. ii. 339.
Neaule, i. 474.

Necica, ii. 334.
Neniicome, i. 182.
Neocæsarea, i. 315.
Νεοκαισάρεια, Νεοκαισαρεύς.
Neoclaudipolis, i. 238.
Neontichos, i. 151.
Νέων τεῖχος, Νεοτειχίτης, et Νεο-
τειχεύς.
Nephelis prom. ii. 323.
Neronias, ii. 339.
Nesiazusa prom. ii. 323.
————— urbs, ii. 323.
Nesaulium, ii. 329.
Nicæa, i. 180.
Νίκαια, Νικαιεύς.
Nicephorium, i. 138.
Nicomedia, i. 185.
Νικομήδεια, Νικομηδεύς.
Nicomedium, i. 215.
Nicopolis Bith. i. 194.
————— Lyd. i. 474.
————— Armen. ii. 150.
Ninoe, ii. 10.
Ninus fluvius, ii. 197.
Nisyrus, Calydn. ii. 218.
————— insula, ii. 222.
Nitazus, ii. 117.
Nolasene, ii. 125.
Nora, sive Neroassus, ii. 132.
Noscopium, ii. 265.
Notium Ion. i. 357.
————— Chior. i. 400.
————— Calydn. ii. 218.
Nymphæum, i. 207.
————— Lyd. i. 440.
————— Cilic. ii. 364.
Nysa, i. 466.
Νύσα, Νυσαεύς.
Nyssa, ii. 117.
Νύσσα, Νυσσηνός.
Oanus, i. 473.
Obrimas fluvius, ii. 54.
Oca, sive Occa, i. 60.
Ochosbanes, sive Ochthomanes
fluvius, i. 228.
Ochras, ii. 146.
Ochyroma, ii. 238.
Octapolis, ii. 265.
Œandenses, ii. 103.

Œcus, ii. 216.
Οἶκους, Οἰκούσιος.
Œdymus Sinus, ii. 191.
Œniandus, ii. 363.
Œnoe, i. 272.
Œnoanda, ii. 272.
Οἰνόανδα, Οἰνοανδεύς.
Œnussæ insulæ, i. 401.
Odogra, ii. 124.
Odryses fluvius, i. 172.
Olachas fluvius, i. 184.
Olba, ii. 333.
Ὄλβα, Ὀλβεύς.
Olbasa, ii. 307.
Ὄλβασα, Ὀλβασηνός.
Olbia Bithyn. i. 185.
————— Pamphyl. ii. 274.
Ὀλβία, Ὀλβιανός.
Olbianus Sinus, i. 185.
Olenus, ii. 97.
Oleoberda, ii. 157.
Olgasys mons, i. 235.
Olotoedariza, ii. 155.
Olympus Mys. mons, i. 178.
————— Lesb. ——— i. 161.
————— Bithyn. — i. 211.
————— Lyciæ urbs et mons,
ii. 257.
————— Cypr. ii. 379, 385.
Ὄλυμπος, Ὀλυμπηνός.
Onopnictes fluvius, ii. 144.
Onugnathos prom. ii. 190.
Ophiogeneis, i. 65.
Ophius fluvius, i. 290.
Ophiusa insula, i. 49.
Ophlimus mons, i. 310.
Ophrynium, i. 82.
Opistholepre, i. 374.
Orbalisene, ii. 150.
Orbanassa, ii. 307.
Orbesine, ii. 150.
Orcaorici, ii. 95.
Orcistus, ii. 91.
Ordinius fluvius, i. 292.
Ordymnus mons, i. 161.
Orgas fluvius, ii. 53.
Orgibate, i. 234.
Oriens Medio, i. 214.
Orminius mons, i. 214.

Oroanda, ii. 300.
Ὀρόανδα, Ὀροανδεύς, et Ὀροανδικός.
Oromandrus, ii. 154.
Orsara, sive Orsa, ii. 154.
Orsena, ii. 150.
Orsinus fluvius, ii. 200.
Orthosia, ii. 207.
Ὀρθώσια, Ὀρθωσιεύς.
Orthronienses, ii. 214.
Ortygia, i. 376.
Orymna, ii. 286.
Otrea, i. 183.
Otrus, ii. 58.
Oxinas fluvius, i. 207.
Oxyopum, i. 142.
Oxyrrhoum prom. i. 194.
Ozdara, ii. 160.
Ozzala, ii. 117.
Pactolus fluvius, i. 441.
Padasea, ii. 144.
Pædopides fluvius, i. 207.
Pæsus, i. 65.
Παισὸς, Παισηνός.
———— fluvius, i. 65.
Pagrum, ii. 161.
Pagus mons, i. 339.
Pagus Iliensium, i. 102.
Paipert, ii. 61.
Palæa Troad. i. 125.
——— Cypr. ii. 379.
Palæapolis, Lyd. i. 474.
———————— Pamph. ii. 286.
Palægambrium, i. 395.
Palæmyndus, ii. 176.
Palæpaphos, ii. 373.
Palæscamander fluvius, i. 93.
Palæscepsis, i. 85.
Palalce, ii. 102.
Palamedium, i. 122.
Palinurus port. Sam. i. 409.
Pampali villa, ii. 133.
Pamphylia, ii. 273.
Pamphylii, ii. 273.
Panacra, ii. 391.
Pancalea campus, ii. 145.
Panemotichos, ii. 286.
Πανεμότειχος, Πανεμοτειχίτης.
Pania, ii. 364.
Panionium, i. 379.

Panormus Cyzic. i. 42.
Panormus Ephes. i. 375.
Panormus Milet. i. 392.
———————— Sam. i. 409.
———————— Caun. ii. 195.
Pantaenses, i. 154.
Pantichium, i. 188.
———————— Bosph. i. 195.
Paphlagones, i. 216.
Paphlagonia, i. 216.
Paphos, ii. 374.
Πάφος, Πάφιος.
Papira, ii. 90.
Papitium, i. 241.
Papyrii Castrum, ii. 365.
Paradisus fluvius, ii. 365.
Paridion, ii. 191.
Parium, i. 63.
Πάριον, Παριανός.
——— mons, ii. 355.
Parlais, ii. 72.
Παρλαΐς, Παρλαιεύς.
Parnassus, ii. 116.
Parparon, sive Perine, i. 153.
Parthenium, i. 141.
Parthenius fluvius, i. 221.
Pasada, ii. 195.
Passala, ii. 201.
Pasarne, ii. 125.
Patara, i. 300.
———— Lyc. ii. 249.
Πάταρα, Παταρεύς.
Patavium, i. 214.
Patmos insula, i. 412.
Patrasys, i. 322.
Pedalia, ii. 364.
Pedalium prom. ii. 197.
———————— Cypr. ii. 380.
Pedasus, Troad. i. 122.
Pedasum, sive Pedasa, Car. ii. 182.
Πέδασον, Πεδασεύς.
Pedieis, ii. 216.
Pednelissus, ii. 312.
Πεδνελισσός, Πεδνελισσεύς.
Pegasæum Stagnum, i. 362.
Pegella, ii. 96.
Peium, ii. 91.
Pele insula, i. 345.

Pelecas mons, i. 56.
Pelinæus mons, i. 401.
Pelope, i. 473.
Peltæ, ii. 22.
Πελταὶ, Πελτηνός.
Peltenus Campus, ii. 22.
Pentademitæ, i. 60.
Pentachira, ii. 60.
Penthile, i. 165.
Pepuza, ii. 58.
Pera, ii. 314.
Percote, i. 69.
Περκώτη, Περκώσιος.
Peræa regio, ii. 191.
Perdiciæ, ii. 247.
Perga, ii. 279.
Πέργα, Περγαῖος.
Pergamum, i. 136.
Πέργαμον, Περγαμηνός.
Perirrheusa insula, i. 345.
Perirrhous prom. i. 194.
Perperene, i. 132.
Persicum, ii. 195.
Perta, ii. 72.
Pessinus, ii. 85.
Πεσσινοῦς, Πεσσινούντιος.
Petræa, i. 189.
Petrossa, ii. 364.
Peucella fluvius, ii. 16.
Phadisana, i. 272.
Phalacrum, ii. 124.
Phalarus, ii. 191.
Phanæ portus et prom. i. 400.
Phanarœa, i. 309, 310.
Pharmacias fluvius, i. 215.
Pharmacusa insula, i. 412.
Pharmatenus fluvius, i. 280.
Pharnacia Pont. i. 200.
————— Phryg. ii. 60.
Pharsalus, ii. 286.
Phaselis, ii. 261.
Φασηλὶς, Φασηλίτης.
Phazemon, i. 301.
Phazemonitis, i. 301.
Phellus, ii. 252.
Φελλὸς, Φελλίτης.
Phiara, i. 310.
Phiela, i. 194.
Phigamus fluvius, i. 272.

Philadelphia, Lyd. i. 456.
—————— Cilic. ii. 332.
Philæa, ii. 329.
Philocalea, i. 283.
Philomelium, ii. 31.
Φιλομήλιον, Φιλομηλεύς.
Philyreis regio, i. 283.
————— insula, i. 283.
Philyres gens, i. 283.
Phocea, i. 330.
Φωκαία, Φωκαιεύς.
Phœbe insula, i. 280.
Phœnicus portus Ion. i. 347.
——————— Lyc. ii. 251.
———— —— mons, ii. 257.
Phœnix mons, ii. 191.
———— castellum, ii. 191.
Phorontis, ii. 213.
Phreata, ii. 115.
Phrixi portus, i. 194.
Phrurium prom. ii. 377.
Phryges, ii. 1.
Phrygia, ii. 1.
———— Epictetus, ii. 10.
———— Hellespontina, ii. 10.
———— Magna, ii. 22.
———— Pacatiana, ii. 10.
———— Paroreos, ii. 304.
———— Salutaris, ii. 10.
Phrygius fluvius, i. 427.
Pthira mons, i. 394.
Phuibagina, ii. 103.
Phuphagena, ii. 154.
Phuphena, ii. 154.
Phusipara, ii. 127.
Phylacesii, ii. 58.
Phyrites fluvius, i. 362.
Phyrocastrum, ii. 124.
Physcus portus, ii. 192.
Piala, i. 319.
Pida, i. 319.
Pidosus insula, ii. 239.
Pigelasus, ii. 216.
Πειγέλασος, Πειγελασεύς.
Piginda, ii. 216.
Πίγινδα, Πιγινδεύς.
Pimolisa, i. 237.
Pimolisene, i. 237.
Pinara, Lyc. ii. 246.

Pinara Cilic. ii. 364.
Πίναρα, Πιναρεύς.
Pinarus fluvius, ii. 360.
Pindasus mons, i. 140.
Pindenissus, ii. 362.
Pionia, i. 125.
Pirossus mons, i. 38.
Pisidæ, ii. 287.
Pisidia, ii. 286.
Pisilis, sive Pilisis, ii. 193.
Pisingara, ii. 154.
Pisonos, ii. 160.
Pisurgia, ii. 328.
Pisye, ii. 216.
Πισύη, Πισυήτης.
Pitane, i. 134.
Pitaum, ii. 190.
Πιτάον, Πιταεύς.
Pitnissus, sive Petnissus, ii. 95.
Pityea insula, i. 64.
—— mons, i. 64.
Pityodes insula, i. 188, 192.
Pityusa insula, ii. 329.
Placia, i. 49.
Placos mons, i. 129.
Plamus, ii. 216.
Πλάμος, Πλαμεύς.
Plarassa, ii. 198.
Πλάρασσα, Πλαρασσεύς.
Platanea, i. 185.
Plataneus, i. 184.
Plateis insula, ii. 266.
Plegra, i. 238.
Pleumaris, i. 320.
Plistarchia, ii. 216.
Plitendus, ii. 35.
Plutonium, i. 468.
———— Hieropol. ii. 37.
Podalia, ii. 265.
Ποδάλεια, Ποδαλεώτης.
Podandus, ii. 134.
Pœcile petra, ii. 335.
Pœmaninus, i. 56.
Pœmen mons, i. 222.
Pogla, ii. 298.
Πώγλα, Πωγλεύς.
Polemonium, i. 272.
Polichna Troad. i. 88.
———— Ion. i. 343.

Polium, i. 165.
Polyandus, ii. 144.
Polyara, ii. 217.
Πολύαρα, Πολυαρεύς.
Polybotus, ii. 31.
Polydora insula, i. 49.
Polymedium, i. 124.
Pompeiopolis Paphl. i. 236.
———————— Cilic. ii. 339.
Pontamus, i. 185.
Pontus, i. 242.
———— Euxinus, i. 195.
———— Polemoniacus, i. 272.
Pordoselene, sive Poroselene,
   i. 165.
Porphyrione insula, i. 49.
Portus Achiv. i. 146.
————Amyci, i. 194.
Posidea, i. 153.
Posidium prom. Bithyn. i. 176.
———————— Mariand. i. 207.
———————— Ion. i. 391.
———————— Chior. i. 400.
———————— Sam. i. 409.
———————— Car. ii. 191.
———————— Cilic. ii. 327.
Potami, i. 127.
Potamia, i. 235.
———— Cepora, i. 240.
Potamonion, i. 194.
Potamosacon, i. 153.
Praca, ii. 365.
Practius fluvius, i. 69.
Prænetus, i. 183.
Præpenissus, ii. 19.
Pramnus mons, i. 411.
Prasmon, ii. 94.
Priaponnesus insula, ii. 239.
Priapus, i.
Πρίαπος, Πριαπηνός.
————insula, i. 402.
Priene, i. 381.
Πριήνη, Πριηνεύς.
Prinassus, ii. 217.
Πρινασσὸς, Πρινασσεύς.
Prion mons, i. 374.
Procne insula, ii. 238.
Proconnesus insula, i. 48.
Progasia, i. 473.

Propontis, i. 34.
Prostanna, ii. 307.
Πρόστανα, Προσταννεύς.
Prote insula, i. 192.
Protomacra, i. 214.
Protopachium, i. 240.
Prusa ad Olympum, i. 176.
Προῦσα, Προυσαεύς.
Prusias ad mare, i. 175.
———— ad Hypium, i. 201.
Prymnesia, sive Prymnessus.
Πρυμνησσὸς, Πρυμνησσεύς.
Prytanis fluvius, i. 292.
Pseudocorasium, ii. 364.
Psile insula, i. 345.
Psilon insula, i. 379.
Psillis, vel Psillus fluvius, i. 198.
Psimada, ii. 78.
Psoron portus, i. 290.
Psychrus fluvius, i. 291.
Psyra insula, i. 401. ii. 239.
Ptanadari, ii. 144.
Pteleos lacus, i. 82.
Pteleum Ion. i. 350.
Πτελέων, Πτελεάτης.
Pteria regio et urbs, i. 263.
Ptolemais, ii. 285.
Ptoson, ii. 145.
Pulcherianopolis, ii. 58.
Pulchra Picea, i. 131.
Pulchrum Coracesium, ii. 335.
Pusgusa, sive Pasgusa palus, ii. 77.
Pydes, ii. 314.
Pydna, ii. 247.
Pygela, sive Phygela, i. 377.
Πύγελα, Πυγελεύς.
Pylacæum, ii. 58.
Pylæ Ciliciæ Cappad. ii. 135.
———————— ii. 361.
Pyramus fluvius, ii. 140, 350.
—————— vicus, ii. 355.
Pyrinthus, ii. 217.
Πύρινθος, Πυρινθεύς.
Pyrnus, ii. 193.
Πύρνος, Πύρνιος.
Pyrrha Lesb. i. 163.
———— Ion. i. 393.
———— insula, ii. 239.

Pyrrha prom. i. 131.
Pystus, ii. 215.
Pytane, i. 273.
Pytheca, i. 178.
Pythium, i. 182.
Pythopolis, i. 181.
Pytna, i. 181.
Pyxites fluvius, i. 292.
Rastia, ii. 103.
Ravene, sive Avarene, ii. 127.
Rax insula, ii. 266.
Regemauricium, ii. 104.
Regesalamara, ii. 286.
Rege trocnada, ii. 104.
Rhebas fluvius, i. 197.
Rhegma, ii. 255.
—————lacus, ii. 344.
Rhizæum portus, i. 292.
Rhizæus fluvius, i. 292.
Rhodia, sive Rhodiopolis, ii. 265.
Rhodius fluvius, i. 76.
Rhodomerus, i. 182.
Rhodus insula, ii. 224.
———— civit. ii. 233.
Ῥόδος, Ῥόδιος.
Rhodussæ insula, i. 192.
Rhodussa insula, ii. 192.
Rhoe portus, i. 199.
Rhœxus, ii. 364.
Rhogmi, ii. 364.
Rhope insula, ii. 251.
Rhopes, ii. 286.
Rhossicus Scopulus, ii. 362.
Rhosus, sive Rhossus, ii. 362.
Ῥῶσος, Ῥωσεύς.
Rhyndacus fluvius, i. 50.
Rhypara insula, i. 412.
———— locus, i. 53.
Ῥοιζοῦσαι ἄκραι, i. 194.
Rignum, sive Riconium, ii. 72.
Rosologiacum, ii. 98.
Ruscopoda, ii. 279.
Rygmani, ii. 327.
Saba, ii. 157.
Sabagena, ii. 125.
Sabalia, i. 320.
Sabalassus, i. 125.
Sabinæ, ii. 313,

Sacoena, ii. 146.
Sacorsa, i. 238.
Sacrum prom. ii. 256.
Sadacora, ii. 147.
Sadagothina, ii. 116.
Saettæ, i. 434.
Sagalassus, ii. 295.
Σαγαλασσὸς, Σαγαλασσεύς.
Sagylium, i. 302.
Sala, ii. 58.
Σάλα, Σαληνός.
Salagena, sive Sadagena, ii. 125.
Salambria, ii. 96.
Salamis, ii. 382.
Σαλαμὶς, Σαλαμίνιος.
Sale palus, i. 437.
Salmacis arx Halicarnassi, ii. 180.
———— fons, ii. 180.
Salone, i. 209.
Sama, ii. 162.
Samonius Campus, i. 117.
Samos insula, i. 402.
————urbs, i.
Σάμος, Σάμιος.
Samus, ii. 192.
Samylia, ii. 217.
Σαμυλία, Σαμυλιανός.
Sancus, ii. 46.
Sandaleon insula, i. 379.
Sandaleon, i. 166.
Sandalium, ii. 300.
Sandaraca, i. 207.
Sandaracurgium, i. 236.
Sandius collis, i. 463.
Sangarius fluvius, i. 199.
Sangia, i. 200. ii. 36.
Sanisene, i. 235.
Sanni gens, i. 286.
Santabaris, ii. 28.
Sannice, i. 290.
Saporda saltus, ii. 294.
Sapra lacus, i. 128.
Saralus, ii. 103.
Saramene, i. 264.
Saravene, ii. 127.
Sarbanissa, i. 320.
Sardemisus mons, ii. 282.
Sardene mons, i. 150.

Sardes, i. 443.
Sardessus, ii. 282.
Σάρδησσος, Σαρδήσσιος.
Sardus fluvius, ii. 144.
Sargarausene, ii. 124.
Saricha, ii. 145.
Sari capita, ii. 349.
Sarmalia, ii. 101.
Sarnaca, i. 142.
Sarpedon prom. ii. 330.
Sarvene, ii. 124.
Sarus fluvius, ii. 138, 348.
Sasima, ii. 114.
Satala, ii. 152.
Satnioeis fluvius, i. 122.
Satrachus urbs et fluvius, ii. 392.
Satala Lyd. i. 455.
———— Armen. Min. ii. 152.
Saurania i. 321.
Sauronisena in the Table, ii. 156.
Scamander fluvius, i. 96.
Scamandria, i. 109.
Scanatus, ii. 155.
Scari, ii. 267.
Scelenta, i. 58.
Scepsis, i. 85.
Σκῆψις, Σκήψιος.
Schedias, ii. 238.
Schœnus Sinus, ii. 189.
Sclerus lacus, ii. 77.
Scolla, ii. 148.
Scopas, sive Scopius fluvius, i. 213.
Scopelos insula Prop. i. 49.
———————— Paphl. i. 232.
———————— Ion. i. 345.
Scorobas mons, i. 240.
Scotius mons, i. 286.
Scydisces mons, i. 286.
Scylace, i. 49.
Scylax fluvius, i. 305.
Scyrmus, i. 49.
Scythini gens, i. 286, 297.
Sebaste Phryg. ii. 58.
———— Gal. ii. 95.
———— Cil. ii. 337.
Σεβάστη, Σεβαστηνός.

Sebastia, i. 317.
Sebastopolis, i. 311.
Secora, i. 238.
Sedisscapifonti, ii. 159.
Selenitis regio, ii. 323.
Seleoboria, ii. 154.
Seleucenses, ii. 103.
Seleucia Pamphyl. ii. 283.
————— Sidera Pisid. ii. 307.
————— Cilic. ii. 330.
Σελεύκεια, Σελευκεύς.
Selge, ii. 307.
Σέλγη, Σελγεύς.
Selinus fluvius Pergam. i. 140.
————————Cilic. ii. 322.
————— urbs, postea Trajano-
polis, ii. 322.
Σελινοῦς, Σελινούσιος,
Selinusia palus, i. 361.
Seminethus, sive Simmethus, ii.
209.
Semisus, ii. 127.
Sepyra, ii. 362.
Seramusa, i. 319.
Seraspere, ii. 127.
Sermusa, ii. 147.
Serna, ii. 286.
Serrepolis, ii. 355.
Sesamus, postea Amastris, i.
222.
Sestus, ii. 392.
Sete, i. 215.
Siala, ii. 137,
Sibde, ii. 182.
Σίβδα, Σιβδάτης.
Siberis fluvius, i. 213.
Sibidunda, ii. 58.
Σιβιδοῦνδα, Σιβιδουνδεύς.
Sibrus, qui et Xanthus fluvius,
ii. 247.
Sidace, ii. 266.
Σιδάκη, Σιδακηνός.
Side Pont. i. 271.
————Pamphyl. ii. 283.
Σίδη, Σιδήτης.
Sidele, i. 395.
Sidene Mys. i. 36.
————— Pont. i. 271.
————— Lyc. ii. 266.

Siderus portus, ii. 261.
Sidussa, i. 350.
————— insula, i. 402.
Sidyma, ii. 251.
Σίδυμα, Σιδυμεύς.
Sigeum, i. 109.
Σίγειον, Σιγειύς.
————— prom. i. 110.
Signia mons, ii. 49.
Sigrium prom. i. 162.
Silandus, i. 436.
Silbium, sive Siblium, ii. 53.
Σίβλιον, Σιβλιανός.
Sillyus, i. 395.
Simana, i. 215.
Simara, ii. 153.
Simena, ii. 253.
Σίμηνα, Σιμηνεύς.
Simyra, sive Zimira, ii. 153.
Simois fluvius, i. 97.
Sinara, ii. 152.
Sindessus, ii. 217.
Σινδησσὸς, Σινδησσεύς.
Singa, ii. 161.
Sinda, sive Sindia, ii. 267, 272.
Σινδία, Σίνδιος.
Singya, ii. 286.
Siniandus, ii. 213.
Sinis, ii. 127.
Sinope, i. 228.
Σινώπη, Σινωπεύς.
Sinoria, sive Sinebra, ii. 152.
Sinzita, sive Sindita, ii. 117.
Sionia, i. 322.
Sipylus mons, i. 437.
————— urbs, i. 437.
Siricis, ii. 162.
Sisium, ii. 365.
Sisyrba, i. 363.
Situpolis, ii. 58.
Siva, ii. 124.
Sminthium, i. 116.
Smyrna, i. 337.
Σμύρνα, Σμυρναῖος.
Smyrnæus Sinus, i. 342.
Soanda, ii. 146.
Soandus, ii. 147.
Soatra, sive Sabatra, ii. 67,
Σαυάτρα, Σαυατρεύς.

Sobala, ii. 217.
Σόβαλα, Σωβαλεύς.
Soli Cil. ii. 339.
Σόλοι, Σολεύς.
—— Cypr. ii. 387.
Σόλοι, Σόλιος.
Solmissus mons, i. 376.
Solonenica, ii. 159.
Soloon fluvius, i. 182.
Solymi, ii. 268.
Solymorum montes, ii. 258.
Soonautes fluvius, i. 207.
Sophianopolis, ii. 272.
Sophon lacus et mons, i. 188.
Sora, i. 238.
Soroba, sive Sobara, ii. 124.
Sorpara, ii. 155.
Sozopolis, ii. 299.
Speluncæ, ii. 156.
Stabiu, ii. 102.
Stabulum, ii. 103.
Stectorium, ii. 58.
Στεκτόριον, Στεκτορηνός.
Steganos insula, ii. 238.
Stephane, i. 227.
Steunos antrum, ii. 16.
Stiphane palus, i. 301.
Stomalimne, i. 93.
—————— Cor. ii. 222.
Stratonicea, ii. 203.
Στρατονικεία, Στρατονικεύς.
Strogola, i. 473.
Struthia, ii. 59.
Στρούθεια, Στρουθεύς.
Suissa, ii. 157.
Sunias fons, ii. 344.
Sunonensis lacus, i. 189.
Sura, ii. 254.
Susarmia, i. 290.
Syagra, ii. 364.
Syagela, ii. 183.
Σουάγελα, Σουαγελεύς.
Syassus, ii. 59.
Σύασσος, Συασσεύς.
Sycæi, i. 213.
Sycea, ii. 334.
Sycussa insula, i. 402.
Syedra, ii. 321.
Σύεδρα, Συεδρεύς.

Syessa, ii. 266.
Syleum Cibyr. ii. 272.
Sylleum Pamph. ii. 280.
Syme insula, ii. 222.
Σύμη, Συμαῖος, et Συμεύς.
Synnada, ii. 26.
Σύνναδα, Συνναδεύς.
Synnaus, ii. 12.
Syria insula, i. 377.
Syriæ Pylæ, ii. 361.
Syrias prom. i. 227.
Syrius fluvius, i. 215.
Syrna, ii. 217.
Σύρνα, Σύρνιος.
Tabæ, ii. 211.
Ταβαὶ, Ταβηνός.
Tabenus Campus, ii. 211.
Tabala, i. 454.
Talauri, i. 313.
Talbenda, ii. 307.
Tamasus, ii. 388.
Τάμασος et Ταμασσός, Ταμάσιος
    et Ταμασίτης.
Tanadaris, ii. 144.
Tantalis, i. 438.
Tantalus mons, i. 165.
Tapura, ii. 154.
Tarandrus, ii. 59.
Τάρανδρος, Ταράνδριος.
Tarantus, i. 215.
Tarbessus, ii. 314.
Tardequia, ii. 358.
Tarrha, sive Tyrrha, i. 473.
Tarseia, i. 215.
Tarsius fluvius, i. 39.
Tarsus Bithyn. i. 215.
—— Cilic. ii. 344.
Ταρσὸς, Ταρσεύς.
Taspa, ii. 74.
Tattæa palus, ii. 66.
Tattæum, sive Tottæum, i. 211.
Tauropolis, ii. 199.
Taurus mons, i. 7. ii. 277.
———— fluvius, ii. 294.
Tebenda, sive Tebenna, i. 319.
Tectosages, ii. 91.
Tegessus, ii. 392.
Τεγησσὸς, Τεγήσσιος.
Tegium, i. 142.

Telandria prom. ii. 217.
———— ins. ii. 247.
Telandrus, ii. 217.
Τήλανδρος, Τηλανδρεύς.
Telemæa, i. 189.
Telendos insula, ii. 264.
Telephi fons, ii. 267.
Telmessicus Sinus, ii. 244.
Telmissis prom. ii. 245.
Telmissus Car. ii. 183.
———— Lyc. ii. 244.
Τελμισσός, .Τελμισσεύς.
Telos insula, ii. 222.
Τῆλος, Τήλιος.
Tembrus, ii. 392.
Τέμβρος, Τέμβριος.
Temenia, ii. 34.
Τεμένεια, Τεμενεύς. Steph. Byz.
    in. v.
Temenothyritæ, i. 60.
Temnus mons, i. 55.
———— urbs, i. 151.
Τῆμνος, Τημνίτης.
Templum Menis Pharnacis, i.
    314.
————Jovis Urii, i. 194.
———— Didymæi Apollinis,
    i. 390.
Tendeba, ii. 205.
Τένδηβα, Τενδηβεύς.
Tenedos insula, i. 111.
———— Pamphyl. ii. 278.
Teos, i. 352.
Τήως, Τήϊος.
Tephrice, ii. 151.
Terea mons, i. 38, 69.
Termera, ii. 176.
Τέρμερα, Τερμερεύς.
Termerium prom. ii. 176.
Termes mons, i. 440.
Termessus, ii. 291.
Τερμεσσός, Τερμεσσεύς.
Termilæ, ii. 240.
Tetius fluvius, ii. 380.
Tetra, ii. 147.
Tetracis, i. 228.
Tetrapyrgia Cappad. ii. 115.
———— Cilic. ii. 115.
Teucila, ii. 159.

Teucri, i. 77.
Teuthranea regio, i. 135.
———— urbs, i. 135.
Teutlussa insula, ii.
Teutobodiaci, ii. 98.
Thabusion, ii. 213.
Thallussa insula, i. 401.
Thapsacus fluvius, ii. 363.
Thariba, i. 241.
Theangela, ii. 182.
Θεάγγελα, Θεαγγελεύς.
Thebais fons, i. 465.
Thebasa, ii. 72.
Thebe Hypoplacia, i. 129.
——— Milet. i. 395.
——— Cappad. ii. 145.
——— Pamphyl. ii. 278.
Thebes campus, i. 129.
——— mons, i. 298.
Thembrimus, ii. 215.
Θέμβριμος, Θεμβριμεύς.
Themissus, ii. 215.
Θεμισσός, Θεμισσεύς.
Theodosiopolis, ii. 145.
Thera, ii. 215.
Therionarce insula, ii. 238.
Therma Basilica, ii. 147.
——— Xanxaris, ii. 147.
Thermæ Phazemonitarum,
Thia, ii. 158.
Thiba, i. 321.
Thibii gens, i. 321.
Thracia Cyzic. i. 43.
Themiscyra, i. 271.
Themisonium, ii. 47.
Θεμισώνιον, Θεμισωνιεύς.
Theodosiopolis, prius Perpe-
    rene, i. 132.
Thermodon fluvius, i. 266, 270.
Thymnias Sinus, ii. 189.
Thoantium prom. ii. 237.
Thoaris fluvius, i. 272.
Thorax mons, i. 461.
Throni urbs et prom. ii. 282.
Throsmos collis, i. 102.
Thryanda, ii. 266.
Θρύανδα, Θρυανδεύς.
Thyaris fluvius, ii. 20.
Thyatira, i. 429.

Θυάτειρα, Θυατειρηνός.
Thydonos, ii. 213.
Thyessus Lyd. i. 472.
———— Pisid. ii. 314.
Thymena, i. 225.
Thymbra Troj. i. 103.
———— Mys. i. 142.
Thymbrara, sive Thymbres fluvius, ii. 20.
Thymbra Lyd. i. 472.
Thymbrium, ii. 306.
Thymbrius fluvius, i. 103.
Thynias insula, i. 199.
Thynus, ii. 364.
Tiare, i. 142.
Tibareni gens Pont. i. 277.
———————— Cilic. ii. 363.
Tiberiopolis, ii. 59.
Tibium mons, ii. 59.
Tichiussa, ii. 170.
Tilius fluvius, ii. 59.
Tilicastrum, ii. 348.
Timæa, i. 214.
Timeles fluvius, ii. 211.
Timolæum, i. 225.
Timoniacenses, ii. 103.
Timonium, i. 241.
Timonitis regio, i. 235.
Timyra, ii. 78.
Tiralli, ii. 143.
Tiriza, i. 241.
Tisanusa, ii. 191.
Titarissus, ii. 127.
Titiopolis, ii. 389.
Tityassus, ii. 314.
Τιτυασσὸς, Τιτυασσεύς.
Tium, i. 207.
Tlos, ii. 265.
Τλῶς, Τλωεὺς, et Τλωΐτης.
Tmolus mons, i. 441.
———— urbs, i. 443.
Tnyssus, ii. 217.
Τνύσσος, Τνυσσεύς.
Tolistoboii, ii. 85.
Tolosochorium, sive Tolistochorium, ii. 91.
Tomarene, i. 474.
Tomisa, ii. 142.
Tonea, ii. 102.

Tonosa, ii. 161.
Tobata, i. 238.
Torrhebia lacus i. 47.
Torrhebis regio, i. 474.
Torrhebus, i. 474.
Trabala, ii. 267.
Τράβαλα, Τραβαλεύς.
Trachea, i. 374.
Trachia porta Cyzic. i. 45.
Tracias, ii. 147.
Tragasæ, i. 116.
Tragiæ insula, i. 411.
Trajanopolis Phryg. ii. 59.
Tralles, i. 464.
Trallicon, ii. 215.
Trampe, i. 395.
Tranipsi gens, i. 215.
Trapeza prom. i. 81.
Trapezopolis, ii. 207.
Τραπεζόπολις, Τραπεζοπολίτης.
Trapezus, i. 287.
Τραπεζοῦς, Τραπεζούντιος.
Trarium Mys. i. 132.
————, sive Trallium Bith. i. 188.
Tremithus, sive Trimethus, ii. 389.
Tresena, ii. 286.
Treta, ii. 376.
Tribanta, ii. 60.
Tricomia, ii. 21, 89.
Trinessa, ii. 60.
Τρινήσσα, Τρινησσαῖος.
Triopium prom. ii. 184.
Tripolis Pont. i. 282.
———— Lyd. i. 469.
———— Car. ii. 217.
Trisca, i. 189.
Trocmi gens, ii. 98.
Trœzene, ii. 213.
Trogilium prom. i. 378.
Trogitis palus, ii. 66.
Troja, i. 100.
Trojanus ager, i. 89.
Turris Isia, ii. 254.
Tyana, ii. 128.
Τύανα, Τυανεύς.
Tyanitis Præfect. ii. 128.
Tymandrus, ii. 313.

Tymbrium, sive Tembrium, ii. 305.

Tymenæum mons, ii. 60.

Tymenna, ii. 267.

Tymnessus, ii. 217.

Tymnus, ii. 217.

Tyndaridæ, i. 207.

Tynna, ii. 143.

Tyriæum, ii. 306.

Tyropæum, ii. 145.

Tyrus, ii. 314.

Tyscon, ii. 35.

Tzamandus, ii. 145.

Tzybitza, ii. 61.

Vadata, ii. 124.

Væsapa, sive Varsapa, ii. 154.

Valenta, ii. 95.

Vasoda, ii. 71.

Ubinaca, ii. 96.

Ucena, ii. 103.

Venasi, ii. 115.

Venecuso, ii. 157.

Vetissum, ii. 96.

Via Mauriana, ii. 365.

Vincela, sive Unzela, ii. 98. 313.

Vindia, ii. 89.

Voturi, ii. 85.

Urania, ii. 386.

Uraniopolis, ii. 298.

Xanthus fluvius, Æol. i. 150.

——————— Lyc. ii. 247.

——————— Lesb. i. 165.

——— urbs Lyc. ii. 248.

Ξάνθος, Ξάνθιος.

Xenagoræ insulæ, ii. 251.

Ximene regio, i. 305.

Xoana, i. 238.

Xyline, i. 295.

Xylene come, ii. 294.

Xylocastrum, ii. 124.

Xylus, ii. 216.

Xystis, ii. 214.

Ξύστις, Ξυστιανός.

Zagatis fluvius, i. 292.

Zagria, i. 238.

Zagora, i. 234.

Zalecus fluvius, i. 234.

Zama, ii. 124.

Zarzela, ii. 294.

Zede, ii. 239.

Zela, i. 306.

Ζῆλα, Ζηλάτης.

Zelea, i. 38.

Ζελεία, Ζελειάτης.

Zenocopi, ii. 157.

Zephyrium prom. Paphl. i. 226.

——————————Pont. i. 282.

———————————et urbs Cilic. ii. 341.

——————————Cilic. ii. 329, 335.

——————————Cypr. ii. 376.

Zeugma, i. 73.

Zigana, ii. 158.

Zimara, ii. 153.

Zipœtium, i. 115.

Ζιπоίτιον, Ζιπоίτιος.

Ziziola, ii. 156.

Zocotessus, ii. 161.

Zompi, ii. 36.

Zoparistus, ii. 127.

Zoropassus, ii. 117.

Zorzila, ii. 294.

Zyganium, ii. 32,

Zygi, sive Zychi gens, i. 295.

Zygopolis, i. 295.

Lightning Source UK Ltd.
Milton Keynes UK
UKOW07f1258121217

314329UK00008BA/561/P